JESUS

JESUS

A Theography

LEONARD SWEET | FRANK VIOLA

NASHVILLE DALLAS MEXICO CITY RIO DE JANEIRO

Published in Nashville, Tennessee, by Thomas Nelson. Thomas Nelson is a registered trademark of Thomas Nelson, Inc.

Leonard Sweet is published in association with the literary agency of Mark Sweeney & Associates, Bonita Springs, Florida 34135. Frank Viola is published in association with the literary agency of Daniel Literary Group, Nashville, Tennessee 37215.

Thomas Nelson, Inc., titles may be purchased in bulk for educational, business, fund-raising, or sales promotional use. For information, please e-mail SpecialMarkets@ThomasNelson.com.

Library of Congress Cataloging-in-Publication Data

Sweet, Leonard I.
Jesus : a theography / Leonard Sweet and Frank Viola.
p. cm.
Includes bibliographical references (p.).
ISBN 978-0-8499-4702-5 (trade paper)
1. Jesus Christ—Biography. 2. Bible—Criticism, interpretation, etc. I. Viola, Frank. II. Title.
BT301.3.S89 2012
232—dc23 2012023804

Printed in the United States of America

12 13 14 15 16 QG 6 5 4 3 2 1

To T. Austin-Sparks,
a choice servant of God whose ability to expound and exalt Jesus Christ from Genesis to Revelation was without peer.
—Frank Viola

To E. Stanley Jones,
a lover of The Story and a writer for all times and climes.
—Leonard Sweet

Contents

INTRODUCTION

The Jesus Story

ACCORDING TO ESTIMATES, APPROXIMATELY 1.25 BILLION CHRISTIANS live in the world today. Many, if not most, have become overly familiar with their Bibles. The same can be said about how they view the Lord Jesus Christ.

A daring statement, you say? Perhaps. How can the two of us think that Christianity has become overfamiliar with the most influential person who ever lived, the most important person who ever walked planet Earth?

As you read this book, we hope you will come to the same conclusion. Better still, when you finish, we expect you will encounter the Scriptures in a fresh way. And as a result, you will encounter your Lord anew as well.

Let's face it. The Bible is often viewed as a disjointed array of stories, events, laws, propositions, truths, ethical statements, and moral lessons.

But as we will demonstrate in this book, the sixty-six books of the Bible are woven together by a single storyline. One of the best ways to look at the twenty-seven books of the New Testament may be to see them as a commentary on the Old Testament. The entire Scriptures, both Old and New Testaments, are unified by a common narrative. And once our eyes are opened to see that narrative, everything in both Testaments gels into a coherent, understandable, and amazing story.

And what is that story? Well, it's not enough to call it "salvation history" as many people do.[1]

No. *It's the story of Jesus Christ.*[2]

The end product of biblical Christianity is a person—not a book, not a building, not a set of principles or a system of ethics—but one person in two natures (divine/human) with four ministries (prophet/priest/king/sage) and four biographies (the Gospels). But those four biographies don't tell the whole story. Every bit of Scripture is part of the same great story of that one person and that one story's plotline of creation, revelation, redemption, and consummation.

TOWARD A NEW KIND OF BIOGRAPHY

Writing about Jesus is like matrimony: not to be entered into unprepared or lightly, but reverently, discreetly, advisedly, soberly, and in awe of God. Not to mention that over the last fifty years, there have been countless books telling, retelling, and reconstructing the life of Jesus of Nazareth.[3] In fact, there are more biographies of Jesus than of any other human—one hundred thousand biographies in English alone.[4]

So why this book?

First, this isn't a biography. It's a theography. Even if you argue that a biography of Jesus is possible, which is hotly debated among scholars today,[5] we are telling the story of God's interactions, intersections, and interventions with humanity through the life of Jesus. We are less concerned with every fact and detail of Jesus' life than we are about the narratives, metaphors, signs, and symbols that reveal pictures of God's touching of humanity through the person and identity of Jesus. In each major scene in the Jesus story, we try to provide "snapshots"—organic freeze-frames and visual markers of Jesus in living color and surround sound to be experienced, breathed, and lived by our readers.

This book lifts up the epic story of Jesus as the single, ascertainable truth that triumphs over all other contingent truths. In other words, human identity is bound up with the story of an individual and the story of a community. In a world that tries to snatch an identity off the racks of an Armani store, or from the marble floor of a BMW showroom, we believe that humanity was created to find its identity in a relationship with God. The story of Jesus as found in the Bible shows us how to do that. Neither of us wants to bend the world to see things through our eyes. But we do want to entice the world to see things through Jesus' eyes.

Virtually every biography of Jesus begins with the nativity account in Bethlehem.[6] The Jesus theography you hold in your hands begins the story of Jesus at "the beginning."[7]

FROM ETERNITY PAST TO THE SECOND COMING

According to Scripture, the Jesus story doesn't begin in Bethlehem or Nazareth. It begins in eternity past, when the Word (Jesus in His preincarnate state) "was with God, and . . . was God."[8] So we will tell the Jesus story, not "from the womb to the tomb," but from eternity past (as the preexistent Son) to His second coming (as the postresurrected, risen Lord).[9]

In addition, we will rehearse the story of Jesus—the greatest story ever told—by following the plotline that stretches from Genesis to Revelation. And we will demonstrate that all the Scriptures are held together by a single narrative: the story of Jesus Christ.[10]

The name Jesus refers to the incarnate Christ who had a human nature. As such, the name Jesus doesn't appear in Genesis or elsewhere in the Old Testament. But that doesn't mean He wasn't present as the preexistent Son through whom, by whom, and to whom all things were created.[11] So in this book, we will use the terms *Jesus*, *Christ*, and *Son of God* interchangeably in a nontechnical way.[12] They all refer to the same person.

As far as we know, there is no biography of Jesus that tells His story from Genesis to Revelation. If this is correct, one may ask, "Why hasn't a book like this been written before?" The reason is simple. Biographies of Jesus have generally been written by those trying to investigate the historical Jesus. In general, such people aren't interested in looking at Jesus in the entire biblical canon. On the flip side, those interested in tracing the biblical narrative from Genesis to Revelation are typically disinterested in historical Jesus studies. So these two approaches have yet to converge.[13]

That's where this book comes in. It brings together historical Jesus studies with a survey of the entire biblical canon.[14] In so doing, it seeks to reclaim the Jesus-shaped narrative of Scripture.[15]

THE CORE NARRATIVE

In many Christians' minds, the Old and New Testaments are two separate entities. Melito (second century) and Tertullian (third century) were the first to call the two halves of the Bible the Old Testament and New Testament.[16] However, the Old Testament and the New Testament belong to the same inspired canon. Thus they are organically united. To underscore this unity, we will be calling the Old Testament the *First Testament* and the New Testament the *Second Testament* throughout this book.

In our experience and observation, countless evangelical, postevangelical, Reformed, charismatic, and mainline Christians are not aware that the main subject of the *entire* First Testament is Jesus Christ. But consider what Jesus Himself said about the Scriptures: "You search the Scriptures because you think they give you eternal life. But the Scriptures point to me!"[17]

It is for this reason that statements such as "according to the prophets," "as it is written," "according to the Scriptures," "that the Scripture might be fulfilled," and "in all the Scriptures" are peppered throughout the entire Second Testament. What is more, the Second Testament authors consistently interpreted the First Testament writings in the light of Christ.[18]

Many believe that the Second Testament writers simply used parts of the First Testament as proof texts to show that Jesus of Nazareth was the promised Messiah of Israel and Lord of the world. But this is not the case.[19]

The Second Testament writers consistently quoted or cited large sections of the First Testament, using them to unfold the Jesus story.[20] But that's not all. The Second Testament authors used the *same* First Testament texts *independently* of one another. And they interpreted them in exactly the same way, often citing the texts in the same order.[21]

This fact alone demonstrates that the Second Testament authors shared a common method of interpreting the First Testament. The questions emerge, then: *Where did they find this method of interpretation? What was their common source?*

The answer is that Jesus Himself was the common source.[22]

JESUS REVEALED THROUGH THE SCRIPTURES

The Gospels tell us that Jesus took His followers through the Scriptures and gave them a divinely inspired hermeneutic (method of interpretation) by which to understand the First Testament. In turn, the Lord's original disciples passed this interpretative key to those whom they influenced (this would include people such as Mark, Paul, and Luke).

Luke suggested this in his gospel when he rehearsed Jesus' encounter with two disciples on the road to Emmaus:

> Then beginning with Moses and with all the prophets, He explained to them the things concerning Himself in all the Scriptures.[23]

Note the words "all the Scriptures." This includes the First Testament—Genesis through Malachi. They said to one another, "Were not our hearts burning within us while He was speaking to us on the road, while He was explaining the Scriptures to us?"[24] Luke went on to say that Jesus opened the Scriptures to His disciples: "Now He said to them, 'These are My words which I spoke to you while I was still with you, that all things which are written about Me in the Law of Moses and the Prophets and the Psalms must be fulfilled.' Then He opened their minds to understand the Scriptures."[25]

In this passage, Jesus unveils Himself through the three parts of the Hebrew Bible: (1) the law of Moses (the Torah); (2) the Prophets (the Nevi'im); and (3) the Psalms, which represent the Writings (the Ketuvim).

These three sections make up the *Tanakh*—the rabbinic name for the Hebrew Bible.[26] The way the Second Testament authors quoted the First Testament forms a pattern—a shared hermeneutic for understanding the First Testament.

It is easy to see, then, that the source of this common hermeneutic was Jesus Himself. Jesus taught His disciples how to understand the Hebrew Scriptures, and this is reflected throughout the Second Testament.[27]

Jesus' use of the First Testament text was revolutionary for His time. As R. T. France points out, Jesus "applied the Old Testament in a way that was quite unparalleled. The essence of his new application was that he saw the fulfillment of the predictions and foreshadowings of the Old Testament in himself and his work."[28] The early Christian church "was founded on this distinctive and revolutionary use of the Old Testament"[29]—a usage that was handed down to the apostles by Jesus Himself. Jesus clearly said that He was the fulfillment of the entire Hebrew Bible (represented by the Torah, the Writings, and the Prophets).[30]

> If you believed Moses, you would believe Me; for he wrote about Me.[31]

> Do not think that I came to destroy the Law or the Prophets. I did not come to destroy but to fulfill.[32]

Consider this question with these texts in mind: If you were to ask Jesus what the Scriptures were about, what would His answer be?[33]

R. T. France comments, "Jesus saw his mission as the fulfillment of the Old Testament Scriptures; not just of those which predicted a coming redeemer, but of the whole sweep of Old Testament ideas."[34] In this regard, Jesus not only *completes* the First Testament story; He *fulfills* it. But fulfilling doesn't happen only in view of the accomplishment of its promises. As you will discover in this book, Jesus actually *embodies* the First Testament. He "fills full" the ancient Text.[35]

In a word, Jesus is the thread that holds all Scripture together. He is the prism that breaks forth its multifaceted colors. He is the lens that puts all of it into focus, the switch that sheds light on its dimly lit quarters, and the key that unlocks its meaning and richness.[36]

We agree with a long tradition of theologians who do not view the Scriptures as a storehouse of propositions on every imaginable subject but instead discover the place from which the Spirit of God makes Christ known.[37] Or as Protestant Reformer Martin Luther has put in epigrammatic fashion: "Scripture is the cradle in which Christ lies."[38] Scot McKnight puts it in more current form: "We have to become a People of the Story . . . we need to immerse ourselves even more into the Story of Jesus. The gospel is that the Story of Israel comes to its definitive completeness in the Story of Jesus, and this means we have to become People of the Story-that-is-complete-in-Jesus."[39]

Our desire is to tell that story.

READING SCRIPTURE AS A WHOLE

Given what we have established so far, the approach we are taking to the Scriptures is both holistic as well as reductionist. It is reductionist in that we are drawing from the best findings of modern historical research.[40] Yet it's holistic in that we are bringing the First Testament stories, events, and accounts into the core narrative of Jesus—just as the Second Testament writers did when they interpreted the First Testament.[41] We are searching for the story the Gospels tell about Jesus in the story found in the First Testament.

The Bible didn't emerge out of a vacuum. It is a historical but also metaphorical and narrative story of truth written within history. Thus, history matters in our interpretation of the biblical text. At the same time, the Bible is a collection of writings that are tied together by a common theme. Therefore, the interweaving of both Testaments also matters in our interpretation of the biblical text.

To use a metaphor, we are not only inspecting each tree in the forest (the reductionist approach) but also stepping away from the trees to view the entire landscape at high altitude, making note of how each tree connects with the others in an ecosystem (the holistic approach).[42] And further, we reveal how we see that forest as nourishing, creative, life-giving, revelatory, and beautiful.

To put it another way, the Bible contains its own hermeneutic.[43] As usual, Augustine has put it best: "In the Old Testament, the New is concealed; in the New, the Old is revealed."[44] This being so, the Holy Spirit often had an intention in Scripture that went beyond its authors' present knowledge.[45]

Understanding the author's intent in a given portion of Scripture is certainly part of the task of biblical interpretation. But it's not the whole task. As you read this book, this fact will become abundantly clear. The Second Testament authors "remain true to the main intention" of the First Testament authors.[46] But they go beyond that intention to the Spirit-inspired meaning found in Christ.[47]

In our theographical snapshots, we will be employing the same method of interpretation that the Second Testament writers used in their interpretation of the First Testament—a method given to them by Jesus Himself. This method of interpretation safeguards us from entertaining subjective, fanciful, and forced allegorical interpretations on the one hand[48] and completely missing Christ in the sacred Text on the other.[49]

Again, the Scriptures are not a library of disjointed, independent, inspired books. The First and Second Testaments are not two separate books bound together between a single cover. Rather, they are a unified canon. All the books of that canon contribute to the plotline of God's covenantal relationship with humanity through Jesus. You can think of the First and Second Testaments as act 1 and act 2 of the same drama. Each book, therefore, must be understood and interpreted within the framework of the greater whole.[50]

Jesus Christ is the glue that binds both Testaments together. As Brevard Childs says, "The completely New of the gospel is formulated in terms of the Old. Herein lies the deep mystery surrounding the two testaments. Separate and yet undivided, two voices yet the sound is similar, an Old Word pointing to the New, yet the New is only known in the Old."[51]

That said, it's a profound mistake to detach Scripture—both First and Second Testaments—from Christ.[52] The Bible has no real meaning unless it is grounded in Christ.[53] The beauty of Scripture for followers of Jesus is to reveal Christ.

THE WITNESS OF THE SECOND TESTAMENT AUTHORS

Here are just a few samples of how the authors of the Second Testament read the First Testament in the light of Christ:

Matthew quoted Hosea about a prophecy concerning Israel: "Out of Egypt I called My Son."[54] But Matthew located its fulfillment in Jesus. He drew similar connections throughout his gospel.[55]

John informed us that Philip declared Jesus to be the fulfillment of the Law and the Prophets: "We have found Him of whom Moses in the law, and also the prophets, wrote—Jesus of Nazareth, the son of Joseph."[56]

John applied words from Isaiah to Jesus, equating Christ with "the arm of the LORD."[57] John's gospel is full of references showing how Jesus fulfills the images and events of the First Testament and of the Jewish messianic expectation.[58]

According to Paul, one cannot understand the First Testament except in Christ. Jesus is the key that unlocks its meaning.[59] Three quick examples:

1. Paul stated that Adam is an image, or a model, of Jesus.[60]
2. Paul argued that Israel's festivals and food laws are embodied in Christ. They are mere shadows that point to Jesus, the reality.[61]
3. Paul said the rock that followed Israel represents Christ.[62]

Paul's epistles are rife with these kinds of connections.

The writer of Hebrews took a promise that God gave to King David and applied it to Jesus.[63] He also stated that the Law foreshadowed what was in the new covenant: namely, Jesus Christ.[64] This is a major theme throughout the book of Hebrews.

According to Peter, the prophets spoke of the sufferings and glories of Christ in ways that they themselves didn't fully understand.[65] Peter applied the words of Isaiah about a stone lying in Zion to Jesus.[66]

In like manner, the church fathers, the Reformers, and countless theologians and scholars of the past and present all testify to this same understanding of the First Testament. With a united voice, they declared that Jesus is the interpretative key of the Bible. (In the appendix, we give a sampling of these post-apostolic witnesses.)

To put it in a sentence:

> In Jesus the promise is confirmed, the covenant is renewed, the prophecies are fulfilled, the law is vindicated, salvation is brought near, sacred history has reached its climax, the perfect sacrifice has been offered and accepted, the high priest over the household of God has taken his seat at God's right hand, the Prophet like Moses has been raised up, the Son of David reigns, the kingdom of God has been inaugurated, the Son of Man has received dominion from the Ancient of Days, the Servant of the Lord, having been smitten to death for his people's transgression and borne the sin of many, has accomplished the divine purpose, has seen light after the travail of his soul, and is now exalted and extolled and made very high.[67]

Many who have rightly taught that Jesus is the hermeneutical key to the Bible have failed to look at *all* Scripture through the lens of Christ. What we will demonstrate in this book is that everything in the Bible points to Jesus—either His person, His work, or His character.

When we fail to see the entire Bible christologically and theographically, the door is opened for the Bible to take on a raft of contradictory interpretations. We believe, therefore, that failure to read the Bible christologically is the cause for the countless divisions among Christians. The internal unity of the Bible is its witness to Jesus. He is the Canon within the canon.

Reading Scripture through a christological and theographical lens is more radical a move than we might think at first blush. In our observation, it's rarely practiced today—even among those who claim to uphold the centrality of Christ. It's one thing to *profess* to read the Scripture christologically or to agree with it in *principle*. But it's quite another to actually *practice* it.

Many Christians read the Bible with modern or postmodern optics, then clip on "Christocentrism" sunglasses. But reading Scripture through a christological lens changes the way we see and approach the entire

Bible, as well as how we regard and handle biblical doctrine.[68] It also prevents us from making the common mistake of missing the drama for the details. Reading Scripture christologically turns Bible reading from two dimensions into 3-D. It transforms it from black-and-white into high-definition Technicolor. We are confident that as you read this book, you will better understand what we mean.

TOWARD A TRUE RED-LETTER BIBLE

Many Christians grew up reading red-letter editions of the Second Testament. Those are the Bibles wherein the words of Jesus are printed in red. Now imagine a First Testament where every reference, every prophecy, every shadow, every image, and every allusion to Christ appeared in red. If such a red-letter First Testament existed, it would glow in the dark. And if Jesus is YHWH,[69] as Dietrich Bonhoeffer, N. T. Wright, Scot McKnight, Richard Bauckham, and others have argued, then it could light up a living room.[70]

As you read this book, we want you to remember the image of a red-letter Bible in which all the letters are red. The reason is because the story of Scripture is the story of Jesus. All of it, therefore, should appear in red.[71]

In this connection, the Bible was written in a narrative arc that ends where it began. In other words, biblical logic defies logic. The Bible was written in a circle.

For the Western mind, this is hard to hear. As the old joke goes, two Christians were once talking about their pastors. The first one bragged, "My pastor's good at foreign languages—he uses Greek a lot." The second one said, "My pastor's good at geometry—he talks in circles a lot." To say that someone "talks in circles" is not a compliment. Yet recent anthropological study and literary scholarship have revealed that when the spoken word became the written word, when bards turned into scribes, the resulting texts were written in a lost art of symmetry and elegance that is now called "ring composition."[72] Not just the Hebrew Bible, but ancient literature in India, Homer's narratives in Greece, as well as texts found in such disparate places as Egypt, China, Indonesia, and Russia, were written in nonlinear configurations where the chapters of the story are connected not sequentially but synoptically. It's not a "story-line" but a "story-circle," where the plot relates to what is across the circle from it, not what is before or after it.

The three main features of ring composition are (1) parallelism, (2) chiasmus, and (3) latch. We are most familiar with *parallelism*, where each section mirrors what is across the circle and is often marked by parallel alliteration and resonance. *Chiasmus* is the turning point, that place in the narrative arc when a climax of meaning drives a loop back, dividing the circle into halves and overlaying one half on top of the other. The *latch* is the journey home, back to where you started, that closes the circle, not so much with a conclusion, as with an arrival home, but at a higher level of integration and increased awareness that is transformative and enchanting.

When humans started writing, why did they write in rings? Because that's how the brain is hardwired. The brain works through symmetry, balanced proportions, corresponding repetition, and parallelisms, just like ring composition. Furthermore, ring compositions are shaped not like straight lines or sine curves but like a torus (think spiral donut), the universal form of self-organizing, self-regulating, self-organizing systems. One more thing: our ancestors wrote stories as the universe moved, not in linear progression but in circles. A story that doesn't build step-by-step, chapter by chapter, book by book, but reaches a climax by syntactical rules that form relationships between parallel rungs of the text, appears odd to people used to linear storytelling.

Ring composition forces one to slow down and pay attention to the details while never losing sight of the whole. It is natural, then, that the most relational book ever written should be written in this relational and beautiful symmetry. And our theography will attempt to draw attention to those rings.

THREE KEY POINTS

In closing, we want to leave you with three key points about this book.

First, *this book is primarily written for a Christian audience.* Thus, when we use the words "we" and "us," we are referring either to ourselves (the authors) or to all followers of Jesus—what the Second Testament calls disciples of Jesus—those who trust in and share in the life of Christ.

There is a sign as you enter the Louvre Museum: "You do not judge the paintings; they judge you." Part of the difference between a biography and a theography is that you move away from a critical stance and reposition yourself to be critiqued by the truthfulness and authority of the entire biblical canon. This repositioning also involves trusting the historical authenticity of the Hebrew Scriptures, the Gospels, the Epistles, and Revelation as they present the story of Jesus.[73]

"All Scripture is given by inspiration of God" (or more poetically, "God-breathed"[74]) is the famous phrasing of 2 Timothy 3:16. This mixture of terms is not found in any previously composed biblical text. Paul coined a new term to convey how important it is to comprehend the authoritative nature of all the Hebrew Scriptures and to contend that they all interpret and illumine the gospel of Jesus Christ.[75]

Consequently, the Bible is an organic, living document. As with every living organism, everything is connected to everything else. You can start anywhere and get everywhere. Each verse is a doorway or dormer that can lead into other venues that have their own portals into God's presence. The whole Bible is a beautiful, intricately woven tapestry—or in digital terms, a measureless interconnected network—where unexpected similarities, surprising parallels, and profound paradoxes can be found. It was this kind of intimacy with the Bible that Jesus the Jew manifested in almost everything that proceeded out of His mouth.

When we interpret Scripture, we are not simply interpreting documents as dead objects, as we would analyze the rings in tree stumps. We are engaged in a transaction with a divine book that was coauthored by humans and a divine person who still lives and speaks. Interpreting Scripture, then, is not simply a scientific, secular enterprise. It requires spiritual insight. It mandates a divine imagination. For this reason Paul argued that the "natural man" cannot comprehend the things of the Spirit.[76]

Jesus is the Logos.[77] He is the Word, or the self-utterance, of God. So when God speaks, it is Christ who is being spoken about. When God breathes, it is Christ who is being imparted. The Spirit is God's breath (the words "Spirit" and "breath" are the same in both Hebrew and Greek). The Second Testament tells us clearly that the Holy Spirit's job is to reveal, magnify, and glorify Christ. Thus, because the Bible is inspired, it all speaks of Jesus.

Again, *Jesus Christ is the subject of all Scripture.* He is the main character of the story. The plot revolves around Him, and the images of Christ are what make the story sing the song of truth. The real and total meaning of Scripture, therefore, is found in Jesus Christ—His person, His mission, and His work. He is the fulfillment of the Torah, the Prophets, and the Writings.

Regardless of whether you prefer to view the Second Testament references to Christ as allusions, applications, types, signs, allegories, shadows, figures, extended meanings,[78] or the literal meaning of the text, Jesus Christ is the focus of the entire Bible—both First and Second Testaments. This point will become obvious as we move forward in telling the Jesus story.

Second, when we get to chapter 4, *we will begin recounting the story of Jesus from His birth in Bethlehem until His second coming.* The chronology we will follow is found in Robert Mounce's classic *Jesus, In His Own Words*—a chronological blending of the four Gospels.[79] We have been amazed at how many problematic passages in the Gospels suddenly become clear when read in chronological sequence.[80]

As we recount Jesus' life on earth, we will be weaving into it references, images, prophecies, and events from the First Testament to show the unity of Scripture as it concerns Jesus. We hope this effort will bring the First Testament alive for you in fresh ways. Our purpose is to connect the dots of the First Testament to the Second, highlighting the Bible's unified storyline. Among other things, you will discover that the entire story of Israel in the First Testament *repeats* itself in the life of Christ in the Second Testament. And it does so in almost every detail.[81] In this regard, Jesus not only fulfills the First Testament narrative but also reenacts, relives, and replays it. This is one of the most fascinating aspects of the Bible.

At times we will quote the authors of the Second Testament in their use of the First Testament to shed light on the Jesus story. Other times we will simply make references to the First Testament without any such quotations. The reason for this is that not all references and allusions to Jesus in the First Testament are mentioned in the Second Testament. To quote Edmund Clowney (former president of Westminster Theological Seminary), "To conclude that we can never see a type where the New Testament does not identify it is to confess hermeneutical bankruptcy."[82] Yet by following the same line of interpretation that the First Testament authors consistently used in their reading of the Hebrew Scriptures, we can discover Jesus Christ afresh all throughout the Bible.

Note that if we unveiled all the references, allusions, prophecies, and foreshadowings of Jesus present in the First Testament, this book would be thousands of pages.[83] We are forced to be highly selective in which ones we choose to highlight. Nonetheless, we hope you will pick up the pattern of interpretation we are using so that you may take it from here and find Jesus throughout the rest of the First Testament yourself.

In a world and a church that has lost the plot of the story and the *cantus firmus* of the music, we need to reclaim the Bible as a whole narrative telling one fluid, coherent story—the Jesus story. After all, the origin of the word *gospel* is *Godspell*, or the "story of God."

Third, *we are not writing this book for scholars but for the general Christian population*. At the same time, we have provided endnotes for the benefit of scholars, academicians, and curious minds who wish to see the sources that have influenced some of our conclusions and to delve deeper into them.

One of our favorite metaphors for reframing how people see the Bible is to approach it as a movie.[84] But not any simple, straightforward movie—one filled with flashbacks, interweaving relationships and plotlines, metaphors and narratives, multiple voices, and circles of meaning, an organic and rich symmetry of dynamic signs, a story that reveals the truth of Jesus Christ in freshness, surround sound, and living color. As with any great story, there are characters, sequence, conflict, climax, and resolution. Unlike any other story, however, this is a never-ending story. This story invites you to become part of it with its main character, who wants to merge His story with yours.

So sit back, relax, and enjoy the story. Stay in your seat. Sit at its feet. Don't try to figure everything out or get everything right. Just let the story unfold. Let the Bible tell its own story to you. Trust the Jesus story as it moves from Genesis to Revelation. And see if the Holy Spirit doesn't open your eyes to see the greatness of Christ anew and afresh.

May your heart burn within you while reading it as it has ours while writing it.

—Leonard Sweet and Frank Viola

CHAPTER 1

Christ Before Time

Every word of the God-breathed character of Scripture is meaningless if Holy Scripture is not understood as the witness concerning Christ.

—G. C. Berkouwer[1]

All Scripture finds its organic center and unity in Jesus. For this reason, the biblical narrative has its beginning in the creation of the universe through Christ, its middle in the earthly life and ministry of Christ, and its end in the reconciliation of all things in Christ. There's an overarching unity to both Testaments. And Christ is the unifying agent.

Part of that statement is not entirely accurate. While Genesis begins the scriptural narrative at the point of creation, the Second Testament tells us that the narrative actually begins somewhere else. The Jesus story doesn't begin in Bethlehem, Nazareth, or even Israel. According to the Second Testament, it begins long before them. It begins in the dateless past, before angels or atoms.

In this chapter, we will narrate the Jesus story as it happened before creation, and we will get a breathtaking glimpse of the preincarnate

Christ—the eternal Son, the preexistent Word, Jesus before time, Christ before creation.

The Second Testament contains numerous texts that give us insight into Christ before time. And the First Testament supports those texts.

BEFORE THE FOUNDATION OF THE WORLD

Considering Jesus before the world began is mind-boggling. We feel we are fumbling in the dark, groping for words to express the inexpressible. It's impossible to find adequate language for what happened before creation. Taken literally, *before creation* is unintelligible because there is no such thing as a "before" or an "after" until there is a creation. According to Einstein's physics, time doesn't exist without mass and matter. Time, therefore, begins with creation.[2]

So on a literal basis, phrases like *time before time* or *before creation* are nonsensical. They only make sense when we see them as intuitively graspable metaphors. When we talk about what God was doing before creation, it's impossible to avoid language that sounds as though we are talking about a time before time.[3] Nonetheless, we will use these metaphors because Scripture uses them. The phrases "before the foundation of the world" and "before the world began" are used frequently in the Second Testament.[4]

Both First and Second Testaments speak much about God's eternality.

> Before the mountains were brought forth, or ever You had formed the earth and the world, even from everlasting to everlasting, You are God.[5]

> To God our Savior, who alone is wise, be glory and majesty, dominion and power, both now and forever. Amen.[6]

It has been said that a student once asked Martin Luther, "What was God doing before He created the world?" Luther responded, "He went into the woods and cut rods with which to punish good-for-nothing questioners!" John Calvin reportedly responded to the same question: "God was not idle but was creating hell for curious questioners!"

While we respect Luther and Calvin, we don't agree with those sentiments toward this question. What happened before God created the world is critical. And it is for that reason that the Scriptures are not silent on the matter. As Paul put it: "So we fix our eyes not on what is seen, but on what is unseen. For what is seen is temporary, but what is unseen is eternal."[7]

What God was doing before creation belongs to the unseen and eternal. And Paul exhorted the Corinthians to fix their eyes on those eternal intangibles. In that connection, let's explore what Jesus Christ was doing before the foundation of the world.

> *Father, I want those you have given me to be with me where I am, and to see my glory, the glory you have given me because you loved me before the creation of the world.*
>
> —Jesus[8]

THE SON AND FATHER LOVED EACH OTHER

Before God the Father said, "Let there be light,"[9] He loved His Son. Before time, the Father and the Son enjoyed a mutual exchange of love, life, and fellowship through the Spirit.[10] All throughout the Second Testament, we see Jesus returning to the Father what the Father has given Him.[11] This reciprocal activity is rooted in His very nature of God Himself. His nature is love.[12] Thus, what Jesus did on earth, He did in His purely divine state as the eternal Son. The loving oneness the Father and the Son shared before time was reflected on the earth as well.[13]

This exchange of love, life, and fellowship is best understood in terms of the triune God.[14] In the trinitarian community, the Father, Son, and Spirit all enjoy the fullness of one another in endless fellowship.[15] Each member loves the other. That is, the Father and Son both empty themselves and pour themselves into each other through the Spirit.[16] It is within this eternal fellowship that we find the headwaters of the mission of God, the church, and the believer's life in Christ.[17]

According to Philippians 2, the Son left the pristine setting of a shared love that flowed between the Father, Son, and Spirit, and made Himself of no reputation as a human being—even a servant.[18] While on earth, Jesus divested Himself of His divine rights and was the recipient of the Father's love, life, and power—just as He had known them in eternity.

Consequently, the incarnation should not be seen as a single temporal act in history. But the divine emptying that it embodied began before creation, continued into the incarnation, and further than that. As Paul wrote, it continued to "even the death of the cross."[19] In the incarnation, the God of eternity gave Himself to humanity by becoming human.[20]

Because we are caught in space-time, the incarnation is something we can approach only from the human side. We know it to be a historical event that took place in the first century. But when we talk about the incarnate Son—Emmanuel, God with us—we're talking about a profound mystery. The incarnation points to an eternal reality. Namely, God's nature is that of *kenosis*, the pouring out of Himself in love into the other members of the Trinity. This pouring out of divine fullness was experienced between the members of the triune God before time.[22] God the Father has always been the God who pours Himself into the Son. He has never been anyone else. And God the Son has always been the God who pours Himself into the Father. He has never been anyone else.[23] When Jesus took on human flesh, the principle of incarnation broke into time and space.

And now, Father, glorify me in your presence with the glory I had with you before the world began.

—Jesus[21]

But that's not all. Before time began, the Son of God lived by His Father's life. This practice continued when He took on flesh and became a man. Jesus repeatedly said that it was not Him but His Father who did the works. It was not Him but His Father who gave the teachings. It was not Him but His Father who made the judgments. Jesus boldly declared that He could do nothing without the Father. And He lived by the Father's life. But this was nothing new. It was true of Jesus in eternity. With the coming of Bethlehem, the key had switched from the divine to the human, but the song remained the same. The Father's life was the source of the Son's being and living—in eternity as well as on the earth.[24] As one theologian put it, the Father is the Source, the Son is the Wellspring, and the Spirit is the Living Water.[25]

THE SON AND FATHER SHARED THE DIVINE GLORY

Before God the Father ever said, "Let there be . . ."[26] He shared His radiant glory with His Son. And His Son returned that glory back to the Father.

God's glory is not something separate from His Being. His glory is another way of talking about who He is. God's glory is His own essential life, with all of the wonder and splendor of what it means to be God. The Hebrew word for glory is *kavod*, and it means the essential weight of something. The very being of God is love,[27] and that love is understood as the mutual sharing of glory with one another "before the world was."[28]

With the birth of Christ, the eternal broke into space and time. And one of the hallmarks of this inbreaking was *glory*. The Lord Jesus left glory to come to a sin-cursed earth. In His High Priestly Prayer in John 17, Jesus recalled "the glory which I had with You before the world was."[29] We can only put our hands over our mouths when it comes to articulating the *glory* that was shared between Father, Son, and Spirit before anything was made.

But, thankfully, the Lord has given us numerous glimpses of His glory in the unfolding drama of history. We will just highlight a few. Keep in mind that these were appearances of Christ, who is "the radiance of His glory."[30]

The pictures, signs, and events that were given by God before Christ came to earth were not random. Hebrews 8:5 states that they were copies and shadows of what existed in heaven before anything was made. In other words, they were the pre-creation heavenly realities flowing out of the eternal Christ.[31]

We know that Abraham encountered the eternal Christ. Jesus told His detractors, "Your father Abraham rejoiced at the thought of seeing my day; he saw it and was glad." They responded by noting that Jesus was not even fifty—"How could you have seen Abraham?" Jesus gave them this astounding response: "Most assuredly, I say to you, before Abraham was born, I AM."[32]

Isaiah said, "In the year that King Uzziah died, I saw the Lord sitting on a throne, high and lifted up."[33] When confronting the Jews' unbelief, John noted, referring to Jesus, "Isaiah said this because he saw Jesus' glory and spoke about him."[34] Thus when Isaiah "saw the Lord," he was speaking of the eternal Christ.[35]

After the exodus out of Egypt, God led Israel by His glory in a cloud.[36] Paul noted that the eternal Christ was the One who was guiding the people of God. He wrote that they "all ate the same spiritual food, and all drank the same spiritual drink. For they drank of that spiritual Rock that followed them, and that Rock was Christ."[37] This literal rock pointed to the spiritual reality of Jesus Christ.[38]

Recall that Moses asked God to show him His glory. The Lord put Moses in the cleft of a rock and covered him with His hand while His glory passed by. Then the hand of God was removed, and Moses saw God's back but not His face, for God said, "You cannot see My face, for no man can see Me and live!"[39] That was then, but later, in the gospel age, Paul said that God made His light shine in our hearts "to give the light of the knowledge of the glory of God in the face of Jesus Christ."[40] John said the same, writing, "No one has seen God at any time. The only begotten Son, who is in the bosom of the Father, He has declared Him."[41]

Jesus is the human face of God. He is also the inbreaking of the eternal into time. This is a good definition of the kingdom of God, which is embodied in Jesus.

After Moses constructed the tabernacle according to the Lord's directions, "the glory of the LORD filled the tabernacle."[42] This was a picture of the Lord dwelling with His people. When Jesus appeared on earth, He "tabernacled" among us, and "we beheld His glory."[43] He was the fulfillment of the earthly tabernacle and the glory that rested upon it.[44]

Given the inexpressible glory that the Father, Son, and Spirit shared before time, and given the amazing and repetitive appearances of the glory of God in history, it is not surprising that the glory of God would explode in the person of the heavenly Man as He penetrated the earth through Mary's womb. Shepherds beheld the glory at His birth.[45]

John saw the coming of Christ stepping into history against the backdrop of the original Genesis account. "In the beginning was the Logos, and the Logos was with God, and the Logos was God. He was with God in the beginning."[46] This One who had full, unabated glory with the Father before time had now entered the confines of time to fulfill the eternal purpose of the Godhead. And what was the chief attribute that captured their attention? "We beheld His *glory*." The glory from above was now functioning on earth. However, before Calvary it was a *veiled* glory.

Luke noted that he and the other apostles "saw His glory" on the Mount of Transfiguration.[47] But then something beyond remarkable happened: "a cloud appeared and enveloped them, and they were afraid as they entered the cloud."[48] This cloud is reminiscent of the cloud that led Israel, came upon the tabernacle of Moses, and filled Solomon's temple. It was the cloud of God's shekinah glory of His awesome presence. Out of this cloud the Lord spoke with clarity, "This is My beloved Son. Hear Him!"[50]

> *To me, the very least of all saints, this grace was given, to preach to the Gentiles the unfathomable riches of Christ, and to bring to light what is the administration of the mystery which for ages has been hidden in God who created all things; so that the manifold wisdom of God might now be made known through the church to the rulers and the authorities in the heavenly places. This was in accordance with the eternal purpose which He carried out in Christ Jesus our Lord.*
>
> —The apostle Paul[49]

Glory is the highest expression of a life. When a flower is in full bloom, we say it is glorified.[51] When God's divine, uncreated life is at its highest expression, Scripture calls it *glory*.[52]

Jesus is the mercy seat.[53] He is the dwelling place of God and the Sin-Bearer. Christ is the fulfillment of all that was signified in the space between the cherubim.[54]

In the end, we are given a spellbinding look at the heavenly city, the New Jerusalem, which comes down out of heaven from God. The city shines with the glory of God.[55] Next, we see the glory of God filling the new heaven and new earth: "I did not see a temple in the city, because the Lord God Almighty and the Lamb are its temple. The city does not need the sun or the moon to shine on it, for the glory of God gives it light, and the Lamb is its lamp."[56] The glory that humanity lost at the Fall has been restored.[57]

THE GODHEAD BIRTHED AN ETERNAL PURPOSE AND SHROUDED IT IN A MYSTERY

Before creation, the Godhead conceived of an eternal purpose. They shrouded that purpose as a mystery in Christ, where it was hid in God for ages. An entire book could be written unveiling God's eternal purpose.[58] But we will summarize it briefly. Before time, the Father, Son, and Spirit counseled together and purposed to expand the fellowship they had with one another. This was the very reason that provoked creation. God wanted to enlarge the love relationship between the Father and the Son through the Spirit.[59] In the words of C. S. Lewis, "The whole dance, or drama, or pattern of this three-Personal life is to be played out in each one of us."[60]

History is not about whim and chance. It is the unfolding of God's timeless purpose in Christ. Paul saw that the creation was designed for the formation of a bride and a body for the Son.[61] With everything being by the Son, for the Son, and to the Son, the perfect eternal communion of the triune God would be expanded through history into a vast, uncountable number of saints ("holy ones"[62]) from all over the earth.

To this end, the church is said to be chosen in Christ "before the foundation of the world."[63] This bride and body constitute the family of

God and a dwelling place for the Father through the Spirit.[64] Therefore, God the Father desired children. He also desired a home through which to express His glory. The Son desired a bride to be His counterpart and enter the divine dance that existed eternally between the Father, Son, and Spirit. She would be the new partner in the dance. The bride would also be the body for the Son's visible expression and movement in a created world. These four aspects of the eternal purpose—a bride, a body, a family, and a house—are all highlighted in Paul's letter called Ephesians. And they can be found from Genesis 1 to Revelation 22. (This point will be explained further in chapters 2 and 3.)

> *His works were finished from the foundation of the world.*
>
> —The apostle Paul[65]

GOD FINISHED ALL THINGS BEFORE HE BEGAN ALL THINGS

Jesus Christ had finished all things before He created all things. This is perhaps one of the most glorious things Jesus Christ accomplished before creation, but it may be the least reflected upon. Imagine a builder standing in front of an empty lot, saying, "What a beautiful house I have constructed." But there is nothing there. Only the Lord can say that His plans in the Son were finished in eternity before they came to pass in history. He completed the masterpiece before He ever painted it.

How can this be? It is because time exists in Christ. Paul told us that in Christ, "all things hold together."[66] That includes creation itself, which includes time.[67] C. S. Lewis drew a brilliant illustration to describe this reality. He said to imagine a straight line on a piece of paper. The line is time. The paper is God Himself. Time is in God just as the line is in the paper. Consequently, He is at the beginning[68] and the end at the same time.[69] As one theologian put it, "God is immediately and simultaneously aware of all events. Whether they be in what we call 'past,' 'present,' or 'future,' they are all in God's 'present.'"[70]

This throws fresh light on the declarations in Revelation that Jesus Christ is the Beginning and the End, the Alpha and the Omega, and First and the Last.[71] It's not that Christ was first the Alpha and then later the Omega. It's that Christ is the Alpha and Omega, the Beginning and the End, at the same moment. How? Because the line of time exists within Him.

Recall when Jesus said to the Pharisees, "Where I am you cannot come."[72] Notice He didn't say, "where I am going," but "where I am." Jesus couldn't have said that unless time was in Him. Christ is the great I AM, the self-existent One, the One "who is and who was and who is to come" all at once.[73] According to John, Jesus used the divine formula "I AM" without the predicate:[74]

> "For if you do not believe that I am He [I AM], you will die in your sins."[75]
>
> "When you lift up the Son of Man, then you will know that I am He [I AM]."[76]
>
> "Before Abraham was, I AM."[77]
>
> "Now I tell you before it comes, that when it does come to pass, you may believe that I am He [I AM]."[78]

It is no wonder the prophets declared that the Messiah would be the Root (the beginning) and the Branch (the end) at the same time,[79] the Root and the Offspring of David.[80]

For this reason, Paul saw God's purpose as both unfolding before his eyes *and* as already completed before the world began: "[Those] whom He predestined, these He also called; whom He called, these He also justified; and whom He justified, these He also glorified."[81]

This is a remarkable statement. In God's reality, we are already glorified. As creatures caught in space and time, our glorification hasn't caught up to us yet. But it has already been accomplished.[82]

It's not that God shot the movie in His head before He put it on film. It's that the movie exists inside of Him and He's at the beginning, the middle, and the end all at the same time. In other words, the Lord is not playing it by ear. He is not improvising and making it up as He goes along. No matter how chaotic things may seem, God has already worked the chaos into His plan and has turned it into good.[83] In fact, Jesus' own death was not an afterthought. Death was His destiny before the foundation of the world. Before lambs were ever created, a Lamb was slain. He is the "Lamb slain from the foundation of the world."[84] This reminds us of the "everlasting covenant" of which Hebrews 13:20 speaks.[85]

But that's not all. Consider what else God did before creation:

- He decided His eternal counsel and purpose before it actually happened.[86]
- He chose us before the foundation of the world, calling us with a holy calling before the world began.[87]
- He wrote our names in the Lamb's Book of Life before the foundation of the world.[88]
- Before the first angel came off of the finger of God, and before He uttered the words "Let there be . . ."[89] He gave us the promise of eternal life and a great inheritance in the Son.[90]
- The very things He would utter while He was on earth were kept secret before the world began.[91]

All of this is good news, even amazing news. Your salvation was established, completed, and sealed before creation itself. Your Lord wrapped it up, won it, and came out victorious before anything ever went wrong. Before creation, Jesus Christ foreknew you, chose you, predestined you, elected you, selected you, and inherited you to be His.[92]

Consider what limits your Lord went to in accomplishing His eternal purpose. Herein do we find the epic greatness and enormity of Jesus Christ. As we put it in *Jesus Manifesto*,[93] He is so much more than Lord and Savior.

The truth is, the *new creation* began in eternity before the old creation was made. All of this was a secret—a mystery hidden in God. But in the fullness of time, Jesus Christ appeared, and the mystery began to be unraveled. A central dimension of Paul's service was "to bring to light what is the administration of the mystery which for ages has been hidden in God who created all things."[94]

What is at the beginning? *Christ.* What is at the end? *Christ.* Both ends of the bottle of time are capped off by Jesus. He is the beginning, and at the same time He is the end. He envelops creation; He envelops time. In Him, everything occurs and is summed up.

THE ETERNAL CROSS

A Lamb was slain on the cross from the creation of the world.[95] That eternal cross reached before creation and extended after creation. It broke into the visible creation in AD 30 on a hill called Calvary, but it existed before the ticking of time. By that cross, Jesus the Christ reconciled a fallen universe to Himself.[96] After His death, His body was laid in an empty tomb for three days. And on the third day, God raised Him from the dead.[97] And the only things that came out of the other side of that cross and that empty tomb were Christ Himself and everything that was in Christ before the foundation of the world.

Everything else died and was destroyed.

Through the eternal cross, Jesus Christ finished all things before He created all things.

What did He finish? He finished the old creation and the Fall. He finished sin. He finished a fallen world system. He finished the enmity of the Law. He finished satan. He finished the flesh. He put you to death and finished you completely. The person you were in Adam was terminated, swallowed up in death. And then He finished His greatest enemy, the child of sin itself, death. If that isn't enough, He did something else beyond the rest: *He raised you up in resurrection life and glorified you.*

All of this flows from the mystery embedded in eternity past, a mystery that Paul of Tarsus declared to be his "gospel":

> Now to him who is able to establish you by my gospel and the proclamation of Jesus Christ, according to the revelation of the mystery hidden for long ages past, but now revealed and made known through

> the prophetic writings by the command of the eternal God, so that all nations might believe and obey him—to the only wise God be glory forever through Jesus Christ! Amen.[98]

God has never had any plans outside of His Son. As the ancient creed says, "Before all worlds" Christ is begotten, not created.[99] Jesus Christ was before all things. He created all things. He holds everything together. He will have preeminence in everything,[100] for everything will be summed up in Him.[101] Christ is the firstborn of all creation and the firstborn from the dead, that He might have the first place in all things.[102] No wonder Thomas said to the resurrected Jesus, "My Lord and my God!"[103]

> *Divine fullness is only going to be reached by a progressive and ever-increasing revelation of Christ and His significance.*
>
> —T. Austin-Sparks[104]

THE PREEXISTENT LOGOS

We will close this chapter with a few thoughts about the Logos, mentioned in John's gospel. The Greek word *logos* has a long history of meaning in the Greek and Jewish worlds. Beginning with Heraclitus in the sixth century BC, the word *logos* meant the principle that gave the universe order, meaning, structure, and harmony. Aristotle used the term to mean reasoned discourse. Other Greek philosophers believed *logos* to be the divine, active reason that animated the created universe. The word has been translated into "word," "speech," "reason," "principle," "language," "logic," and "story." The Jewish philosopher Philo believed the *logos* to be the bond of everything that held all created things together. He taught that the *logos* acted on behalf of God and was His instrument in creating the universe.

With all of this as a backdrop, John came along and announced that the Logos was God, the Logos was with God, and the Logos created all things.[105] But the mind-blowing statement with which John followed this up is, the Logos took on human flesh and became a man dwelling among us![106]

The Logos is Jesus of Nazareth. He is the speaking Word—God enfleshed.

The Logos is also associated with God's wisdom. Proverbs 8:22–31 depicts a divine wisdom speaking in the first person as being in existence in eternity, before creation. Jeremiah says that God established the earth by His wisdom and His power.[107] The psalmist wrote that "by the word [Greek, *logos*] of the LORD the heavens were made, and by the breath of his mouth all their host."[108] Paul taught that Jesus Christ is the wisdom of God and the power of God.[109] This wisdom, or self-expression, ordered and harmonized the universe.[110]

Consequently, the Logos brought together Hebrew ideas of creation and Greek ideas of a universal harmony. It is the Creator's self-expression that harmonized the universe. What John brought in his gospel was not a new idea, but a new fact: this divine self-expression that harmonizes the universe is an actual human being. And neither Hebrew nor Greek could grasp that.

We agree with Lutheran theologian Robert Jensen that Christ as the Logos should be seen not just as God's revelation of Himself to us but as God's own self-knowledge.[111] And as we borrow from Augustine and the Eastern fathers, God knows who He is through being Father to the Son. Thus Jesus is God's own knowledge of Himself. Therefore, everything that makes up divine revelation in the First Testament is part of that self-knowledge.

> *God dwells in eternity but time dwells in God. He has already lived all our tomorrows as He has lived all our yesterdays.*
>
> —A. W. TOZER[112]

When that self-knowledge becomes incarnate in the flesh of the man Jesus, then the entire content of the First Testament revelation is included in the incarnate Son. In God, the duality between movement and eternity is overcome. God is both eternal and eternally moving. Theirs is a consistent *kenosis* (self-emptying) of each member of the Trinity into the others. The constant total surrender of Father, Son, and Spirit to one another is the life of God. This eternal, divine life is an eternal movement. From another perspective, Jesus is the space and time in which humanity gets caught up into the movement of God. Thus God's movement becomes a movement of the divine and the human in Jesus. Jesus, therefore, is the movement of the incarnation. In short, Jesus is God's self-understanding enfleshed. God knows Himself to be what He is when He sees the Son.

In Colossians 1:15, Paul called Jesus "the firstborn over all creation." This indicates two things: First, Christ existed before creation. He was there before anything came into existence. Second, Jesus has primacy over creation, being the heir to all created things.[113] As Hebrews puts it, Christ was "appointed heir of all things, through whom also He made the worlds."[114] Jesus is both the source and the sustainer of creation.[115]

A separate volume could be written on the preincarnate Christ. In this chapter, we simply wanted to give you a glimpse of the biblical witness on the matter. Let's now shift gears and look at how the creation account in Genesis 1 and 2 also narrates the Jesus story.

CHAPTER 2

Christ in Creation: The Macro Version

The whole Bible is about God's mission, with Christ as the central character.

—Michael Horton[1]

The Bible is centered on a great narrative. Jesus taught us that He is present at the very beginning of that narrative all the way through to its climactic end. Consequently, if you read Scripture in a way that doesn't point to Christ, you don't have Christianity; you have a religion.

Jesus Christ is God's language. When God wants to communicate, He does so through His Son. In Genesis, God spoke through types, shadows, stories, and events that embody Christ and His work. In Exodus, He revealed Christ through Israel's exodus and the tabernacle of Moses. In Leviticus, He revealed Christ through various ceremonies, sacrifices, and rituals. In Numbers, He revealed Christ through each station of Israel's wilderness journey. In Deuteronomy, He revealed Christ through commandments and testimonies. In the prophetic and historical books, He revealed Christ through prophetic declarations, predictions, and the actions of prophets and kings. In the Writings, He revealed Christ through songs, poems, and proverbs.

God's language hasn't changed. It has just become more refined.

> In the past God spoke to our forefathers through the prophets at many times and in various ways, but in these last days he has spoken to us by his Son, whom he appointed heir of all things, and through whom he made the universe.[2]

In the past, God spoke about His Son. Today, He speaks straight through Jesus' lips.

Out of the abundance of the heart the mouth speaks.[3] The treasure in God's heart is Christ. Therefore, Christ is what God speaks. For this reason, John called Jesus the Logos, the very utterance and Word of God.[4]

CREATION DECLARES THE STORY OF JESUS

An entire book could be written expounding Jesus Christ from Genesis 1 and 2. These two chapters together are the key that unlocks the entire Bible. The themes that appear in these chapters can be traced throughout the rest of the Scriptures until their dramatic climax, when they reappear in their fullness in Revelation 21 and 22.[5] In this chapter and in chapter 3, we will simply highlight some of the main features of Genesis 1 and 2 as they relate to the Jesus story.

Before we can grasp the spiritual significance of the creation account in the First Testament, we must turn to the writers of the Second Testament.

In Colossians 1:16, Paul declared that everything in the visible creation was created by Christ, through Christ, and for Christ. John stated the same, saying, "All things were made through Him."[6] The universe was framed by God's Word, who is Christ—the visible was created by the invisible.[7] This being so, all of creation reflects Jesus in some way. Just as an artist puts something of Himself into His artwork, the Lord did the same when He crafted the heavens and the earth.

Creation testifies to the glory of God, which is in the face of Jesus

Christ.[8] This sheds fresh light on Romans 1:20: "For since the creation of the world God's invisible qualities—his eternal power and divine nature—have been clearly seen, being understood from what has been made, so that men are without excuse."[9]

When Paul wrote of the "eternal power and divine nature" of God in Romans 1:20, He was speaking of Christ.[10] For it is in Jesus that "the fullness of the Godhead" resides bodily.[11] Consequently, when God created the world, He embedded into the physical universe pictures of His greatest passion, Jesus, His own Son. In like manner, the psalmist wrote:

> The heavens declare the glory of God; the skies proclaim the work of his hands. Day after day they pour forth speech; night after night they display knowledge. There is no speech or language where their voice is not heard. Their voice goes out into all the earth, their words to the ends of the world. In the heavens he has pitched a tent for the sun, which is like a bridegroom coming forth from his pavilion, like a champion rejoicing to run his course.[12]

Day after day, the heavens and the earth testify of Christ. Jesus is the "image" of God and "the brightness of His glory."[13] In the words of the psalmist, Christ is the knowledge of God, the sun, the Bridegroom, and the champion of the universe.

In 2 Corinthians 5:17 (NIV), Paul wrote that "if anyone is in Christ, he is a new creation; the old has gone, the new has come!" Note the word "creation" here. This throws us back to the first seven days. The creation of the heavens and the earth is a shadow of the re-creation of the human spirit in Jesus Christ. The first creation is a picture of the second (spiritual) creation in Christ—a foreshadowing of the "new creation" of 2 Corinthians 5:17.

John's gospel makes this point loud and clear. He began his gospel just like Genesis, with the words "In the beginning." In John 1 and 2, we are presented with the new creation in the midst of the old creation. For this reason, the gospel of John is the new Genesis.[14]

The language of John 1 and 2 reminds us of the seven days of creation. The phrase "the next day" is used repeatedly. Also one day John the Baptist answered the priests and the Levites, saying that he was "the voice of one crying in the wilderness."[15] In Genesis 1:2, we are told that the earth was formless and void, like a wilderness. Strikingly, the Hebrew word for "without form" is translated "wilderness" in other places in the First Testament.

> *The truth of the faith can be preserved only by doing a theology of Jesus Christ, and by redoing it over and over again.*
>
> —Karl Rahner[17]

On another day Jesus was baptized and the Spirit descended upon Him "like a dove."[16] In Genesis 1:2, the Spirit descended with wings, "hovering" over the waters of creation. And on and on it goes.

With these thoughts in mind, let's turn our attention to the seven days of creation, with an eye to discovering the Lord Jesus and His marvelous work of re-creating us into God's image.

Day One: His Birth

Genesis 1:2 opens with the state of the earth: "And the earth was without form, and void; and darkness was on the face of the deep. And the Spirit of God was hovering over the face of the waters." Here we see a picture of unregenerate humanity. It perfectly describes women and men without God. Fallen humankind is a wasteland—full of darkness, emptiness, devoid of God's light and life. Isaiah described the wicked as "like the troubled sea, when it cannot rest, whose waters cast up mire and dirt."[18] It is only when the Spirit of God broods upon a fallen person that he or she encounters life.

So on day one of creation, God declared, "Let there be light."[19] This is the mantra of regeneration. Here we have new birth—the Word of God that brings the impartation of God's life.[20]

When Jesus was born, the Light of the World made its entrance onto this planet. And the light penetrated the darkness.[21] Following the literary format of Genesis 1, John told us that in Christ "was life, and the life was the light of men. And the light shines in the darkness, and the darkness did not comprehend it."[22] According to John, Jesus Christ is "the true Light."[23]

How does the new birth take place? By God's Spirit and by God's Word.[24] This is pictured beautifully on the first day of creation, when the Spirit of God moved upon the face of the waters,[25] and God commanded light to dispel the darkness by His Word.[26]

Paul drew an analogy connecting the day God said, "Let there be light," with our new birth: "God who commanded light to shine out of darkness . . . has shone in our hearts to give the light of the knowledge of the glory of God in the face of Jesus Christ."[27]

Through God's speaking, His Word, we are awakened spiritually and our spiritual eyes are opened. As a result, we are delivered from the dominion of darkness, translated into the kingdom of light, and we can *see* the things of the Spirit.[28]

The principle of regeneration and new birth repeated itself in Noah's day, after the floodwaters covered the old creation. According to Peter, the old world perished under water in the Flood.[29] And eight souls were saved in the ark. For Peter, this was an allusion to the salvation that baptism represents.[30]

Just as God's first creation passed away under the flood of Noah's day, so, too, our old selves passed away when we came into Christ.[31] The burial of the old earth through the Flood is a picture of how our old sinful nature (which belonged to the old creation) has been buried through water baptism. Do you recall how the dove set foot on the earth only after the Flood waters had receded and the new world was manifested? So, too, the Holy Spirit will abide only in the new creature in Christ.[32] Similarly, the dove that rested on Jesus at His baptism was a signpost that God was heralding a new world with Christ, echoing Genesis.

Day Two: His Death

On day two, God created the firmament (the heavens) to separate the waters. Consequently, there is water above (presumably fresh water) and water below (the sea, containing salt water). The emphasis here is on the division of things above from things below.

All throughout the Bible, we have the principle of separation. God divided the clean from the unclean, the earthly from the heavenly, the carnal from the spiritual.[33] The cross is God's instrument of separation and division. The death of Jesus divided the pure from the impure, the spiritual from the unspiritual, the earthly from the heavenly. Therefore, the second day illustrates the principle of separation, which reached its climax in the death of Christ.

Paul told us repeatedly that when Jesus Christ died, we also died with Him.[34] He not only nailed our sins there, but He also put us to death. Through our co-death with Christ, we have been separated from the things of this fallen world system.[35] The authors of the Second Testament describe the world system as those things that are "beneath" or "of this world"—and the things of God as those things that are "above."[36]

Separation from the world and the flesh is a first principle in the Christian walk, and it is only through an application of the cross that we are set apart. This is the meaning of baptism. Through it, we are separated from this fallen world system.[37] Baptism is immersion into and union with the death of Christ.[38] For through the cross of Jesus we are crucified to the world system and the world system is crucified to us:

> And those who are Christ's have crucified the flesh with its passions and desires. . . .
>
> But God forbid that I should boast except in the cross of our Lord Jesus Christ, by whom the world has been crucified to me, and I to the world.[39]

The Word of God, bringing the power of the cross into our lives, also brings division. God's Word separates soul from spirit, the natural from the spiritual, the earthly from the heavenly.[40]

When we recognize our co-crucifixion with Christ and reckon it to be true, we begin the journey of embracing the way of suffering, denying ourselves and losing so that He can gain. By this the heavenly is separated from the earthly, the spiritual from the unspiritual, the Spirit from the flesh.[41] The second day of creation reminds us of these realities.

Day Three: His Resurrection

On day three, God gathered the waters together and allowed the dry land to appear. The dry land then began to bear fruit. This was the first sign of life. And it appeared on the third day. Three is the number of resurrection. The Second Testament repeatedly tells us that Jesus was raised on the third day.[42] The resurrection on the third day was also foreshadowed by the prophet Hosea.[43]

Following the great divide of the cross, we see our resurrection with Christ typified by the third day of creation. The waters below—which became the sea—remind us of death. Recall the parting of the Red Sea under Moses and the Egyptians who perished in it.[44] Paul taught us that this was a picture of baptism through death.[45] Throughout Scripture, the sea is often associated with death.[46] Water baptism itself is a picture of death.[47] At the final consummation of the ages, there will be no more sea and no more death.[48]

On day three of creation, the waters of death that once buried the dry ground were parted. The dry ground appeared, and it produced life. This was the first appearance of life in God's good creation. Trees and herbs came forth and began bearing "seed" and "fruit."[49] Jesus referred to Himself as plant life that emerges out of death and produces "many seeds": "The hour has come for the Son of Man to be glorified. I tell you the truth, unless a kernel of wheat falls to the ground and dies, it remains only a single seed. But if it dies, it produces many seeds."[50] Here the Lord was speaking about what would happen on the third day, after He was put to death.

Jesus also spoke of Himself as the "true vine" and bid His disciples to "feed on" Him.[51] Solomon described plant life "from the cedar tree of Lebanon even to the hyssop that springs out of the wall."[52] Both cedar and hyssop are mentioned throughout the Bible. When we think of the hyssop, we think of Christ's meekness and lowliness. When we think of the great cedar tree, we think of the regal majesty and power of Christ. In like manner, wheat is analogous to death, while barley is analogous to resurrection.[53] Our co-resurrection with Christ enables us to bear fruit unto God.

Paul's words in Romans 7 contain echoes of the third day: "So, my brothers, you also died to the law through the body of Christ, that you might belong to another, to him who was raised from the dead, in order that we might bear fruit to God."[54]

The fertile land, which appeared on the third day, reminds us of the fullness of Christ. Imagery of the good and plentiful land of Canaan as a picture of the unsearchable riches of Christ abounds in the books of Ephesians and Colossians.[55] The people of God lived off the land. They drew all their resources from the land. They shared the fruit of the land with one another. Thus the wheat, the barley, the figs, the olives, the fruit of the vine "that makes glad the heart of man,"[56] all represent different aspects of Christ.

Resurrection out of death. Multiplication. Seed. Fruit. Fullness. All these thoughts are captured in day three of creation. Not only have we been crucified with Christ, but we have also been raised with Him.[57] This is the meaning of the third day for every believer.

Day Four: His Ascension

Ascension follows resurrection. On day four, our focus shifts from the earthly to the heavenly. It moves from the ground to the skies. God created the sun, the moon, and the stars and put them in the heavens. These are all light-bearers, for they embody light. They also mark times, signs, and seasons.

When we consider the sun, we cannot help but think of Jesus. He is the embodiment of God's light. He is the source of all light, and He stands high above the earth in His ascended state. He is light contained in a body.[58] In the words of Malachi, Jesus is "the Sun of Righteousness . . . with healing in His wings."[59] Zechariah, the father of John the Baptist, prophesied that Christ would be "the rising sun" that "will come to us from heaven."[60] Both John and Peter called Jesus the "bright Morning Star."[61]

In the natural realm, all life on planet Earth depends on the sun. In the spiritual realm, all life depends on Christ. Recall the Lord's own words: "Without Me you can do nothing."[62] Indeed, Jesus is the reality of the sun.

When we behold the moon, we are reminded of the church. Like the sun, the moon is also an embodied light. But it is not a light source. Rather, the moon *reflects* the light of the sun. The darkness of the world cannot see the real light. But it can behold the body of Christ, the church, which reflects the light.

As the moon, the church reflects the light of Christ and is a faithful witness to His light in a dark world.[63] Scripture tells us that we as individual Christians are like stars, distant suns that expel darkness by their light.[64]

In the divine thought, the church is seated in heavenly places with Christ.[65] In that position, the church stands victorious over satan.[66] Yet the beauty of the gospel is that Christ has become one with His church in resurrection and ascension. For this reason, the church will share in the glory of the Son of God and "shine forth as the sun in the kingdom of their Father."[67] Speaking of the beloved maiden's beauty, Solomon asked the question, "Who is this that appears like the dawn, fair as the moon, bright as the sun, majestic as the stars in procession?"[68] Christ and His beloved share the glory depicted by the sun.[69] The sun and moon are temporary shadows that point to a divine reality, which is fulfilled in God Himself.[70]

In Genesis 1:14, we are told that the sun and the moon are to divide the day from the night. This reminds us of Paul's words in 1 Thessalonians 5:5: "You are all sons of light and sons of the day. We are not of the night nor of darkness." Thus he asked the Corinthians, "What fellowship can light have with darkness?"[71] In the New Jerusalem, there will be no more night.[72]

The sun and moon were also created "to mark seasons and days and years."[73] In Colossians, Paul wrote that the yearly festivals, the monthly new moons, and the weekly Sabbaths are all shadows of Christ: "Therefore do not let anyone judge you by what you eat or drink, or with regard to a religious festival, a New Moon celebration or a Sabbath day. These are a shadow of the things that were to come; the reality, however, is found in Christ."[74]

So the fourth day reminds us of our ascension with Christ and all it entails.

Day Five: His Indwelling Life

While the risen Christ is ascended at the right hand of God the Father in the heavenly realm, Jesus lives in and through His followers by the Spirit. The fifth day reminds us what it means to live by the indwelling life of Christ.

On day five, God created a life that is higher than the unconscious plant life of the third day. He created conscious life in the waters (the fish) and in the heavens (the birds). Notice that the added light of day four (the sun, moon, and stars) came before these higher life forms. Herein lies an important spiritual principle: *with more light comes higher life.*

Although we are ascended with Christ in heavenly places in the spirit, our experience as believers is here on this earth. Spiritually speaking, our spirits are now in Canaan (the heavenlies), our flesh is in Egypt (the world system), and our experience is in the wilderness (the realm of God's testing).

The fifth day teaches us that Christ's life can live in death. Salt water represents death. Few life forms can live in it.[75] The fish lives in the death waters of the sea. The life that we receive in regeneration is a life that has passed through death and overcomes it. It is a life that enables us to swim in the death waters of trial, tribulation, suffering, and persecution. It is a life that conquers the evil things that emerge from the salty seas.[76]

The salted death waters cannot penetrate the fish. (When you eat fish, you detect no salt.) Jesus Christ cannot be touched by death. The same is true for His followers.[77] It is no accident that the early Christians used the sign of the fish (Greek, *ichthus*) to represent Jesus and His followers. Tertullian, in his essay on baptism, said that the Christian, like his Lord, is "born in water."[78] So it is with the Christian's experience on earth.

But that's not all.

After we taste of Christ's life in the waters of death, He lifts us up to soar as the birds of the heavens. The birds know no hindrance. They are not limited to earthly things. They are heavenly creatures. While they can land on the earth and mingle with it, their citizenship is in the heavens.[79] Like the One who created them, they are in the world, but not of it.[80] Like the eagle, they soar above the things of the earth with grace, power, and majesty.[81]

Jesus referred to Himself as a bird.[82] The dove symbolizes the Holy Spirit.[83] But ever since Christ was resurrected, He has come to us in the

Spirit. This is the reason Paul used the Spirit and Jesus synonymously.[84] When predicting His resurrection, Jesus used Himself and the Spirit interchangeably as well.[85] This is because Christ is now in the Spirit, and we experience Him as such.

Like the bird, Jesus is called the "Man . . . from heaven," or the heavenly man.[86] As the heavenly man, the resurrected life of Christ is not bound to this earth. Because it comes from a different realm, it is unchained to this world and cannot be overcome by it.[87] Yet it has contact with the world and is *for* the world. God's ultimate desire is to bring heaven and earth together. This is the meaning of the garden of Eden—the joining together of heaven and earth. And it is what we find at the end of the story in Revelation 21 and 22. In Jesus Christ, heaven and earth are joined together. So Jesus is the reality of both fish and bird.

Romans 8:11 (NIV) sums up the meaning of the fifth day, saying, "And if the Spirit of him who raised Jesus from the dead is living in you, he who raised Christ from the dead will also give life to your mortal bodies through his Spirit, who lives in you."

Day Six: His Rule

On day six, God created the land animals. This includes the cattle of the field. The land animals depict yet another aspect of Christ. Jesus is the real Lamb.[88] He is also the real Lion.[89] He is the embodiment of the bullock, the ram, the red heifer, and all the other animals that were used for Israel's sacrifices.[90] Jesus is the real sacrifice.[91]

The creation of the land animals was followed by the apex of His creation—humanity.

Following regeneration (day one), the work of the cross (day two), our resurrection with Christ (day three), our ascension with Christ in the heavenlies (day four), and the Holy Spirit's work of forming Christ within us in our daily experience (day five), there is only one thing that remains. Paul described it in 1 Corinthians 13:10–12: "But when that which is perfect has come, then that which is in part will be done away. . . . For now we see in a mirror, dimly, but then face to face. Now I know in part, but then I shall know just as I also am known."

At the end of the Christian walk, culminating in the return of the

Lord Jesus Christ, we will be perfected. "We know that when He is revealed, we shall be like Him, for we shall see Him as He is."[92] When Jesus returns, He will bring everything under His control and "will transform our lowly body that it may be conformed to His glorious body."[93] In that day, we will bear the image of Christ in its glorious fullness.[94]

In Romans 5:14, Paul wrote, "Adam is a symbol, a representation of Christ, who was yet to come."[95] In 1 Corinthians 15:45 and 47, Paul called Jesus "the last Adam" and "the second Man [Adam]." Jesus is God's perfect and full thought for humanity. He is the human prototype.[96] On this score, the great theologian Karl Barth rightly said, "As the man Jesus is himself the revealing Word of God, he is the source of our knowledge of the nature of man as created by God."[97]

According to Genesis 1, Adam was created in God's image. Jesus Christ is the perfect image of God. To see Him is to see God.[98] It is by looking at Jesus that we discover who God is. He is the human face of God. In Jesus, true humanity begins anew and reaches its zenith.

Just as Adam was given authority to rule the earth and exercise dominion over it, so Christ, the Second Adam, bore God's image in the earth and exercised His authority. In this way, Adam was a king and a priest on this earth. He was a king to exercise authority and dominion, and a priest to bear God's image and serve the garden.

Note that Adam's dominion was over "every living thing that moves on the earth."[99] We see the fulfillment of this in Jesus' ministry when He cast out demons and healed those who were oppressed by the devil.[100] Recall the Lord's words to His disciples: "Behold, I give you the authority to trample on serpents and scorpions, and over all the power of the enemy, and nothing shall by any means hurt you."[101]

Jesus is the Second Adam—the real King and the real Priest of the earth. He is Lord of both heaven and earth. Like the first man, Jesus embodies God's image and God's rule. And He will visibly rule the entire earth at His second coming and judge the living and the dead.[102] At that time, the saints of God will share His glory and will reign with Him.[103] Through Him the world becomes submitted to God.

Jesus is also "the last Adam."[104] As the last Adam, Christ has finished the old creation. He has put to death all negative things and has brought forth the new creation in which He is Head. As the last Adam, Christ has become a life-giving spirit, imparting the life of the new creation to all who trust in Him.

Today He reigns.[105] And we reign with Him.[106] But at the end of the age, the full inbreaking of His reign will cover the entire earth. This was God's intention from the beginning. Right now, we live in the presence of the future, tasting of the powers of the age to come.[108] The already-but-not-yet lordship of Jesus is upon us. We have bowed the knee today. But tomorrow, every knee shall bow.[109] And if we suffer with Him today, we shall reign with Him tomorrow.[110]

> ***Part of the difficulty is that Jesus was and is much, much more than people imagine. Not just people in general, but practicing Christians, the churches themselves.***
>
> —N. T. Wright[107]

Day Seven: His Rest

On the seventh day God rested from His labors. After Christ reigns supreme, there will be a new heaven and a new earth. And the age of eternal rest shall begin.[111] Following the seventh day (the Sabbath) there is no more mention of evening or morning. This is because the seventh day speaks of the perfect day of eternity that is to come when God will be fully satisfied and find His rest.

Gold will be poured into gold, and light into light, and the *bride* of Christ will become the *wife* of God.[112] (A bride is a married virgin.) The marriage of Adam and Eve that was foreshadowed in Genesis will be consummated between the Second Adam, Christ, and the second Eve, the church. She will enjoy eternal rest in the bosom of her Lord. Jesus Christ will sum up all things into Himself, the kingdom will be given to the Father, and God will become "all in all."[113]

Jesus Christ is the rest of God. He is, as N. T. Wright has put it, "the fulfillment of the sabbath."[114] By taking Christ as our rest, we cease from our labors just as God did from His.[115] Christianity, therefore, begins not with a *do*, but with a *done*—"It is finished!"[116] We enter into God's rest, and we labor from there.

The Sabbath was merely a shadow, as Paul put it. It was a signpost pointing to Jesus Christ, who is the reality of the Sabbath, our true rest and Jubilee.[117] Yet the rest of God will one day fill the universe. The Prince of Peace will establish His rule over all things, the lion will lie down with the lamb, and the knowledge of God will cover the earth as the waters cover the sea.[118] The seventh day of creation points to all of these realities.

Day Eight: His Bride

In Genesis 2, we have another account of creation.[119] Here we find the first appearance of Eve. Some scholars view Eve's formation as occurring on the sixth day. Others, however, view it as having occurred on the eighth day.

If the second interpretation is correct, then the reference to male and female in Genesis 1:27 is a reference to the fact that Adam had a female inside of him (metaphorically). This was before God "split the Adam" and took Eve from his side.[120]

What makes this interpretation attractive is that the number eight in the Bible is connected with resurrection, regeneration, and newness of life.[121]

Eight is the number after seven. Many Bible students believe the number seven in the Bible points to completeness or perfection. Eight, therefore, seems to represent a new series, the beginning of a new order. For example, the eighth day is the first day of the week after the seventh (the Sabbath). There were eight souls saved in the ark to greet a new creation and begin a new world.[122] Israelite males were circumcised on the eighth day, which foreshadowed the circumcision of the heart that occurs during regeneration.[123] The firstborn sons were to be given to YHWH on the eighth day.[124] David, the man who would begin a new dynasty in Israel, was the eighth son.[125] Jesus was raised again on the first day of the week, or the eighth day.[126]

The church was born on the eighth day. The old creation was part of the seven-day cycle; the new creation emerged on the eighth day. For this reason the early church "celebrated the first day of the week as 'the Lord's day.'" [127] The first day of the week is the eighth day.

Even if you disagree as to the precise time of Eve's formation, one thing is clear. Paul taught us that Adam prefigured Jesus Christ—God's perfect thought for man.[128] And Eve is analogous to the church, which is one body with Christ.[129]

One of us described the formation of Eve in another place, saying:

> Recall that creation is finished. Day seven has passed. We are nearing the end of the eighth day—the first day of the week. It is evening. And God does something extraordinary: He puts His man into a deep, deathlike sleep. This may be the first time that unfallen man had ever slept. If so, a deep sleep was no small thing for Adam to experience.
>
> Behold, I show you a mystery: *There was a woman hidden inside of Adam.*
>
> I want you to imagine Adam lying on the ground in a hypnotic, deathlike sleep. Watch his still body as the Almighty comes down to him and breaks open his side. The angels of heaven hide their eyes over what is about to take place. Out of Adam's very being, the Lord God extracts another being. The Almighty takes out of Adam a part of Adam, and by it He fashions another Adam. God takes a human out of the first human and builds a second human. And that second human has within its pounding heart all that is part of the first human, including his passion.
>
> God did His most magnificent work while Adam was asleep. This episode contains an important insight: *When man rests, God works.*
>
> So out of Adam's side, God "fashioned" a woman (Gen. 2:22, Hebrew text). This woman is not part of the first creation. She appears after creation, on the eighth day. Consequently, this woman is a *new creation.*[130]
>
> Adam's drastic surgery is over, and he awakens from God's anesthetic. As Adam wipes the slumber from his eyelids, he turns and looks. What he sees is beyond telling. Before his very eyes stands a living, breathing, pulsating being. Another human. But not just another human, she is Adam in another form.
>
> Immediately, he notices that she has a hand just like his, a hand to hold. She has lips just like his, but fuller and more inviting. At that

> moment, Adam realizes that he is no longer alone. He has a counterpart to match him. He has a companion. Instantly, the two are hypnotically drawn to each other. Adam falls deeply in love with her and she with him.
>
> According to the Hebrew text, when Adam saw this new creation, he uttered these words: "At last . . . this is bone of my bone and flesh of my flesh" (Gen. 2:23). "Finally . . . I am no longer alone!"
>
> "Finally . . . the passion of my heart has an outlet!" "Finally . . . the love that has been beating inside my chest has a home!" *"Finally . . ."*
>
> Adam had stood on this earth alone. He had been the loneliest creature on the planet. Single and solitary. But now, on the first day after creation, he stood in the presence of one who was just like him. She was Adam in a different form. And in a blinding flash of insight, Adam realized that his loneliness had vanished. His passion had a place to break forth. It could now find release.[131]

All of this contains a pre-echo of John 19–20. In John 19, Pilate looked at a beaten, dejected Jesus, the Second Adam, and declared, "Behold the Man!"[132] Pilate's words remind us of day six, when the first Adam appeared in creation.[133] We then read about the crucifixion of Jesus, when He died. His last words were "It is finished!"[134] The word "finished" reminds us of Genesis 2:1, when the first creation was completed.

After three days of being in what might be described as a "deep sleep," Jesus was resurrected. When Mary Magdalene saw the resurrected Lord, she believed He was the gardener, a throwback to the garden of Eden.[135] We are now in the presence of a new Eden—a new beginning, a new creation, a new day.[136] The first (old) creation was finished at the cross. The new creation has emerged. The grave has become a garden, and the resurrected Christ has become the last Adam. Jesus then breathed His Spirit upon His disciples.[137] In His resurrection, the Second Adam became a life-giving spirit.[138] The church, the body of Christ, the bride of the Lamb, was born. Interestingly, John was careful to point to the language that Genesis 1 repeatedly used, "morning" and "evening."[139]

Just as Eve was inside Adam before she appeared, the church was "in Him [Christ] before the foundation of the world" before she appeared.[140]

Just as God put Adam into a deep sleep, Jesus was put into the deepest sleep of all—death.[141] Just as God opened Adam's side to bring forth Eve, the side of our Lord was opened on the cross. Out of it flowed water and blood—the outstanding marks of birth.[142]

The pierced side of Jesus is the womb from which the bride of Christ was born. The water that poured out of Him reminds us of the living waters that poured forth from the rock when Moses struck it in the presence of Israel.[143] Paul told us "that Rock was Christ."[144]

The water speaks of the life of God that awakens our dead spirits, and the blood speaks of that which redeems us from sin.[145] Eve, the bride of Adam, was formed after the first creation was finished. She is part of a second or "new creation." The same is true for the new Eve, the church, the bride of the Second Adam. She is part of the new creation. She is that which comes out of Christ, just as Eve came out of Adam.

> *"Truth unchanged, unchanging" is ever moving forward to the completion of God's purpose, and that purpose is being fulfilled, and will be consummated, in the immutable Jesus.*
>
> —F. F. Bruce[146]

In short, Jesus Christ is the *real* Adam, and the church—the Lord's counterpart—is the *real* Eve. Paul called this "the mystery which has been hidden from ages and from generations, but now has been revealed"—the open secret that has been in God's beating heart from before time.[147] There are two aspects to this divine mystery. The mystery of God is Christ,[148] and the mystery of Christ is the church.[149] And the mystery of all mysteries is that Christ and the church are united together in oneness.[150]

BACK TO THE GARDEN

In Genesis 2:15, God commanded Adam to cultivate and keep the garden. The Hebrew word for *cultivate* is *abad*, and the Hebrew word for *keep* is *shamar.* These same Hebrew words are used to describe how the priests cared for the tabernacle of Moses.[151] (The tabernacle was a precursor to the temple of Solomon.) The priests were to cultivate (*abad*) and keep (*shamar*) the tabernacle. In addition, we are told that God walked in the garden (Hebrew, *hawlak*) during the cool of the day.[152] God also walked (*hawlak*) in the midst of the temple.[153]

The meaning is clear. The garden was a temple for God. Like the temple, the garden was the joining together of God's space and man's space—the intersection of the heavenly realm and the earthly realm. For this reason, Isaiah called it "the garden of the LORD,"[154] and Ezekiel called it "the garden of God."[155]

The parallels between the garden of Eden, the temple, and creation are striking. Let's first compare the garden with the temple of Israel.

THE GARDEN AND THE TEMPLE OF ISRAEL

The garden of Eden faced east.[156] The tabernacle and temple faced east.[157] The garden was placed on a mountain.[158] The temple was also placed on a mountain.[159] The trees of the garden were pleasing to the eye.[160] In like manner, the temple of God is always associated with beauty.[161] Palm trees, pomegranates, lily blossoms, and open flowers were graven in the walls of the temple.[162] These all contain echoes of the garden.

The cherubim (plural of *cherub*) were embroidered into the curtains of the tabernacle and temple, guarding the Holy of Holies.[163] The cherubim were also placed on both sides of the bloodstained mercy seat of the ark of the covenant, guarding it just as they guarded the garden of Eden.[164] This is why the First Testament says that the Lord dwells in the midst of the cherubim.[165]

Gold, silver, and precious stones filled the temple.[166] Gold, pearl,[167] and precious stones flowed from the garden of Eden. Interestingly, gold and onyx were in the temple—the same elements mentioned in Genesis 2.[168] But why is silver mentioned in the temple and not pearl? Consider Paul's words in 1 Corinthians 3:12–15, when he spoke of gold, silver, and precious stones in the context of building the church. In the temple (both the shadow and the reality), silver replaces pearl. This is because silver typifies redemption.[169] Before the Fall[170] and after the Fall is removed,[171] silver is unnecessary. So we have pearl instead. But between Genesis 2 and Revelation 21, silver is necessary.

It is no accident that the ancient Hebrews and rabbis regarded the garden of Eden to be God's first temple.[172] Both the tabernacle of Moses and the temple of Solomon constantly remind us of the garden.[173] But they also remind us of creation itself.

The tabernacle was built in seven distinct stages.[174] The temple of Solomon was built in seven years,[175] and it was dedicated in the seventh month.[176] God created the heavens and the earth in seven days, and then He rested. Moses rested after he built the tabernacle.[177] And once the temple of Solomon was built, God found rest.[178] It's not surprising, then, that the psalmist regarded the temple as a microcosm of heaven and earth.[179]

Jesus Christ is the reality of the temple. (In the Greek, John 1:14 says Jesus "tabernacled among us.") He is also the reality of the garden. He is the real Tree of Life[180] and a flowing river.[181] In Christ, God's space and man's space are joined together. But Christ is also the reality of the seven-day creation, as we have seen. He is, as the Second Testament declares, the head or firstborn over all creation, including the new creation.[182]

> *The Christian faith begins not with a big DO but with a big DONE.*
>
> —Watchman Nee[183]

In the temple, God's glory and presence dwelled on the ark of the covenant in the Holy of Holies. The Holy of Holies was a perfectly cubed room. It grew in size from its dimensions in the tabernacle to its dimensions in the temple of Solomon. But it still retained its perfectly cubed shape. In the temple Ezekiel saw in his vision, the Holy of Holies grew even larger.[184] In the book of Revelation, we are introduced to the New Jerusalem—a colossal-sized, perfect cube.[185] In other words, the entire city is the Holy of Holies. God dwells there. The Tree of Life; the flowing river; and gold, pearl, and precious stones all reappear in the city. And the city is a bride.

The gold, pearl, and precious stones all reflect different aspects of the nature and work of the Godhead.[186] In Revelation 21–22, the garden of Genesis 2 has been transformed into a city—the very dwelling place or "house" of God. The bride of Christ is the house of God. From the beginning of creation, God has been building His house, which is also the bride of Christ. Interestingly, in Genesis 2:22, we are told that God "built"—a Hebrew word translated "made"—a woman out of Adam's side.

The imagery is clear. God began His creation with clay. Humans are but jars of clay.[187] We were designed to contain God's life. The Tree of Life appears in the midst of the garden. And women and men are invited to eat from that tree and live by it. The Tree of Life is God's life in consumable form. The reality of the tree, of course, is Jesus Himself. The words of the Second Testament quickly come to mind: "I am the vine . . . without Me you can do nothing." "He who feeds on Me will live because of Me." "It is no longer I who live, but Christ lives in me." "Christ . . . our life."[188]

By eating from the Tree of Life and drinking from the flowing river, clay is transformed into gold, pearl, and precious stones for the building of God's dwelling place. This dwelling place is not a physical building. Rather, the New Jerusalem is a magnificent symbol of the glorious church, the bride of the Lamb. This dwelling place is pictured by Eve, whom God built from Adam's side. She is the new creation birthed after the first creation was finished. And she and her husband, Jesus Christ, are united in spirit. Note Paul's remarkable words in 1 Corinthians 6:16–17 (NIV): "Do you not know that he who unites himself with a prostitute is one with her in body? For it is said, 'The two will become one flesh.' But he who unites himself with the Lord is one with him in spirit."

In Christ, the garden of God, which is the temple of God, will fill the entire cosmos.[189] Together with our Head, we—the body of Christ—are the real temple of God, which God is seeking to enlarge to the entire creation.[190]

N. T. Wright wraps it up nicely, saying, "I have already hinted strongly enough, I think, that Jesus saw his own work, his own public career, his own very person, as the reality to which the Temple, sabbath, and creation itself were pointing."[191]

There is so much more. But we hope these points will throw new light on the word of our Lord Jesus when He said, "If you believed Moses, you would believe Me; for he wrote about Me."[192]

ANOTHER PERSPECTIVE ON CHRIST IN CREATION

Before we shift our attention to a small village called Bethlehem, we want to go deeper in unveiling Jesus in the first two chapters of Genesis. In this chapter, we presented a survey of the main points, largely focusing on Genesis 1 (the macro version of creation). In the next chapter, we look more closely at Genesis 2 in the light of Christ (the micro version of creation). Augustine said the first chapter of Genesis is creation in the mind of God, and the second chapter is creation in time and space. He went on to say that you can take it the other way around if you want.[193] That's the genius of a great story. You can always take it the other way, look at it upside down, inside out, sideways and crossways, and find new insights and inspirations.

So the first two chapters of Genesis give us different but complementary tellings of the same story—the greatest story ever told. And that story is the narrative of Jesus Christ and God's timeless purpose in Him.

CHAPTER 3

Christ in Creation: The Micro Version

Heat cannot be separated from fire,

or beauty from the eternal.

—Michelangelo[1]

God's art of communication is incarnation, which began with the sound of a big bang that pierced the silence with "Let there be light" and crescendoed as sound became sight and creation blossomed forth. Then one day, the star of Bethlehem bloomed, and the ultimate act of communication took place—the human incarnation of the eternal Word, the Light of the World, when God took human flesh in Jesus, who was the Christ, the human One, the bright and morning star.[2]

The people who walk in darkness
Will see a great light;
Those who live in a dark land,
The light will shine on them . . .
For a child will be born to us, a son will be given to us;
And the government will rest on His shoulders.[3]

The universe is so big, it takes two versions, a micro and a macro rendering, to tell the creation story, just as Jesus is so big, it takes four gospels to tell His story. Although, as we are trying to show in our expositions of Genesis 1 and 2, you can start anywhere in the Bible and tell the whole Jesus story.

THE STORY STARTS WITH DIRT

The first image in the Genesis 2 micro version?

Dirt. At least dirt is where the micro creation account launches the birth story of the universe: no shrubs, no plants, just dirt and dust. The Bible begins with a disquisition on dirt. Biblical faith is a down-to-earth faith.

That image of dirt is presented in poetic form, in terms of what it isn't rather than what it is, but the dirt is inescapable. The Latin word for "dirt," *humus*, is from whence we get the word *humble*. Something can be as dry as dust and lifeless as dirt, with scant or scrawny growth. Or something can be as rich as topsoil, the humus of life, when the ground has been fertilized by its past. Out of humble dirt comes life. Far from dirt being "matter out of place,"[4] matter is dirt placed to order. But not without water, H_20, the union of opposites. Hydrogen burns; oxygen promotes burning. But when united together, they put out fires.

Suddenly in the story, streams rise up from within and below. The surface of the ground is watered.

Wait a minute: When dirt and water mix, what do you get? Mud. Clay. How were you and I created? The Bible begins with an artistic image of God as a Potter fashioning humans in God's image. But no potter can work with dry clay. In order for the Master Potter to mold and make a human according to divine design, the clay must be moist. The most important questions every human being must answer, and can only answer for him- or herself, are these: What keeps your clay moist? What moisturizers keep our clay pliable and susceptible to the Master's touch?

GOD PLAYS IN THE DIRT

God, the Master Potter, scooped out of the ground a clump of clay, molded and made it into the first human, and then breathed into that human the breath of God. Until God breathed the divine spirit into Adam, humans were just a mass of matter, a moist duvet of dirt. But when matter united with spirit, and that spirit was God's Spirit, a soul was conceived, and the first Adam became a human being. God created *adam* from *adamah*, earthling from earth, and added spirit to the mix to create a living soul. When spirit is removed—from dust and dirt we came; to dust and dirt we return.[5]

The earliest image of God in the Bible? God is playing in the dirt, making mud pies. Maybe we were meant to play in the dirt, and to get our hands dirty and wet.[6] The first time we meet God, we see that our Creator is not afraid of getting dirty. The Bible begins with God getting the divine hands dirty and wet. The more we know about the human body, the more we realize that a healthy human needs exposure to dirt to protect from disease. Getting dirty is at the heart of keeping physically fit and spiritually clean.

What makes a being "human" is soul. Humans are "God-breathed."[7] Human beings don't have souls. Humans *are* souls. But humans aren't born with fully developed souls. They must grow in soul. Soul moments are growth spurts in loving God with our whole hearts, minds, and spirits.

There is a difference between cold hearts and dirt hearts, or between cold souls and dirt souls. Dirt souls are undeveloped souls, souls to which water hasn't been added.

Every human is born with a dirt soul. You grow a dirt soul into a soul that bears fruit, but to grow a fruit-bearing soul, you need to add water and spirit—not just any spirit but God's Spirit. It is the undeveloped soul that is the source of our problems today, not so much the cold soul or mean soul as the underdeveloped soul, the unwatered and underbreathed soul.

THE GARDEN OF GOD'S TEMPLE

In the macro creation account of Genesis 1, there is the portrayal of God establishing the cosmos as the Lord's temple, meant to be filled and flooded with God's presence. This is why God "rested" on day seven, a verb that is used almost exclusively in ancient Near Eastern literature to describe how divine beings take up residence in their temples.

The first, the fairest garden that ever was, Paradise, He [Christ] was the gardener, it was of His planting. So, a gardener. And ever since it is He that as God makes all our gardens green, sends us yearly the spring, and all the herbs and flowers we then gather . . . but He it is who gardens our "souls," too, and . . . waters them with the dew of His grace, and makes them bring forth fruit to eternal life.

—Lancelot Andrewes[10]

But every temple needs a garden, and every garden a temple. In Genesis 2, the garden is a microcosm of the cosmos and God's mission for the macrocosm. Garden and temple, the two places that pinnacle and ritualize the divine presence.[8]

The first things we know about the garden of Eden are twofold. First, God put Adam there, as it later says, "to tend and keep it [the garden]."[9] The world's oldest profession is not what we think it is. You might call this the real prime directive: we are all gardeners—groundskeepers, housekeepers, beekeepers, earthkeepers. Our relationship with the world is as gardener to garden—a symbiosis of mutual care and dependence. Gardening and shalom-making are the same: be the image of God to the part of the world where God has placed us.

But notice there are two parts to God's prime directive: conserve and conceive. We are to conserve what God created. Not *preserve* but *conserve*. You preserve pickles. You don't pickle the planet. Our directive is more than giving this garden planet nursemaid-like attention in an ecological purism that snubs everything not aboriginal. Nor is our directive to do whatever we feel like doing to the planet and its resources, as if the garden is here to serve us or we're in the liquidation business. Cruelty and cupidity are not what the Creator had in mind when entrusting humans with "dominion" over creation.[11] This is made clear at the end of the story, when part of each person's divine judgment includes the question: How have you cared for the earth?[12]

> ***The time has come to begin the begat . . .***
>
> —Adam to Eve in the musical *Finian's Rainbow* (1947)[13]

Gardens are the result of collaboration between human and divine, between art and nature. God planted the first garden Himself but left the garden unfinished. We are put there to continue what the Master Gardener started and to bring the planet under cultivation. Adam and Eve couldn't garden the earth alone. They needed to cultivate new Adams and Eves. Of course, part of cultivating is leaving some wild alone. But it is also taking what God gives and doing something wondrous with it. God does not call humanity to simply receive, to merely consume. God calls us to give back and participate, to procreate and conceive, to take the wilderness and make it marvelous. Not to wipe out the wilderness, but to make the wilderness wonderful.

OUR PRIME DIRECTIVE

While giving humans the responsibility for conserving what God has created ("tend the garden"), we are to continue God's creativity and "conceive" ("till the garden"). God created humans not just to take care of the garden but to make it more beautiful and marvelous. Augustine's classic *The City of God* may have been better called *The Garden City of God*.

God did not put us here to consume but to conceive. The prime directive gives us an ethic of conception ("I conceive, therefore I am"), not consumption ("I consume, therefore I am"). This is the real meaning of originality: going back to origins and recapitulating the new out of the original. "Conceiving" is not "co-creating," but "sub-creating" (as J. R. R. Tolkien liked to put it).[14] We are subcontractors who are privileged to participate in God's creation project. God creates the "new." Our prime directive is to sub-create the new out of the old, the old-new. What Isaiah and then later Jesus called "a new thing"[15] are those things that are always present but undetected until now in the Master's storehouse. The future beats with an ancient vibe. Humans are created in the image of a God who has been cultivating the earth. Thus, our mission is to cultivate the earth.

Second, God is an arborphiliac and chlorophiliac. God loves trees, and God loves green. The first things the Lord put in the garden were trees, which makes one wonder if God's favorite color isn't green. This garden planet called Earth in the garden galaxy called the Milky Way is miraculously conceived so that the waste product of trees (oxygen) is the life-breath of humans, and the waste product of humans (carbon dioxide) is the life-breath of trees. Deforestation is a form of lung removal (pneumonectomy).

THE TREES IN THE GARDEN

There were two kinds of trees God planted in the garden, however. The first were designed to bear fruit—"good for food."[16] But there was another kind of tree that God created, making one wonder if God isn't, besides an arborphiliac and chlorophiliac, also a venustraphiliac: trees that had no other function than to be "pleasant to the sight."[17] From the very beginning, God was in the beauty business, which (as it is defined today) is better called the ugly industry, since ugliness (sin, death, lust) is consumption without conception. The Creator evidences a beauty bias. God wants to beautify our lives. Beauty is not something that stimulates or satisfies an appetite for something else. Beauty is its own reward. It is the scent of God on the universe, a keyhole-peek of the kingdom in the here and now and a sonogram of God's own heart. This is why art is so powerful—it can rival the God it is created to reveal.

For Russian icon painters in training, it all begins with the transfiguration. Apprentices traditionally dip their first brush tips onto a palette dedicated to the creation of an icon of the transfiguration of Christ. Of all the events in Jesus' life, the transfiguration most manifests God's transfiguring beauty, which is integral to the integrity of the divine-human relationship, a transfiguring beauty that icon painters aspire to infuse in all their art.[18]

> ***The real sin against life is to abuse and destroy beauty, even one's own—even more, one's own, for that has been put in our care and we are responsible for its well-being.***
>
> —KATHERINE ANNE PORTER[20]

Of all the trees in the garden of Eden, two are highlighted as being in the "midst" and being of special importance: the Tree of Life, and the Tree of Knowledge of Good and Evil.[19] The Tree of Life is the fount of eternal life. The Tree of Knowledge is a tree that invites the feeder to enter into a relationship with the mystery of good and evil, a mystery reserved for God alone. In Hebrew the word for "knowledge" really means "intercourse with," and "intercourse" means the highest degree of intimacy possible between two entities. To eat of the fruit of "good and evil" is to unite oneself to "good and evil," to "know" it personally. The garden was then crossed by four rivers, a layout for a dream garden that still goes by the name of "paradise garden" to this day.

What comes next is extremely important. This is the first time in the Bible that God spoke to humans. First words are always remembered and celebrated. What were the first words out of God's mouth? "And the LORD God commanded the man, saying, 'Of every tree of the garden you may freely eat.'"[21] The first words out of God's mouth are positive, not negative. God speaks "yes" before "no": "but of the tree of the knowledge of good and evil you shall not eat, for in the day that you eat of it you shall surely die."[22] If the first commandment in the Bible is "Eat freely," one wonders what the last commandment might be.

> *He who has an ear, let him hear what the Spirit says to the churches. To him who overcomes I will give to eat from the tree of life, which is in the midst of the Paradise of God.*
>
> —JESUS[25]

If we quickly jump ahead to the end of the story, and leap from Genesis to the maps, we find ourselves where we began in the story. This time, though, we're in a garden city with the Tree of Life and River of Life flowing from the throne of God. There we receive the promise of the coming of Jesus, God's ultimate "Yes!"[23] And the last commandment in the Bible is this: "Let anyone who desires drink freely from the water of life."[24]

The Bible has bookend commands: The first command is "Eat freely." The last command is "Drink freely." And everything in between is a banquet.[26] Not a snack. Not a smorgasbord where we choose what we like and leave what we don't like. Rather, a life-course meal on which we feast on Him in our hearts with thanksgiving. The Jesus life is a dinner party . . . or more precisely, a garden party.

JESUS MEETS ALL HUMAN NEED

It is no surprise, therefore, that Jesus was repeatedly presented as food.[27] And He had a great deal to say about food and eating.[28] Jesus, in a word, is the reality of what food points to. He is the reality of what drink points to. Christ is real food and real drink; what we consume on earth is but a shadow.

In this regard, the gospel of John (which is the new Genesis) portrays Jesus as meeting all human need:

- He is life.[29] Life is the beginning of all human need.
- He is light.[30] No life can live without the sun, the light of the world.
- He is air.[31] "Spirit" means "breath" in Greek. We need air to live.

- He is food.[32] Life doesn't exist without food.
- He is drink.[33] Life doesn't exist without water.
- He is shelter.[34] We need a place to abide in order to live.

I am the food of grown people.

—AUGUSTINE[35]

THE FIRST NEGATIVE NOTE IN THE BIBLE

Suddenly, something is not right. The first negative note struck in the Bible is here: "It is not good that man [*adam*] should be alone."[36] Aloneness is what God had been creating against. God exists in relationship[37] and created Adam to enable the Creator to be in relationship with the creation. But *adam* was alone, and aloneness is the ultimate anti-force in the universe. Long before sin entered the picture, the God who filled the void with light and life and color and clamor identified aloneness as a "not good" state of being.

In a stunning turn in the story, the next thing God created to correct this condition was the animals. In as high a doctrine of creation as one can find in all of ancient literature, the first candidates for companionship were the beasts of the field (represented by the lion, the king of the beasts and symbol of Mark's gospel); the birds of the air (represented by the eagle, the king of the birds and symbol of John's gospel); and the domesticated livestock (represented by the bull, the king of farm animals and symbol of Luke's gospel). The last things God created were the earthlings, *ish* and *ishah* (represented by the human, the capstone of creation and symbol of Matthew's gospel).

Up until now, there was only a whole perfect being called *adam,* who came from the *adamah*. When Adam named Eve *ishah*, he also called himself into a new state of being and named himself: *ish*. Man and woman found their identity together and in each other. In Hebrew *ish* is "man"; *ishah* is "woman." The *ishah* physically comes from *ish*, from his "side," his "rib," a place that is neither superior nor inferior to its source.[38]

> *Freely you have received, freely give.*
>
> —Jesus[39]

The word we weakly translate as "helper" in Hebrew is *ezer*. But astonishingly, *ezer* is masculine in gender, even though it refers to Eve. Ever more amazingly, the word *ezer* is most often used to refer to YHWH in relation to Israel. YHWH is Israel's *ezer*, Israel's "strong deliverer," "mighty companion," "saver." Here Eve, the woman to the man, the *ishah* to the *ish*, saved Adam from his isolation and solitariness. She was his *ezer*—his "deliverer," his "companion," his "saver."

THE BRIDE IS CONCEIVED

When God prepared to create the perfect *ezer* for *adam*, the literal translation of God's intent was this: "I will make for him a partner according to what is in front of him." The verbal root *neged* ("in front of") suggests a face-to-face union of equals. There is no hint of superiority or inferiority between Adam and the *ezer* that is God's gift. This is also why all the animals that initially auditioned for the role of *ezer* failed to qualify. The fact that they were, like Adam, created out of the dirt put them literally under his already created feet. Adam tried his hand at partnering with God in sub-creating—naming each creature as it passed before him. But no beast, no bird, and no farm animal could go face-to-face with Adam. Thus none could be his *ezer*.

The Almighty created the first Adam out of matter that God had already created: dirt. Adam's "companion" (*ezer*) was fashioned differently. To create a genuinely new *ezer* for Adam, there was only one raw resource that met the criterion: *adam*. The ultimate partner would come from the same source. So God split the *adam*.

It required surgery to separate the *ishah* from the *ish*. The *adam* was put into a divinely induced deep sleep (*tardemah*), so he was oblivious to any pain and to the surprising, side-splitting action God took on his behalf, creating a wholly new creature drawn from half of him: wo-man. The word *sex* comes from the Latin *secare*, which means "to cut or divide."

Once the woman was split apart from him, God "brought her to the man,"[40] an image that foreshadows the bridal attendant taking the bride to the bridegroom. The sudden appearance of this new human being inspired the man to shout (and maybe even speak) for the first time. Although he was not privy to how the woman had been created, the face-to-face and beside quality of the one standing before him was immediately discernible: "bone of my bones and flesh of my flesh."[41] Up to this point in the text, the man has been consistently referred to as *adam*. Now, confronted with his new *ezer*, a final naming ritual took place. "Adam" named both of them together—she was "woman," *ishah*, and he was declared to be "man," *ish*.

When the first Adam's side was split, a bride was conceived, a bride worthy of the husband leaving home and family to join in marriage.[42] It is a striking image, since the wife left the homestead and father in ancient Near Eastern marriages, just as Jesus left His home and Father for His bride.

Both "forsake" and "cling" are terms used to describe Israel's covenantal relationship with YHWH.[43] The relationship between man and woman, husband and wife, is framed as a covenant. Marriage is not about improving land holdings, upping your status, or picking up a new herd of sheep. A covenant relationship means a loyalty and faithfulness that sometimes require the groom to leave home and father and be united to a bride.

Male difficulty in showing emotions wasn't there from the beginning. It was something *ish*es learned over time. When the first *ish* was introduced to the *ishah*, what did Adam do? He started gushing with a gully-washer of emotions. His language made the first, stammering attempts at connection—"At last!"[44] Was *ish* excited or what?

THE BROKEN RELATIONSHIPS

It was an idyllic existence for both human and divine. God's favorite thing to do was walk in the garden with Adam and Eve "while the dew is still on the roses," as the hymn writer put it.[45] Ask any gardener when is the best time to walk a garden, and he or she will tell you the same thing:

while the dew is still on the roses—early and dark (dawn) or late and light (dusk). These were the last Adam's two favorite times of day, which He mostly spent in prayer. Prayer is walking in the garden with God.

> *What is a charitable heart? Is it a heart which is burning with a loving charity for the whole of creation, for me, for the birds, for the beasts. . . . He who has such a heart cannot see or call to mind a creature without his eyes being filled with tears by reason of the immense compassion which seizes his heart: a heart which is so softened and can no longer bear to hear or learn from others of any suffering, even the smallest pain, being inflicted upon any creature. This is why such a man never ceases to pray also for the animals . . . pray even for the lizards and reptiles.*
>
> —Isaac of Syria (seventh century)[46]

One day, God walked the garden—and Adam and Eve were nowhere to be found.

"Adam, Eve, it's our time together. . . . Adam? Eve? Where are you?"

"We're hiding."

This was the first broken relationship of human existence: a broken relationship with God. We are all, in one form or another, hiding from our Maker.

"Why are you hiding?" God asked.

"We're naked."

This was the second broken relationship of human existence: a broken relationship with ourselves. We're all wearing masks, facades, and trying to be something other than what God made us.

"Who told you you were naked? Why did you eat of that tree? I gave you thousands of trees and said, 'Eat freely. Go there.' Only one tree I said, 'Don't go there.' Why did you disobey Me?"

Adam replied, "The woman *You gave me* made me do it."

Eve replied, "The serpent made me do it."

This was the third broken relationship of human existence: a broken relationship with each other, with the companions God has given us, human and animal. The great unresolved issue of the human species is this: how to get along with one another.

Then God banished the humans from the garden, which was the fourth broken relationship of human existence: a broken relationship with creation. Creation needed redemption; it was fallen, like the rest of us. From now on humans would not function in a paradigm of play, where vocation and vacation are synonymous, but a paradigm of work: "Eve, you'll labor, and Adam, you'll labor." From now on, nature and humans would go their separate ways. In biblical Hebrew there is no word for "nature" because "nature" was not supposed to be something separate from us: we were created to be a part of it, and it a part of us. After the Fall, all creation joined humans in the trail and travail of brokenness, awaiting the day of its redemption.

To prevent Adam and Eve from returning to the garden, God posted great winged creatures called cherubim and their fiery, flashing swords to guard the gate to the Tree of Life.

THE REST OF THE STORY

The rest of the story, from Genesis to the genuine leather, is the story of God's initiatives to repair and restore, redeem and mend those four broken relationships so as to bring humans back to God's eternal purpose, which was in God's heart from before the Fall. Thus the mission and purpose of God are not redemption, as is commonly taught. Redemption is the contingency program put in place to get us *back to* God's purpose—a purpose that predated Adam's fall into sin. Consequently, the history of humanity comprises three parallel stories:

- the story of God's original purpose, which stands apart from the Fall and redemption—a purpose that God has never let go of
- the story of human attempts to find loopholes to avoid the legacy of the Fall
- the story of God's various strategies for corralling humanity back through the gates of Eden

There is no event in history unrelated to these three stories.

God tried everything.

God tried a flood, which one Asian theologian calls "God's tears."[47] God was so hurt by our rejection, stubborn rebelliousness, and refusal to be in a right relationship that God couldn't stop crying.

God tried a covenant. Not just a covenant with Noah but a covenant with all creation, with "all flesh that is on the earth."[48] That's why YHWH kept sending Moses back in his negotiation with Pharaoh. A partial release of "My people" wasn't good enough. Liberation had to apply to men, women, and children as well as all creation. In some of the most stunning words of ancient literature, "Not a hoof shall be left behind."[49]

God tried prophets.

God tried a king.

God tried a temple.

Nothing worked.

Finally God decided to go for broke: God stepped in. Literally. God sent the Son to be the Second Adam, the last Adam to stand firm where Adam didn't, to lead the life that Adam wouldn't, and to pay the price that Adam couldn't. By assuming our humanity, Jesus made all creation sacramental and gave God a human voice.

The mission of the Second Adam? To show us how to be the kind of humans God created us to be, and to bring us back into a garden relationship with God. Luke recorded Peter preaching Jesus, "the author of life."[50] What kind of life? Human life living by divine life. Jesus returned to us our full humanity. The Creator's original thought for human beings was that they would live by God's divine, eternal, uncreated life. God wanted Adam and Eve to live by the Tree of Life. Adam, however, tragically chose to live by the wrong tree instead. Jesus, the Second Adam, lived by the life of His Father. And He has called all humans to live by His life just as He lived by His Father's life.[51]

On the cross Jesus probed the limits of what it means to be human, enabling us to become fully human ourselves and thereby to participate in Jesus' divine life. As the second-century church father Irenaeus explained it, just as the Spirit of God created a life at the beginning of time, the Holy Spirit created new life in Mary—a fresh start for humanity.[52] The kingdom of God proclaims the possibility of a new person, a new human being. "Put on the new man," Paul wrote.[53]

From beginning to end, the Bible shows us how to be a Jesus kind of human, the kind of garden human we were designed to be. How do we know the mission of that Second Adam is accomplished?

Mary Magdalene was the first person to whom Jesus appeared after His resurrection. Did Mary recognize Him? No, she thought He was the gardener.

What God has started lovingly, God will finish lovingly. In His life, death, and resurrection, Jesus redeemed and restored all four broken relationships. Only a redeemed human nature can truly radiate the divine nature, can radiate Christ. Jesus is the fulfillment of all God's promises and the flowering of humanity. In coming to know Jesus, we come to know God, ourselves, others, and creation.[54]

Solon (c. 638–c. 558 BC) said, "Know thyself."

Menander (343–292) countered, "Know other people."

God (infinite) says, "Know Jesus, and you'll know both."[55]

CHAPTER 4

Jesus' Birth and Boyhood

The birth date of our God has signaled the beginning of good news for the world.

—First-century stone inscription announcing birth of Caesar Augustus

Jesus was born "before Christ" (BC). Probably 4 or 5 BC.[1] Jesus is always one step ahead.

> And she brought forth her firstborn Son, and wrapped Him in swaddling cloths, and laid Him in a manger, because there was no room for them in the inn.[2]

In some manger straw, Jesus was born. A defenseless baby lying amid the stench and stain of animal dung.

What was God's answer to saving the world and righting all wrongs? God became small and dirty.

A CULTURE OF PARADOX

Great power resides in the small, spare, simple.

A box cutter brought down a skyscraper and nearly bankrupted a nation.

A pamphlet on common sense sparked a revolution.

A song about overcoming changed the world.

A little town birthed the Messiah.

And a small room on the lower level (a dirty room called a stable) cradled the Son of God.

> ***I bring you good news that will bring great joy to all people. The Savior—yes, the Messiah, the Lord—has been born today.***
>
> —ANGEL TO SHEPHERDS[3]

Little is large if God is in it.

A large room on the upper level (a bare open chamber called the upper room) cradled the Spirit of God.

The word for both upper and lower rooms is the same. "Inn" translates as *katalyma* in Greek, which is mistakenly portrayed as a first-century "Best Eastern." The only other time Luke used *katalyma* was to describe the Upper Room where Jesus and His disciples gathered for their Last Supper.[4] When Luke did mean to indicate an "inn," a rooming house for travelers, he used a different term, *pandocheion*. In the parable of the good Samaritan, the badly beaten man is taken by the compassionate Samaritan to a *pandocheion*, an "inn," to recover.

In other words, by the time Mary and Joseph arrived at the home of Joseph's Bethlehem relatives, the guest room was already occupied. The most common design for simple, first-century homes consisted of two levels. The upper floor was where the family slept and where a guest room might be available. The lower floor was used for ordinary daytime living and where the animals were kept at night. A separate stable for livestock would only be found among the well-off. The body heat from the first-floor animals would warm the air and rise to the upper sleeping quarters. Think of it as a very early form of radiant floor heating.

So it was probably into the lower level of a relative's home, a house already overcrowded with kin, that Jesus was born. There was no cozy stable with well-tended stalls and lots of fresh straw on the ground. What was on the floor was waiting to be shoveled out in the morning so it could be dried out and then burned as fuel in the cooking fire. Comfort was over a century away from even being a concept. The lower level was a plain, open space where people could gather during the day and animals could be gathered at night. The only furniture available for the new mother to use for her baby was the feeding trough used by the animals, a manger.

The Bible does not say what animals were fed from that one Bethlehem trough, but the earliest depictions of the nativity portray an ox and an ass present at the manger.[5] We do know what lives in straw, however: itch mites that bite. It seems that all God's creatures were part of the reception party for Emmanuel, God with us.

In the Bible, Jesus always comes in surround sound. If you hear only one thing, you aren't hearing Jesus. It is a sign of Jesus' greatness that one thing can be said about Him and the opposite be true at the same time. Jesus is a paradox and an oxymoron rolled into one.

That makes Christianity a culture of paradox. Swiss theologian Emil Brunner pegged it right: "The hallmark of logical inconsistency clings to all genuine pronouncements of faith."[6]

The Living Water gospel is a cocktail of opposites, a paradoxical brew of hydrogen and oxygen, fire and wind, "Lord I believe" and "help my unbelief," as well as . . .

Come and live. Come and die.

Be as wise as serpents, innocent as doves.

My yoke is easy, my burden is light.

You want to be first? Be last.

You want to find yourself? Lose yourself.

You want to be famous? Be humble.

The Prince of Peace came bringing a sword.

Give to Caesar what is Caesar's, and to God what is God's.

Jesus never tried to unknot His contradictions. Rather, He used these knots as rungs in the ladder to enable us to climb higher in truth and revelation.

Man has been made more sacred than any superman or super-monkey . . . His very limitations have already become holy and like a home; because of that sunken chamber in the rocks, where God became very small.

—G. K. Chesterton[7]

What brings the opposites together and connects them is the sign of the cross. The Bible in general (and John's gospel in particular) is sometimes called the Book of Signs. But the sign above all signs is the cross, which brings together the vertical and the horizontal. Jesus' love is *agape* love. Agape love is made up of two dimensions: love of God and love of neighbor. The horizontal and the vertical go hand in hand. How do you show love of God, love of neighbor, and vice versa?[8]

The gospel goes parabolic beginning with Jesus' birth, where God works little large with the whole of faith encapsulated in a very small package: one little act of love. Jesus is the definitive localization of the Creator's universality. The incarnation is the original "small is big."

UNTO US A CHILD IS BORN

There are 184 verses in the birth narratives of the Second Testament. These 184 verses presuppose or repeat the words of 170 verses from eighteen different books of the First Testament. Let's start with John, the birth narrative that no one reads at Christmas, and then explore the more recited ones.

John's gospel tells the story of Jesus' birth in as storyless a way as possible. John's account of how God made the longest Word short has no ox and ass or straw and shepherds—only philosophy: "In the beginning was the Word, and the Word was with God, and the Word was God. . . . The Word became flesh and dwelt among us."[9]

John's birth narrative is structured in the signage of seven I AM metaphors, which function as a menorah that highlights the birth of Jesus just as the seven-branch golden lampstand called the menorah ("tree of life") illuminated the ark of the covenant in the Holy of Holies, and the original Tree of Life lit up the garden of Eden.

The seven I AM metaphorical statements of Jesus in the gospel of John are followed by their corresponding circumstances in the story of Jesus' birth:

> ***I see a solid gold lampstand with a bowl at the top and seven lights on it, with seven channels to the lights. Also there are two olive trees by it, one on the right of the bowl and the other on its left.***
>
> —ZECHARIAH[10]

"I am the bread of life."[11]

Jesus was born in Bethlehem, which means "house of bread."[12]

"I am the light of the world."[13]

Jesus was born under the light of the star of Bethlehem.[14]

"I am the door of the sheep."[15]

The doors of the guest house were closed to Mary and Joseph, but the gate to the stable was open.[16]

"I am the good shepherd. The good shepherd gives His life for the sheep."[17]

Baby Jesus was sought by shepherds looking for a baby wrapped in swaddling bands (used for birth or burial), and lying in a manger.[18]

"I am the resurrection and the life."[19]

Jesus survived King Herod's attempt to kill Him.[20]

"I am the way, the truth, and the life."[21]

Wise men found their way to Him, recognized the truth about Him, and defied King Herod's evil plot.[22]

"I am the true vine."[23]

Jesus was born in Bethlehem Ephrathah, which means "fruitful."[24]

The parabolic curving of opposites into connection and conversation is evident right here and becomes one of the most distinctive features of John's gospel. There is no higher understanding of Jesus' divinity as the "Son of God" than John's gospel. There is no fuller understanding of Jesus' humanity as the "Son of Adam" (or "the Human Being") than John's gospel. John is the "I AM" gospel because Jesus appears in His mysterious "I AM–ness" as part of the triune life of the Godhead while Jesus is also present in His concreteness as "I am the door," "I am the true vine," "I am the Good Shepherd," and so on. In the gospel of John, Jesus stands with His head in eternity and His feet in Eden.

The Spirit of God forms in us cross-shaped minds, bodies, and spirits. Christians live a cruciform life. And a cruciform life is a well-connected life that brings together the polarities: the ebb and flow of love and hate, belief and unbelief, joy and suffering, trust and uncertainty, saintliness and sinfulness. The cross is what bridges the banks, binds the ends, and marries the extremes of being. If anyone should be prepared for a future where polarities coincide, it is Christians, whose faith is friendly toward ambiguity, simultaneity, and double exposure. That's why those who live the Jesus story have such sharp noses for incongruities and ironies. For biblical story-catchers, paradox can be paradise.

> *The money in which the Roman poll-tax is paid [the denarius], . . . is, as it were, the star under which he was born in Bethlehem, where—according to another evangelist, Luke—his earthly parents had gone for registration for tax purposes.*
>
> —James Buchan[26]

If discipleship is the cruciform life, then the cross is the ultimate symbol of orthodoxy as paradoxy.[25] The cross brings opposites into relationship, not so much as a dialectic to be synthesized, but more as a double helix to be embraced and lived. In Christ, all opposites are not so much reconciled as transcended in the oneness of twoness. We are born for ontological tension: we are in, but not of, the world. We are made for the harmonious oscillation of abundance and austerity, celebration and asceticism. Before Lent? Carnival. Before Ash Wednesday? Shrove Tuesday. Holy Saturday brings together the opposites: fire and water, light and darkness, hell and heaven, death and life.

The first arm of the cross is the vertical, our relationship with God. The second arm of the cross is the horizontal, our relationship with others, ourselves, and creation. If you just pick up one arm of the cross, it becomes a stick most often used to beat other people with. If we are, in Jesus' words,[27] put on earth that we may learn to bear the cross, the crossbeams of love, we must pick up and carry a cross with both arms crossed. Heresy is one-arming truth. Unorthodoxy is the cross uncrossed. From the very beginning of the Jesus story, we discover the essence of faith: living the cruciform life.

On the heavy wooden door of an old Scandinavian church, there is a large handle shaped in a circle and made of wrought iron. Inside the circle is a large cross cradled in a wrought-iron hand. To open and close the door, you grasp the cross. In grasping hold of the cross, the hand points directly at you. Every door that opens in life is a question: What does the cross mean to me? To you? What are we going to do about it? It's the question that even opens the door of Jesus' birth.

THE LINEAGE OF JESUS

Jesus is fully God and fully human. John's gospel gives us a clear look at His divinity, while the other gospels show us His humanity. Through the lens of His divinity, we see the outline of the king-priest Melchizedek, who was "without father, without mother, without genealogy, having neither beginning of days nor end of life, but made like the Son of God."[28] Of the two more-traditional narratives of Jesus' birth, Matthew and Luke, Matthew's account spends more time tracing the genealogy of Jesus than it does telling the story itself.[29]

What kind of story is a genealogy? A genealogy was important, a legal document often structured so it could be committed to memory.[30] The genealogy of Jesus proved three things that identified one big thing: first, that Jesus' lineage started before Abraham with Adam, the first human;[31] second, that He was a descendant of Abraham (a Jew); third, He was related to King David (a contender for Israel's throne). Those three things identified Jesus as the authentic Messiah in the eyes of the Jewish people.

Matthew's genealogy begins with the Greek expression *biblos geneseos,* which means "the book of genesis." This mirrors the beginning of the micro creation account in Genesis 2:4—"This is the *biblos geneseos* of heaven and earth"—and Genesis 5:1—"This is the *biblos geneseos* of Adam." Matthew was narrating the record of the new creation with Christ coming into the world as the new Adam. Significantly, Luke called Adam "the son of God" in his genealogy.[32] And as we have already seen, John's gospel is a replay of Genesis.

When we peel back the genealogy of our Lord from both Mary's and Joseph's sides, we come to a startling revelation. God the Father chose some of the worst examples in human history to be blood kin to the Son of God Himself. Consider the Lord's kinfolk:

- Judah—a Jew who had sex with his daughter-in-law, thinking she was a prostitute
- Tamar—a Gentile who bore two sons out of incest
- Rahab—a Canaanite prostitute[33]
- Ruth—a Moabite (the Moabites' lineage began with incest between Lot and one of his own daughters)
- David—a king who committed adultery and murder
- Bathsheba—a woman who committed adultery

Can you imagine a more embarrassing lineage? It's certainly no lineage suited for a king. Yet these were the ancestors of the spotless, holy Son of God. They are His great-great-great-grandmothers and great-great-great-grandfathers. This was no accident. It was the sovereign choice of a sovereign God, who chose each of these people to be the blood kin to our Lord.

This poses good news for every child of God. In the words of Hebrews, "He is not ashamed to call them brethren."[34] Jesus Christ was willing to come from a humiliating lineage—a lineage His Father chose for Him—to show us that no past is so shameful that God cannot make it beautiful. No matter what you may have done in your past, Jesus Christ is not ashamed to call you His brother or sister. What comfort and rest we find in that kind of a God.[35]

The most humble of all places for this particular King to enter into the world was never beneath His dignity. No more than the genealogy from which He came. Yes, this babe born in Bethlehem was the promised seed of the woman who would bruise the serpent's head.[36] He came without a proper bed, without a proper shelter, without robes, chariots, or processionals. His mother and nonbiological father were not rich enough to offer a lamb. So they offered a pair of turtledoves and pigeons when Jesus was circumcised.[37]

God made His entrance into this earth in the least expected of all places through the least expected of people. And as such, the worst and the best, the richest and the poorest, and the first and the last will seek Him out then and now. The conditions of Jesus' birth demonstrate to us that no one and no place is beneath His dignity or His reach. He hallows and sanctifies all things, all places, and all people with His presence. This is Luke's story in his remarkable gospel.

Of all the holy haze that mists the story of Jesus' birth, the greatest miracle was the conception. We often hear the phrase "the virgin birth." While a virgin did give birth to the Messiah, the real miracle was in the conception.[38] His Father was God Almighty—not in some metaphorical sense, but in reality. In Jesus we have the first motion of the new creation in the midst of the fallen creation. His DNA is human, but it is also divine. He is God "manifested in the flesh."[39] Hence He would be called "the Son of God" and "the Son of Man."[40]

Jesus, while being fully God, was fully human. He came as human flesh to undo what had become a marred, warped, and distorted humanity. His incarnation was God's making of Himself available to all human beings. God came as the last Adam, the Second Man, to set right a fallen humankind. He inaugurated a new creation but also a new humanity—a new race—a new kind of human where there was neither Jew nor Gentile but which would embrace all and live by the life of God. He also came as a human to be the unblemished and perfect sacrifice, having been tempted in all points, but "without sin."[41] Jesus' sinlessness isn't a myth; it enabled Him to reverse what Adam had done.

For all these reasons and more, God sanctified the womb of a virgin Galilean girl to bring into the earth the Creator of all things. In the birth

The omnipotent, in one instant, made himself breakable. He who had been spirit became pierceable. He who was larger than the universe became an embryo.

—Max Lucado[43]

of Jesus, we have the greatest glory and the gravest humility displayed. (The same can be said about the cross, which awaited Him some thirty years later.) As George MacDonald once put it, "They were looking for a king / To slay their foes and lift them high: / Thou cam'st a little baby thing / That made a woman cry."[42]

Herod was told that the child would be born in Bethlehem of Judea, as opposed to the lesser-known Bethlehem of Galilee.[44] Jesus was born in Bethlehem, the birthplace of David and site of his coronation.[45] But Jesus always comes in surround sound. If where Jesus was born was a royal city, where He grew up was a royal pain.

CAN ANYTHING GOOD COME OUT OF NAZARETH?

Jesus grew up in Nazareth, a nondescript, Jewish agricultural village with probably fewer than four hundred inhabitants, and one of the southernmost villages in Galilee.[46] Isaiah prophesied that the Messiah would come from Galilee.[47] It was such a Podunk place that for Mark, the first miracle was the fact that Jesus came from Nazareth. Or as Nathaniel put it, "Can anything good come out of Nazareth?"[48]

Bethlehem was a little town in Jesus' day. Only about a thousand people lived in the area, and infant mortality throughout Judea stood at about 30 percent in the first century.[49] Most people know that Bethlehem means "house of bread" in Hebrew. What more fitting place for the "Bread of Life" to be born than in this breadbasket where Ruth gleaned in the barley fields of Boaz, the great-grandfather of King David, of whose lineage came Joseph, wedded to Mary, who gave birth to Yeshua known as the Messiah.[50] Through the centuries, wheat and barley (the poor man's wheat) have grown on Bethlehem's east side.

But you can predict that where grains grow, close by, you will find the animals that feed upon them. And sure enough, on Bethlehem's northwest side, there are the sheep to go with the wheat. There is an Arabic side to go with the Hebrew side. For the Arabic cognate of Hebrew *lechem* is meat, flesh. In Arabic "beth-lehem" translates into *bet lahm* (*bayt lahem*) or "house of meat." In fact, the Syriac gospel and Peschitta[51] use the Aramaic cognate for *lachma* for bread (house of meat). Even in Hebrew, *lechem* can mean food in general and in at least one instance refers clearly to meat.[52]

Angels stand, but a holy person moves on.

—OLD HASIDIC SAYING

When Jesus suggested that this bread is His flesh, He was bringing together the east and west hills of Bethlehem, something connected in the minds of His hearers that we have lost.

JESUS: THE LAMB FROM BETHLEHEM

In spite of all that has been written about that little town of Bethlehem, which lies just inside the West Bank, many of its most important features have yet to be explored. What is postcard familiar is that Bethlehem birthed princes, and as a boy, David tended sheep in the very northwest hills where today shepherds still tend their flocks of sheep and goats.

But what is less widely known and what connects with the Arabic translation of "Bethlehem" as a "house of meat" is this: the kind of sheep cared for by Bethlehem shepherds was a special kind that made the name "Bethlehem" synonymous with fields full of lambs ripe for slaughter. Bethlehem carried another brand identity alongside "house of bread": "house of meat."

In the midst of the butcher shop, incarnation.

Bethlehem shepherds were not just any shepherds tending sheep. They were descendants of David, tending "David's flock"—sheep destined for the temple (another possible translation of "*Beth*" besides "house of" is "temple"). Jerusalem was only a short two miles from those Bethlehem slopes. You may even think of Bethlehem shepherds as outsourced employees of the temple, royal shepherds.

The ox knows
its owner,
And the donkey
its master's crib
[phatne];
But Israel does
not know,
My people do
not consider.

—God to Isaiah[53]

If truth be told, the center of religious life in Judaism was the massive slaughter of animals. According to the Torah, every day two lambs were required for sacrifice in the temple. That's 730 lambs each year. The twice-daily offering of a male lamb was known as the *tamid*, or "the continuous offering." It was the first offering and the last offering of each day.[54] During the hour of the final sacrifice of the day, the Final Sacrifice was offered.

On top of that, thousands of lambs were needed by Jewish families at Passover and other religious rituals. One of the most widely observed of the Jewish holidays, Passover required a lamb to be sacrificed for every household that could afford it. All the lambs were ritually killed at the same time in the same place.[55] But before they were slaughtered, each lamb was required to be a pet in the family for at least four days.

So the day after the final Sabbath before Passover, shepherds from the Bethlehem hills drove thousands of lambs into Jerusalem, where they were taken in by Jewish families for at least two days and treated as members of the family. Before sacrificing the lamb, the Jewish priest would ask, "Do you love this lamb?" If the family didn't love the lamb, there would be no sacrifice. When Jesus asked Peter three times, "Do you love Me?" He affirmed His identity as the sacrificial Lamb of God.[56] When we love Jesus, we receive the gift of His sacrifice—redemption from death and a resurrected life.

We celebrate "the day after the final Sabbath before Passover" by a different name: Palm Sunday. There were two processions on that first Palm Sunday. One was an unwilling procession of thousands of perfect lambs herded into the city by Bethlehem shepherds. The other was a willing procession of the one perfect Lamb of God who takes away the sins of the world.[57]

Bethlehem's priestly shepherds had to learn and follow special techniques and rituals during the lambing season. Bethlehem lambs born for slaughter were special lambs. To prevent harm and self-injury from thrashing about after birth on their spindly legs, newborn lambs were wrapped in swaddling cloths. Then they were placed in a manger or feeding trough, where they could calm down out of harm's way. After careful inspection by the shepherd, any spot or "blemish,"[58] no matter how slight, meant instant rejection (slaughter). The Hebrew word *tamiym* (translated for lambs "without spot or blemish") means "complete, whole, entire, sound."[59]

> *And you, O tower of*
> *the flock* [Hebrew:
> *Migdal Eder*[60]],
> *The stronghold of the*
> *daughter of Zion,*
> *To you shall it come,*
> *Even the former*
> *dominion*
> *shall come,*
> *The kingdom of*
> *the daughter of*
> *Jerusalem.*
>
> —MICAH[61]

The shepherds who gathered around the Bethlehem stable where the Lamb of God was born were not witnessing anything new, except who was in the manger: the most important sacrificial Lamb who had ever been born, the Lamb who would close down the slaughterhouse of sacrifice, the perfect Lamb of God.

Everything about Jesus' birth foreshadowed the purpose for Jesus coming into the world: "The next day John saw Jesus coming toward him, and said, 'Behold! The Lamb of God who takes away the sin of the world!'"[62] Even the ox and the ass, straight from Isaiah 1:3, testify to the fact that the promised one would come out of Israel's promises and prayers. As in Balaam's story[63] the star of David came "to lead the wise of the world to the place where Israel's king is born."[64]

Jesus is the three shepherds: the good shepherd,[65] the great Shepherd,[66] and the Chief Shepherd.[67] Jesus presented Himself as both sheep and shepherd, the good shepherd who lays down His life for the sheep. It was a way completely different from the meat sacrifices of the old temple. The sheep now have a good shepherd who feeds them and does not slaughter them. The sheep now have a good shepherd who is one of them and understands them as one of them. The sheep now have a good shepherd who covers up all their spots and blemishes and presents them spotless and blameless.

Mortality rates for both lambs and ewes are high at birth. It is not uncommon for up to 30 to 40 percent of the lamb flock to be lost between late pregnancy and weaning.[68] Ewes are notorious for not accepting orphan sheep. So every shepherd learns some methods to get a mother sheep to accept an orphan lamb. One is to take the mother's placental blood and fluids and smear the orphan lamb with her smell. That will work some of the time. But what works best, but requires the most work, is to wash the orphan lamb in the blood of the dead lamb.

When Jesus proclaimed Himself the "door of the sheep" and the "good shepherd,"[69] the Good Shepherd and the sheep became one.

Jesus died on the cross at the ninth hour (about three o'clock in the afternoon) when the Passover lamb would be sacrificed in the temple.[70] Christ, the Paschal Lamb, was slain to atone for the sins of humanity and to open the gate of the true temple that promises God's salvation for all people.

> ***'Twas much that man was made like God, long before. But that God should be made like man, much more.***
>
> —John Donne[71]

The "house of meat," the temple rituals of sacrifice and slaughter, was transformed into the "house of bread." Jesus, the One who was born in *Bethlehem*, in old Hebrew the "house" (*beth*) of "bread" (*lehem*), declared that the sacrifice of "meat" would no longer be the gateway to God's salvation and God's presence. Bread would become His body—His flesh, meat—and God's presence would now be found around tables as much as at temples. In shutting down the slaughterhouse, Jesus moved us from the temple to the table.

THE STAR OF BETHLEHEM AND THE CROSS OF CALVARY

The Christmas story revolves around a tree. But it's not a Christmas tree. And it comes already adorned.

The beginning of the Jesus theography is a star-crossed love story that brings together the star of Bethlehem and the cross of Calvary. The adoration of the Magi,[72] one of the most frequently painted scenes in all of Christian art, testifies that this birth has relevance not just to Israel but to all humankind. This would be a Savior not just of the house of Israel but of all houses of all humankind.[73] The day after Christmas, December 26, is when many churches celebrate the martyrdom of Saint Stephen. Still during Christmastide, on December 28, many churches remember "the massacre of the innocents," the firstborn sons whom Herod killed.[74]

The Christmas story is part of a larger story that addresses a world of injustice, suffering, and even death. The joy of that first Christmas wasn't a cute joy but a joy that overcame obstacles and barriers, even moved mountains and liberated sheep.

The cross is where incarnation and resurrection meet. When we accept Christ to be born into our lives, we're all virgin Marys. For "unto you" a son is born. For "unto us" a child is given. His name? Emmanuel, which means "God with us." In the words of Teri Hyrkas, "'With' is Emmanuel's middle name."[76] That means it is also *unto us* that a child is born, a son is given.

> *If in your heart you make*
> *a manger for his birth,*
> *then God will once again*
> *become a child on earth.*
>
> —German poet Angelus Silesius[75]

A COLLISION OF TWO KINGDOMS

Appropriately, Matthew embedded Jesus' birth into three biblical narratives. Jesus is "Immanuel," the embodiment of God's presence with His people.[77] He is the new Joshua, bringing God's people into the promised land.[78] He is the new David, born in Bethlehem, the city of David.[79]

Many Christians are familiar with Micah 5:2, where the prophet predicted where the Messiah will be born: "But you, Bethlehem Ephrathah, though you are small among the clans of Judah, out of you will come for me one who will be ruler over Israel, whose origins are from of old, from ancient times."[80] But they are less familiar with the rest of the text: "He will stand and shepherd his flock in the strength of the LORD, in the majesty of the name of the LORD his God. And they will live securely, for then his greatness will reach to the ends of the earth. And he will be their peace."[81] The prophet declared that the coming Messiah, the One who would be born in the lowly village of Bethlehem, would bring peace. And His greatness would reach to the ends of the earth. In other words, He would rescue the people of God from her enemies. In Micah's time Israel's enemy was Assyria. And the writers of the Second Testament would have connected the dots to Israel's present enemy, Rome.

Herod, about sixty years old when Jesus was born, represented pagan rule and oppression. Herod also brought peace, but by murder. He had to kill to acquire it and he would have to continue to kill to sustain it. Jesus, the new King just born, posed a great threat to Herod, for He was another King. And He, too, would bring peace, as the prophet foretold. But His peace would come about through a radically different way.

In Herod (the old king) and in Jesus (the new King) we have the collision of two kingdoms. Two kingdoms representing two different powers, two different glories, and two different kinds of peace. The true King of the Jews was born under the nose of the evil king. And for that reason, Jesus entered the world He created with a price tag on His head.

These two kingdoms would meet head-to-head again when Pilate confronted an adult Jesus. The One whom Isaiah declared to be the Prince of Peace would encounter another political leader who would bring peace by the sword (Pilate). The circumstances surrounding Jesus' birth would repeat themselves in His death.

Look again at the babe from Bethlehem and see a King who was destined to redefine power, glory, and peace. And He would do it by subverting the kingdoms of this world by a cross—an instrument made of the same material that composed the manger into which He was born: wood. Even so, God's glory was revealed not in the manger but on the cross. And therein lay His destiny.

JESUS IN LIVING COLOR: EARLY CHILDHOOD AND MESSIANIC IDENTITY

If Jesus' birth resonates in surround sound, then His early childhood shines forth in living color. Jesus' messianic identity was not just a self-proclaimed announcement from a thirty-year-old, mission-driven rabbi. Both First and Second Testaments describe the coming Messiah, and from the time of His birth, Jesus the child was identified through revelations, prophecies, and encounters by others as the messianic prophecy revealed and fulfilled through Scripture and the story of the Jewish people.

> *I will see him for*
> *myself.*
> *Yes, I will see him*
> *with my own*
> *eyes.*
> *I am overwhelmed*
> *at the thought!*
>
> —Job[82]

On the eighth day of His life, Jesus underwent the rite of circumcision. Thirty-two days later (forty days after His birth), He was formally presented in the temple according to the law of Moses. Here Simeon the priest took the young infant into his arms and blessed Him. Simeon's prayer revealed that Jesus is the central person in all of history.

In Jesus' day it was customary for parents to bring their firstborn son to the temple to be presented for the *Pidyon HaBen* (presentation of the firstborn son). But Jesus' presentation in the temple astounded even His parents, as both Simeon (a righteous seer) and Anna (the daughter of Phanuel) made prophetic proclamations about the young child, calling Him the redemption of Jerusalem, the light to the Gentiles, glory to Israel.[83] In Him, they saw the messianic identity. Jesus was only one month old.

The *Pidyon HaBen* is an important ritual in the Jewish lifeline and in the understanding of Jesus as both Messiah of the new covenant and redeemer of Israel. In fact, the account of Jesus' flight to Egypt with His parents—taking place most likely one to two years after His presentation in the temple—to escape Herod's slaughter of innocents echoed the First Testament redemption of the Hebrew people. Jesus' coming out of Egypt echoed the words of the prophet Hosea when he said of Israel, "Out of Egypt I called My son."[84]

In the Judaism of Jesus' day, one could offer an animal sacrifice. Some who could afford it might offer a lamb or goat. Others could offer two pigeons or a pair of turtledoves. Poorer families could offer a pancake made of grain and flour.[85] The ceremony of *Pidyon HaBen*, called the "redemption of the firstborn son," occurred forty days after birth. "This ritual symbolically relieves the child from service to the priesthood."[86]

Additionally, Jesus' role and identification by both Simeon and Anna as the Redeemer of God's people, at the time He was being symbolically released from priestly service, acted as powerful indicators of His messianic birthright and His future as one who, like Moses, had escaped Pharaoh's death decree. Where Moses was raised as a prince of Egypt, Jesus—the Prince of Peace—stayed in Egypt until Herod's death, when His family returned with Him to their hometown of Nazareth, where Jesus spent the rest of His early years. Likewise the One "redeemed" in the temple would become the redeeming sacrifice for all.

At the end of the book of Genesis, Joseph (son of Jacob) brought his family to Egypt. Years later as the family multiplied and prospered, Pharaoh issued an order that the firstborn of all babies born to Hebrew mothers[87] must be killed. In the tenth plague God issued upon Egypt, every firstborn Egyptian was killed, save those whose doors were washed in the blood of the lamb. These were passed over. Hence the Passover feast. Jesus, the Paschal Lamb, first escaped death at birth to become the sacrificial Lamb whose blood would save and redeem. But in the new covenant the saved include not only Israel but all God's people. The redemption of Israel is the redeeming of the Gentiles: "A light to bring revelation to the Gentiles, and the glory of Your people Israel."[88]

The history of the presentation ritual goes back to the First Testament Exodus.

> The firstborn son (*bechor*) was to be the priest (*kohen*) of the Jewish family. As the *bechor*, he was responsible to offer *avodah* (sacrifice) on behalf of other family members. God said "the first issue of every womb among the Israelites is mine" (Exodus 13:2). Thus firstborn sons were sanctified and obligated to serve as *kohanim* (priests) from birth. We see evidence of this in the lives of the early patriarchs, Abraham, Isaac, and even Jacob, who received the blessing of the firstborn through transfer from Esau. And because firstborn sons (*bechorim*) were consecrated as *kohanim*, during the Exodus from Egypt, God spared them when He issued the 10th *makkah* (plague)—the death of the firstborn.
>
> After the Exodus from Egypt, however, the Israelites committed the grievous sin of the Golden Calf, of which only the tribe of Levi was not guilty. Consequently, the Lord declared that the Levites were to take the place of the firstborn sons of Israel (Num. 3:11–12). But since a firstborn son is technically a (disqualified) *kohen*, he had to be substituted with a *kohen* from the tribe of Levi, and therefore God required that all firstborn sons (who were not themselves Levites or *kohens*) must be redeemed from service to God by means of paying five shekels of silver (see Num. 18:15).[89]

In the Second Testament, as the sacrificial sign of the new covenant, Jesus Himself becomes the sin offering of humanity. In fact, Jesus' very words on the cross, "It is finished!" ("*Kalah.*"), are the words used by a priest at the conclusion of the sacrificial offering in the temple. In the ancient days, when the Jewish priest had killed the last lamb of the Passover, he uttered the Hebrew word *Kalah*, "It is finished."

THE VISIT OF THE MAGI

Jesus was not only recognized at the temple in Jerusalem; upon His return to relatives in Bethlehem, He was visited and identified also by a group of Magi. The Magi from the east were most likely a group of those versed in astrology; the medicinal and healing properties of herbs, salves, and precious stones; the interpretation of dreams; and other healing arts, as was the custom of the day. In the first-century world, many times, these "wise ones" would give to families of wealth or stature honorary birthing gifts that would include medicines for healing and prevention of disease and death for the child and mother. Since both childbirth and early childhood were precarious times, and the mortality rate for children was abysmally high, these gifts would have been highly cherished in value for their salvific properties in addition to their monetary value, as such items were rare and expensive. The gifts given to Jesus at the home of His family—relatives in the line of King David—consisted of gold, frankincense, and myrrh.[90]

The visit of the Magi, most likely, according to the records of Josephus, was at a time when Jesus was between one and two years of age.[91] Matthew 2:11 says they came to find not a baby but the "Child" in the "house" with Mary. And the gifts presented to Jesus would have been well welcomed. But these gifts had not only practical value; they were also symbolic of Jesus' messianic identity. Gold, in addition to having known healing qualities in the first century, was a gift given to kings. Gold not only reminds us of Jesus' royal blood but also, according to many Bible teachers, is an allusion to His divinity.[92] Jesus, as King, would represent the Messiah to the Gentile populations.

Frankincense was a valuable and expensive sacred oil used in temple rituals and celebrations. Some scholars believe it symbolizes Jesus' salvific and priestly function to humanity and His role as redeemer of Israel. Some also believe that frankincense symbolizes the sacred temple, into which Jesus will usher in the new covenant. Frankincense was additionally used in households to worship and for fragrance. Jesus as Messiah is the anointed one, and this was an oil of celebration and of inauguration into His messianic role.

Finally, myrrh was used in birthing and swaddling a newborn baby, in healing and pain relief, as well as in salving wounds. The Egyptians additionally used it as an embalming oil. Nicodemus saw to it that Jesus' body was smoothed with myrrh and aloes at His death before swaddling

Him and sealing Him into the tomb. And myrrh was offered to Jesus to ease His pain on the cross—an offering He refused.[93]

At His birth, Jesus received the myrrh. At His death, He rejected it. Jesus' earthly ministry centered on alleviating human suffering.[94] He was the personification of myrrh. In His crucifixion, however, He was bearing the full brunt of human pain, suffering, and agony on the cross. He bore our shame and sorrows. So He rejected the myrrh and the wine that came with it.[95] Jesus took the full dose of suffering for sin on the cross so we wouldn't have to. And He rejected the myrrh so we would be able to receive it.

Symbolically, then, myrrh foreshadowed Jesus' sacrificial death, His burial, and His future as one who would die and see the tomb, before rising as the true anointed one of all people. Psalm 45:6–8 tells us that Christ's "garments are scented with myrrh and aloes." In the wake of His death, as His garments were shed, there was a scent of the resurrected Christ. It was the scent of myrrh.[96] In short, the gold reminds us of the divine kingship of Jesus, the frankincense reminds us of His priestly ministry, and the myrrh reminds us of His Saviorhood.

THE MESSIAH THE PROPHETS FORETOLD

Jesus' early years and His identity as the long-awaited Messiah were predicted poetically, literally, and metaphorically throughout the First Testament. The prophetic voice resounded through the Law, the Writings, and the Prophets in preparation for the Son of man.

The First Testament prophets predicted that Jesus would be born in Bethlehem.[97] He would be born from a virgin.[98] He would crush the head of the serpent,[99] and He would be a blessing to all the nations.[100] He would be the root and offspring of David[101] and would come from the royal line of Judah.[102] He would be a son, a child, and He would sit on the throne of David forever.[103] He would be called out of Egypt by God, His Father,[104] and He would be raised in the despised town of Nazareth in the fameless region of Galilee.[105]

Like the rainbow of the covenant, Jesus' identity stands out in living color from Genesis to Revelation as a robe that winds around the incarnational, covenantal gift of God—God come down. The word of YHWH has become the Word in the flesh, the light to the Gentiles, and the glory to God's people, Israel.

> And the Child grew and became strong in spirit, filled with wisdom; and the grace of God was upon Him.[106]

As Jesus grew in wisdom, stature, and divine grace, He would mature in His identity and take on the powers of the world in the name of God, redeem the Lord's creation, and return the world and its peoples to walking the garden with God.

Let's now shift our attention to one of the most controversial parts of the Lord's life on earth: His boyhood.

CHAPTER 5

Jesus' Missing Years

I tell you that if these should keep silent,

the stones would immediately cry out.

—JESUS[1]

"AS GOD IS MY WITNESS, AS GOD IS MY WITNESS THEY'RE NOT going to lick me. I'm going to live through this and when it's all over, I'll never be hungry again."[2] These words, spoken by the unbending Scarlett O'Hara in Margaret Mitchell's 1936 Pulitzer prize–winning novel, *Gone with the Wind*, embody the spitfire and grit of the Old South. Contrary and accusatory, Scarlett's words testify to the land's rejuvenating power, the people's raw determination to live, and the author's faith in the human spirit.

Jesus' metaphorical promise of moaning stones needs to be heard similarly as words of resolve and rescript. With these words about stones that sing, Jesus boldly and directly accused the prevailing temple power-brokers of the Sanhedrin, threatening them with the knowledge that the whole of creation testified to their bloody skullduggery, that God had felt the breaking of the covenant, and that nothing could silence or assuage their guilt.[3]

What does Jesus know? Enough to take on the entire Jewish

power structure with the authority of someone who could bring them down.

Jesus' words resonate from passages found in Habakkuk: "For the stone will cry out from the wall, and the beam from the timbers will answer it"[4]—and Genesis: "The voice of your brother's blood cries out to Me from the ground."[5] The Habakkuk image is a builder's metaphor and a temple image. The Genesis image is that of the gardener, creator, covenant maker. These two semiotic flares of gardener and builder light up a constellation of links in the Hebrew understanding of temple and garden, and they provide a key to Jesus' identity as both rabbi and Messiah, alpha and omega of Scripture and of life.

With that simple phrase of singing stones and others like it, Jesus identified Himself both as an expert in the intricacies of the language of the Hebrew Bible and one who has the knowledge and platform to accuse the reigning religio-political establishment of the murder of brothers. Jesus made His accusation as He rode on a donkey into Jerusalem amid palms and hosannas from followers. In the cheering crowds were Gentiles of the region, despised by the ruling Sanhedrin and temple authorities. His speech bore all the marks of an educated rabbi and mission-driven challenger, while His actions were symbolic of the long-awaited Hebrew Messiah. The explosive power of this combined message was lost perhaps to some, but it hit the educated elite right between the eyes.

> *When He marked*
> *out the foundations*
> *of the earth,*
> *Then I was beside*
> *Him as a master*
> *craftsman.*
>
> —The Excellence of Wisdom[6]

Yet they didn't arrest Him. They plotted to figure out a way.

Jesus went on into the temple courtyard, overthrowing the money tables that had occupied the area where Gentiles had previously been allowed to pray.[7] Then He proceeded to teach and preach in the temple at the high holy days, just as He had done time and time again.

Yet no one arrested Him or even stopped Him. Why?

THE STONES CRY OUT

Stones are eyewitnesses. Stones are living testimony to the truth. Stones mark the sign of the covenant. They are the signposts of the Lord. The prophet Joshua quoted a longer version of the stone metaphor as testimony: "Behold, this stone shall be a witness to us, for it has heard all the words of the LORD which He spoke to us. It shall therefore be a witness to you, lest you deny your God."[8]

God's covenant, made not only with humankind but with all creation, testifies from the very *adamah* of the created world. This same covenant was chiseled initially into stone and later carved into the cardiac-caves of humankind:

- to guard the entrance to the garden of Eden: a stone
- the place where Jacob called Bethel "the house of God": a stone
- the treasure cradled in the ark of the covenant: stone tablets
- the foundation slab on which the ark of the covenant was placed in the temple: stone
- the foundation of Solomon's temple: stone

Then there are the prophetic words of Isaiah declaring the coming cornerstone of God,[9] YHWH, the Rock of Israel.[10] Even the propagation language of the covenant can be found in the metaphor of the stone.[11] In the Hebrew Bible, references to stones serve both as testimony and signs of the messianic prophesy. Genesis proclaims, "From there is the Shepherd, the Stone of Israel."[12] Daniel described the metaphor of the Messiah as the "stone . . . cut out of the mountain without hands."[13]

Throughout the Second Testament and especially in the Gospels, these stones become not only the stones of creation and of the foundation of the physical temple but also the living stones of the disciples of Jesus[14] and the living stones of Christ's spiritual temple. Christ Himself is the incarnated and resurrected foundation and cornerstone, the eternal kingdom, the garden paradise, the covenant.

> You also, like living stones, are being built into a spiritual house.[15]

> You are God's building. According to the grace of God which was given to me, as a master builder I have laid the foundation, and another builds on it.[16]

> In whom the whole building . . . grows into a holy temple in the Lord, in whom you also are being built together for a dwelling place of God in the Spirit.[17]

There is a treasure in the earth that is a food tasty and pleasing to the Lord. Be a gardener. Dig and ditch, toil and sweat. Turn the earth upside down and seek the deepness and water the plants in time. Continue this labor and make sweet floods to run and noble and abundant fruits to spring. Take this food and drink and carry it to God as your true worship.

—JULIAN OF NORWICH (AD 1416)

In Hebrew theology, the stones can be equated with the seed of the earth, which requires gardening. Both represent the Word of YHWH, the Torah, the covenant. In Genesis, to garden (conserve and conceive) the earth is to garden (conserve and conceive) the covenant. When the covenant is broken, the earth and the stones cry out. All creation testifies to the power of the presence of the Lord, to the indissoluble relationship of God and God's people.

Jesus, a master of the Torah, was still in the gardening business. In the mind of a Jewish scholar, the words of YHWH were the seeds of the ground. To study the Scriptures is to be a "keeper of the garden," a keeper of the Word, someone who cultivates and cares for the Word of YHWH. A true disciple is a gardener of God's Word.

You can't be a gardener without digging. To conserve and cultivate God's Word, one has to go digging in the garden.[18] And when digging in the dirt, one finds treasures of testimony to the living Christ and to the person of Jesus. Just because some seeds are buried in the ground, some stones are baked and caked in dirt, doesn't mean they don't bear fruit or that they display no gemstone testimonial. The Word of Christ as attested in the Gospels bears witness to the truth of Jesus' identity.

Every word represents the Word. Jesus' identity cries out from His very language, from the narratives and metaphors ("narraphors") of His discourse in the Gospels. All four Gospel writers, as well as other writers and disciples of Jesus, recorded only what was relevant to the message they needed subsequent disciples to hear, as a witness to the identity of Jesus. Jesus' own words and the words of those following Him testify to His identity, both human and divine, as rabbi and Messiah.

Let the stones bear witness. Jesus Himself becomes the Word. In the defining parable of the sower,[19] we are to tend the Word of YHWH, the seed of the ground, and to plant it everywhere. You never know where it will take. Jesus is the Torah seed in the flesh. This is one of the "mysteries of the kingdom," Jesus reveals.[20]

JESUS' HIDDEN YEARS AREN'T REALLY HIDDEN

The text of our lives goes on, whether or not it is written down. It is the same with Jesus' life and His "missing years" from twelve to thirty. What if Jesus' "missing years" aren't missing at all but simply hidden in His words, His parables, His actions, His signs? In a sense, the signs around us are like stones, witnesses to the work of the Holy Spirit in our midst. When our text is interrupted, signs shine through what is said and what is left unsaid. *We need merely to connect the dots*, to fill in the missing words that are not so much missing as invisible to the eye.

As Jesus would say in His favorite phrase, "Pay attention." Or elsewhere, "Let those with eyes see, those with ears hear."[21] To be aware is to look for the signs in all of their manifestations.

Jesus' divinity has become a catchword, a rhetorical blindfold rather than the recovery of sight to the blind. The only reason the Gospels and Epistles were written, and the only passages chosen to record, was to witness to the truth of the living cornerstone, the messiahship of Jesus, the divinity of Christ, who was more than the phenomenal and controversial man everyone knew. Without the testimony of the Gospels, Jesus would have gone down in history as the most astute and amazing rabbi in Jewish history.

But to deny Jesus as divine Messiah is to negate the entire gospel story, the purpose of His ministry, the reason for His death, and the magnitude of His resurrection. Truth is not a construction (although truth emanates from Christ in concepts that are communicable and constructible). If Jesus taught His disciples anything, He taught that His identity was the very foundation of His ministry and the cornerstone of our faith. The way, truth, and life for Jesus are themselves the fulfillment of the scriptural promise, the renewal and reconstitution of the original covenantal relationship with God and the return of humanity to the garden.

THE GARDEN RELATIONSHIP WITH GOD

When in a garden relationship with God, humanity had no need of the Torah, for we had the Tree of Life. The Torah was the Tree of Life reborn, and Jesus was the Torah reborn. The PaRDeS[22] of the Torah, the Word of YHWH is Jesus Himself. In the act of resurrection, the stones of the temple, which confined God's favor to a chosen few, are reframed into a spiritual house: the City of God becomes the *paradeiso*, the garden of Eden, the eternal life.

The symbolism of the garden of Eden as Torah, as ark of the covenant, and as temple pervades Hebrew texts as well as the Jewish spiritual tradition. Even the scroll of the Torah itself is symbolic, with each pole called the "tree of life" and the manuscript its "leaves." Within those leaves lies the seed of YHWH, buried in the garden of the Torah. The seven-branched golden lampstand known as the menorah,[23] hammered out of pure gold into an almond-tree design (which was sometimes called the "awakening tree"), symbolized the Tree of Life. The most common symbolism of Judaism, the menorah stood to the side of the ark, giving it light and reminding the Hebrew people that they are chosen to be a "light to the Gentiles."[24] The little town called Nazareth means "branch." Nazareth was the dead branch[25] that would restore the Tree of Life[26] spoken of in the book of Revelation, whose leaves give the nations healing.[27]

This incarnational presence moves in the new covenant from Torah to Jesus Himself. The living stones become the testimony to the living PaRDeS, the foundational stone of the spiritual temple of God, the garden of Eden, the gateway to the Tree of Life, where there is restored relationship to the Creator and eternal life in God.

The design of Solomon's temple likewise echoes this garden imagery. The eastern gate models the gate of the garden of Eden. The inner sanctum, where the ark of the covenant resides, is strewn with garden designs. "He carved all the walls of the temple all around . . . with carved figures of cherubim, palm trees, and open flowers."[28] The ark itself is set upon stone and guarded by two angels, like those guarding the eternal garden.

The entire resurrection story is crammed with this garden symbolism. Jesus as the way, truth, and life assumes the role as gateway, gardener, garden, and Tree of Life. Jesus not only brings the new covenant; He is the new covenant. The way is *through* Him: "No one comes to the Father except through Me."[29] When Mary found the empty tomb in the garden, she found the stone had been rolled away (metaphorically, the stone guarding the garden of Eden), and two shining angels guarded the head and foot of Jesus.

The resurrected Christ serves as the new entryway to the garden *paradeiso*. Mary recognized her master first as the "gardener."[30] When Jesus spoke to the thief on the cross, He told him, "You will be with Me in Paradise [*paradeiso*, "the garden"]."[31] When Mary addressed Jesus, she used the term "Rabboni": "my most esteemed master."[32] Her eyes were opened, and she recognized Jesus for who He was.

Basalt became basal: the covenant of inorganic stone (the Hebrew Torah, the Law) became the new organic covenant, the fulfillment of the original intent, the living and spiritual stone, the return to the garden: "To him who overcomes I will give to eat from the tree of life, which is in the midst of the Paradise of God."[33] In Genesis God told Cain that a sin offering would be placed at the door of the garden.[34] Now Christ, God's sin offering, was standing at the door. Not only standing at the door and knocking, but He Himself *is* the gateway for the opening of the door.[35] Jesus welcomes inside not only Israelite nor only Gentile but all humanity. With the tearing of the temple curtain, the breaking of the sacrificial body and blood of Jesus, the final barrier between us and God has been broken: "Therefore, brothers and sisters, since we have confidence to enter the Most Holy Place by the blood of Jesus, by a new and living way opened for us through the curtain, that is, his body . . ."[36]

In the Genesis account, Adam (the stones of the earth and the disciples of the covenant) was commanded to conserve and conceive the garden, to watch and ward the covenant. When Adam failed and Cain spilled his brother's blood, God's people were variously expelled. Jesus, the Second Adam, broke the seal of the rock, and the entryway was opened once again for humankind and God to commune together.

Only through Jesus the Messiah, the sacrificial offering, can this spiritual temple, this garden paradise, be reestablished. Jesus, the master builder, teaches us that truth is not a construction. Truth is a relationship. It is a garden of relationships. Truth is an organic, breathing, binding covenant relationship with the Master Architect, the Creator of the universe.

Jesus said, "I am the way and the truth and the life."[37] He is the means, the beyond real, the livingness without beginning or end. Every gospel account bears witness to Jesus' identity: "Let those with eyes see, and those with ears hear."

Nature abhors a vacuum, and so do historians. When there is insufficient evidence to say anything with certainty, scholars are increasingly using something called "scenario thinking" to present a best-case scenario, worst-case scenario, and status-quo scenario. Colloquially these scenarios are called "the good, the bad, and the likely." In the next section and in the following chapter, we will present a scenario of what the stones might say about our Lord's "missing years." We are keenly aware that any scenario needs to be made with deep humility and tentativeness. And it is with such an attitude that we will explore this piece of Jesus' amazing life.

THE MAN WHO FITS NO FORMULA

Eduard Schweitzer rightly described Jesus as "the man who fits no formula."[38] N. T. Wright echoed this sentiment, observing that Jesus "burst the boundaries of all expectations."[39]

The Gospels tell us that Jesus was born in Bethlehem, He grew up in Nazareth in northern Palestine, and He visited the temple in Jerusalem at age twelve. Beyond that, they are mostly silent on what He did for the eighteen years in between. We say "mostly" because we do have some hints from Jesus' own lips and from the lips of His contemporaries. It's not a great deal, but it's enough to gain some insight into His preparation for ministry.

So the first thing to be said about the so-called missing years of Jesus is that no one can be certain about the details. The Gospels are virtually silent. The same is true for the rest of the Second Testament.

This vacuum of information has become fertile ground for the birth of all sorts of theories, some with more scriptural backing than others. Some of the more speculative sources say Jesus went to India to study under Eastern gurus. Others say He studied with the Essenes. Others even say He visited Great Britain. Some recent studies suggest that Jesus went to Jerusalem to be trained as a rabbi. Many scholars still claim Jesus to be a fringe revolutionary. Still others claim that He was merely a poor, uneducated but charismatic outsider. Not surprisingly, most want to fit Jesus into their own image of His hidden years. But the real question is,

The point is that God has put right down into this world, into the midst of mankind, a new kind of Man, Who is not just better, more or less, than other men, but different altogether from other men; and has, in effect, said, "That is the Man that I have in view, and eternally it has been My purpose to conform to that image." How important it is, therefore, for us to understand the real nature and meaning of the life of our Lord Jesus as lived here on this earth. It is not just a beautiful story, about a man living and working and teaching, in a country somewhere in this world, far away and long ago. But, right up to date, a Man is presented to us, as altogether different from us in constitution and yet as God's pattern for His working in us.

—T. Austin-Sparks[40]

which can be most backed up by scripture? What makes for good story doesn't equate to what actually happened.

JESUS' MISSING YEARS WERE NOT UNUSUAL

We will set forth one scenario of the lost or hidden years based on the data that we have from the Gospels and from other first-century sources. According to the scenario presented in this chapter, the so-called missing years in Jesus' life aren't lost or missing at all. They simply didn't contain the kind of drama that would compel the Gospel writers to write much about them.

Let's begin with two pertinent texts on the subject:

> And he came and dwelt in a city called Nazareth, that it might be fulfilled which was spoken by the prophets, "He shall be called a Nazarene."[41]

> Then He went down with them and came to Nazareth, and was subject to them, but His mother kept all these things in her heart. And Jesus increased in wisdom and stature, and in favor with God and men.[42]

These two accounts are immediately followed by the account of Jesus being baptized in the Jordan by John the Baptist. This seems to imply that Jesus' baptism was the next significant event in His life (at least in the minds of the Gospel writers). According to Dr. David Instone-Brewer of Tyndale Fellowship, ancient biographers rarely wrote about the childhood of the people they chronicled. Their custom was to detail their births, their lives, and then their deaths. Unless someone had an unusual upbringing, they wouldn't mention his youth.[43]

The reason the Gospel writers were silent about these years may be because Jesus' youth was similar to that of most Jewish boys who grew up in Nazareth. There wasn't anything out of the ordinary about His upbringing. (At least not on the surface.)[44] Perhaps that's the point the Gospel writers were trying to communicate to us about those years.

Jesus' youth was very human. It was like that of most Jewish boys of His day: "Therefore he had to become like his brothers and sisters in every respect."[45]

The fact that the people of Nazareth were taken aback by the way Jesus taught as an adult seems to confirm this:[46]

> And all were speaking well of Him, and wondering at the gracious words which were falling from His lips; and they were saying, "Is this not Joseph's son?"[47]

> He came to His hometown [Nazareth] and began teaching them in their synagogue, so that they were astonished, and said, "Where did this man get this wisdom and these miraculous powers? Is not this the carpenter's son? Is not His mother called Mary, and His brothers, James and Joseph and Simon and Judas? And His sisters, are they not all with us? Where then did this man get all these things?"[48]

> When the Sabbath came, He began to teach in the synagogue; and the many listeners were astonished, saying, "Where did this man get these things, and what is this wisdom given to Him, and such miracles as these performed by His hands? Is not this the carpenter, the son of Mary, and brother of James and Joses and Judas and Simon? Are not His sisters here with us?" And they took offense at Him.[49]

What is more striking is the reaction of the Jews in Jerusalem when they heard Jesus teach in the temple courts:

> Now about the middle of the feast Jesus went up into the temple and taught. And the Jews marveled, saying, "How does this Man know letters, having never studied?"
>
> Jesus answered them and said, "My doctrine is not Mine, but His who sent Me."[50]

The Jews in Jerusalem were amazed at Jesus' teaching, wondering *where* He had gained such knowledge and insight "having never studied."[51] Jesus' response is telling: His tutoring came from His Father. He was not taught by any man but by God. N. T. Wright has underscored this point, saying,

> Teachers in Judaism would normally have studied the law with one or more rabbis. They would have spent years perfecting their knowledge of the finer points of interpretation. Jesus had never attended such classes, and yet he obviously knew the scriptures extremely well and was able to expound them in a fresh and vivid way. Where had he got it all from? . . . In verse 16 [of John 7] Jesus states his response baldly: his teaching comes from God, and he didn't make it up himself.[52]

WHERE THE HISTORICAL EVIDENCE POINTS

Jesus' hometown was a village that resided in lower Galilee, called Nazareth.[53] The word *Nazareth* comes from *netzer* and means "branch" or "shoot." The town was called the "branch" town because it was a place where descendants of the royal line of David settled. "A shoot will come up from the stump of Jesse; from his roots a Branch will bear fruit; He grew up before him like a tender shoot, and like a root out of dry ground."[54] This could explain why Mary and Joseph settled there in God's providence.

Nazareth was worthy of its lowly name. It held the lowest place in public estimation. Nathanael's question reflects this fact: "Nazareth! Can anything good come from there?"[55] The larger town just next to Nazareth was Sepphoris.[56] According to the best scholarship we have, Nazareth was small. It probably had a population of fewer than four hundred, and it was not very well-to-do.[57]

As the son of an artisan, Jesus would not have been poverty-stricken. Artisans were not at the bottom of the social strata; they certainly were not peasants. Tenant farmers, shepherds, and agriculture workers were poorer.[58]

At the same time, many scholars believe that to call Jesus "middle-class" or "rich" isn't accurate either. Jesus was certainly familiar with poverty. Paul said of Him, "Though He was rich, yet for your sakes He became poor, that you through His poverty might become rich."[59] The riches Paul mentioned here may have referred to the riches of the heavens that Jesus possessed before His incarnation, a wealth He forfeited by becoming a man born to a nonwealthy family.

Although not extremely poor, from scriptural evidence we can assume that Mary and Joseph were likely not wealthy.[60] While prosperity teachers have tried to take certain portions of the Gospels to transform Jesus and Joseph into opulent men, their arguments have been strongly challenged.[61] N. T. Wright has put it this way:

> Jesus, with all the "riches" of his life in the glorious mystery of God's inner being, became "poor," both in the sense that becoming human was an astonishingly humbling thing and in the sense that the human life he took on was not royal, rich and splendid in the world's terms but instead poor, humble and eventually shameful.[62]

Some scholars believe that Joseph and Jesus worked in Sepphoris. Sepphoris was roughly an hour's walk from Nazareth, about four or five miles away. Bible scholar and archaeologist Jerome Murphy O'Connor asserts that Joseph and Mary settled in Nazareth because of its proximity to Sepphoris.[63] After 3 BC, Sepphoris was the center of a building boom and provided daily work opportunities for artisans like Joseph. It's certainly possible that Jesus worked in Sepphoris as well as in Nazareth, but there is no proof one way or the other.[64] So while the idea that Jesus was an illiterate, uneducated, landless peasant doesn't fit the evidence, the notion that He was rich is built on questionable scholarship as well. It is clear from the Gospels that Jesus could read.[65] Josephus pointed out that it was expected that Jewish children be taught to read.[66] And Armin Baum has concluded that the evidence is overwhelming that first-century Jews memorized large portions of the Torah.[67] Jewish people emphasized education more than most cultures (this was recognized even by Gentile writers). Thus literacy among Jews was generally higher than among most people groups in the Roman world.[68]

It appears that Jesus gave the bulk of His teachings in Aramaic, He had a basic knowledge of Hebrew, and He knew at least some Greek.[69] Like most Jewish males of His day, His primary education took place in the synagogue. This is where He would have learned to read.[70] Jesus would have also learned the Scriptures at the local synagogue in Nazareth, which He attended every Sabbath.[71] And His parents would have trained Him in the Jewish way of life. The fact that Jesus had tassels on His garment indicates that He was a Law-observing, pious Jew.[72] There is no question that His parents, Joseph and Mary, were devout Jews as well.[73]

A PEEK INTO JESUS' YOUTH

The only peek into Jesus' youth that the Gospels give us is found in Luke 2:42–50. A twelve-year-old Jesus went up to Jerusalem with His family to celebrate the Passover feast. After a day passed on their journey home, the Lord's parents suddenly realized Jesus was missing. They searched for Him among the caravan of relatives and friends, but He was nowhere to be found. Frantically worried, Mary and Joseph headed back to Jerusalem to look for Jesus. After three days of searching, they found Him in the temple courts, sitting among the teachers, listening to and quizzing them.

Mary and Joseph were astonished and asked Him why He didn't return with them. Jesus responded, "Didn't you know I had to be in my Father's house?"[74] He then returned to Nazareth and "was obedient to them."[75]

There are echoes in this story of the burial and resurrection of Jesus. In both cases, Jesus was lost, and three days later He was found. Luke used the phrases "after three days" and "the third day" to describe these events.[76] Jesus' responses in both situations were similar: "Why did you seek Me?"[77] . . . "Who are you looking for?"[78] And in both cases, we have women remembering the event: "His mother kept all these things in her heart"[79] . . . "And they remembered His words."[80] Luke seemed to see this story as an anticipation of the resurrection.

The story also gives us a window into understanding that Jesus was a precocious young man—so much so that He confounded the Jewish teachers with His probing questions and deep understanding. Jesus was, in effect, assuming the posture of a teacher—sitting. He would assume this posture again when He turned thirty and began teaching in the synagogue in Nazareth.

Interestingly when Mary found Him, she said, "*Your father* and I have sought You anxiously." Jesus responded by saying, "I must be about *My Father's* business," speaking of God.[81] Jesus was surprised that His parents didn't expect Him to be in the temple. At age twelve He was clearly aware that God was His Father, and He had a special mission on earth.

We must understand that a twelve-year-old boy in the ancient Jewish world was not viewed as a child any longer. So Mary and Joseph shouldn't be regarded as bad parents for losing sight of Him. The extended family was very powerful in Jesus' day. So Mary and Joseph naturally assumed He returned home with relatives.

Luke went on to say, "Jesus increased in wisdom and stature, and in favor with God and men."[82] In other words, He grew physically in height and age, and He grew mentally and spiritually in wisdom and insight.[83] And God's favor was upon Him.

WHAT DID JESUS LOOK LIKE AS HE GREW INTO MANHOOD?

As far as Jesus' appearance goes, nothing is said about it in the Gospels or Epistles. This is interesting because the human memory recalls human faces better than it does words and actions. Thus the absence of a physical description of Jesus appears intentional. The post-apostolic literature that claims to describe Jesus' physical appearance is flimsy at best, and most scholars consider them to be forgeries. Perhaps the truth of Plato's "beauty is in the eye of the beholder" is nowhere more evident than in the question of what Jesus looked like. For Isaiah, Jesus is plain-looking if not ugly: "There was nothing beautiful or majestic about his appearance, nothing to attract us to him."[84] But then there is the Messianic psalm: "You are the most handsome of all."[85]

The Isaiah description fits the entire narrative of Jesus. Jesus entered into this planet in a way no one anticipated. His birth was the exact opposite of what one would expect for a king, let alone the King of the world, God's own Son. He wasn't born in a palace, and He constantly associated with the lowly and downtrodden. Humans put great emphasis on outward appearances. This was just as true in the ancient world as it is today. Recall when Jesse put forth all of his sons before the great prophet Samuel. Samuel assumed that the best-looking and tallest was God's choice. But it wasn't.

> When they arrived, Samuel saw Eliab and thought, "Surely the LORD's anointed stands here before the LORD."
>
> But the LORD said to Samuel, "Do not consider his appearance or his height, for I have rejected him. The LORD does not look at the things man looks at. Man looks at the outward appearance, but the LORD looks at the heart."[86]

God's choice was the youngest of Jesse's children, the shepherd boy, David. No one expected this. To be sure, there is unspeakable beauty in the new David, Jesus. But just like the tabernacle of Moses, the beauty of Christ resides inwardly. Outwardly, the tabernacle was covered with badgers' skins, which were dull, drab, and mundane. From the outside, the tabernacle was a plain and ordinary sight. But inside, the house was filled with gold, fine-woven white linen embroidered with blue, purple, and scarlet thread. It was a glorious sight to behold, "full of grace and truth."[87] Jesus is the real tabernacle of God.[88]

The words of Frederick Buechner sum it up well:

> The faces of Jesus then—all the ways he had of being and being seen. The writers of the New Testament give no description of any of them because it was his life alive inside of them that was the news they hawked rather than the color of his eyes.[89]

Yet Jesus was incarnated in human form, and as human beings, we can make some assumptions about what He may have looked like as a Jewish male in His culture at that time. Most male Jews in Jesus' day did not have *long* hair, defined as shoulder-length hair or longer. Long hair was a sign of rebellion and dissent. *Short* hair wasn't cropped but lay trimmed neatly along the neck. Jesus is presumed to have had this kind of short hair because Paul stated, "Isn't it obvious that it's disgraceful for a man to have long hair?"[90]

Whatever the length of his hair, however, Jesus was careful about grooming: "when you fast, put oil on your head and wash your face, so that it will not be obvious to men that you are fasting."[91] Or in other words, *do not look gloomy*. Jesus combed His hair, looked good, and smiled.

Perhaps His smile is the most telling feature of Jesus. The ancients knew it was the content of the Lord's character, not the quality of His appearance, that mattered.

This all provides the backdrop to how God the Father prepared Jesus for His incredible ministry.

CHAPTER 6

Jesus' Preparation for Ministry

> *Preach Christ . . . He is the whole gospel. His person, offices, and work must be our one great, all-comprehending theme.*
>
> —Charles Spurgeon[1]

N. T. Wright has pleaded for the importance of doing responsible historical and biblical reconstruction on Jesus, saying, "If we don't make the effort to do this reconstruction, we will, without a shadow of a doubt, assume that what Jesus did and said makes the sense it might have made in some other context—perhaps our own."[2] According to Wright, if we don't interpret the available evidence correctly, "we shall simply squash Jesus into the little boxes of our own imaginations rather than seeing him as he was."[3]

While every interpretation has some element of subjectivity, we do have one possible scenario of what Jesus was doing between the ages of twelve and thirty to prepare for His adult ministry. Based on a plausible reading of Scripture and the cultural information of His era, let's go back in time, and imagine.

TWELVE-YEAR-OLD BOYS IN AD 8

It is the year AD 8, and we are in the town of Nazareth. If Jesus was born in 4 BC, as many scholars suggest, Jesus is now twelve.

Throughout Galilee, other young men, part of a select group, are also twelve. They are part of the tribe of Levi. These young men are planning to relocate to Jerusalem to be trained for the priesthood. Older priests will apprentice them, teaching them the details of the Law and tutoring them in the temple sacrificial system. They will learn how to manage the furniture inside the Holy Place. They will learn how to slaughter bullocks and lambs and how to remove the fat according to the Law. They will be trained to be expert butchers. They will also learn all the rituals associated with the temple. This training will go on for years. They will not be able to receive their ordination and begin their priestly service until they reach age thirty.[4]

There is another group of young men who are twelve. They will soon begin their education as scribes. Each is being tutored by an older scribe under whom the boy has chosen to study. Some are studying under village scribes. Others, desiring a more advanced education, are moving to Jerusalem to study. They will learn the rare skill of writing and be schooled in the fine points of the Law as well as the oral tradition. They will seek to master how to preserve, apply, and defend the Torah. (In the first-century world, rabbis didn't recruit or select students. Students chose the rabbis under whom they wished to study, much as a student today chooses a professor under whom to study.)

There is yet another group of twelve-year-old Jewish males who have selected rabbis to disciple them.[5] (Paul of Tarsus was tutored under the rabbi Gamaliel, for instance.[6] Again, rabbis were simply teachers. The rabbis of Jesus' day could be likened to the pastors and Bible teachers of our time, where the scribes could be likened to our Bible scholars and theologians.)

But what is *God* doing in AD 8 at age twelve?

Jesus could have trained to be a scribe. And He could have been trained as a rabbi. Those two choices were before Him. He could have gone the route of the religious professional.[7]

But that's not what He did.

Think back to how He came into this world. He was born in the place where animals were kept. No priest, scribe, or rabbi was present at this birth. Who showed up? Shepherds. And some time later, some pagan astrologers.

No, God incarnate did not choose any of the accepted forms of "religious training" of His day. Here again, our Lord burst the boundaries of all expectations. His ministry preparation was to become a craftsman—part of the working class. Jesus, God incarnate, chose to be a blue-collar worker.[8] That was His preparation for spiritual service.

A BLUE-COLLAR MESSIAH

Since it was the practice of a father to teach his son his trade or skill, we can assume that Joseph trained Jesus for the vocation of being a *tekton*. (The fact that Matthew 13:54–56 says Joseph was a *tekton* and Mark 6:2–3 says Jesus was a *tekton* confirms this.) The Greek word *tekton* used in Matthew 13:55 and Mark 6:3 has been commonly translated "carpenter." However, the wide consensus among Greek scholars today is that the word means "artisan"—someone who works with stone and wood.[9]

So Jesus of Nazareth was a builder. He was a craftsman who worked with His hands. And for the next eighteen years, He would work in an artisan's shop as well as on outside projects. He would perspire. He would toil. He would get His clothes dirty. He would become exhausted. He would learn the physical labor of cutting wood, mixing mortar, hauling stone, and working with a mallet, ax, and trowel. He would know the agonies of labor as well as its joys. Just like most of us.

After Jesus' visit to Jerusalem at age twelve, Joseph is never mentioned. So it's probable that Joseph died sometime after Jesus turned twelve.[10] This would have meant that Jesus, being the oldest son of the family,[11] would have been largely, if not fully, responsible for supporting His mother, His four brothers, and His sisters.[12]

If that's the case, Jesus knew the pressures of having steady employment to put food on the table, not just for Himself but for others. The idea that because Jesus was the Son of God, He simply snapped His fingers and created tools, buildings, furniture, or even coins out of thin air goes against the grain of how the Gospel writers portrayed Him. Jesus came in the likeness of sinful flesh and lived as an ordinary human being yet without sin.[13] He didn't live like a superhero.

> *Angels watched as Mary changed God's diaper. The universe watched with wonder as the Almighty learned to walk. Children played in the street with him. And had the synagogue leader in Nazareth known who was listening to his sermons . . . Jesus may have had pimples. He may have been tone-deaf. Perhaps a girl down the street had a crush on him or vice-versa. It could be that his knees were bony. One thing's for sure: he was, while completely divine, completely human.*
>
> —Max Lucado[14]

Think about it: Jesus the craftsman, falling and scraping His knee while running to make an appointment. Jesus the journeyman, hitting His thumb with a hammer after overshooting the nail by a centimeter. Jesus the artisan, with hands callused and scarred from years of plying His trade.

Watch Him after a full day's work, with splinters in His fingers and sawdust in His hair. His toe was bruised and swollen from a falling stone. He was physically spent. He would have loved to spend the next day resting to recover, but He must rise early in the morning to finish a job He had begun. Day in and day out, He worked, He sweated, and He dealt with fallen human beings, whom He was trying to serve.

The artisan from Nazareth who worked with stone was the very person who created stone with the words of His mouth. The iron in which His tools were crafted was extracted from the ore that He created. The water that so refreshed Him when He perspired in the scorching Eastern sun was the water that He Himself spoke into existence. And the wood with which He was so familiar, the material upon which He would one day be crucified, came from His own hands.[15] The Second Testament states five times that Jesus died on a tree.[16] And not only were trees all created *by* Him, but they were created *for* Him.[17]

Jesus knew not only the rigors that came with manual labor but also the boredom that was attached to it. For eighteen long years He filled His days with the mundane. Sure, some days were probably more exciting than others, but there was no glory there. There were no miracles there. There were no crowds there. There was only perspiration, toiling for hours in indescribable heat, and the pleasure and pain of dealing with customers. All in all, it was an ordinary—sometimes boring—occupation.

Human nature doesn't change. And neither do the challenges that come with working for others. So we can assume that Jesus knew the scourge of unsatisfied customers. Imagine: A local farmer in Nazareth has hired Him to repair one of his plows. Jesus spends three days fixing it. It's not an easy project. It turns out to be more complicated than first assumed. The job is finished, and the farmer sees what Jesus has done. But he's not satisfied, so he spreads word around Nazareth that Jesus does poor work.

Another person hires Jesus to do some work on his home. Jesus spends a solid week accomplishing the task. It's one of the most difficult of His career. The person never pays Him. This isn't the first time this has happened. Not a few times Jesus worked without being paid. Not a few times did unhappy customers browbeat Him with unfair complaints and condescending insults. Are we suggesting that Jesus didn't do quality work? Not at all. But we know human nature. And so do you. Sometimes people aren't pleased with even the very best work. In short, Jesus knows what it feels like to be slighted, to be unappreciated, to feel used.

He is tempted to feel anger toward these individuals. He is tempted to argue His case. He is tempted to defend Himself. He is tempted to set the record straight. The pressure of having to take care of His family in the face of all of this just increases the temptations.

> For we do not have a High Priest who cannot sympathize with our weaknesses, but was in all points tempted as we are, yet without sin.[18]

> Though He was a Son, yet He learned obedience by the things which He suffered.[19]

> No temptation has overtaken you except such as is common to man.[20]

But Jesus never gave in to the temptations. Instead, He yielded to His Father's life within Him, a life that knows how to die. A life that loses instead of fights to win.[20] This was His pattern of living. And it would eventually lead Him to suffer the ultimate loss: *His own life.* His years in the artisan's shop, working with and for fallen mortals, was incredible training in this area.

But perhaps more encouraging than all of this is that Jesus Christ, in becoming an ordinary working man, made work a holy thing. He made toil sacred. And He destroyed the secular-versus-sacred myth by blessing the mundane, hallowing the ordinary, and sanctifying the routine.

Many modern Christians still have in their minds that "spiritual" work (being "called to full-time ministry," going to Bible school or seminary, and being ordained) is somehow more valuable to God than doing "secular" work (being a construction worker, a secretary, a dental assistant, or a computer engineer; changing diapers, preparing meals, and cleaning houses; you name it). The Lord's life on earth teaches us that this is simply not true. Whatever is done for the glory of God is valuable in His eyes. The so-called secular becomes spiritual when done for the Lord.

> Therefore, whether you eat or drink, or whatever you do, do all to the glory of God.[22]

Keep this in mind when you grow weary of the drudgery of doing the same thing every day. Keep it in mind when you are worn out from your job and deem it trivial and unimportant. Recall it when you are being treated unfairly at work and you're being undervalued, underpaid, and unappreciated. Remember, you are not wasting your time, no more than Jesus was wasting His time in that artisan's shop. Jesus Christ has made sacred every minute, every hour, and every day that you spend earning your wage. He identifies with your sweat, your toil, and the agonies that go along with it.

Indeed, when the Romans crucified the Son of God, they not only put to death the Savior of the world, but also crucified a working man . . . they killed a craftsman. And it was a blue-collar worker who rose again from the dead. For that's what He was most of His life.

THE TEACHER WHO TAUGHT JESUS

There was something else going on in that artisan's shop that was part of our Lord's preparation for ministry. In the gospel of John, Jesus repeatedly told us what it was:

> "By myself I can do nothing; I judge only as I hear, and my judgment is just, for I seek not to please myself but him who sent me."[23]

> "As the living Father hath sent me, and I live by the Father . . ."[24]

> Jesus answered, "My teaching is not my own. It comes from him who sent me. If anyone chooses to do God's will, he will find out whether my teaching comes from God or whether I speak on my own."[25]

> So Jesus said, "When you have lifted up the Son of Man, then you will know that I am the one I claim to be and that I do nothing on my own but speak just what the Father has taught me."[26]

> "For I did not speak of my own accord, but the Father who sent me commanded me what to say and how to say it."[27]

> "Don't you believe that I am in the Father, and that the Father is in me? The words I say to you are not just my own. Rather, it is the Father, living in me, who is doing his work."[28]

"He who does not love me will not obey my teaching. These words you hear are not my own; they belong to the Father who sent me."[29]

Jesus made many of these statements in response to the religious authorities who challenged Him about His teaching and where it came from. His answer was consistent and telling: "I can do nothing of Myself. I do not speak on My own accord. My teaching comes straight from My Father. It is not Mine. The Father has taught Me all the things I teach. He tells Me what to say. He shows Me what to do. I do nothing without My Father's leading. He sent Me here, and He lives within Me."[30]

While Jesus worked as an artisan, He was in constant communion with His Father. From a young age, He had learned how to recognize His Father's voice.[31] His communion with His Father mostly took place inside of Him. We can deduce this from the fact that the Gospels only record Jesus praying aloud a few times. And in one instance, He indicated that praying aloud wasn't the typical way He spoke to His Father.[32]

Having an enormous capacity to retain information (as most people in the ancient world did), He probably recited to Himself portions of the Law, the Prophets, and the Writings He learned in the synagogue from His childhood and throughout His adulthood. He probably communed with His Father about those texts. From His youth, Jesus began to understand who He was, for He began to recognize Himself and His mission.[33] He even remembered some of what happened in His preincarnate state, before He stepped out of eternity to become human.

"Your father Abraham rejoiced at the thought of seeing my day; he saw it and was glad."

"You are not yet fifty years old," the Jews said to him, "and you have seen Abraham!"

"I tell you the truth," Jesus answered, "before Abraham was born, I am!"[34]

God the Father was the One who had tutored Jesus. Because Jesus was in constant communion with His Father, He learned the extraordinary habit of seeing the ordinary through the eyes of God. Let me give you an example of how it may have happened.

A POSSIBLE SCENARIO

Imagine Jesus at age eighteen. He is taking a long walk in Nazareth. He's not had work in weeks, and He is out of money. The pressure is mounting, and He is tempted to worry. One of His sisters accidentally damaged her last set of clothes, and she is need of something to wear. Jesus is flat broke and cannot buy new clothes for her. Disturbing thoughts flit through His mind. *What will happen if I can't feed My family?* As He walks, He communes with His Father about the situation.

He passes a meadow and notices the Middle Eastern lilies. Some birds fly overhead and catch His eye. Then the Father speaks within Him, saying, *My Son, look at these birds. I take care of them, and they don't worry a second about food. Look at the beautiful lilies before You. They don't worry about what they will wear, for I clothe them. How much more are You, Your sisters, Your mother, and Your brothers worth to Me than these things? You have nothing to worry about. I will provide for You. Do not doubt. Only believe. Continue to seek Me and My kingdom above all other things, and You and Your family will have everything you need.*

Years later, Jesus will sit down on a hill and say to His disciples,

> Therefore I tell you, do not worry about your life, what you will eat or drink; or about your body, what you will wear. Is not life more important than food, and the body more important than clothes? Look at the birds of the air; they do not sow or reap or store away in barns, and yet your heavenly Father feeds them. Are you not much more valuable than they? Who of you by worrying can add a single hour to his life?
>
> And why do you worry about clothes? See how the lilies of the field grow. They do not labor or spin. Yet I tell you that not even Solomon in all his splendor was dressed like one of these. If that is how God clothes the grass of the field, which is here today and tomorrow is thrown into the fire, will he not much more clothe you, O you

> of little faith? So do not worry, saying, "What shall we eat?" or "What shall we drink?" or "What shall we wear?" For the pagans run after all these things, and your heavenly Father knows that you need them. But seek first his kingdom and his righteousness, and all these things will be given to you as well.[35]

Did this actually happen? Probably not. But given what the Gospels tell us about the source of all that Jesus taught, we suspect it's not too far off the mark.

JESUS BEGINS HIS MINISTRY

After eighteen years of living life as a craftsman, the Father led Jesus to transition to full-time service. So at age thirty, Jesus began His ministry of teaching. And when He did, what was the people's response? "Is not this Jesus, the son of Joseph?"[36] They did not take Him seriously because He didn't have the proper credentials. He wasn't ordained. He wasn't tutored by a scribe or a recognized rabbi. *What does He think He's doing?*

It is clear from the Gospels that Jesus' main audience was never the religious leaders. Jesus wasn't trying to persuade or convert the Jewish establishment. Exceptions, like Nicodemus (and probably Joseph of Arimathea), came to Jesus. But Jesus was addressing the common people who gave Him a hearing. Thus He kept to the villages,[37] staying away from the large Galilean towns, like Sepphoris and Tiberias.[38] (Interestingly, the Gospels don't mention these two cities, which were the largest in Galilee.)

The religious elite ignored Him as long as they could. But as His influence grew (which was rather quickly), they were forced to listen to and engage Him.[39] Robert McIver has suggested that at least sixty thousand people would have witnessed some aspect of Jesus' earthly ministry.[40] Consequently, the religious establishment had to take Him seriously. Here's a summary of their critique against Him: "By what authority are you doing these things?" they asked. "And who gave you this authority?"[41]

The Jewish establishment constantly leveled this challenge at Jesus.

They were essentially saying, "You didn't come through the proper channels. You aren't qualified. Where are your ordination papers? What school did you graduate from, and where is your degree? Who gave you the authority to teach as you are doing?"

Jesus' authorization to teach was *not* based on institutional sources. He wasn't trained in the oral tradition of the elders, like the Pharisees. Neither was He a member of the priestly class, like the Sadducees. He spoke in the capacity of a prophet, and His authority came from God.[42] In today's language, Jesus was a layman. Yet He believed "He had authority over and above the Torah."[43]

I understand God's patience with the wicked, but I do wonder how He can be so patient with the pious.

—George MacDonald[44]

In addition, Jesus didn't argue like other teachers or later rabbis. Their method of teaching was to exegete Scripture by quoting other rabbis. Jesus, however, never used footnotes. He claimed God was His only authority. In his book *Jesus the Sage,* Ben Witherington expounds on this further, arguing that Jesus taught as a sage, not primarily as an exegete. (Neither the Talmud nor the Mishnah existed in Jesus' day, and He showed no knowledge of either.)[45] Instead, Jesus taught in parables, aphorisms, riddles, and one-liners—the teaching methods of sages.[46] Although He was a prophet, Jesus never used the prophetic formula, "Thus says the Lord." This isn't surprising since Christ, being "greater than Solomon," is both the wisdom of God and the Logos of God incarnate.[47]

LESSONS GLEANED

So what does Jesus' ministry preparation have to teach us today? It teaches us that God understands what it means to toil by the sweat of our brows and earn a living. It teaches us that God values work. He blesses the mundane, He sanctifies the ordinary, and He forges no division between the secular and the sacred. It teaches us that God knows what's involved in putting food on the table. He knows firsthand the challenges, and even the suffering, that are tied up with being part of the working class, including the temptation to worry and fret. It also teaches us that communion with God can happen in the midst of the ordinary things of life.

But beyond all this, it holds valuable insight for those who would walk in the same steps as Jesus with respect to His teaching ministry.

Imagine a young man publicly teaching about the things of God today. He has no formal theological training. He possesses no official ordination papers. He's part of neither the clergy nor the religious academic world. He's read the Scriptures deeply for years, and He's familiar with what the scribes (the scholars) and the rabbis (pastors) of His day have said on many subjects.

People listen to Him and are amazed at His insight into the Scriptures. They are taken aback by the depth in which He expounds the things of God. Interestingly, much of what He teaches runs against the grain of the religious establishment. It flies in the face of the reigning orthodoxy. It contradicts and confronts the status quo. Those who listen to Him regard Him as a prophet, a great teacher, a needed voice.

Their initial response is, "Where did this man get all this wisdom and insight from, seeing that He's never been to seminary?" To wit, His teaching is not for the religious establishment, but for the masses of God's people. They are His audience. He cares little about what the religious establishment thinks or says.

The religious elite ignored Him as long as they could. Since Jesus sported no theological degrees and wasn't part of the pastors guild, they didn't take Him seriously. He was not credible in their eyes. But they could only follow this course for so long. His influence grew so large that they couldn't ignore Him any longer. So they must extend to Him the credibility of engagement.

They came out with all guns blazing, seeking to refute Him. First, their pushback was targeted at the content of His teaching. But after realizing that they couldn't successfully discount what He said, they downshifted to an ad hominem assault. Personal attacks became their new weapon for dismissal: "He has no authority to say what He's saying." "He's not seminary trained." "He has no ordination papers." "He's not a scholar."

Then it escalated: "He was born as the result of fornication."[48] "He's a blasphemer."[49] "He's deceptive."[50] "He's a glutton and a drunkard."[51] "He's a false prophet."[52] And the ultimate attack: "Satan is working through Him!"[53]

Strikingly, this same story has been played out on virtually every bloodstained page of church history.[54] And unfortunately the destiny of many who have followed in Jesus' steps has been the same as His: persecution, suffering, and even execution.

> "Remember the words I spoke to you: 'No servant is greater than his master.' If they persecuted me, they will persecute you also. If they obeyed my teaching, they will obey yours also."[55]

Human nature changeth not. Nor do the systems men create, be they secular or religious. The reactions are all the same. When men feel threatened, the evil they are capable of in the name of God (and while defending Him) defies sanity. Jesus was put to death chiefly because of jealousy.

> For he [Pilate] knew it was out of envy that they had handed Jesus over to him.[56]

The favor and anointing of God will always garner the jealousy of those who do not possess them. Abel, upon whom God looked with favor, is not alone in those who were persecuted by a jealous Cain. Jealousy still lives and breathes in the hearts of the religiously ambitious and insecure.

> Crowds gathered also from the towns around Jerusalem, bringing their sick and those tormented by evil spirits, and all of them were healed.
>
> Then the high priest and all his associates, who were members of the party of the Sadducees, were filled with jealousy. They arrested the apostles and put them in the public jail.[57]

> When the Jews saw the crowds, they were filled with jealousy and talked abusively against what Paul was saying.[58]

> Some of the Jews were persuaded and joined Paul and Silas, as did a large number of God-fearing Greeks and not a few prominent women.
>
> But the Jews were jealous; so they rounded up some bad characters from the marketplace, formed a mob and started a riot in the city.[59]

The ways of God changeth not either.

According to rabbinical scholar David Instone-Brewer, Jesus "wasn't educated within the system." He was instead an "outsider." And as such, "He was rejected from the start . . . He stood out as someone having great authority, but outside the system."[60] Jesus threatened the status quo, a move that garnered the trust of the poor, oppressed, and marginalized. But it threatened the wealthy and powerful.

Again, others interpret the biblical and historical evidence differently. And so they come to different conclusions about Jesus' ministry preparation. But regardless of what theory one may hold, two things are indisputable: (1) Jesus' primary tutoring came from His Father, and (2) Jesus was not received by the religious establishment of His day. These two themes will reemerge again and again throughout the rest of this theography. Let's now turn to the beginning of Jesus' incomparable ministry.

CHAPTER 7

Jesus' Baptism and Temptation

Water is at the origin of the world,

the Jordan is at the origin of the Gospels.

—SAINT CYRIL OF JERUSALEM[1]

JESUS CHRIST'S PUBLIC MINISTRY WAS UNVEILED AND INAUGURATED at His baptism in the Jordan River at the hands of John the Baptist.[2] Luke tells us that Jesus was around thirty, the age when the priests of Israel could begin to be ordained.[3] Although Jesus didn't need a baptism Himself for the remission of sin, He was ritually washed on behalf of Israel and of all humanity. Jesus' baptism was a sign of His identity and mission, foreshadowing both crucifixion and death, as well as resurrection and new life—in the redemption of the world.

JOHN THE BAPTIST

A few words about John the Baptist.[4] The First Testament predicted the coming of this one whom Jesus regarded as the greatest person to ever penetrate the womb of a woman.[5] Isaiah foresaw Him as the voice crying in the wilderness, preparing the way of the Lord.[6] Malachi foresaw Him as God's messenger, sent to prepare the way before the Lord.[7]

He was known as John the Immerser.[8] His prophetic ministry included a baptism of repentance. To be baptized by John meant that you were being purified from your sins. That you were being freed from the burden of the filth of your past and loosed from the burdens that were attached to it. It meant you were starting all over again. Or in a more Jewish understanding of John's baptism, being plunged into the waters was the symbol of a people who would "turn" from sin and pride and "re-turn" to right relationships with God. The Greek word for "repent" is *metanoia*, which means to turn back, to turn around, to return to the waters of creation and to the wellspring of God's covenant. Baptism symbolized the restoration of a right covenant relationship between God and the people of Israel. When Jesus, the new Noah of Israel, came up out of the waters and saw the dove, the covenant was once again sealed. Jesus' baptism signifies the ultimate restoration of that covenant relationship.

Although water initiatory rituals were not uncommon among various first-century religions, John's use of the rite raised both eyebrows and questions. There was nothing and no one quite like John the Baptizer.

First, he did it for you—you didn't baptize yourself. Unlike the self-baptizing of Gentile converts to Judaism or the daily dunkings self-administered by the Qumran sectarians, John immersed those who came to him.

Second, and even more unsettling, he issued a demand for repentance and emphasized the need for baptizing to a Jewish audience—those who were by definition already God's chosen, privileged people. John's baptizing practices were controversial, and those most concerned with issues of proper purification, the Pharisees, demanded some additional explanation.

Third, John made the repentent enter a river, and he plunged them into the water. Even more, the Messiah got into the water right with His followers and submitted to John's baptism.

Fourth, John based this new baptism not on cultic practice or commandments but on a coming kingdom. It was future oriented, not past.

John the Baptizer was the new Elijah, hanging out in the Jordan River region that was Elijah's old stomping grounds[9] and wearing a fur mantle. But where Elijah withheld the dew and rain, John the Baptizer gave back the water if there was repentance. Elijah's message was "Repent or no water." The new Elijah's message was "Repent and receive water." Elijah baptized the pagan altar with water, drenching it with so much water it became an island, and God provided the fire. John the Baptizer said he would come baptizing with water, but Jesus would baptize with fire.[10]

THE HINGE BETWEEN THE TWO COVENANTS

With John the Baptizer, God was turning a new page in the human drama. John was the hinge from the old covenant to the new covenant. With John the Baptizer, the era of Moses and the Law was coming to an end. The era of grace and truth brought about by the promised Messiah was beginning.

John was the result of a miraculous birth. His mother, Elizabeth, was well along in years, past the age of conception. His father, Zechariah, also well up in years, was a priest.[11] John was filled with the Spirit of God when he was in his mother's womb—something both mysterious and inexplicable. John was six months older than Jesus.[12] His mother, Elizabeth, was Mary's older cousin.

At the time John met Jesus, he had been living in the wilderness.[13] All the Gospel writers tell us that John's ministry was foretold by Isaiah and Malachi.[14]

At some point, John began his ministry of preaching repentance and baptizing. It was no small feat to come out to hear John. The desert's scorching heat would sometimes reach 170 degrees in the day, with the temperature dropping to below zero in the evening.

As far as outward appearances go, John was a spectacle. His skin was probably calloused by the blistering heat of the Judean desert. His hair was never cut. Perhaps it reached to his waist. He lived on a diet of locusts and wild honey, which may or may not have been a Spartan diet.[15] His clothing was woven from camel's hair, and he donned a belt of leather.

This is the one whom God chose to raise the curtain for the promised Messiah, the King of the world.

If you lived in that day, John didn't come to your town to preach.

You went out to see him.[16] People from all over Judea came to see John in the desert, arguably by the hundreds. They came to see and hear this rare spectacle of humanity.[17] Joseph Ratzinger points out that Israel didn't have a genuine prophetic voice for many years preceding John. This made John quite a sensation.[18]

> *Yesterday he was the historical Jesus; today he is the Christ of faith. But it is the identical Jesus Christ with whom we have to do, whether we think of him as he was in the early decades of the first century, or as he is in the closing decades of the twentieth century, or as he ever will be. The Christ of faith, if disunited from the Jesus of history, is apt to be a figment of the pious imagination.*
>
> —F. F. Bruce[20]

In addition, John's message wasn't exactly positive. He took dead aim at everything. He declared war on the spirit of the age in the fashion of the thundering prophets like Elijah. John rebuked, corrected, warned, threatened, and laid bare the sins of Israel . . . including that of its religious leaders. To the Pharisees and Sadducees, his words were sharp and pointed—"Brood of vipers!"[19] But it was his specific rebuke of the king of Israel at the time, Herod, that eventually got him beheaded.

Indeed, John was seeking to straighten the crooked paths, take down mountains, and exalt the low places. To accomplish this, he used an ax instead of a surgeon's knife.

Yet amid his consistent denouncements, John announced the Messiah. As "the friend of the bridegroom," John the Baptizer introduced the heavenly Bridegroom to His much-loved bride, the people of God.[21] Let's go back and try to recreate the scene.

A PROPHET MEETS THE MESSIAH

The day has arrived. John, this unusual prophet who was molded by the hands of the Almighty, is baptizing people in the Jordan. The people are well aware what the Jordan signifies. It is the spot where Israel received her inheritance.[22] The Jordan stands for death; the gateway to a new beginning. It was the transition between the old world and the new world of Canaan—the land of promise—the goal of the exodus.

Israel crossed over the Jordan and entered the land. And it was there in the Jordan that the Lord commanded Israel to take twelve stones from the middle of the river and write the names of each tribe of Israel on each. The twelve stones were piled in the land to which they had entered, as a memorial of the occasion. Joshua then took another twelve stones and dropped them into the river, where they remained.[23]

The Jordan is an apt picture of death and resurrection. It signifies the burying of the old and the beginning of the new. The twelve stones Joshua buried in the river remind us of death; the twelve stones that were laid by the river remind us of resurrection. And now, John the Baptizer was standing in that same river, keenly aware of the rich history that lay behind it.

Crowds had come to confess their sins and be baptized. And Jesus arrived from Nazareth.[24] What Jesus did next stunned John. Jesus asked John to baptize Him.[25] Understandably, John didn't want to. He knew that Jesus was the Messiah—the Savior, the One who removes sin. Why then should He undergo a water burial?

Again, baptism means burial. It means the burial of the old life and the beginning of the new. What sin did Jesus have to be cleansed of? What sins did He need to confess? What in His life needed to be buried? From what did He need to be set free?

The answer is *nothing*. Jesus' baptism was a revelation to Israel, not a reflection of His own cleansing. In this act of fulfilling righteousness, Jesus was bringing Himself into solidarity with all humans. He was foreshadowing what He would do on the cross—that is, bear the guilt of humankind. Thus Jesus began His ministry by stepping into the shoes of every sinner. He was anticipating the cross, which He would later refer to as a baptism.[26] He was acting as the new Jonah, who said, "Pick me up and throw me into the sea."[27] In His baptism by John, Jesus was identifying Himself with all of humanity and foreshadowing the cross.[28]

The only way to make seed produce fruit is to bury it in the ground, to plant it in the darkness.

From that point forward, the earthly ministry of Jesus Christ began, and it would always have the mark of the cross (death to self) upon it.

As John baptized Jesus in the Jordan, Jesus was communing with His Father.[29] The heavens were ripped open, and the Spirit of God descended upon Him in the form of a dove. Suddenly the Father spoke from the heavens, saying, "You are My beloved Son; in You I am well pleased."[30]

Echoes from the First Testament were loud. In God's pleasure in Jesus, we are reminded of Isaiah, the "suffering servant": "Here is my servant, whom I uphold, my chosen one in whom I delight; I will put my Spirit on him."[31] In the dove descending on Jesus, we are reminded of when the earth was created formless and void, like a wilderness (as we have seen, the Hebrew word for "without form" is translated "wilderness" in other places in the First Testament). In John the Baptist's appearance as "the voice of one crying in the wilderness,"[32] we are reminded of God's voice in the void that turned sound into sight and light. The dove symbol connects the Jesus story in the Jordan waters to the creation story, where the Spirit descends with wings, "hovering over the face of the waters" of this new creation,[33] as well as to the Noah story, with a renewed covenant and a rainbow promise. The imagery is clear: Jesus is the new creation that has come to earth.

Thus the Spirit of God descended upon Him. This one simple scene, so packed with complexity, gives us a peek into the triune God operating together—the Son being baptized, the Spirit anointing, and the Father speaking.

But the baptism of Jesus means more than His voluntary solidarity with fallen humans. Priests, kings, and prophets were all anointed for spiritual service. The baptism of Jesus also signifies the anointing of the Spirit for ministry. Here the Spirit of God, who indwelled Jesus, now empowered Him for service.[34]

The new David (Jesus) was anointed by the new Samuel (John) with the oil of the Spirit (the dove). The new Melchizedek and the new Aaron was anointed for His priesthood.[35]

Jesus was the new Moses, anointed to be the mouthpiece of God

Himself. Jesus the King was anointed for the service of representing God before humans. Jesus the Priest was anointed for the ministry of representing humans before God. Jesus the Prophet was anointed to bring the present and living word of God to His people. *Christ* (*Messiah*) actually means "the Anointed One."

Interestingly, David was thirty when He was anointed king of Israel.[36] David was a king, but he acted as a priest (he wore the linen ephod and ate from the table of showbread, which only priests could do), and he functioned as a prophet.[37] Jesus is the new David. He is the real prophet, the real priest, and the real king.

Jesus was anointed for a ministry of power and authority at His baptism. Although the Spirit was within Him at birth, He was now clothed with the Spirit's power, something that would happen to His followers after His ascension:

> God anointed Jesus of Nazareth with the Holy Spirit and power, and . . . he went around doing good and healing all who were under the power of the devil, because God was with him.[38]

> "Jesus of Nazareth was a man accredited by God to you by miracles, wonders and signs, which God did among you through him."[39]

> "I am going to send you what my Father has promised; but stay in the city until you have been clothed with power from on high."[40]

Consequently, the popular idea that Jesus did miracles, discerned people's minds, and healed the sick "because He was God" is false. Jesus did all of those things as a human being anointed by the Holy Spirit. Keep in mind that Peter also did miracles, discerned people's minds, and healed the sick.[41] The same is true for Paul of Tarsus.[42] And neither Peter nor Paul was divine. They were operating by the same Spirit that empowered Jesus. In this regard, Jesus truly is our example, the prototype of a human being.

The Gospels strongly imply that Jesus did no miracles before His baptism. He healed no sick people. He proclaimed no new messages.

He was simply a *tekton* (artisan) from Nazareth. There was no indication that He was a prophet, let alone the Son of the living God. All that went on in His life before His baptism was preparation.

JESUS' MINISTRY BEGINS

Now His ministry began. This is confirmed in Luke 4. The wilderness temptation account ends in Luke 4:13. In verse 14, Luke said, "Jesus returned to Galilee in the power of the Spirit, and news about him spread through the whole countryside" (NIV). Then in verses 18–19, we have the words of Jesus Himself laying out His mission statement (more on this in chapter 9):

> The Spirit of the Lord is on me, because he has anointed me to preach good news to the poor. He has sent me to proclaim freedom for the prisoners and recovery of sight for the blind, to release the oppressed, to proclaim the year of the Lord's favor.[43]

Isaiah's prophecies converged on Jesus in the Jordan River.[44] The four spices that made up the holy oil that was used to anoint the priests of Israel came rushing together as "the Spirit of the Lord" anointed Jesus to preach the good news, set the captives free, heal the blind, and release the oppressed.[45]

Later the chief priests, scribes, and elders challenged Jesus concerning the source of His authority, and He responded with a question regarding John's baptism.[46] The implication is that Jesus' authority to proclaim Himself as God's authority came from His anointing of the Spirit at John's baptism.

At His baptism Israel's Messiah was unveiled to the nation. This world's true King made His appearance. The Jews believed the promised Messiah of Israel would rule the world.[47] Hence throughout the Second Testament, Christ ("Messiah" to the Jew) and Lord ("King" to the Gentile) signify the same thing: Savior and Ruler of the world.

At the Jordan River the Father's voice was heard from the heavens, saying, "This is My beloved Son, in whom I am well pleased."[48] Consider those words for a moment. Before His baptism, Jesus had done no ministry yet. He had healed no sick person. He had set no one free. He had not selected His disciples, or done any mighty works for God. And yet the Father's full pleasure was upon Him.

There is a message here for every adopted child of God. God's pleasure is not based on what you do for Him. It's based on whether you are His child. If you are in Christ, you are a child of God, and He accepts you because you are in Christ. Because the Father is pleased with His Son, He is also pleased with you. You are, as Paul put it in Ephesians, "accepted in the beloved."[49] The Christian, therefore, does not work *toward* the pleasure and acceptance of God. The Christian lives *from* the pleasure and acceptance of God.

If Jesus' immersion into water anticipated the cross, then His rising out of the water anticipated His resurrection. Both Luke and Paul wrote that Jesus was declared to be the Son of God by His resurrection.[50] When Jesus came up out of the Jordan, the Spirit fell upon Him, and God the Father spoke from heaven audibly, declaring that Jesus is the Son of God.

A short time later John publicly declared that Jesus is the Lamb of God who takes away the sins of the world.[51] Jesus is the fulfillment of the Passover Lamb—the blood that would save Israel from the death angel. Jesus is the reality of the Passover Lamb—the meat that gave Israel the strength to leave Egypt. Indeed, the Lamb made the exodus possible.

Why Jesus? Because he is the most fascinating person in the world.

—WILLIAM WILLIMON[52]

The Second Testament repeatedly witnesses that Jesus is the reality of the Passover Lamb, and every sacrificial lamb whose blood was spilled for the sins of Israel. We find this witness in Paul,[53] John,[54] Peter,[55] and the writer of Revelation.[56] Jesus' baptism foreshadowed His ministry of being the Suffering Servant, the Lamb, bearing the sins of many.[57]

A PERFECT HUMAN VERSUS A FALLEN ANGEL

After Jesus was empowered and anointed for ministry, the first thing the Holy Spirit did was lead Him into the wilderness to be tempted by the devil. From the heights of the Jordan River, where Jesus' mission was affirmed, Jesus then went into the depths of the desert, where His mission was besieged. The most dangerous point in anyone's life is when he is riding the crest of a wave.

The desert in the Bible is a double symbol. It means first a place of encounter with God, and second a place of testing. Many times, the two are related. But a stretch in the wilderness in the biblical drama is not an escape but an engagement, often a face-to-face encounter with God and a higher level of encounter with one's mission field. *Peirazo* means "trial" or "test." This is the same word used when Abraham was "tested" to sacrifice Isaac.

In the wilderness we had a replay of Genesis 2. In the garden of Eden, there was a battle between a fallen angel (disguised as a serpent) and a human. In the wilderness, we had the same battle. But it was between the old serpent and the new Adam. Jesus the *tekton* (artisan), versus satan the fallen angel. This was satan's first appearance in the Second Testament. The word used, *satan*, is the Greek taken from Hebrew meaning "adversary," one who opposes us in our mission. It is the same word used by Jesus to Peter: the one that would stop him in his mission of God.

In the wilderness Jesus fasted for forty days and forty nights. There is no doubt that He lost much of His body weight during that time (the typical human body cannot survive more than forty days without food), not to mention His strength. Consequently, Jesus was physically and emotionally depleted. And until that point, He had been untested, as far as we know. At His baptism, He was anointed as the new David. But just as David was hunted by Saul in the wilderness after His anointing by Samuel, so, too, the new David was being hunted by Lucifer in the wilderness.

The Greek word for "devil"[58] is *diabolos*, and it means "accuser" or "slanderer." Herein we discover the very nature of satan himself: to accuse, to slander, to smear. His other name, *satan*, means adversary. The Greek word for "tempt" also means "test." Satan is the tempter. The first Adam succumbed to satan's temptation. The last Adam didn't.

The entire universe was at stake in this drama. In Genesis 1, God created Adam in the image of God and commanded him to be fruitful and multiply and fill the earth with God's image. Adam was supposed to subdue the earth, which means that if things got out of line, Adam was to put them back in line. But Adam failed in his mission.

God made humans trustees of that portion of God's estate called earth.[59] Through disobedience, however, Adam handed the title deed to the earth over to God's enemy. Satan (embodied in the serpent) became "the god of this world,"[60] "the prince of the power of the air,"[61] and "the ruler of this world."[62] This would be confirmed later in one of the temptations. This does not mean that creation is evil, but that the blood of Cain has slithered over the earth, which groans and strains from the stain and awaits its day of redemption.

> ***There is a world of difference between tempting God and putting Him to the test. The former is forbidden; the latter welcomed.***
>
> —Watchman Nee[63]

Now in the wilderness, the Second Adam made His entrance. And He faced off with the same enemy to gain back the real estate that God entrusted to humans. If satan could have successfully tempted Jesus into sin, he would have won the victory, and Christ's mission would have failed. It would have been a repeat of the drama that befell the first Adam. However, since Jesus won and kept on winning, He then proclaimed, "The ruler of this world is coming, and he has nothing in Me."[64] There was no ground upon which satan could operate.

THE OVERLOOKED NATURE OF SATAN'S ATTACK

A point that is often overlooked in this story is the nature of satan's attack. Satan's temptations toward Jesus in the wilderness were all concentrated on luring Jesus to fight satan on the divine level rather than on the human level. Only a human could rob satan of his power because it was humans who gave him the title deed of the earth. If satan could get Jesus to react to him as a divine being rather than as a human being, satan could keep the earth. Satan repeated this strategy when he returned at the crucifixion, where he tried each one of these temptations one last time ("I thirst"; "If you are the Christ, save yourself and us"; and so on).

This becomes clear throughout the temptation scene. Satan quoted from the Psalms in order to allure Jesus, while Jesus countered with quotes from Deuteronomy.[65]

It's also confirmed when Jesus cast out demons. Notice what the demons said to Jesus: "What do you want with us, Son of God?"[66] And on another occasion, "Ha! What do you want with us, Jesus of Nazareth? Have you come to destroy us? I know who you are—the Holy One of God!"[67]

The demons were challenging Jesus' authority on the grounds that He was the Son of God. They weren't dealing with Him on the level of a human being—the Son of man. But Jesus responded as the new Adam, a human being, who had authority over the creeping things, such as serpents and scorpions, symbols of the demonic world.[68]

In some ways, Jesus' struggle with satan was not a conflict between satan and the Messiah but between Jesus and messiahship. Each one of the temptations challenged the standard idea of what the "messiah" was. And each one of the temptations invited Jesus to embrace His superpowers and divine might to bring about the expected messiahship that would seize political power from the Romans and establish Israel as a political reality.

God entrusted humans with the responsibility of enacting and enforcing God's intentions on the earth.[69] Humans guarded the garden of Eden, presumably from the impending threat of the serpent.[70] The fact that God chose to deal with satan through human beings explains why the demons could say, "What have you to do with me, Jesus, Son of the Most High God? I beg you, do not torment me."[71] The demons invoked God's authority because they assumed Jesus was acting in the capacity of the Son of God. But Jesus wasn't. He was acting as a man anointed by the Holy Spirit.

Recall that John exhorted us to "test the spirits," and then said every spirit that confesses that Jesus Christ has come in the flesh (as a human being) is of God. And every spirit that denies that Jesus came in the flesh is not of God.[72] The demons were seeking to deny Jesus His humanity, for they knew it meant their demise.

Jesus was a new creation on the planet. He was the first human incarnation, the first human being indwelled by God Himself. In His resurrection, He multiplied that new creation on the planet. This is the meaning of Jesus' metaphor about the one grain multiplying into many grains. "Unless a grain of wheat falls into the ground and dies, it remains alone; but if it dies, it produces much grain."[73]

Jesus was the one grain. Consequently, satan knew that Jesus was something different from a fallen human being. Jesus, as it were, is an endangered species. If satan could defeat Jesus, there would be no way for Jesus to "be fruitful and multiply and fill the earth" as the new Adam. And there would be no way for Him to take back the title deed of the earth and return it to humans.

THE FIRST TEMPTATION

The evil archangel approached a hungry, starving man. Jesus was thin and weak. His skin was blistered by the scorching wilderness sun. He probably looked as if He had not bathed in weeks.

Using the Lord's hunger as a point of temptation, satan said to Him, "If You *really* are the Son of God, turn these stones into bread and eat."[74]

Notice that the temptation was to lure Jesus into drawing on His divine power. Consider Jesus' response: "*Man* shall not live by bread alone but by every word that God speaks."[75]

Look at the dialogue carefully. Satan said, "If You're the Son of God . . ." Jesus responded with the word *man*, as if to say: "I am a *man*. I am the real human—the new Adam. And by being a real human, I will defeat you. For Adam, who was also a man, was defeated by you. I am man; and as a man, I live by God's words, God's life, God's Spirit. This is what is written in the Scriptures."

As Paul put it, Jesus laid aside, or emptied, Himself, of His divine power, but took upon Himself the form of a servant, and was made in the likeness of men.[76] We need to pause for a moment to grasp what is happening here. Humans, we are told, were made a little lower than the angels.[77] Jesus is the Son of God. But He laid aside His divine powers to live as a human being without divesting Himself of His divine nature. Jesus did not take advantage of His full equality with God the Father while He lived on earth. While He still had access to His omniscience and omnipotence, He limited Himself and refused to draw on those powers. (Therefore, when Jesus said He didn't know the timing of His second coming in Mark 13, He wasn't bluffing.) Jesus rejected being a Muscle Messiah. Instead, He *truly* became human and participated in the limitations and frailty of our humanity. Even to the point of death.

The temptations that satan leveled against Jesus in the wilderness were targeted at obliterating His true humanity and His solidarity with humans. Jesus was tempted to betray His mission, to abandon His vocation, to "be His own man" and be the divine being He was, thus inaugurating the kingdom of God not by suffering and death but by politics and economics.[78] If Jesus had taken the bait and drawn on His divine powers as the Son of God, He would have ceased living as a human being. And He would have ceased being the Second Adam, "Adam-gone-right." Satan wanted Jesus to dedicate His ministry to changing the world, not saving the world. Jesus could inhabit His divine self to save people from their hungers. Or He could inhabit His human self to save people from their sins.

Satan is an angel. As an angel, his particular life form is higher than that of human beings. But Jesus was living as man anointed by the Spirit of God and living by God's words and God's life. In these words, "Man shall not live by bread alone, but by every word that proceeds from the mouth of God,"[79] Jesus gave us an insight He would repeat over and over again: that He was a man who was living by the indwelling life of His Father—the very thing Adam was called to do by eating from the Tree of Life in the garden.

THE SECOND TEMPTATION

The second temptation began. Jesus was standing on the highest point on the temple, where the ram's horn was blown. The Lord of creation, now in the form of a human being, was under great distress. Satan taunted Him to show His stuff and jump: "If You *really* are the Son of God, then jump, and Your heavenly messengers will protect You as promised."[80] Satan was challenging Jesus to survive capital punishment, which is death by stoning, with the one being "stoned" often hurled off a high precipice onto the stones below.

Once again satan refused to acknowledge the humanity of Jesus. Instead, He appealed to His divinity as the Son of God. Jesus responded with words that were given to mere mortals: "It is written again, 'You shall not tempt the LORD your God.'"[81]

The man, Jesus, won the second battle against the fallen angel.

THE THIRD TEMPTATION

Then satan brought forth the third and final temptation in the wilderness. It seems that satan realized he was unsuccessful at getting Jesus to do battle on the basis of His divine nature. So he quit this strategy and tried to tempt Jesus with His humanity.

The third temptation brings us back to the garden itself. In Genesis 3, Adam violated his trustee relationship with God by bowing his knee to Lucifer instead of obeying God. Satan wished to hand it all back to a human, the Second Adam, if He would simply worship him in return.

We don't know what this scene looked like, but in some mysterious way, satan was able to display to Jesus all the kingdoms of the world with all their glory. His offer: "I won them in the garden, and I own them now. But I will give them all to You. And You will rule the earth. I will hand the kingdoms of the earth back over to You if You will only bow down and worship me." Ever wonder how important worship is? Ask satan. So highly does satan value worship that he was willing to give up everything if Jesus would worship him: "Fall down and worship me."[82]

Even Herod, who wanted to kill the Christ Child, pretended that he wanted to worship Him. Pretenders are the modern Herods. Pretension is one of the church's greatest threats.

Jesus never disputed that satan owned the kingdoms of the world. Instead, He seemed to acknowledge that they belonged to him when He called satan "the ruler of this world."[83]

What was Jesus thinking at that moment? Perhaps He was thinking, *No suffering. No cross. No death. But instantly, I can sit on the throne. Instantly, I can receive the glory of the world. Instantly, the kingdoms of the earth will be Mine.*

Jesus again responded on the level of a human being and uttered without reserve, "Away with you, Satan! For it is written, 'You shall worship the LORD your God, and Him only you shall serve.'"[84] God doesn't worship God. It is human beings who are to worship God. Again, Jesus reaffirmed His humanity and responded from that vantage point. The authority He exercised over satan was the authority God gave to Adam back in the garden of Eden. Jesus exercised such authority as the Son of man (human), not as the Son of God (divine):

> For as the Father has life in Himself, so He has granted the Son to have life in Himself, and has given Him authority to execute judgment also, because He is the Son of Man.[85]

When Jesus said to satan, "Get behind Me,"[86] He was acknowledging that we all live with the devil. We cannot escape evil on this earth. But as long as we are in *front* and he is *behind* us, we are protected. The devil ought not to be in our line of vision but in our shadow.

After the third temptation, satan left Him. As James stated, "Resist the devil and he will flee from you."[87] Angels came to attend to Him. In the garden, Adam and Eve spoke the language of beasts. They lived in harmony with creation. Everything changed after the expulsion from the garden. In fact, Judaism developed extensive animal taboos. No images of beasts were allowed in the temple—only cherubim and seraphim and wings covering the ark. Animals were worshipped in the goddess cults of Asia Minor; hence, the creation of the golden calf, which when elevated meant the god was present and that sexual rioting was not just permitted but encouraged. The Jesus story countered this prevailing attitude with positive animal connections, beginning with His being born in a manger among animals, and here He spent time in the wilderness with wild beasts, along with the angels who ministered to Him.[88]

Although satan failed in the wilderness, he would return to tempt the Son of man.[89] For this reason, Jesus was "in all points tempted as we are, yet without sin."[90] Jesus suffered temptation so He could help those who are being tempted as well.[91]

> ***We need the whole Jesus. The complete Jesus. Everything he said. Every detail of what he did.***
>
> —EUGENE PETERSON[92]

In other words, Jesus entered the drama of human existence and experienced the whole gamut of humanity so He could transform it. The battle between satan and Jesus continued, reaching its zenith at the cross.[93]

A REPLAY OF THE FIRST TESTAMENT

The temptation of Jesus was a playback of two episodes in the First Testament.

First, *it's a replay of the first temptation in the garden of Eden*. John tells us that the three enemies of the Christian are "the lust of the flesh, the lust of the eyes, and the pride of life."[94] Each of these temptations was in play in the temptation of Adam and Eve in the garden:[95]

- The fruit was "good for food" = the lust of the flesh.
- The fruit was "pleasant to the eyes" = the lust of the eyes.
- The fruit was "desirable to make one wise" = the pride of life.

God created the garden of Eden for humans to enjoy and eat freely. But there were limits to human freedom. Free does not mean a free-for-all or free fall.

The temptations that satan leveled at Jesus in the wilderness struck the same three chords. Here is the order presented in Luke 4 (paraphrased):

- "Turn these stones to bread" = the lust of the flesh.
- "I will give you the kingdoms of the world and their glory" = the lust of the eyes.
- "Cast yourself down from here and angels will protect you" = the pride of life.

In the garden, the first Adam ate the wrong food. In the wilderness, the Second Adam ate the right food—the Word of the living God.[96]

When the garden scene closes in Genesis 3, we are left with an angel posted at the gate, commanding the first Adam. When the wilderness scene closes in Luke 4, we are left with the last Adam commanding an angel—"Get behind Me, Satan!"[97]

> *The main line of interpretation of the Old Testament exemplified in the New is not only consistent and intelligent in itself, but also founded upon a genuinely historical understanding of the process of the religious—I should prefer to say the prophetic—history of Israel as a whole.*
>
> —C. H. Dodd[100]

Jesus, the one grain: Jesus, the new Adam, was now in a position wherein He could be fruitful and multiply the earth with God's image. Three and a half years later, the new Adam died on a cross. Three days later, He became "the firstborn among many brethren," bringing forth "many sons unto glory."[98] The one grain fell into the earth and died to bear many grains like unto itself.[99]

This is the meaning of resurrection, among other things. The *ekklesia* (church) will become the inheritor of the image of God on the earth. She will become the image-bearer of the Almighty, the body of Jesus on the earth again.

Second, *in the wilderness temptation we see how Jesus relives the story of Israel*. Jesus is not just the new Adam; He is the new Israel. Israel was in the wilderness of testing for forty years. And like Adam, they failed the test. So the forty years of Israel's temptations in the desert incarnated in Jesus' forty days of temptation in the desert. And for each temptation, Jesus quoted the words Moses gave to Israel when Israel was being tempted:

- "Man shall not live by bread alone; but by every word of God."[101]
- "You shall not tempt the LORD your God."[102]
- "You shall worship the Lord and serve Him only."[103]

Compare the wording of these two texts from Deuteronomy and Matthew:

> Remember how the LORD your God led you all the way in the desert these forty years, to humble you and to test you in order to know what was in your heart, whether or not you would keep his commands. He humbled you, causing you to hunger and then feeding you with manna, which neither you nor your fathers had known, to teach you that man does not live on bread alone but on every word that comes from the mouth of the LORD.[104]

> Then Jesus was led by the Spirit into the desert to be tempted by the devil. After fasting forty days and forty nights, he was hungry. The tempter came to him and said, "If you are the Son of God, tell these stones to become bread."
>
> Jesus answered, "It is written: 'Man does not live on bread alone, but on every word that comes from the mouth of God.'"[105]

N. T. Wright has isolated the point, saying, "The story of God's people is being encapsulated, recapitulated, in his [Jesus'] own work."[106] Indeed it is. Out of Jacob's struggle with God came "Israel" in the First Testament.[107] Out of the wilderness struggle came the new Israel, the Messiah who saves and propagates the new covenant of the Second Testament.

When Jesus orders satan to leave, he must leave. The wilderness scene closed with satan leaving and angels coming to minister to Jesus. This reinforces that Jesus was the new Israel.[108] The ministry of angels to Jesus reminds us of the stairway that Jacob saw connecting heaven and earth, from which angels descended and ascended.[109] Jesus identified Himself to be that very stairway in John 1:51. Psalm 91:11–12, a psalm written to Israel, promises that the angels of God will keep charge over you, preventing you from dashing your foot against a stone.

> ***If you want to understand the Scripture in the spirit in which it is written, you have to attend to the content and to the unity of Scripture as a whole.***
>
> —JOSEPH RATZINGER[110]

Israel was to be the corporate Adam, fulfilling the commission God gave to Adam—to be "a kingdom of priests." Adam was called to bear God's image and to exercise His dominion in the earth. Israel was called to do the same.

Regrettably, Adam failed in the garden, and Israel failed in the wilderness. But where Adam and Israel failed, Jesus succeeded. Praise His name!

> For just as through the disobedience of the one man the many were made sinners, so also through the obedience of the one man the many will be made righteous.[111]

Didn't Jesus pray, "Do not bring us to the time of trial"?[112] If so, did Jesus' prayer go unanswered? After all, at the beginning of His ministry, He was tempted. At the end of His ministry, He was brought literally "to the time of trial."

> Christians believe that because Jesus freely accepted this time of trial and dreadful death on our behalf, he himself became God's answer to the plea in the Lord's Prayer "deliver us from evil." He taught us to ask that we might be delivered from evil, but he himself knew the price of

that deliverance would be his own blood. He was willing to pay that price as an act of love for all humanity.[113]

FROM NAZARETH TO CAPERNAUM

After John the Baptist was arrested, Jesus moved from His hometown of Nazareth to the city of Capernaum, fulfilling the words of Isaiah the prophet.[114] Unlike the obscure town of Nazareth, Capernaum was a fishing center on the shores of Lake Galilee. It was also a tax collection station containing a Roman garrison of one hundred soldiers. The population was estimated to be between six hundred and fifteen hundred, making it one of Galilee's larger villages.[115]

Apparently, the city had no paved streets or channels for running water or sewage. The streets were irregular, narrow, and packed with earth and dirt. The construction of houses was of low quality, and it seemed to lack public buildings, such as shops, a theater, and storage facilities. There were no signs of wealth there.[116]

After He moved to Capernaum, Jesus began to preach that the kingdom of God was at hand.[117] From that point on, He regarded Capernaum as His "own city,"[118] and He taught in the synagogue there,[119] not always to applause.[120]

Why Jesus made Capernaum the new base for His mission is anyone's guess. James D. G. Dunn suggests that He may have been given a room in a house by one of His followers.[121] Because Capernaum was close to the edge of Herod's territory on the lake, living there would have allowed Jesus to slip out of Herod's jurisdiction when the need arose.[122] Jesus would travel widely throughout Galilee,[123] even returning to Nazareth to preach.[124] Josephus reported that there were 204 villages in Galilee. They ranged in size from a few inhabitants to large towns of several thousand.[125]

After Jesus was baptized, He was on a constant road trip. He was, so to speak, God in motion, moving all throughout Galilee, Judea, and even Samaria. Even to places where He wasn't invited. The Gospels present us with a Jesus who was a living, speaking, and moving God. A person who was anointed by the Spirit of God to accomplish the will of God and bring forth the kingdom of God. A person who met people where they were, but who never left them the same. A person who constantly breaks out of our expectations.

The heavens opened at Jesus' baptism. And Jesus continued to live under an *open heaven* and hear His Father speak in and through Him.[126] This, in fact, became the source of His fruitful ministry. Let's continue the story by looking at whom Jesus chose to be His disciples and why.

CHAPTER 8

Jesus Chooses His Disciples

This dirty dozen became his chosen people.

—Stephen M. Miller[1]

In first-century Palestine, the word *disciple* didn't mean what it means today. It did not refer to a pupil in school who learned from notebook to notebook via a credentialed teacher. Rather, it meant apprentice. A disciple was someone who learned a skill or way of life from a teacher. With respect to Jesus, a disciple was a *follower*—not just of a set of teachings but of an entire way of living.[2]

Throughout His short ministry on earth, Jesus called many people to follow Him. The Gospels tell us that Jesus ministered to multitudes.[3] He had a countless number of disciples,[4] as well as some close friends who supported Him.[5] However, at some point during His ministry, Jesus specifically selected twelve men out of all His disciples to live with Him and eventually carry on His ministry.[6]

> Jesus went up on a mountainside and called to him those he wanted, and they came to him. He appointed twelve—designating them apostles—that they might be with him and that he might send them out to preach and to have authority to drive out demons.[7]

Notice that Jesus selected the disciples He wanted to apprentice. This ran against first-century custom. The word "designating" in Mark 3 is similar to the word used for the appointment of priests to the priesthood in the First Testament.[8] In Jesus' day, disciples chose their masters (teachers). As the famous rabbi Gamaliel admonished those who wanted to become schooled in spirituality, "Find a teacher and lose your ignorance."[9] Jesus reversed this order and chose His disciples. "You did not choose Me, but I chose you."[10] To follow Jesus was a matter of personal invitation. It was a *call.*

> *Even cursory glances through the Gospels confirm that the work Jesus did in the lives of his disciples occurred because the disciples were in relationship, not simply with him, but with one another.*
>
> —Richard Lamb[11]

Jesus didn't pick anyone until He "went up on a mountain to pray, and he prayed to God all night. At daybreak he called together all of his disciples and chose twelve of them to be apostles."[12] Since Jesus acted only when the Father directed Him to act, the choice of the Twelve was the Father's choice as well.[13] Luke refered to these twelve men with the shorthand phrase "the twelve."[14]

THE NEW ISRAEL

Why not thirteen disciples? Why twelve disciples and not fifteen, twenty, thirty, fifty, or three hundred? Because in calling twelve disciples, Jesus was symbolically reconstituting the kingdom of Israel.

This answer becomes obvious when we look at Jesus against the backdrop of the First Testament. Jesus is the New Israel, the new Jacob. The twelve disciples correspond to the twelve tribes of Israel—the twelve sons of Jacob. Jesus was establishing the new Israel; He was restoring the true people of God.[15]

Jesus made this explicit at the Last Supper.[16] John made this explicit at the beginning of his gospel. John 1 and 2 are unique in all the Bible.

We have already seen how John 1 begins very much like Genesis 1: "In the beginning." John 1 and 2 present us with the new creation in the midst of the old creation. As such, John 1 and 2 are the new Genesis.

Jesus found Nathanael and told him, "You shall see heaven open, and the angels of God ascending and descending upon the Son of Man."[17] This is a replay of Jacob's dream in Genesis 28. Jacob was the first Israelite (his name was changed to Israel in Genesis 32). Before his name change, Jacob was full of deceit. When Jesus met Nathanael, He said to him, "An Israelite indeed, in whom is *no* deceit!"[18]

The stairway Jacob saw in his dream finally made its appearance on earth. That which Jacob called "the house of God" arrived on the planet in the person of Christ. Jesus is the One who connects the heavenly realm with the earthly realm. He is the One who joins God with humanity. He is Emmanuel: "God with us," where God's space and humanity's space intersect. Jesus is the temple—the gateway connecting the invisible with the visible. He is the house of God (more on this later).

In John 4, Jesus met a Samaritan woman at Jacob's well. The entire chapter is an echo of Jacob's encounter with Rachel at the well in Genesis 29. Strikingly, Jesus met this woman at noon, the same time Jacob met his wife Rachel. And the well was named after Jacob.

But there is so much more. For example:

- In Hosea we read the words, "When Israel was a child, I loved him, and out of Egypt I called My son."[19] Matthew applied those words to Jesus.[20]
- God called Israel to be a light to the nations.[21] Jesus declared Himself to be the light of the world,[22] and so are His followers.[23]
- In Isaiah 49:3 (GW), we have the words "my servant Israel," and the entire chapter is a prophecy about the coming Messiah. Jesus is God's servant, Israel, and He fulfills the prophecies in Isaiah 49, one of the servant songs that is developed famously in Isaiah 53.[24]
- When Paul called Jesus the "Seed" of Abraham, he was effectively saying that Jesus is the real Israel.[25]

- Paul stated that all of God's promises are inaugurated and fulfilled in Jesus, God's "Yes."[26] This, of course, would include the promises for and about Israel.

Bible scholar Christopher Wright has astutely remarked that "the New Testament presents him [Jesus] to us as the *Messiah*, Jesus the *Christ*. And the Messiah was Israel. That is, the Messiah was Israel representatively and personified. The Messiah was the completion of all that Israel had been put in the world for—i.e., God's self-revelation and his work of human redemption."[27]

To be sure, the Twelve were the Lord's agents to free Israel with the message of Jesus. But they were also called to embody the new Israel. Jesus is the true Israelite, and the Twelve gained their status and identity in Him. Bible scholars have emphasized this in boldface. Here is N. T. Wright: "Jesus came as the true Israel, the world's true light, and as the true image of the invisible God. He was the true Jew, the true human."[28] And G. K. Beale writes: "Israel was not faithful and disobeyed, and . . . God raises up a true Israel. I think that Jesus is the true Israel."[29]

> *It is the most important thing in life to understand the Lord Jesus.*
>
> —T. Austin-Sparks[31]

In chapter 2 we showed how Adam was the first priest-king. Israel was called to be a "kingdom of priests."[30] In a sense, then, Israel was the corporate Adam. The story of the First Testament is how both Adam and Israel failed in their tasks. However, Jesus Christ came to embody the new Adam and the new Israel. Jesus, as it were, is the real priest (He bears God's image in the earth and serves Him) and the real king (He exercises God's dominion).

AN UNEXPECTED BAND OF YOUNG MEN

It was radical enough that Jesus chose His disciples. But then look at the disciples He chose. Not the best scholars, the best leaders, the movers and shakers, those who would make Him look good, or the ones with the most promise. The people Jesus chose to be part of the Twelve were not what anyone could have predicted. They were "unusual suspects." But then again, when you understand how Jesus Himself failed to meet virtually all Jewish expectations about the coming Messiah, it begins to make sense. Consider this motley mix of chosen ones:[32]

1. Andrew—a fisherman and Peter's brother: he was originally a disciple of John the Baptist.
2. Bartholomew (also called Nathanael): we have no knowledge of his background or trade.
3. James, son of Zebedee—a fisherman and John's brother: Jesus nicknamed the brothers the "Sons of Thunder," probably because of their fiery tempers and undisciplined zeal.[33] Being a fisherman, James (along with John, Peter, and Andrew) did better than most financially.[34]
4. James, son of Alphaeus: he was the brother of Jude (though some scholars believe he was Matthew's brother).
5. John, son of Zebedee—a fisherman and James's brother: some scholars believe he is the unidentified disciple of John the Baptist mentioned in the gospel of John.[35]
6. Judas Iscariot (Matthias later took his place[36])—a Jewish nationalist: Judas was possibly part of the fanatical Zealots movement. The Zealots were prepared to resort to violence and terror to restore Israel's freedom.
7. Jude (also called Judas, Lebbaeus, and surnamed Thaddaeus): he was a Jewish nationalist.
8. Matthew (also called Levi)—a tax collector: tax collectors colluded with Rome in oppressing the Jewish people. Thus Matthew was viewed as a traitor by his own people, a turncoat who decided to suck the blood out of his fellow Jews. Also, as a tax collector, Matthew would have had the ability to write (a rare commodity in the first century).
9. Peter (also called Simon)—a fisherman, Andrew's brother, and likely a disciple of John the Baptist:[37] he partnered with James and John in the fishing business.[38]

10. Philip—probably a fisherman: He is believed to originally have been a disciple of John the Baptist.[39]
11. Simon Zelotes (also called Simon the Canaanite)—a Jewish nationalist: Simon was part of the fanatical and violent Zealots movement.
12. Thomas (also called Didymus): we know little about his background or trade.

These were the Twelve whom Jesus chose to be His closest friends and interns: four fishermen, one tax man, a couple of freedom fighters, and a significant number who met while they were apprenticing with John the Baptist (Andrew, John, Peter, James, and maybe even two more, Philip and Nathanael), which Jesus gathered on the shore of the Jordan when He was staying with John. He chose ordinary folk with no special training in the Scriptures[40] from His native neighboring villages in Galilee. There is one singular exception and one striking omission. Judas was from Iscariot, a Judean village in southern Israel.[41] Jesus chose no one from His hometown, no one from His first thirty years.

People from diverse walks of life. Fishermen and tax collectors would have been economically mobile, but they weren't part of the elite.[42] A raggedy, rugged bunch. Again, none were priests, rabbis, or scholars. In fact, Jesus underscored why He didn't select His closest disciples from the religious establishment:

> Then John's disciples came and asked him, "How is it that we and the Pharisees fast, but your disciples do not fast?"
>
> Jesus answered, "How can the guests of the bridegroom mourn while he is with them? The time will come when the bridegroom will be taken from them; then they will fast.
>
> "No one sews a patch of unshrunk cloth on an old garment, for the patch will pull away from the garment, making the tear worse. Neither do men pour new wine into old wineskins. If they do, the skins will burst, the wine will run out and the wineskins will be ruined. No, they pour new wine into new wineskins, and both are preserved."[43]

New wine cannot be put into old wineskins. The Twelve were the new wineskins for the new wine Jesus was bringing. They were the foundation stones of the church He was building.[44]

When the Lord found them, the Twelve were all observant Jews waiting for the deliverance of Israel. But their views on how Israel would be restored to salvation were at opposite ends from each other (tax collectors worked hand in glove with the Romans, while the Zealots wanted to slaughter them).

It must be understood that life in the first century was short. It wasn't unusual if a Jewish man died before he reached age thirty.[45] People entered into adulthood at puberty. Jewish females married around thirteen or fourteen years of age, males a little older. In the Greek world, vocational training began in the midteens. Bible scholar Craig Keener surmises that most of Jesus' disciples were in their midteens. Peter, having a family, may have been older—perhaps eighteen.

Beginning with the Twelve, Jesus was creating the renewed people of God, "the renewed remnant of Israel."[46] His way of bringing in the kingdom ran contrary to that of the Zealots or the Essenes. Jesus taught we are both of this world, and a world apart. Or as He put it in definitive form: we are to be "in" the world but not "of" the world, but not "out of it" either.[47]

Unlike his cousin John the Baptist, Jesus was called a glutton and a "winebibber" by His critics.[48] He did not separate Himself from the mainstream. But His kingdom-come mission was antithetical to a nationalist revolution. His agenda was subversive but in an extraordinary way. In His meals with sinners (including tax collectors), Jesus showed that when God is in charge of the world, it means radical embrace and forgiveness. It means turning the other cheek, giving away the second coat, walking the extra mile, and taking up one's cross. This is how the new Israel was to live, breathe, and have its being. This is how the renewed people of God would reveal the true nature of their King.

Jesus was announcing that He was the real Jubilee, the One who would bring deliverance to God's people. He was telling all who would listen that He was the real Joseph, protecting and caring for His people while they were living in the land of oppression. He was proclaiming to Israel that He was the real Moses, delivering them from bondage. He was announcing that He was the real Joshua, bringing Israel into the fullness of her calling—a calling the nation had lost sight of. He was revealing that He was the real David, acting as prophet, priest, and king to God's people and gathering the building materials for His living house. He was announcing that He was the real Solomon, demonstrating the wisdom of God and building the Lord's true temple. Jesus was declaring the end of Israel's long exile and the coming to pass of God's promise of shalom. But not in a way that anyone expected.

> *"With" is Emmanuel's middle name.*
>
> —Teri Hyrkas[49]

Through the Twelve, Jesus was restoring Israel's vocation as the light of the world, the salt of the earth, a city set on a hill to be a blessing to all the nations. Not by war, not by violence, but by radical love. *The very nature of the King Himself.* God was going to take down the earthly temple with its corrupt political and religious system and establish a new Temple, the One the old temple had foreshadowed. Jesus was reconstituting the people of God—Israel—around Himself.

LIVING WITH GOD IN HUMAN FORM

Jesus called the Twelve to be with Him—that is, the Twelve lived *with* Jesus. Day in and day out, they observed the peerless life of Christ. They lived with God in human form and observed Him from morning till evening. But more than that, they watched a man living by divine life—something that they would experience themselves after Jesus rose again from the dead and became "a life-giving spirit."[50]

The Jesus they saw with their eyes, touched with their hands, and heard with their ears would one day take up residence inside of them. And they would learn to live by His indwelling life just as He lived by His Father's indwelling life.[51] But for now, the Twelve would get to know Jesus at close range as He "went in and out among" them.[52]

After His resurrection, Jesus would send them out, and their calling as *apostles* ("sent ones") would be fulfilled. The time they spent living with Jesus was their preparation for missional living. It's no wonder that when they began to preach, teach, and heal, their message was Jesus Himself.[53] Elsewhere, one of us has written in some detail about how Jesus specifically trained the Twelve.[54]

It should be noted that in choosing the Twelve, Jesus again replayed the life of David. At the cave of Adullam, a group of unpolished men joined David in his mission.[55] They recognized David to be the anointed king, even though he was being hunted by Saul. These men would later become David's "mighty men of valor."[56] David would later found the city of Jerusalem and seat the tabernacle of God on Mount Zion in Jerusalem—something the new David will eventually do also—though it will be the heavenly Jerusalem.[57]

Jesus will also end up putting the Twelve in charge.[58] His method of leadership, which He modeled and passed on to the Twelve, was very different from any form of leadership yet modeled in both the Jewish and Gentile worlds, not just in *style*, but in its very *substance* and *structure*.[59] In fact, Jesus warned against even using the word *leader*: "Do not be called leaders; for One is your Leader, that is, Christ. But the greatest among you shall be your servant. Whoever exalts himself shall be humbled; and whoever humbles himself shall be exalted."[61]

> *In the last days, God says, I will pour out my Spirit on all people. Your sons and daughters will prophesy, your young men will see visions, your old men will dream dreams. Even on my servants, both men and women, I will pour out my Spirit in those days, and they will prophesy.*
>
> —Peter[60]

When Jesus' disciples got into an argument among themselves about "who then is greatest in the kingdom of heaven?"[62] and asked Him to referee the dispute, almost every word of their question was wrong.

The same thing could be said of the request of history's first recorded helicopter mom, when Mrs. Zebedee got down on her knees and asked Jesus to make her boys His right- and left-hand men: "Grant that these two sons of mine may sit, one on Your right hand and the other on the left, in Your kingdom."[63] It is a constant comfort that the disciples were most often the "duh-ciples"! Their "confessions of faith" were as much "confusions of faith."

While all other rabbis called their disciples to follow the Torah, Jesus called His disciples to follow Him. He was the personification of the Torah. In addition, first-century rabbis wanted their students to equal or surpass them. But Jesus told His disciples that they should strive to be *servants* of all, not the master.[64]

THE WOMEN[65]

Before we look at the Lord's female disciples, let's go back a few steps and get the broader context. Generally speaking, the Jews of Jesus' day had a dim view of women.[66] Jewish women were not allowed to receive an education. Hence, they were largely uneducated. Their only training was in how to raise children and keep house.

Women were also largely excluded from worshipping God. In Herod's temple in Jerusalem, there was a special court that stood on the very outside. It was called the court of the Gentiles. The Gentiles could go into that court, but they were limited to that area alone. Five steps above the Gentiles' court was the women's court. The women were limited to that one area. Fifteen steps above that was the Jewish men's court. Men were given far more privileges to worship God than were women.

A woman had no voice in her marriage. Her father decided whom she would marry, when she would marry, and why she would marry. A woman couldn't divorce her husband under any condition. Only a man could initiate a divorce.

Jewish women were to be seen as little as possible in public. In fact, young men were warned about talking to women in public, so much so that it was a shame in ancient Israel for a man to talk to a woman in public. Consequently, most women stayed out of the streets.

Women were regarded as inferior to men. In the Talmud, one hundred women equal two men.[67] Women were regarded as property, just like cattle and slaves. Jewish males prayed a daily prayer of thanksgiving, which ended:

> *Praise be to God who has not made me a non-Jew.*
> *Praise be to God who has not made me an ignorant person.*
> *Praise be to God who has not made me a woman.*[68]

This was man's view of a woman in first-century Israel. It was not much better in other cultures. In fact, ever since the fall of humanity, women have been regarded as second-class citizens, inferior to men. But something happened that changed all that.

Jesus came.

In Jesus Christ we find God's view of a woman. Not man's view.

Jesus Christ is God made flesh. As such, He embodies all of God's opinions. In His earthly life, Jesus was the visible expression of God Himself. By His actions and His words, we discover God's view of a woman. And that view was utterly contrary to the prevailing view of His day. It was not goddess worship that issued equality for women. It was Jesus.

Consider this: When God decided to make His entrance upon this planet, He visited a woman. He chose a woman to bring forth the Eternal Son, the Messiah—the Anointed One for whom Israel had waited thousands of years. The life of God was first placed in the womb of a woman before He got to you and me. And God was not ashamed.

As Jesus ministered, He ripped down all social conventions that were pitted against women. On one occasion, He rose to the defense of a woman caught in adultery. He became her attorney and saved her life. And He was not ashamed.

Jesus was noted for befriending sinners. He ate with prostitutes and tax collectors. We are told in one gospel that He made a point of meeting one particular woman and then did something that shocked everyone, including the disciples: *He talked to her in public.* And He was not ashamed.

Not only was she a woman; she was a divorcée. Not only was she a divorcée; she was actively living in immorality. But not only was she a woman, a divorcée, and an adulteress living in sin; she was worse than a Gentile. She was a Samaritan—a half-breed. (Samaritans were people with whom Jews were never to talk.) Jesus talked unashamedly to this divorced, adulterous Samaritan woman in public, and He forgave her of her sins.

Jesus Christ had a custom of using women in His parables and making them heroes. He talked about the woman who searched and found her lost coin. He spoke of the woman who was relentless in the presence of the unjust judge who honored her for her persistence. He told of the widow who dropped all the money she had into the temple treasury and praised her for doing so.

Once, Jesus was dining with a self-righteous Pharisee.[69] In walked a woman. But this was not just any woman. She was a woman of the streets—a prostitute. Upon seeing the Lord, she dropped to her knees and did something unsettling. In the presence of Pharisees, this woman unbound her hair and poured costly perfume upon the feet of our Lord. This unclean woman touched Jesus Christ in public. She wept, washed His feet with her tears, and dried them with her hair. This scandalous and improper act mortified the self-righteous Pharisees. At that moment, these religious leaders lost all respect for Jesus and doubted that He was a true prophet. But He was not ashamed.

Without shame Jesus allowed an unclean woman to touch the hem of His garment. In fact, He praised her for it. He even paid a Canaanite woman, who was viewed as a dog in the eyes of Israel, one of the highest compliments He ever gave anyone. He also traded barbs with her as an equal and healed her daughter—and he felt no shame about it.

A RADICAL VIEW OF WOMEN

In the Lord's last hours on this earth, He stayed in a small village called Bethany. It was there that He would spend His last days before giving His life on Calvary. In Bethany lived two women whom Jesus loved: Mary and Martha. They were His friends, and they received Him. And He was not ashamed. One well-known occasion that occurred in Bethany gives us a lot of insight into just how radical our Lord's relationship was with His female disciples:

> Now it happened as they went that He entered a certain village; and a certain woman named Martha welcomed Him into her house. And she had a sister called Mary, who also sat at Jesus' feet and heard His word. But Martha was distracted with much serving, and she approached Him and said, "Lord, do You not care that my sister has left me to serve alone? Therefore tell her to help me."
>
> And Jesus answered and said to her, "Martha, Martha, you are worried and troubled about many things. But one thing is needed, and Mary has chosen that good part, which will not be taken away from her."[70]

This story is usually interpreted as an example of the tension that exists between those who are given to outward service and those who are given to inward worship. Maybe this way of looking at the story has some merit. But there is something even greater going on.

Let's consider some historical background that throws fresh light on our story. In Jesus' day, homes were divided into the male space and the female space. The kitchen was the women's domain. (This is still the case in some countries, like Ethiopia.) Men did not enter it.

The public room was for the men. For a woman to settle down in the public room with the men was considered very inappropriate. Scandalous, even. The only two places men and women shared was the marital bedroom and outside the house, where the children played.

Martha escorted Jesus and the Twelve into the public room—the space for the men. Jesus didn't request a meal. Instead, He wished to teach. So He began speaking. The Twelve were all gathered around Him, sitting at His feet. But there was something strange about this picture. A woman was also present. And she, too, was seated at His feet.

Mary had breached two social boundaries. First, she was sitting in the men's space. Second, she was sitting in the posture of a disciple.

Now, why is that significant? Because every rabbi in that day had only male disciples. Jesus was the exception. He welcomed women to be His disciples also.

Let's go over to the kitchen and look in on Martha. She had one thing in mind: she wanted to give the Lord a proper welcome. She was preparing a *large* meal for Jesus and His disciples. She was slaving in the kitchen, preparing the food, getting the plates out, taking out the best silverware, and so forth.

But as the minutes went by, Martha began to fume. Her sister wasn't helping her at all. Instead, she was in the public room, seated at Jesus' feet, like one of His male disciples. In other words, Mary was acting like a man!

Martha continued to work in the kitchen, hoping that Mary would get up and help her. She broke a sweat. Finally, she just couldn't take it any longer. She stormed into the public room and protested to Jesus, "Mary isn't helping me! Don't You care? Tell her to help me!"

Martha was in effect saying, "My sister is in the public room, acting like a man, when she should be in the kitchen—helping me!"

Notice that in the midst of Martha's protest, Mary was silent. She didn't defend herself. She let the Lord defend her. And He did.

The Lord's response to Martha was tender. "Martha, Martha, you are worried and troubled about many things. Mary is concerned with only one thing. And it is the only *necessary* thing. It is the better thing, and I won't take it away from her—*being My disciple.*"[71]

Martha became an important figure for the early church. Her comment to Jesus after the death of her brother, Lazarus—"You are the Christ, the Son of God"[72]—almost exactly matches Peter's confession in Matthew 16:16.

JESUS' FEMALE DISCIPLES

When Luke wrote his gospel, he referred to the twelve disciples with the shorthand phrase "the twelve." But he also used another shorthand phrase: "the women" or "some women":

> The Twelve were with him, as well as *some women*: Mary called Magdalene; Joanna, the wife of King Herod's cupbearer; Susanna; and many others. They provided for them out of their resources.[73]

> And *the women* who had come with Him from Galilee followed after, and they observed the tomb and how His body was laid.[74]

> These all continued with one accord in prayer and supplication, with *the women* and Mary the mother of Jesus, and with His brothers.[75]

Jesus and His disciples were not beggars; discipleship did not equal destitution. Jesus and the Twelve had financial backers who supported the ministry, many of whom were women. In fact, they had sufficient funding not only to warrant a treasurer but to elicit Jesus' insistence that His and the disciples' taxes be paid to Rome.

The Twelve lived with Jesus for three and a half years. They followed Him everywhere. But Jesus also had a group of female disciples. Luke used his shorthand phrase for them, "the women,"[76] the same way he used "the twelve." They were the Lord's disciples also—the female counterpart to the Twelve. The women followed the Lord wherever He went, and they tended to His needs. And He was not ashamed.

There is no question: the greatest disciples of Jesus Christ were not the Twelve. They were the women. The reason? Because they were more faithful.

When Jesus Christ was taken to die, the Twelve fled. They checked out. All the disciples except John said, "See ya!" But the women stayed with Him. They didn't leave. They followed Him up to Calvary to do what they had been doing all along—comforting Him, taking care of Him, tending to His needs. And they watched Him undergo a bloody, gory crucifixion that lasted six long hours.

To watch a man die a hideous death is something that goes against every fiber of a woman. But these women would not leave Him. They stayed the entire time, close enough to Jesus to experience the full impact of the blood, sweat, tears, and other bodily fluids that rained down from the crosses of those being tortured. Yet He was not ashamed of their presence.

Following His death, it was the women who first visited His grave. Even after His death, they were still following Him. They were still taking care of Him.

And when Jesus rose from the dead, the first faces He met—the first eyes that were laid upon Him—belonged to women. And it was to the women He gave the privilege of announcing His resurrection, even though according to Jewish law their testimony wouldn't hold up in court. Later, on the day of Pentecost, these women were also present in the Upper Room along with the Twelve, waiting for Him to return.

> ***Though Mark says that Jesus had four brothers and several sisters, Jesus' family plays a remarkably negligible role in his story.***
>
> —William Willimon[77]

Unlike Jesus' male disciples, the women never left Him. They followed Him to the end. Their passion for and dedication to Jesus outshined that of the men. And God was not ashamed.

Throughout the Lord's life, it was the women who tended to His physical needs. It was the women who looked after Him and funded Him.[78] It was the women who cared for Him up until the bitter end, as well as at the glorious climax. *Not the men.* The women were indispensable to Him. And He was not ashamed.

While the Twelve and the women were part of the Lord's inner circle of interns, Jesus also had a wider band of followers. In Luke 10, for instance, He commissioned seventy disciples on a trial mission.[79]

Why seventy? The ancient Jews believed that there were seventy nations on the earth.[80] Perhaps the seventy disciples represented the fact that the message of Jesus would eventually go out to all nations, not just to "the lost sheep of the house of Israel."[81] In addition, Moses appointed seventy elders to help lead Israel to their complete exodus.[82] Consequently the Lord's act of sending seventy disciples seems to symbolize the new exodus that Jesus (the new Moses) was leading—an exodus that would bring deliverance, salvation, and healing to the people of God and eventually to the whole world.

A NEW FAMILY

It is hard for us to hear how Jesus repeatedly overturned traditional family roles and values.[83] Why? Because Jesus was creating a new kind of family, in which relationships were not based on blood, clan, or patriarchy but on participation in the kingdom of God. Jesus Himself said that those who did His will are His family and friends.[84]

Consequently the call to follow Jesus meant a radical break with the past. Those who followed Jesus left everything. That sometimes included family[85] and jobs.[86] But His promise was that they would receive a new family in return.[87] The community (*ekklesia*) that comprised the disciples became that new family.[88]

Interestingly not all of Jesus' disciples left their homes. For instance, Mary, Martha, and Lazarus (who were among Jesus' closest friends) stayed in Bethany and made their home His home.[89] Jesus also appeared to have different circles among His disciples. Peter, James, and John enjoyed a more intimate relationship with Jesus.[90] John seems to have been the closest to Him. Even though Peter is always named first among the Twelve,[91] Jesus was tough on him. The breaking of God is proportionate to the quality of ministry one will have later in life. This principle emerges in bold relief in the way Jesus trained Peter.

Despite the fact that Peter was repeatedly exposed and failed his Lord many times, he was the object of Jesus' unending love. Even after he denied Jesus three times,[92] Jesus never mentioned the tragedy after His resurrection. Instead, Jesus gave Peter the opportunity to express his love for Him the same number of times that he denied Him. Then He commissioned him to feed His sheep.[93] On the day of Pentecost the same man who denied his Lord three times preached the gospel and opened the door of salvation to thousands of Jews. And as he preached, the other disciples stood faithfully by his side.[94]

In times of failure keep two words in mind: *Remember Peter.*[95]

JESUS' NEW FAMILY

Jesus regarded His followers as His own family.[96] In His resurrection they would become His kinfolk in a very real sense. Jesus, in His resurrected state, would impart His divine life to His followers, and "the only begotten Son" would become "the firstborn among many brethren."[97] And He would not be ashamed to call them "brethren,"[98] a term used often throughout the Second Testament to include females. After His resurrection Jesus specifically called His disciples "brethren."[99] Even so, while Jesus was on the cross, He anticipated the birth of His new family (and healed a rift between His disciples and His family) by introducing John and His mother as "son" and "mother."[100]

In short, the Twelve were the embryonic expression of the church.[101] For that reason the family is the dominating metaphor used for the church all throughout the Second Testament.[102] Family language is peppered throughout the Epistles. Jesus was creating not only a new Israel but a new family, the bond of which was shared divine life instead of blood ties. This brings us back to God's eternal purpose, which is to obtain a bride for the Son, a house for the Father, a body for the Son, and a family for the Father.[103]

Jesus' choice of the Twelve was an integral part of His mission. The Twelve constituted the future Israel, the recreated people of God, the foundation stones of the *ekklesia* that Jesus came to build. And the Twelve, along with His other disciples—the women—would carry on His work and fulfill His mission statement.

CHAPTER 9

Jesus' Mission Statement

For this purpose the Son of God was manifested, that He might destroy the works of the devil.

—The apostle John[1]

Jesus taught His disciples how to take their work home with them. Even more, Jesus made it clear that life comes with a take-home final.[2] There can be no dividing line between what we do for a living and whom we live to serve. There can be no distinction between our Monday-to-Friday work lives and our "Sunday selves." That is because Jesus claims to be "at home" with us wherever we go and whomever we encounter[3]—so much so, in fact, that divine judgment will be based on how we respond to the presence of Jesus in our midst.

At the resplendent moment, Christ the King will portray His lofty perch of lordship and the throne of glory from which He will judge all the nations of the world. At that very glorious moment, Jesus dethroned Himself. The emperor wore a purple robe. The only time Jesus wore a purple robe was when others put one on Him, as the soldiers did when they stripped Him naked, twisted a crown of thorns into His head, and draped the kingly purple robe over Him to mock Him before leading Him up the hill.[4] There they would crucify this "king" on a cross on which was posted a message from Pilate: "JESUS OF NAZARETH, THE KING OF THE JEWS."[5] Christ the King reigns from a cross.

Our "take-home final" is one we take throughout our whole lives, and it is this: to find Christ the King in "the least ones." Not the easy ones, but the queasy ones. Not the established religious leaders, whom Jesus called "whitewashed tombs,"[6] but the ne'er-do-wells, the ones Jesus Himself hung out with: the misfits, the outcasts, the unclean, the disgraced, the disabled, the failures, the ostracized, the enemy. It would have been impossible for Jesus to imagine a Jewish Israeli going through life without knowing, let alone befriending, a Palestinian. For Jesus there were sheep and goats,[7] but no category of "other." Even the goats were not an "other," but part of one another.

> *Jesus left us with a commandment and a commission—to love him with everything we've got and to obey him with everything we've got.*
>
> —Bill Hull[8]

Some people don't start life at ground zero, or plus with plush, but at minus four or minus five. These are the people with whom Jesus spent the most time. We have a Messiah who, from the very beginning, befriended the weak and wretched of humanity—manger-born, stable-mansioned refugees on the run—and expects us to do the same. This essential feature of the Jesus story, the identification with the rejected and broken, was for Nietzsche the fatal flaw in Christianity.[9]

Jesus' "take-home final" revolutionizes the world's understanding of success and failure, big and small, good and bad. Smallness and bigness have nothing to do with numbers or size. The biggest love the world has ever seen was wrapped in the tiniest bundle of flesh, and tied with a red ribbon of sacrificial giving.

Our "take-home exam" is based on Jesus' challenge to us. Jesus gave His apostles their mission statement in what were among some of His last words: "Go therefore and make disciples of all the nations, baptizing them in the name of the Father and of the Son and of the Holy Spirit."[10] Or in Mark's rendering, "Go into all the world and preach the gospel to every creature."[11]

JESUS' ONE-MINUTE MISSION STATEMENT

But while Jesus gave His apostles a mission statement, He had His own mission statement as well. It was not John 3:16; rather, it came from the prophet Isaiah, a passage Jesus selected for His inaugural message. Jesus made His mission statement into His first "sermon."

Jesus' first message was not the so-called Sermon on the Mount but the one He delivered in His hometown, when He went to the Nazareth synagogue on the Sabbath and opened up the scroll of the prophet Isaiah, chapter 61, and read these words:

> *"The Spirit of the Lord is on me,*
> *because he has anointed me*
> *to preach good news to the poor.*
> *He has sent me to proclaim freedom for the prisoners*
> *and recovery of sight for the blind,*
> *to release the oppressed,*
> *to proclaim the year of the Lord's favor."*

> Then he rolled up the scroll, gave it back to the attendant and sat down. The eyes of everyone in the synagogue were fastened on him, and he began by saying to them, "Today this scripture is fulfilled in your hearing."[12]

That was it. Those last eight words may have been the shortest message Jesus ever preached.

But Jesus was a master of the One-Minute Message. In poetic form, He could have delivered the Sermon on the Mount in less than a minute. In poetic form, the Lord's Prayer can be recited in Hebrew in less than a minute, and almost every parable takes only a minute to tell. Jesus' One-Minute Messages were in marked contrast to the standard prayer practices of His day. First, prayer was conducted most often at set times in the day: morning, afternoon, and evening, usually at 9:00 a.m., noon, and 3:00 p.m. Second, the pious would stand, rather than kneel or bow, for prayer. Third, seldom would prayer be spontaneous. Rather, the pious would recite collections of prayer, most often from what was called the *Amidah* (Hebrew for "standing"), or in more ancient lingo, the *Shemoneh Esrei* (Hebrew for "eight plus ten"). Finally, praying would be timed and situated so the supplicant could be seen and heard praying long prayers in public places.

> ***And each morning and evening they stood before the Lord to sing songs of thanks and praise to him.***
>
> —Ezra[13]

Jesus broke the rigid pattern and advocated praying in private, encouraged spontaneous prayers from the heart, and advocated short, simple prayers, like the minute appeal Elijah prayed before the fire fell, thereby mocking the babbling entreaties of the 850 prophets of Canaanite gods. Like the first Adam, the Second Adam chose to pray before daybreak[14] and late in the day.[15] But beyond all of that, Jesus modeled for us the highest form of prayer of all: *fellowship*. Jesus was in constant fellowship with His Father throughout all His waking moments—a fellowship into which He has called us as well. It was something deep, internal, and very real. For Jesus, prayer was walking the garden with the Father in the dew of the day. In fact, the phrase "speaking out of the whirlwind" in Hebrew is similar to "hearing God walking in the garden in the cool of the day."[16]

Jesus spent His entire life living His One-Minute Mission Statement, and taking His Father's "take-home final."

> Jesus went throughout Galilee, teaching in their synagogues, preaching the good news of the kingdom, and healing every disease and sickness among the people. News about him spread all over Syria, and people brought to him all who were ill with various diseases, those suffering severe pain, the demon-possessed, those having seizures, and the paralyzed, and he healed them.[17]

When John the Baptist sent two disciples to ask Jesus, "Are You the Coming One, or do we look for another?"[18] Jesus answered them by referring to His mission statement: "Go and tell John the things you have seen and heard: that the blind see, the lame walk, the lepers are cleansed, the deaf hear, the dead are raised, the poor have the gospel preached to them."[19] In other words, Jesus was saying, "Am I fulfilling My mission or not?"

Whether you call it the "Sermon on the Mount" (Matthew) or "the Sermon on the Plain" (Luke), this greatest sermon ever preached was a masterpiece of Jesus' mission statement. Jesus turned conventional Jewish spirituality on its head as He outlined the holy attitudes that are blessed, and then followed them up with the holy actions He honors and rewards: "Be perfect"; "Love your enemies"; "Don't worry about tomorrow." The law of Moses, a set of rules and regulations, a covenant "cut" with the blood of a lamb, would now be written in the heart and cut with the blood of the Lamb of God: "I will put my law in their minds," Jeremiah prophesied, "and write it on their hearts."[21] What Jesus preached on the hill where He gave the Sermon on the Mount, He practiced on the hill called Golgotha. God's reign is no longer found in a legal code etched in stone but in a love code of living etched in a new heart. It's a change from within that moves outward:

> ***A disciple, who is not inwardly the same as outwardly, will not be allowed to enter the House of Study.***
>
> —Rabbi Gamaliel[20]

> For a good tree does not bear bad fruit, nor does a bad tree bear good fruit. For every tree is known by its own fruit. For men do not gather figs from thorns, nor do they gather grapes from a bramble bush.[22]

Without new hearts there can be no new world.

JESUS' MISSION STATEMENT IS OUR TAKE-HOME FINAL

Jesus has come, and that changes everything. With one definitive act on an old, rugged tree, Jesus turned His personal mission statement into our take-home final. Like all take-home finals, there is no time limit. We have all of life and our resources to draw upon. We can edit and redo our responses throughout our lifetimes. We are to "take home" this final wherever our "home" may be, whatever circumstances we may be living in. But we are always to take this mission, this message of Christ's presence in "the least ones," home with us.

Instead of the Torah Ten (the Ten Commandments), Jesus had what one might call His Heaven Seven—seven actions the world can't live without:

1. Feed the hungry and give drink to the thirsty.
2. Welcome the stranger.
3. Clothe the naked.
4. Visit the prisoner.
5. Care for the sick.
6. Befriend sinners.
7. Side with the weak and least.

This is what it means to inherit the kingdom. We act out the Heaven Seven in a meal (the Lord's Supper) because food connects us through our sensory and spiritual selves to unite us into a group. At the same time, it sets us apart from others and gives us a unique identity. For Jesus, the very thing that sets His followers apart is what unites them as a group: "Inasmuch as you did it to one of the least of these . . . you did it to Me."[23]

Assume a Jesus identity—and do it with others as part of the kingdom community.

What we will say next is, for us, the missing ingredient to many exhortations to follow the Sermon on the Mount and obey the teachings of Jesus. That missing ingredient is the fact that we simply cannot.

The Sermon on the Mount should not be viewed as a new law or rule to obey by grit, by gut, or by gumption. Instead, it is first and foremost a *description* of the character and nature of Jesus Christ. Consider it a biographical sketch of the Lord Himself. That said, only Jesus can fulfill it. Look carefully at all the demands of that sermon and try living them without fail for a year. We're confident that, after failing miserably, you'll agree with us. Only Jesus can live out what He taught, and He does so in and through His people. This brings us back to the issue of living by the indwelling life of Christ.

As we stressed in our book *Jesus Manifesto*, Jesus said, "I can do nothing without My Father," and then He turned around and said to His disciples, "Without Me you can do nothing."[24] Jesus lived by the indwelling life of His Father, and Christ has come into every believer through the Holy Spirit to live out His indwelling life in us. When this happens, the characteristics of the Sermon on the Mount become visible in a local community of believers—the community of the King.

The Sermon on the Mount wasn't given to an individual. It was given to Jesus' disciples as a whole. As such, it can only be fulfilled in a local *ekklesia*. The local *ekklesia* is the community of the kingdom. None of us can pull it off on our own. The same is true for the Lord's mission statement in Luke 4; this is a joint endeavor. Jesus is on the earth today but not as an individual. He is here as a collective body, the *ekklesia*. The church is Christ on the earth, carrying out His mission. It is something corporate, not individualistic; embodied in face-to-face, shared-life communities, though it certainly has individual dimensions.

That said, in the course of our lives, as we progress through our "take-home final" on the Heaven Seven, we should see Christ more and more clearly in the lives of those we encounter everywhere, every day, every way. Christ is King because His presence permeates every part and parcel of our lives. Christ is no King if His reign is only for a few hours on Sunday morning. Jesus' reign is not observing formalities and performing functions. Jesus' reign is about taking things personally.

Jesus encouraged His disciples to do more than take the big picture. We are instructed to take everything and everyone personally. Jesus takes personally every action we have taken throughout our lives. Every time we drop a dollar in someone's cup. Every bit of clothing we donate to a shelter. Every drop of human kindness we extend to those thirsty for a meaningful life. Every extension of ourselves beyond ourselves, beyond our comfort zone, beyond our definition of *safe* and *secure*.

We enthrone Christ the King by personalizing and personating Jesus in the world. When we personate Jesus in and to the world, we become part of the Jesus story, a fifth gospel, a third testament. The strength of the church is not the strength of its institutions but the authenticity of its witness.

Jesus not only takes things personally but also takes us person by person. Jesus does not judge according to the big picture, the long view, the undifferentiated median, or the massified middle. Jesus insists, with the consequence of judgment, that we take life as we encounter it, that we take people as we experience them, that we meet the needs of others as they come to us—day by day, person by person, moment by moment. Our person-to-person experiences are the take-home final for our lives.

> ***If Jesus made the kingdom of God the center of his message and the center of his endeavor, the greatest need of man, as I see it, is to rediscover the kingdom of God.***
>
> —E. Stanley Jones[25]

Every day, every moment, every person is a test of Christ's kingship. Will we discern His presence in the "least ones" and be a Jesus for them? "Inasmuch as you did it to one of the least of these My brethren, you did it to Me."[26] It is the heart of Jesus' gift to us of a world-changing faith.

THE MISSION STATEMENT—PAST AND PRESENT

The Gospels, in essence, are the story of how God has come to reign through Jesus Christ on earth as He reigns in heaven. When He spoke, He spoke as if He was in charge. When He rose again from the dead and ascended, His disciples acted as though He really was in charge . . . still.

What does the world look like when God is reigning in the earth? What does it look like when God is in charge? It looks like this: physical healing; deliverance from evil spirits; feasting with outcasts, prostitutes, tax collectors, and thieves; the embracing of Samaritans; hardened hearts softened; forgiveness granted to those who have sinned; freedom from bondages; and mourners finding joy in God. All of these elements featured prominently in Jesus' ministry. They all testify to the inclusiveness of the kingdom of God. They all bear witness to what it looks like when God is reigning on the earth.

During His ministry, Jesus spoke on four issues more than He did anything else:

1. *The kingdom of God*—the manifestation of God's ruling presence, here now and yet coming.
2. *Life*—the eternal life that is embodied in Himself. A life that would be imparted to His followers after His resurrection. A life that they would live by.
3. *His Father*—the offer to have a relationship with God as Father, the *same* relationship He had with the Father.
4. *Himself*—He (Jesus) was the fulfillment of the entire First Testament story and promises.

All the other things Jesus spoke about were supplemental to these four things.

Eternal life is the life of God's new age that has broken into the present one. It is Christ Himself in the Spirit. Modern Western Christian movements have taught us that Jesus has a kingdom, but it's not part of this world. It's the equivalent of heaven after you die. This interpretation is based on various misreadings of certain things Jesus said (some of which we've dealt with in this book). Jesus taught, however, that the kingdom of God comes from somewhere else. It comes from another realm. But it is ultimately for this world, and it will ultimately fill the physical universe. What is more, it can be experienced now.

Jesus said, "If I cast out demons by the finger of God, then the kingdom of God has come upon you."[27] Remember His prayer: "Your kingdom come. Your will be done on earth as it is in heaven."[28] This kingdom petition does not stand alone. It goes hand in hand with Jesus' parting words before His ascension: "All authority has been given to Me in heaven and on earth."[29] Jesus of Nazareth is in charge of this earth. He announced it at the beginning of His ministry. And He executed it by His death and resurrection.

As we argued in our book *Jesus Manifesto*, Jesus and His message do not fit neatly into either liberal or conservative boxes. Jesus announced the kingdom of God—which was a royal inauguration that challenged the existing kingdoms of the world. But His kingdom message didn't fit into today's left-versus-right spectrums. We simply cannot put Jesus into our political grids.

Jesus is the true King of the earth, whose kingdom comes in a totally unexpected and radically counterintuitive fashion. It was foolishness to the Roman officials. And it was a scandal to the Jewish elite.

The kingdom of God is the sovereign rule of Israel's God on earth as in heaven, exercised through David's true son and heir. This is what the ancient Scriptures foretold. And God chose to bring that kingdom by an event that most Jews and Gentiles found incomprehensible: a brutal death on a Roman cross.

The prophets foretold that God would return to Jerusalem one day (after He had abandoned it during the Babylonian captivity), that He would deliver His people from their oppressors, and that He would be King over the whole world, bringing forth peace and justice, and removing sin and corruption.[30]

But the Scriptures also predicted that God would rule through the Lord's "anointed" Son, and He would rule from Zion.[31] They prophesied that God would reign through the Davidic King from the land of Israel and would rebuild the temple.[32] But they missed how God would do it. They missed that God would return in human form.[33] Even though it was written in the prophets, they didn't expect that the King would have to die[34] and that His death was the means by which He would bring forth the new covenant[35] and the new creation.[36] Nor did they expect that God would extend an arm to accomplish this.

> He saw that there was no one, he was appalled that there was no one to intervene; so his own arm worked salvation for him, and his own righteousness sustained him.[37]

> Who has believed our message and to whom has the arm of the LORD been revealed? He grew up before him like a tender shoot, and like a root out of dry ground.[38]

An arm is a part of someone. It is an extension of himself. Jesus, the arm of God—Jesus, the kingdom-bringer and the cross-bearer—announced that a new government was taking over. He announced that God's reign was now breaking into the earth. He announced that He was walking in the footsteps of David. That God was ending the exile and proclaiming the "acceptable year of the LORD," the year of Jubilee—the year of freedom and deliverance to God's people.[39]

After Jesus' death, God the Father raised Him from the dead, vindicating Him before men and angels. Resurrection is the life of heaven, the life of the new age, now come to earth. And today, Jesus is enthroned as Israel's Messiah and the world's true King. As a result, we are now living in the new creation wherein a new world has dawned in Christ. As followers of Jesus, we have a task before us. That task is to work *for* the kingdom. To continue the ministry of Jesus in the power of the Holy Spirit . . . to bear witness to the sovereign lordship of Christ . . . to embody the message that Jesus is both Lord and Savior, not just of our personal lives but of the entire world. And to find creative ways to manifest that kingdom where we live and travel.

A legitimate question to ask is, "If Jesus is now Lord of the world, why is it still filled with evil, wickedness, pain, and chaos?"

The answer: Jesus, the ruler of the world, has chosen to rule in and through His people. For this reason, the Scriptures call us "kings and priests" on the earth.[40] Or as Peter put it, "a royal priesthood,"[41] bringing us back to God's original intention for human beings.[42] When Jesus was on the earth, God was establishing His rule on earth as it is in heaven through Him. Today, Jesus is seeking to further establish His rule on earth as it is in heaven. But He has chosen the church to be the instrument for its accomplishment.

The church, therefore, is the means by which Jesus Christ continues to work, to teach, and to establish His sovereign rule in the world.[43] And He will continue to do so until the kingdom of God comes in its fullness, and heaven and earth can be seen by one another again.

CHAPTER 10

Jesus: Healer and Miracle-Worker

We beheld His glory.

—THE APOSTLE JOHN[1]

PROVENANCE IS A FAMILIAR WORD TO ANYONE WHO HAS EVER WATCHED the television show *Antiques Roadshow*. An antique gold ring is literally worth its weight in gold. But an antique gold ring given to your great-grandmother by Pablo Picasso along with a thank-you note for doing such a good job cleaning his studio? That's called "provenance," and such a provenance makes that gold ring worth much, much more than its weight in gold. A story is what adds value and luster to a plain piece of jewelry.

God established Jesus' provenance at the transfiguration, a pivotal moment marking the beginning of a new phase in Jesus' mission and ministry—His movement toward Jerusalem and the cross. Taking with Him His inner circle—Peter, James, and John—Jesus headed for Mount Tabor, where a miracle happened.

THE TRANSFIGURATION OF JESUS

The transfiguration gave Jesus a perfect, unimpeachable provenance. Every word and image celebrated the past, evoking the history of

Israel—and captured the future, revealing the power of God's covenant promise. This mountaintop experience took place "six days" after Jesus had foretold His death and resurrection.[2] The reference to six days, coupled with a mountaintop excursion, surely reminded Jewish readers of the six days that Mount Sinai was shrouded by the cloudlike glory of God.[3]

> *[When the Messiah appears] . . . the* LORD *will create over all of Mount Zion and over those who assemble there a cloud of smoke by day and a glow of flaming fire by night; over all the glory will be a canopy.*
>
> —ISAIAH[4]

Like the greatest prophets of the past, Jesus journeyed upward first. Mountaintop experiences involve high altitude to increase divine amplitude. As the disciples watched in amazement, Jesus' face and clothing took on all the classic features associated with heavenly beings. His face radiated and shined with light. His clothes glowed with dazzling whiteness.[5] All of this leads one scholar to call the transfiguration "The Restored Face."[6]

Suddenly Jesus and the disciples were no longer alone. Two of the most important figures in Israel's history were with Jesus, engaging Him in casual conversation. Moses, the one who led Israel out of Egypt, who climbed Mount Sinai and brought the Torah to the people, now stood on the land he was prohibited from entering at his death. Also standing before them was Elijah—Israel's most powerful prophet, the one who was mysteriously transported to heaven without suffering death and who must return before the final days of judgment will occur. Both Moses and Elijah were linked to messianic and eschatological (last-days) expectations.[7]

Peter's construction proposal for "shelters" or "tabernacles"[8] recreates the Feast of Tabernacles, where temporary shelters are erected as a commemorative sign of Israel's long wilderness wandering. Peter wanted to provide human shelter for these heavenly visitors, shelters that would remain long after this epiphany had faded away.

But any human participation in this event was squelched by yet another sudden appearance—a cloud rolled in and a voice echoed out. The "bright cloud" that "overshadowed" the mountaintop[9] is a familiar image for God's divine presence throughout Israel's history, both in the wilderness and in the sanctuary.[10] Later Jewish writing described this cloudlike phenomenon of the divine presence as the *shekinah*, the glory of God made visible to human eyes.

Even as Peter, James, and John found themselves being overshadowed by that shekinah glory, they heard nothing less than the voice of God: "This is My beloved Son, in whom I am well pleased. Hear Him!"[11] The voice that accompanied the divine presence on this mountaintop exactly echoed the baptismal declaration.[12] But here it added a directive to the earlier decree: "Hear Him!" This "listen up" order once again recalls the promise of a prophet "like Moses," whom the people are instructed to heed.[13]

The disciples' response to the vision and voice was distinctly different from Peter's cheerful offer to pitch a few tents for the heavenly crew. As is normal for any miraculous encounter between God and humans, they were terrified and respectfully fell prostrate on the ground.[14]

It was Jesus Himself who comforted His cowering cohorts: "Do not be afraid."[15] The vision had vanished when the disciples looked up. Jesus's final word on what had just happened was a command for silence about this "vision" (*horama*) until "the Son of Man is risen from the dead."[16] This sneak peek of Jesus' future glory was not yet ready for prime time. Now it was time for Jesus to return to His mission of teaching, preaching, and healing.

Perhaps Peter was more theologically savvy than we give him credit for. What had just happened was steeped in symbols and studded with the most important figures in Israel's past. Keeping memories alive was one of Israel's strengths. If this was to be a new milestone along the path of faith, it needed to be marked in some way.

When the ark of the covenant finally crossed over the Jordan River and into the promised land, Joshua commanded the priests carrying the ark to pause in the middle of the river. A representative of each of the twelve tribes was instructed to stop midstream and collect a plain stone from the miraculously dried-up riverbed.[17] The reason for this rock hounding was so "these stones [would] be for a memorial to the children of Israel forever."[18] The stones would remind the people of the miracle that brought them and the ark into the promised land. Once the people reached the other side of the river, Joshua oversaw the erection of all twelve stones at Gilgal, making a permanent marker to commemorate the miracle and to serve as a reminder to the people.

The cairn tradition of rock stacking has been with humans ever since we first began to mark moments with memory tools. Gilgal commemorated a pivotal moment in Israel's history, the moment the people and the ark of the covenant finally entered the promised land. Peter's offer to build "shelters" or "tabernacles" for Jesus, Moses, and Elijah is most often associated with the Feast of Tabernacles, the annual Jewish festival during which small, temporary shelters were built to celebrate and remember the years of wilderness wanderings. If building "tabernacles" was Peter's impetus, they would be powerful symbols to "remember this place."

But the transfigured Christ was too unique, too unprecedented, to be commemorated in cairn or canvas, both of which celebrated the journey and arrival of God's people at a particular place. The moment Peter wanted to domesticate the divine presence, the glory of God came down to disclose a greater revelation. At precisely the moment Peter suggested tying Jesus to a location, God bared the divine will.

God's command was not to commemorate a place. It was to connect to a person: "This is My beloved Son, in whom I am well pleased."

God's next command was to respond to that person: "Hear Him!"

Jesus is the new ark of the covenant.
    "Hear Him!"
He leads the way.
    "Hear Him!"
He tells the truth.
    "Hear Him!"
He brings life to living.
    "Hear Him!"

The world may be in the process of being transfigured, and we may become changed "from glory to glory,"[19] but mission in the real world awaits. The three disciples who climbed the mountain with Jesus and wanted to stay, Jesus led back *down* the mountain, back into the valley, where they were immediately met by human suffering and hurt. A father pleaded for his child: "'Lord, have mercy on my son,'"[20] whereupon the boy was healed.

There is a famous painting called *The Transfiguration* (1516) by the great Italian artist Raphael. Raphael died at the age of thirty-seven. As he lay in state, the painting commissioned as a high-end altarpiece was placed at the head of his coffin. The striking thing about the painting is that the top half depicts Christ and the three apostles in their mountaintop bubble of glorious intimacy with God. But the bottom half of the painting depicts the lunatic boy and his father in the agony of their pain and need. The disciples are trying to heal him and failing. Only Jesus can heal the boy. When Goethe looked at the painting, he said this: "The two are one: below the suffering part, in need of help, above, the effective helpful part, both of them linked together . . . Can the connection between the conceptual and the real be severed?"[22]

> *Jesus went throughout Galilee, teaching in their synagogues, preaching the good news of the kingdom, and healing every disease and sickness among the people. News about him spread all over Syria, and people brought to him all who were ill with various diseases, those suffering severe pain, the demon-possessed, those having seizures, and the paralyzed, and he healed them.*
>
> —Matthew[21]

JESUS REBUKED SICKNESS

According to the Bible, sickness came into the world through Adam's sin. Sickness is incipient death. Romans 5:12 says, "Therefore, just as through one man sin entered the world, and death through sin, and thus death spread to all men, because all sinned . . ."

Since sickness initially came into the world as the result of sin, it's not something God originally intended. As such, sickness will not be part of the new creation when it arrives in its fullness.

For this reason, Jesus rebuked sickness[23] and attributed many diseases to satan or evil spirits.[24] Consider the following passages:

> God anointed Jesus of Nazareth with the Holy Spirit and with power, who went about doing good and *healing all who were oppressed by the devil*, for God was with Him.[25]

> For this purpose the Son of God was manifested, that *He might destroy the works of the devil.*[26]

In Galatians 3:13–14, Paul wrote that Jesus redeemed us from the curse of the law so that the blessing of Abraham may be given to the Gentiles.[27] What is the curse of the law? According to Deuteronomy 28:15–61, sickness and disease are part of the curse. What are the blessings given to Abraham's seed? One repeated promise is health:

> The Lord will take away from you all sickness.[28]

> "I will put none of the diseases on you which I have brought on the Egyptians. For I am the Lord who heals you."[29]

> Bless the Lord, O my soul, and forget not all His benefits: who forgives all your iniquities, who heals all your diseases.[30]

> Fear the Lord and depart from evil. It will be health to your flesh, and strength to your bones.[31]

> Give attention to my words. . . . For they are life to those who find them, and health to all their flesh.[32]

So sickness appears to be part of the curse of the law, and healing appears to be one of Abraham's blessings. Galatians 3:16 says that Christ is Abraham's Seed and that the promises were made to Him. Furthermore, Galatians 3:29 says, "And if you are Christ's, then you are Abraham's seed, and heirs according to the promise."

SICKNESS IN THE JEWISH MIND

The Jews in Jesus' day believed that if someone was ill, it meant that he had sinned in some way to cause the illness. Sickness, then, was regarded as judgment from God.[33] They also attributed sickness to demonic power.[34] Consequently, sickness represented sin, and healing represented forgiveness.[35] In addition, if someone was the instrument of healing, it signified that he was sent from God, for only God heals.

While there was no normative set of expectations of the Messiah that all Jews shared in the first century, most of them believed that the Messiah would fulfill a kingly role as well as a priestly role.[36] Thus many ancient Jews believe that the coming Messiah would perform unusual healings. John the Baptist appeared to have such an expectation:

> At that very time Jesus cured many who had diseases, sicknesses and evil spirits, and gave sight to many who were blind. So he replied to the messengers, "Go back and report to John what you have seen and heard: The blind receive sight, the lame walk, those who have leprosy are cured, the deaf hear, the dead are raised, and the good news is preached to the poor."[37]

And so did many of the Jews:

> Still, many in the crowd put their faith in him. They said, "When the Christ comes, will he do more miraculous signs than this man?"[38]

One Jewish scholar has argued that the ancient Jews regarded the following three miracles to be "Messianic":

1. The cleansing of lepers.
2. The casting out of demons that caused muteness.
3. The healing of blindness.[39]

It is interesting to note that whenever Jesus performed one of these miracles, the Jewish response was radically different from when He performed other types of miracles. For example, when Jesus cast out a demon that caused muteness, the Jews responded, saying, "Could this be the Son of David?"[40] After Jesus healed a leper, the Pharisees and scribes came from "every village in all Galilee and Judea, as well as from Jerusalem" to see Him.[41]

Jesus clearly had authority over disease and demons.[42] And much of His ministry was dedicated to healing the sick and casting out demons, as well as forgiving sins.[43] Even after His resurrection, Jesus was still healing the sick through His followers.[44] In fact, He commissioned His followers to carry on His ministry of healing.[45]

Note the words of Isaiah that were fulfilled in Christ:

> He was despised and rejected by men, a man of sorrows, and familiar with suffering. Like one from whom men hide their faces he was despised, and we esteemed him not. Surely he took up our infirmities and carried our sorrows, yet we considered him stricken by God, smitten by him, and afflicted. But he was pierced for our transgressions, he was crushed for our iniquities; the punishment that brought us peace was upon him, and by his wounds we are healed.[46]

Matthew applied this text to the healing ministry of Jesus while He was on earth.[47] Peter pointed out that this ministry is still in effect.[48] Jesus Christ is Healer, both for the body and the spirit.

But this was all a signpost. When Jesus came to town, it meant that healing, deliverance, joy, celebration, forgiveness, transformation, and rescue soon followed. This is the consistent testimony of the Gospels. Jesus healed, He forgave, He celebrated through feasting with people (usually the outcasts of society), He delivered, and He transformed lives—not by changing the outside of the cup, as the

Pharisees did, but by curing hardened hearts and cleansing them from the inside.

Jesus' healings demonstrated that the arrival of God's rule over evil was breaking into the present. For Jesus, healings and the casting out of demons were signs of the dawning kingdom. They indicated that God's future had arrived. They were tangible signposts that the kingdom of God was coming to earth as it is in heaven.

> "But if I drive out demons by the Spirit of God, then the kingdom of God has come upon you."[49]

By healing the sick and casting out demons, Jesus was effectively saying, "This is what happens when God is running the world. This is what it looks like when God is King of the earth. The time has come; the dominion of God is breaking into the present. This is what happens when God becomes King on earth as He is in heaven. And contrary to popular opinion, God's rule will benefit those who are regarded as being the most unworthy."[50]

> *Jesus of Nazareth was a man accredited by God to you by miracles, wonders and signs, which God did among you through him.*
>
> —Peter[51]

To put it in a sentence: Jesus is God's future in person. That is what His healings announced. To encounter Jesus was to encounter God's rule in human form.

So Jesus went all throughout Galilee, heralding that God was taking the throne. And His healing ministry pointed to that. The religious leaders, who had a completely different understanding of how the kingdom would come, didn't recognize it when it was actively breaking forth in their midst.

THE SEVEN SIGNS OF JESUS

In addition to His healings, Jesus did many miracles or "signs." The miracles of Jesus were His parables and teachings in action.[52]

Jesus' signs and wonders were his calling card, one of the proofs that the kingdom of God had come.

—John Wimber[53]

For example, John wrote his gospel around seven miracles that he called "signs." A sign is a pointer to a deeper spiritual reality.

Each sign in John's gospel sets forth what life in the kingdom of God practically means. To put it another way, the seven signs reveal the nature of eternal life—a life that has been given to us now in Jesus Christ.[54]

Jesus Christ as eternal life is the central theme of John's gospel:

- In Him was life.[55]
- Whoever believes in Him shall have eternal life.[56]
- Whoever drinks the water He gives shall have a well of water springing up into eternal life.[57]
- People would not come to Him that they might have life.[58]
- He is the bread of life.[59]
- Whoever follows Jesus shall have the light of life.[60]
- Jesus came that we might have life.[61]
- Jesus is the resurrection and the life.[62]
- Jesus is the way, the truth, and the life.[63]
- This is eternal life: that we might know the Father and Jesus Christ, whom He sent.[64]
- By believing, we have life through His name.[65]

We could easily write a separate book expounding the seven signs of John's gospel, but here's a brief survey:

1. Turning water into wine—demonstrates how eternal life reverses human failure and removes mortal shame.
2. The healing of the nobleman's son—demonstrates how eternal life is unlimited by space, time, and matter.

3. The healing of the palsied man at the pool of Bethesda—demonstrates how eternal life delivers us from the bondage to sin and death.
4. The feeding of the five thousand—demonstrates how eternal life is always sufficient and can never be exhausted.
5. Jesus walking on water—demonstrates how eternal life transcends and is victorious over the force of nature.
6. The healing of the man who was born blind—demonstrates how eternal life gives spiritual sight.
7. The raising of Lazarus from the dead—demonstrates how eternal life overcomes death in all of its degrees.

JESUS IS THE REAL TEMPLE

Earlier we pointed out that healing and forgiveness of sins go together. This is abundantly clear in both Testaments. In this connection, the ancient Jews understood that the temple was the place where sins were forgiven. The Gospels are clear that Jesus was the Temple of God in living, breathing, walking, and talking form. He was the embodiment of what the temple meant. Consider the following:

- The Jews understood that the temple was the one place on earth where heaven and earth intersected. It was the extension of the garden of Eden, the playground of angels and humans. Jesus was God and man. He was the joining together of God's dwelling and the dwelling of humans. Jesus is the reality of *Bethel*, the "house of God," which is marked by commerce between the heavens and the earth. (Recall Jacob's dream in Genesis 28, where angels ascended and descended from heaven to earth, and Jesus' words to Nathanael in John 1 that Jesus is the fulfillment of God's house.)[66]
- Jesus identified Himself as the tabernacle of God, the fulfillment of the tabernacle of Moses, where God's glory rested.[67] The words of John 1:14, He "dwelt among us," literally mean He

"tabernacled among us." In the same text, John went on to say "and we beheld His glory."

- In John 2:19, Jesus said to the Jews, "Destroy this temple, and in three days I will raise it up." John then informed us, two verses later, that Jesus was speaking of the temple of His body.
- In Matthew 12:6, Jesus announced that He is greater than the physical temple. The physical temple was a signpost. Jesus is the reality.
- In Colossians 2:9, Paul says that all the fullness of the Godhead dwells in Jesus in bodily form. In other words, Jesus is the dwelling place of God.
- In John 20, Jesus breathed into the disciples. They were now a new creation. He then gave them the word of proclaiming forgiveness to sinners. Forgiveness was the rule of the temple in Jerusalem. The temple afforded forgiveness of sins by the sacrifices that were offered there. Now Jesus, the real Temple and the real Sacrifice, offered forgiveness. And those who were part of the Temple, His disciples, declared it as well.[68]
- In His ministry in Galilee, Jesus was acting and living as though He were the temple itself. He was fulfilling all of the temple's functions. To have your sins forgiven in that day, you had to go to the temple. Jesus was subverting this system by offering forgiveness Himself.
- After the temple of His body was destroyed, Jesus rose again on the third day. Fifty days later, at Pentecost, thousands of Jews were converted to Christ. They were the "living stones" that were "hewn out of the one Rock," which is Christ. In Mark 14:58, one of the witnesses at Jesus' trial said, "We heard him say, 'I will destroy this man-made temple and in three days will build another, not made by man.'"[69] These living stones became the building blocks for the house of God. Jesus, the real Temple, had increased. Now the church has become the temple of God on earth.[70]
- In Acts 2, an unusual event occurred on the day of Pentecost in the city of Jerusalem. The Spirit of God fell on 120 disciples of Jesus. They spoke in tongues, and tongues of fire appeared on

their heads. The real temple of God was being born right in the midst of the old physical temple. The tongues were the reverse of what happened in Babel. At Babel sinful men tried to achieve unity by creating a tower to reach the heavens. God judged their effort and confused them by scrambling their languages. At Pentecost the Spirit of God united them, they spoke in other tongues, and they understood one another. The fire on their heads is reminiscent of the fire that fell from heaven on the temple when it was dedicated.[71] The new temple of God is not built with human hands.[72]

- The temple was a signpost of a future reality. It was God's dwelling place. It was the place of forgiveness, redemption, restoration, and wholeness. It was the place of God's presence on earth.

So Jesus was the Temple of God in person—the overlap of heaven and earth. In Jesus, God's will was being done "on earth as it is in heaven."[73]

What does this have to do with the Lord's healing ministry? A great deal.

In addition to certain miracles many first-century Jews believed the Messiah would do the following:

- He would cleanse and restore the temple.
- He would triumph over Israel's enemies.
- He would end Israel's exile.
- He would bring God's peace and justice to the whole world.[74]
- He would be of Davidic descent.[75]

The First Testament books of Jeremiah, Daniel, Ezra, and Nehemiah all witness to the fact that Israel's exile was the result of their sin and rebellion. Israel, therefore, longed to be forgiven (corporately) and to be released from exile. (They were under the thumb of the Romans during Jesus' day.)

In their eyes God had left the earth after the temple at Jerusalem was destroyed by the Babylonians and Israel was taken into exile. He was no longer called "the God of heaven and earth." He was only called "the God of heaven."[76] The temple and the land, possessed by God's people, gave the Lord a foothold in the earth.

For this reason, the First Testament prophets predicted that God would someday return to Zion. When this happened, the long, bitter exile of Israel would end and their sins would be forgiven. To put it another way, if the sin that caused Israel to be exiled was forgiven, it meant that Israel's long exile was over.[77]

Jesus' healing ministry, therefore, was not simply evidence that He was the promised Messiah or that the kingdom of God was breaking into the present. It was not simply evidence of the compassion of God to alleviate human suffering, reversing the curse that sin produced. *It was also a visible expression that Jesus was re-creating the new Israel and that her exile had come to an end.* The healings Jesus did demonstrated that the forgiveness He offered was in fact effective.[78]

JESUS' CLEANSING OF THE TEMPLE

In like manner stands Jesus' act of cleansing the temple, which was a dramatic symbol that the temple and its corrupt system were under God's judgment. The city of Jerusalem and the temple that stood in it—the place of God's presence—were to be the light of the world. Instead, they came to symbolize the commercial oppression of the poor. The place where God chose to put His name rejected Him when He appeared.[79] Jesus' "temple tantrum" demonstrated, in active parable, that the city and the temple would be destroyed.[80] Jesus was declaring and portraying that God's judgments against His people and their temple in the past were repeating themselves again. When Jesus cleansed the temple, He was acting in the role of a king, for only kings held the exclusive right to cleanse and reestablish the temple. This act of cleansing the temple is what most likely got Him killed.

Jesus was replacing the old temple with Himself. At the consummation of all things, the temple of God—Christ and those who are in Christ—will fill the earth and be among humans.[81] Thus, God's intention to expand the garden to cover the entire globe will eventually reach fulfillment. As Zechariah prophesied hundreds of years beforehand, the "BRANCH" would rebuild the temple, sit on His throne, and rule.[82] In that day fasting will turn into feasting.[83]

In short, Jesus fulfilled the chief criteria of the Messiah: He would be of Davidic descent (Jesus was born of the seed of David, and His life would echo David's life in many respects). He would cleanse and restore the temple (Jesus cleansed the temple and, in His resurrection, restored its reality). He would triumph over Israel's enemies (Jesus conquered all of God's enemies in a way that no one expected—on a Roman cross). He would end Israel's exile (Jesus did this in His death and resurrection). And He would bring God's peace and justice to the whole world (Jesus inaugurated this in His healing ministry, and He will consummate it at His return).

> *We must look for the fulfillment of the New Covenant within, the covenant not of laws but of life. The Spirit of Christ Himself is to be within us as the power of our lives.*
>
> —Andrew Murray[84]

CURING AND HEALING

Jesus never met a condition He couldn't cure. Jesus even healed the weather—sounds strange but true.[85] But there is a big difference between healing and curing.[86]

Nels Ferré was born in Sweden in 1908, one of ten children of a strict Swedish Baptist clergyman. At thirteen, he was sent to find his future in America on his own. At the train station on the day of his departure, Nels's family formed a prayer circle around him as his father prayed first. Then each member of the family blessed him with a prayer. Nels boarded the train and sat by the window, watching his family wave to him and cry. As the train rolled out of the station, his mother ran down the wooded platform alongside it. He slid the window open and leaned out just in time to hear her calling, "Nels! Nels! Remember Jesus! Remember Jesus!"[87]

Ferré became a respected theologian, sometimes with rather strange notions, and taught at some of the most prestigious educational institutions in the United States. While teaching at Andover Newton Theological School, he developed rheumatoid arthritis. Two of his graduate students took it upon themselves to provide transportation for him to and from his home to the campus. His physicians warned Ferré that the disease was progressing fast enough that eventually he would never walk again. But Ferré said he lived in the "citadel of faith," not the "borderlands of doubt." So he refused to accept that diagnosis. Instead, Ferré asked his seminary students to leave his car farther, and farther, and farther away from his house. Gradually, Ferré lengthened the distance he could walk to the point where he asked the students not to bring the car at all.

He struggled and stumbled to the classroom. But when he arrived at the door, he burst into the room, singing Martin Luther's great hymn "A Mighty Fortress Is Our God." He sang so loudly he could have startled people for miles around.

Was Nels Ferré cured? No. All the determination in the world did not change the course of the disease. His joints still swelled. His hands became disfigured. Fibrous tissue still grew in the wrong places, and the linings to his lungs were reddened. His mobility decreased as the pain increased.

Was Nels Ferré healed? Absolutely. He experienced the only kind of healing that counts in the end because it is the only kind of healing that lasts to the end—unto eternity. He "remembered Jesus." And in that remembrance he found healing, the healing that only Jesus can bring.

God sometimes cures. God always heals. Sometimes death is the final healing act. But death is never a "blessing." The blessing is not in the death, which is part of the powers and principalities Jesus has already overthrown. The blessing is in the healing that comes after all the curatives of earth have been tried and failed.

CHAPTER 11

Jesus: Teacher and Preacher

Not only do we know God by Jesus Christ alone, but we know ourselves by Jesus Christ alone. We know life and death by Jesus Christ alone. Apart from Jesus Christ we know not what is our life, nor our death, nor God, nor ourselves.

—Blaise Pascal[1]

For three years, Jesus traveled the kingdom of Herod with twelve envoys and an entourage of women and men He had healed. He traveled from place to place with His disciples, walking the roads connecting the cities and villages of Galilee to the north, Samaria in the center, and Judea to the south. The team of twelve was mostly dependent on the hospitality of others,[2] although they did have their own treasurer.

Repent, for the kingdom of heaven is at hand.

—Jesus[3]

They often met in private homes,[4] but one of Jesus' favorite places to preach was on the Sea of Galilee. Jesus pioneered voice amplification for large crowds by using a boat as His podium, the water as a sounding board, and the sloping hills and curving coves where people would sit as a natural amphitheater.[5]

Jesus' beginning message was an oxymoronic mixture of good news and bad:

- "Repent"—the bad news
- "The kingdom of heaven is at hand"—the good news[6]

Herod's patch of the planet was about the size of Massachusetts, but it was a micro mosaic of the universe that showcased the whole with green Galilee, rocky Judea, desolate Negev and the desert south of Jericho, the sunken Dead Sea, the lush coastal plains of the Jezreel Valley, the mountains of Tabor and Meron, and the balmy shores of the Mediterranean and Sea of Galilee.

THE TEACHING OF JESUS

It is hugely significant that Jesus left us no writings, no "book" or "words of the founder" to read. This is why bibliolatry does not fit with Christianity. You can't worship a book when the Founder didn't give us a book, only Himself and stories from others about Him. Jesus was killed by the Scripture-toting-and-quoting people of His day. A literalist treatment of the Torah (which included oral traditions) is what got Jesus killed.

Yet Jesus is steeped in the Scriptures. In fact, the Second Covenant knows the First Covenant: the Second Testament quotes the First Testament more than 320 times, and that does not include times when biblical writers, searching for the scriptural reference, were reduced to admitting that "somewhere" it reads thus and so.[7] Scholars have made the mistake of not identifying Jesus in terms of the Judaism of His day. In fact, it is the thesis of this book that the life of Jesus was the Hebrew story déjà vu. In what some believe to be the earliest Christian creed, Paul affirmed that everything Jesus did was "according to the Scriptures."[8] Or as the German philosopher Friedrich von Schelling said in the eighteenth century, the life of Jesus "had been written long before his birth."[9]

A couple of examples will suffice.

First, in the feeding of the five thousand, Jews saw Moses in Jesus and the Exodus Israelites in themselves, stranded in a "deserted place."[10] The story of Jesus feeding barley bread (barley was the poor man's wheat) to empty bellies not only was the story of Moses and manna redivivus but also echoed the story of the prophet Elisha, who fed a hundred people with twenty loaves of barley.[11] It was the one time we know for sure Jesus fed the crowds that followed Him till their bellies were full. In the Beatitudes, Jews saw Moses in Jesus, especially as "He went up on a mountain."[12] Moses climbed a mountain alone to receive the laws of the old covenant, written on tablets of stone and delivered in a cloud that hid God from their eyes. Jesus climbed a mountain with a crowd of followers to reveal the laws of a new covenant, written on the heart and revealing how God could be.[14] When Jesus raised the cup of wine at the Last Supper, a quasi-Passover meal, He toasted the "new covenant": "This cup is the new covenant between God and His people—an agreement confirmed with my blood, which is poured out as a sacrifice for you."[15]

> *I will incline my*
> *ear to a proverb;*
> *I will solve my*
> *riddle to the music*
> *of the lyre.*[13]
>
> —THE SONS OF KORAH

Second, when Jesus argued that healings should be allowed on the Sabbath because circumcisions were permissible,[16] He was demonstrating His knowledge of a ruling (*halakah*) that is found not in the Hebrew Bible but only in rabbinic literature.[17] The same for His insistence that "the Sabbath was made for man, and not man for the Sabbath,"[18] an almost exact quote from Rabbi Simeon ben Menasia. While these statements can be found in later rabbinic tradition, some scholars believe they reflect early Jewish thinking.

JESUS' RADICAL APPROACH TO THE SCRIPTURES

There were three differences from the other rabbis in Jesus' approach to the Scriptures.

First, Jesus taught and acted "as one having authority, and not as the scribes."[19] The rabbis said, "Thus says the Torah" or "Thus says a particular rabbi." Jesus used neither the traditional rabbinic terminology, "Thus says the Torah," nor the traditional prophetic formula, "Thus says the Lord." But He did say repeatedly in His listen-up mannerism, "You have heard that it was said . . . But I say to you" and "I tell you the truth."[20] Jesus didn't hide behind the authorities. Jesus didn't use the traditional rabbinic terminology but rather fronted almost everything He said with, "I tell you the truth." He did this twenty-five times in John's gospel alone. He was not passing on the teaching of some school or teacher but was on His own opening windows to the divine with a fresh reading of the ancient Scriptures. For Jesus, the "Word of God" was not Torah text or inanimate words but a latent force to be activated in the hearts of believers by the Holy Spirit of God and the communication of the Word.

You might even call Jesus "the One Who Came in His Father's Name." In answer to the question, "Who do you say that I am?" the church fathers realized early on that they couldn't describe Jesus as an entity all by Himself because He was always bringing His Father into the picture. "He who has seen Me has seen the Father"[21]; "I am in the Father and the Father in Me"[22]; "I do nothing of Myself; but as My Father taught Me, I speak these things"[23]; "I have come in My Father's name, and you do not receive Me; if another comes in his own name, him you will receive."[24]

The issue of Jesus' teaching "as one having authority, and not as the scribes"[25] is not so much Jesus' authority to teach as the freshness of His message. In an age where the "old" was sanctified and the "new" was suspect, Jesus' teaching reframed Judaism in a new metaphor landscape. Metaphor is not just something we use for communicating. Metaphor is how we think and reason, how we continually make sense of our continually changing world. Our actions are congruent with our metaphors. In reframing Judaism in new metaphors, Jesus generated new ways of living, thinking, and feeling.

There is a common phrase: the need of each generation to "wash the face of Jesus." Staying faithful in the midst of persecution is, in a sense, "washing the face of Jesus." But there is another sense in which it is used. Each generation and each culture has "dirtied" Jesus' face by various accommodations and accretions. Succeeding generations need to rediscover His beauty and let it be seen in them by "face washing." Jesus washed the face of Judaism and then showed that His face was God's face.

So far from Jesus "hardly ever citing the Holy Scripture,"[26] almost everything that came out of His mouth was a voicing of the Scripture. Neither the Talmud nor the Mishnah were in written form in Jesus' day, but He knew the oral tradition well enough to argue Mishnaic principles with the Pharisees.[27] Jesus never directly quoted a sacred text for a reason. The more you marinate your mind and soak your soul in the Scriptures, the more the Word becomes your words—the more its words become part of the warp and woof of your life, including your unique phrasings and idioms.

When Jesus returned to His hometown of Nazareth, the residents struggled to recognize Him.[28] He went to the community center on the Sabbath. The men of Nazareth were probably without a dedicated synagogue, and the Sepphoris synagogue was an hour's walk away, which was too far to walk on the Sabbath. The men of His hometown handed Jesus the scroll of the prophet Isaiah, not just to read from it but to teach it.[29] After reading the passage He had chosen, He looked at them and began His teaching with an announcement: "Today this Scripture is fulfilled in your hearing."[30]

I want you to show mercy, not offer sacrifices.

—Jesus[32]

Jesus' messianic reading of Isaiah was so shocking,[31] so presuming, that Jesus' own family took offense at Him. His wild prophetic claims had brought so much shame to the family that they schemed to conduct an honor killing to protect the family dignity. Jesus' family and hometown friends plotted to stone Him—to "throw Him down over the cliff."[33] To profess to be the Messiah was a crime to die for. But then, look at what He taught—not the Law, but God.

Other people marveled at Jesus' teaching, but not His kin. "Even His brothers did not believe in Him."[34] His mother was at the cross by herself, with none of her other sons (Jesus' brothers) by her side. He shamed a family with a proud pedigree . . . and He was buried by a non-family member, not by His brothers.[35]

Though they were not in Jerusalem for the crucifixion, at least some of Jesus' brothers were present at the ascension.[36] Two of Jesus' brothers, James and Jude, the ones whose writings are in the Second Testament, saw the resurrected Christ.

JESUS EMBODIED THE TORAH

Second, Jesus didn't trash the Torah. He embodied it. Yet He also didn't interpret the Scriptures the way the leading Jewish scholars of the day did. Jesus knew the oral law but did not demand rigid adherence to it from His disciples and derided it at times as "rules taught by men."[37] Jesus honored those who "sit in Moses' seat"[38]—but not what they did, only what they said. Much of Jesus' moral teachings were not new. The values and norms He upheld were the best Judaism had to offer.

The adulterous woman was still guilty of adultery in Jesus' eyes. Jesus' life principles were strongly opposed to adultery. But there was something that trumped principles, and that was relationship. A paraphrase of the exchange between Jesus and the adulterous woman might go like this: "You are lovely. Does no one love you?" She answers, "I don't know." Jesus says, "I do. Let Me be enough." She says to herself, *Can He be? Can He really, truly be . . . enough?* He is. When Jesus is in first place, all of life falls into place and you no longer feel misplaced.[39]

Sin is mentioned more than thirteen hundred times in the Bible. Sin is not something Jesus took lightly. But Jesus loved in a way that didn't compromise the truth yet expressed God's mercy, which is why Jesus was infamous for hanging with sinners and for loving them. He didn't recoil in horror at their sight or plight. He loved them. But He also required those who followed Him to leave their past behind. When we follow Jesus, we will need to leave something behind. Each time we hear Jesus say, "And will you, too, leave?" what if we responded, "What do we need to leave behind to follow Jesus better?"

Jesus called both the sinners and the righteous to repent, not by doing ritual penances, like fasting and mourning and praying, all of which were good things, but by living lives that forwarded God's mission in the world. For Jesus, it is not enough to repent and confess Him as the Christ, the Son of God.[40] He taught His disciples to incarnate the divine soul of love that motivates the ongoing forgiveness that faith provides. Without this love, there is no genuine faith. Jesus, Himself, is love. Love is the nature of the divine life that Jesus so frequently talked about and lived by. (He used the words "eternal life" and "life" to describe it.) After His resurrection, that life would penetrate His followers and become the source of their living. We have no power to love others without such life. We are fooling ourselves if we think we do. Hence Paul's words, "It is no longer I who live, but Christ lives in me."[41]

To follow the Law makes you observant. To follow Jesus makes you a servant—one who is observant not just about fulfilling legal codes but who is observant about loving God and neighbor. They are not the same. We worship God. We don't worship neighbors. But when people asked Jesus how to find God, He answered their question in stories that said in one way or other that if you find a neighbor to love, you will find God.

"Who is my neighbor?" asked the rich young ruler.[42] The answer in Jesus' day was, in essence, "fellow Jews and those who worship YHWH." Jesus gave a different answer.

Jesus does not propositionalize love, give norms and precepts for what love is, give applications for its use, or spell out in detail what love looks like in every situation—because love requires imagination and creativity and customization. What is Jesus looking for in response to His teaching? Not penitential acts or a Jesus worldview but a Jesus life and a daily living of love.

One scholar has computed that the words of Jesus compose 20 percent of the Second Testament. That's the equivalent of twelve sermons, a total of thirty minutes long.[43] What makes Jesus unique is more than His words or teachings. It's what the last Adam did: He died on the cross to save us from our sins; He rose from the dead; He ascended into heaven; He descended in the Spirit to impart His divine life to all who receive Him, thereby creating His body on the earth; and He's coming back physically. The person of Jesus, not the red letters, is the crux of the story. The righteousness of God is revealed in red on the cross, not in red ink on the page. Even Jesus' vision of peace harks back to the best of Judaism. Chief rabbi of England Jonathan Sacks is right about this: "The prophets of Israel were the first people in history to see peace as an ideal. The Hebrew Scriptures stand as 'the world's first literature of peace.'"[44]

Jesus is God's self-revelation in its fullest form. Not only did He teach, but He was the teaching. The Torah was wisdom for the Jews, but now Wisdom is embodied in Christ. He is the real Torah—a living person. He is the real wisdom—the Logos of God, the living utterance of deity.

JESUS PREACHED THE KINGDOM OF GOD

In the modern era, the attempt was made to rationalize Christianity into a system of belief and worldview—or to turn Christianity into a system of morality with Jesus of Nazareth no more than its original teacher and model of right behavior. The story of Jesus makes both systems indefensible. It is true: Jesus' theological fights with the Pharisees focus most often on issues of purity and holiness. But Jesus taught that the kingdom was not a list of legalisms or a menu of moralisms. Rather, He taught, "the kingdom of God is within you."[45] In essence, the kingdom isn't a code of ethics. Jesus is the embodiment of the kingdom. And after His resurrection, He would indwell His followers.

There is a dismissive dictum that Jesus preached the kingdom of God while the church preached Jesus. What completes the loop without damaging it is the oft-forgotten fact that you can't have a kingdom without a King, and Jesus is the King of kings and Lord of lords. Indeed, the reference is not only to the kingdom of God but also to the kingdom of Christ.[46] As we argued in *Jesus Manifesto*, Jesus is the kingdom incarnate. In fact, the most widely quoted scriptural text in the Second Testament is Psalm 110:1, which points to the cosmic consummation of the salvation story and the restoration of the original temple: "The LORD said to my Lord, 'Sit at My right hand, till I make Your enemies Your footstool.'"[47]

This was the mission of His entire ministry. But for Jesus' peers, a life of holiness, or kingdom living, involved round-the-clock vigilance in keeping oneself separate and uncontaminated from any uncleanliness.

And the "unclean" in Jesus' mind was another word for "in need," which came with a call, not to stay away but to come close. It was in the nature of Jesus to explode boundaries between cultures, sexes, races, divine and human, pure and impure—to exalt the humble and humble the exalted.

Jesus invested most in the least "clean" people of His day. Any Gentile's house was ritually unclean. If a Jew entered the house of a Gentile, cleansing rituals (including a bath) were necessary before a pious Jew could worship God again. Tax collectors were also unclean: "If a tax collector goes inside a house, everything in the house becomes ritually unclean and needs to go through purification rituals."[48]

Jesus could not abide such standoffish, holier-than-thou attitudes, and He flaunted a reckless freedom about hanging out in "unclean" circles. Jesus was invited to a dinner party where members of the order of Pharisees were present. One of them remarked in a smug, self-satisfied fashion, "How pleasant it will be to dine in the kingdom to come." Jesus responded, "Don't be so sure! There'll be surprises."[49] True holiness was an exercise not in hubris but in humility.

In Jesus' day, shepherds had a terrible reputation as unclean and shameful. In rabbinic literature, shepherding was often listed as one of the despised occupations. So for shepherds to be the first to hear the "good news" and the first to visit the Messiah was truly for the "last to be first." The humble were also exalted when Jesus presented positive images of the "least" and "last," including Himself as the Good Shepherd.[50]

> *The central miracle of the gospel is not the raising of Lazarus or the multiplication of the loaves or all the dramatic healing stories taken together. The miracle of the gospel is Christ, risen and glorified, who this very moment tracks us, pursues us, abides in us, and offers Himself to us as companion for the journey!*
>
> —Brennan Manning[51]

Jesus took the holiness code of His day and turned it, like a sock, inside out until it was back in its intended form. After all, for ancient Israel at its best, holiness did not mean the achievement of kept laws; it meant the keeping of a covenantal relationship with God. For Jesus, what was inside was more important than what was outside. A pure heart didn't always mean keeping your hands pure. Sometimes it involved putting your hands in the dirt and grime of humanity. Jesus physically touched the lepers He healed.[52] Purity codes and principles of cleanliness were trumped by relationships and people in need. How many of us are like the one who, graced with the very presence of Jesus reclining at his table, could only see dirty hands?[53]

All of this explains, in large part, why Jesus was so vehemently opposed and frequently run out of town. He loved and embraced "sinners" while declaring that the "righteous" were strangers to the kingdom of God. He ate with the "wrong people" and dismissed the "right people."

BETWEEN THE "ALREADY" AND THE "NOT YET"

Jesus taught that the kingdom had now arrived, and He was the embodiment of it. But we live between the "already" and the "not yet." With Jesus, the future has broken through and is "already" here. But the fullness of fruition is "not yet," requiring our participation for the "already" and the "not yet" to become one. Jesus gave a foretaste of this paradoxical already-but-not-yet kingdom in His healing ministry, an earnest of the *eschaton*, where there will be no more suffering, no more alienation, no more tears. It was said of the Messiah that He would do certain healing functions: giving sight to the blind, cleansing the lepers, and giving other signs of the kingdom breaking in.

Jesus spent His whole ministry doing three things: preaching, teaching, and healing. Of the three, we tend to forget His healing ministry. But in many ways, it was Jesus' most important ministry. All three of His ministries were ministries of signs. He taught in signs. He preached in signs. He healed in signs.

There is one story of the feeding of the five thousand. There is another story of the feeding of the four thousand.[54] Some scholars say they're the same story told differently. We don't think so. When Jesus was talking to His disciples later about the bread of life, He said, "When I fed the five thousand, how many baskets were there left over?" And they said, "Twelve." Jesus continued, "And when I fed the four thousand, how many were there then?" In other words, Jesus was saying, "How many times do I have to do this before you get it or are convinced?"[55]

Jesus healed at least thirty-five people—at least that's the total number of healed people mentioned in all four Gospels. He probably healed hundreds, if not thousands, more. When talking about Jesus the Healer, it is important to distinguish between healing and curing. Jesus never met a disease He couldn't cure. But He didn't promise to cure every disease. Every person Jesus cured eventually died. But, as we mentioned in chapter 10, God always heals. Sometimes death is the final healing act.

JESUS' TEACHING WAS AUDIENCE-SPECIFIC

Third, the greatest communicator who ever lived had a nontraditional communication style. Jesus did not speak as other speakers or as an exegete. He did not present Himself as a footnote to other rabbis (such as, "Rabbi Gamaliel says on the authority of Rabbi Hillel"). He did not engage in "Midrash Pesher" on Hebrew Scripture.[56]

What He is, however, is a storyteller, metaphor maker, and sage[57] who is always ready with a proverb, aphorism, riddle, and other one-liners. Whether the Sermon on the Mount was one cohesive unit delivered on one specific occasion or a Matthew miscellany of Jesus' favorite sayings, the whole "sermon" can be found mostly in Psalms and Proverbs. Whatever form of communication Jesus used, He was audience-specific, highly participatory, and scripturally tethered.

> ***What do you seek?***
>
> —JESUS, TO HIS DISCIPLES[58]

Jesus began with His listeners. For example, Jesus asked the Samaritan woman for a drink. Then He gave her the metaphor of Living Water. Jesus resurrected Lazarus, having announced, "I am the resurrection and the life."[59] More than half the time, Jesus derived His preaching from the people more than He delivered a message. The people set the agenda. Ralph Lewis calls it "Jesus' start-from-scratch, listener-centered attitude."[60]

Jesus didn't preach to a "point," the thing teachers strive to get to eventually. The crux of what He was really saying was seldom a point, sometimes a conceptual truth, but most often a metaphor or story. Jesus "made known" God. Or put differently, Jesus is God made known.[61] The word translated "made known" *(exēgeomai)* traditionally means "to draw out in narrative."[62] Jesus reasoned with people, not through argument and points but through symbols, signs, stories, and sometimes simply silence.[63]

Jesus taught with more than words. He used meals and feasts, walks and signs, questions and conversations as favored ways of enacting biblical stories in a new guise. Jesus is always ready to parry a criticism with a biblical story and reference. For example, when His disciples were criticized for plucking some grain on the Sabbath to eat, He countered with the story of David and company fleeing from Saul and eating the bread that only priests were allowed to eat.[64]

Jesus often asked questions. Jesus was second to none, not even the master questioner Socrates, in asking great questions:

> "Who do people say I am?"[65]
> "What are you doing more than others?"[66]
> "What good will it be for a man if he gains the whole world, yet forfeits his soul?"[67]
> "Why are you thinking these things?"[68]
> "What do you think?"[69]
> "What is written in the Law?"[70]

Jesus does not have Q and A sessions. He has Q and Q sessions.

—TOM HUGHES[74]

One biblical scholar has argued that if you were to meet Jesus on the street, He would be more likely to ask you something than tell you anything.[71] Another scholar notes that 153 of Jesus' questions have been preserved.[72] In fact Jesus was more likely to answer a question with a question than an answer.[73]

But the Gospels are all about affirmations, not queries or even answers to questions. And all the affirmations orbit around one central question: "Who do you say that I am?"[75]

The number one affirmation of the entire Bible is this: Jesus is Lord. Jesus is the Messiah.

TEACHING IN PARABLES

There are two things to keep in mind in any exploration of Jesus' unconventional teaching and preaching methods. First, Jesus was a Jewish preacher, not a Greek preacher. He majored in images and stories, not in ideas, syllogisms, and propositions. But Jesus chose to communicate biculturally: He had to speak to Greco-Roman linear thinkers and to Hebrew nonlinear thinkers. Jesus, Paul, and Peter showed us how to do crosscultural communication. Baptist preacher Carlyle Marney once said that preachers learn to preach in Greek when we ought to learn to preach in Hebrew. By that he meant that Greek is the language of words while Hebrew is the language of images.

Second, a more holistic way of knowing God had always been a hallmark of Hebrew piety. For example, every item of Passover food symbolizes a key feature of the Hebrew story so that to eat one meal is to experience the original Passover once again. In the Sukkoth (which can mean "circle dance" as well as "hut") festival, there is the elevation of one simple fact of life: everything a person does should be connected to God.

But Jesus took this even further until, you might say, every one of His parables is a miracle, every miracle a parable. Jesus' "parables" were designed to give birth to the very thing they were talking about: not matter-of-fact truths, but life-and-death truths.[76] There are about twenty miracles recorded in Matthew, Mark, and Luke. As discussed in chapter 10, John reported seven miracles, each one a "sign" that Jesus is the Messiah and a parable about what His messiahship birthed and put to rest:

1. Jesus turned water into wine—joylessness is dead.
2. Jesus healed a boy long-distance—distance is dead.
3. Jesus healed the lame on the Sabbath—time is dead.
4. Jesus fed the five thousand—hunger and thirst are dead (Jesus is the Bread).

5. Jesus walked on water—laws of nature are dead.
6. Jesus healed the blind—disease is dead.
7. Jesus raised Lazarus from the dead—death is dead.

In Jesus' public ministry, Mark wrote, Jesus never taught without using parables.[77] Jesus Himself said that parables fulfill a prophecy: "I will open My mouth in parables; I will utter things kept secret from the foundation of the world."[78] What did Jesus use to lift the veil of the secrets of the universe? Not philosophical reasoning. Not mathematical formulas. But parabolic storytelling.

In fact, Jesus' parables are part of the secret of the kingdom. Jesus refused to explain His messages. They contained hidden meaning, partly to keep the authorities at bay, partly as a means of winnowing out those who sought the Presence from those who sought presents.[79] Those who got it found new insight and intimacy with Christ. Those who didn't get it found resentful alienation and incomprehension.

Jesus' parables refused to yield up ready meanings to the hearer, even the disciples. Jesus spoke in public through parables. But Jesus conducted private tutorials with the disciples: "when he was alone with his disciples, he explained everything to them."[80] During these seminars, Jesus often asked questions to judge whether or not His followers understood. And vice versa: the disciples asked Him questions and asked for further clarification.[81]

In the Jewish language chain, Hebrew is the language of the Torah and thus "the language of holiness"; Aramaic is the language of the Talmud and thus "the language of explanation." Torah and Talmudic study fostered an inquisitive mind-set. The basic unit of discussion for the Talmud would come to be known as the *sugya*, which focuses not on consensus around and submission to definitive doctrines and laws but on an ongoing conversation (which often sounds like an argument) that is built around questioning the Scriptures and finding new ways to look at stories and practices.

Professor Marc Bregman, distinguished professor of Judaic studies at the University of North Carolina–Greensboro, gave the best description of *sugya* when he wrote that for a really accomplished Talmud scholar,

> a sugya is like a whole symphony and the scholar is like the conductor or even composer. It is said that Mozart and others like him could conceive of a whole symphony, not in the time it takes to play it, but in an instant—the whole complex piece of music completely present in their minds. That's the way the master scholars do Talmud. A sugya is not a linear discussion but a whole organic mechanism that they see working and then analyze where something unusual is going on—like master mechanics.[82]

You can see what would come to be the *sugya* at work with Jesus' tutorials with His disciples, although for Jesus, too, many of the questions of the Pharisees (there was one in rabbinic Judaism about how many stars must be visible before reciting the evening prayer) majored in minors and minored in majors. When the disciples wanted to know the difference between "clean" and "unclean," Jesus answered them, but He also pushed back on their dullheadedness and dimwittedness.[83] Even with all this back-and-forth, there was a lot the disciples still didn't get. "Have you understood all these things?" Jesus asked. "Yes, Lord," they replied, not always with utmost honesty.[84] When Jesus' disciples asked Him why He taught using such a teaching method, He said, "You are permitted to understand the secrets of the Kingdom of Heaven, but others are not. To those who listen to my teaching, more understanding will be given."[86]

> *Have you ever wondered why some of Jesus's stories seem to complicate or even obscure truth rather than clarify or simplify it? Perhaps it's that God, who knows us better than we know ourselves, is not content to speak simply to the rational intelligence, but informs us instead through imagination, intuition, wonder, and epiphany.*
>
> —Luci Shaw[85]

A parable was not a new communications device with Jesus. Plato and Aristotle had used parables as well. Historians have identified some two thousand parables from ancient Jewish sources, the most famous being Nathan's parable of the lamb before King David. Some scholars have even claimed to have found more than thirty-five parables from first-century rabbis.[87]

But no one used parables with more mastery than Jesus. And no one but Jesus used them as the defining mark of His teaching technique. Jesus told between thirty-one and sixty-five parables (depending on who's counting). Scholars can't agree whether some are parables or not.[88] But most will admit that at least one-third of Jesus' teachings are parables. They were His brand signature.

By blood and origin, . . . I am Albanian. My citizenship is Indian. I am a Catholic nun. As to my calling, I belong to the whole world. As to my heart, I belong entirely to the heart of Jesus.

—MOTHER TERESA[89]

The parables of Jesus are not heroic legends or tales of the heavens. They are ordinary stories of ordinary people doing ordinary things, like fishing, farming, tending sheep, and gardening.

This appeal to the common and the use of the common touch is hard for us to appreciate today. One of the most cutting slurs to sling at an academic is, "How common!" The worst thing that can be said of a scholar is that he or she "plays to the galleries." A teacher deemed common is often considered to be inferior and weak. To "play to the galleries" is to use nonlinear methods of persuasion or suprarational attempts to "move" one's audience. We pat ourselves and others on the back for preaching that is standoffishly alien.

In contrast, Jesus prized the common, especially the common people and the common touch. Jesus respected the burble of everyday life, the bauble of everyday things. The Master's touch was the common touch. Jesus' conviction that God has "hidden these things from the wise and learned, and revealed them to little children"[90] was also symbolized in the rending of the curtain. God is no longer guarding the entrance to the garden, symbolized by the cherubim on the ark of the covenant (Tree of Life), for which the entire temple was built in the first place. And the Holy of Holies is no longer reserved for the elite but is available to all. Indeed, Jesus' experience of intimacy with His Father, as evidenced in the use of the familiar kinship term "Abba," is reproducible and available to all, even the "least of these."[91]

In giving us the Lord's Prayer, Jesus built on the *kaddish*, or the "holy prayer." It was not unusual that Jesus called God "Father." Jews often did that in prayer. What is unusual is twofold: first, the oxymoronic "Our Father who art in heaven." You can't get more horizontal, more intimate, more immanent than "Our Father." But as soon as those "near" words are out of our mouths, we are whiplashed in the "far" opposite direction: ". . . who art in heaven." Never forget God is transcendent, vertical, wholly other, above and beyond what we can even comprehend.[92]

Second, Jesus' "Abba" appellation is based on an intimate relationship with God as Father and with the understanding that we are the sons and daughters of this Father God. In the First Testament, the primary metaphor for God is "King." This image wins out over all other contenders, hands down. Only rarely is God addressed as "Father."[93] In the preaching and teaching of Jesus, however, God as Father replaces God as King, which almost drops out entirely.[94] At the heart of Jesus' understanding of the kingdom was a divine Father, not a divine despot—a loving and trustworthy "Abba," or "Daddy." Before Jesus, "Father" was a term of respect when used of God. After Jesus, "Father" was a term of relationship and intimacy when used of God.

In medieval German villages, a person was designated to go around the houses to awaken people to come to the synagogue service in the morning. This person was called the *beadle*, or more popularly, the *knocker-up*. The beadle would first give one knock, then two, then another one, standing for the letters *alef* and *bet*, one and two, and hence forming the word *abba* ("father"), as if to say: "Rise up to serve Father." Every prayer is a knocker-up to awaken us to a deeper relationship with God.

JESUS BRINGS LIFE AND JOY

Any study of the concepts of delight and joy in the Bible gives an overall picture of rejoicing and laughter in the here and now, as well as in heaven beyond. Indeed, the reuniting of God's people with Him is likened to a bride and groom, joyfully celebrating their wedding.[95]

Jesus didn't perform a wedding, but He did turn water into wine. Jesus wouldn't turn stones into bread for Himself, but He did turn water into wine for friends. In fact, it is not surprising that the first miracle of the Jesus who said, "I am the vine," should be turning water into wine. For that's what every true vine does—turn water into wine.

It did not happen by chance that the miracle Jesus chose to launch His ministry was not to raise the dead or heal the sick but to bring life to a party.[96] The "sign" of wine at the wedding of Cana was a sign of Jesus' entire ministry—a ministry of pouring out, where He Himself would become body and blood, bread and wine for a hungry humanity, and there would never be a short supply—only an overabundance. In addition, the first plague in Exodus was water turned to blood. And the last plague was the death of the firstborn. Jesus' first sign in John was water turned to wine, and His climactic preresurrection sign—the raising of Lazarus from the dead—was His last sign in John.[97]

> *He who made wine that day at the marriage feast . . . does this every year in vines. . . . But we do not wonder at the latter because it happens every year: it has lost its marvelousness by its constant reoccurrence.*
>
> —Augustine[98]

Cana was six miles north of Nazareth. Jesus' mother, Mary, seems to be more than a guest in the story. She knew what was happening to the wine before the host, the groom, and the emcee. The servants followed her instructions. Perhaps Mary was related to the bride and groom, lending credence to a tradition that says the groom was John, the writer of the story, one of Jesus' closest disciples, and that Mary and John's mother were sisters (making Jesus and John cousins).

It was a serious offense to run out of wine, so much so that some guests sued their hosts when they didn't receive the hospitality they believed they were due. We are told that Jesus filled six stone jars, each one of which held twenty to thirty gallons.[99] That's enough wine to render more than one thousand guests unfit to drive home.

Over and over again, Jesus connected His kingdom proclamation to eating and drinking. Feasting at the table was both thanksgiving for the past and celebration of the promise of the future. For Jesus, it was truth with teeth that mattered. Eating is a mundane, normal part of life. Yet Jesus talked about it. A lot. Whenever Jesus ate, it was a sign that He desired to invade even the mundane aspects of our lives. Our love for Him—our intimacy with Him—extends to all that we are and all that we do. Even eating can become an act of worship. We glorify God in how we eat and in how we respond to what others cook for us.

What Jesus' mother said to the servants at Cana may be the best capstone to Jesus' teaching and preaching: "Whatever He says to you, do it."[100] Mary's words would later be divinely reinforced and echoed from the heavens as the transfigured Jesus' true identity was revealed in His face, which "shone" as if on fire, and in the divine voice that spoke from the epiphanic cloud, a cloud long missing from the temple but present with Jesus: "Hear Him!"[101]

Listening to Jesus is listening to God.

CHAPTER 12

The Human Jesus

So if I am asked, "Do you believe in the divinity of Christ?" I answer, "Yes, otherwise how could he have been so wonderfully human?" And if I am asked, "Do you believe in the humanity of Christ?" I answer, "Yes, otherwise how could he have been so profoundly oriented toward God?"

—CANADIAN THEOLOGIAN DOUGLAS JOHN HALL[1]

PEOPLE OUTSIDE THE CHRISTIAN TRADITION SPEND THEIR TIME arguing the divinity of Christ. People inside the Christian tradition spend their time arguing the humanity of Christ.

One of the least famous but most revealing thoughts of Albert Einstein is this: the truest sign of intelligence is not knowledge but imagination.[2] What was Jesus' imagination like?

THE IMAGINATION OF JESUS

As far as we have been able to tell, there has been no book written on the imagination of Jesus. Only a few authors have even asked the question of what kind of imaginative life Jesus displayed.[3] The most striking and obvious feature of Jesus' imaginal life is that He did not have the imagination of merely a carpenter or an artisan who worked only with tools. He showed a skill with stone stories and metaphors, which one would expect of a mason or master builder. He used a carpentry metaphor only once, along with a stab at humor: "Don't criticize the speck of sawdust in someone else's eye, when their own eye has a plank stuck in it."[4] But even this was a rabbinic saying that circulated widely in rabbinic culture.[5]

What seemed to really arouse Jesus' imagination was nature. You might even say He had the imagination of a gardener. He drew many of His stories from the natural world—from the birds in the sky, the flowers in the field, the planting of the soil. Rembrandt made this explicit in his 1638 painting *Christ and St. Mary Magdalene at the Tomb*, where Jesus is portrayed holding a spade and wearing a gardener's hat. When Jesus told us to pay attention to the "lilies of the field,"[6] He could have been referring to any and all kinds of wildflowers that grow in the meadows of Galilee or in the wheat fields. Or He could have been thinking specifically of the purple anemone, which echoes the royal purple of Solomon. The one thing He definitely was not thinking of was our trumpet-fragrant Easter lilies.

> *The Shema means that you have to love God intellectually ("with all thy heart"), emotionally ("with all thy soul") and practically ("with all thy might").*
>
> —Mordecai Kaplan, at age ninety, after a lifetime of studying Judaism[7]

We will speak elsewhere in this book of Jesus' mastery of metaphor, His facility with language, and His ability to reach multiple audiences at the same time. But all of Jesus' imagination seemed dedicated to one end: bringing the Word of God to people in new and imaginative ways that would connect to their lives and lead them into right relationships with their Creator and creation.

THE EMOTIONS OF JESUS

There is another arena of Jesus' life in which many Christians have been woefully disinterested—His emotional life. As far as I know, there has been no portrayal of the dynamics of the emotional life of Jesus. We have only presupposed His psychological reality through a cognitive lens. Yet if there is one thing we have learned from thirty years of leadership literature, it is this: a greater predictor of success than IQ (intelligence quotient) is EQ (emotional quotient). Rudolf Bultmann argued that we can know very little about the personality or preferences of Jesus.[8] That is true in terms of what was His favorite color, when He felt most rejected and dejected, what was His preferred food, or whether He was enchanted by whimsy, laughed loudly, or pined for moody skies.

> *Great faith requires a great sense of humor.*
>
> —John H. Armstrong[9]

But we do know more than we think we know about Jesus' personality—including what landscapes ravished His soul, what emotions nurtured His spirit, and the nature of His prayer life, including His favorite places and ways to pray. Even though the chiaroscuro may be obscure, Jesus often proclaimed emotional truths and bared His primary-color emotions. In contrast to the Stoics, who argued that a true sage and philosopher would not countenance emotions, Jesus was not afraid to bare His.

❧

Jesus expressed human characteristics as widely diverse as exhaustion—so wiped out He slept through a storm[10]—stress,[11] hunger,[12] compassion,[13] and grief,[14] to name an obvious few. He was not afraid to show His feelings, and He painted life with a full palette of emotions.[15] Jesus declined anything that would diminish His full experience of human hurt and suffering. Myrrh, a reddish sap harvested from Commiphora bushes, was used medicinally to reduce pain when mixed with wine. Jesus refused it on the cross.[16]

JESUS' SENSE OF HUMOR

The only feature of Jesus' emotional life that has been even slightly studied is His laughter. Even then the discipline of historical context has been largely missing. Some of Jesus' utterances were obvious guffaws—such as, "It is easier for a camel to go through the eye of a needle than for a rich man to enter the kingdom of God."[17] People would have snickered when Jesus said, "When you do a charitable deed, do not sound a trumpet before you."[18] In other words, "Don't toot your own horn." His slams on the scribes and Pharisees would have drawn a lot of laughter—except from the scribes and Pharisees![19] It would not surprise us if Jesus laughed by day with His disciples but wept at night with God.

> *Humor is not a mood but a way of looking at the world.*
>
> —Ludwig Wittgenstein[20]

Most characteristically, however, Jesus' humor was subtle, sophisticated, and sensitive to His context. "Enter into the joy of your lord" is an invitation to lightness and laughter.[21] For laughter to be real, there must be faith in a framework of providence and purpose. The more you trust in God, the more comedy is possible. That's why the Great Come-Down (incarnation) birthed the Great Comedian (the Incarnate One). The promises of the Beatitudes, for example, are that those who mourn or weep will be comforted and able to laugh. Nietzsche was right about satan: "serious, thorough, profound, solemn . . . the spirit of gravity—through him all things fall."[22] Jesus was the spirit of lightness through whom all things rise and hold together.

Jesus was criticized for many things. He enjoyed life a little too much—that was one rap on Him. Joy is the hallmark and heart of a Jesus-spirituality. There is the joy that comes from submission to the will of God, a kind of transcendental joy. Then there is the joy of the Lord, which is the strength of everyday life. Jesus and His disciples were not known for fasting, even though they did. They were known for feastings and rejoicings, especially alongside those with whom others refused to eat and rejoice.

The Pharisee school of Shammai, the reigning school of Judaism in Jesus' day, despised Gentiles and registered disgust even at the sight of one. Gentile converts to Judaism were shunned by the Shammaites, since only Jews could be beloved by God. Part of the "Eighteen Measures," the eighteen *gezerot* passed by the Sanhedrin to clarify Jewish-Gentile relationships, was that you couldn't even enter the house of a Gentile, much less purchase or take food from him or any other of the "ignorant masses."[23] Disgust is arguably the most virulent of human emotions, which is why every warring party plays this emotional card and imputes to the enemy disease, wretchedness, and filth, wreaking havoc on the souls of everyone. Jesus taught His disciples to be disgust-free. Where the religious establishment looked for ways to give the coup de grâce (death blow) to outcasts and sinners, Jesus looked to give the same people the coup de *grace* (touch and turn of mercy).

Jesus, the master Torah teacher and linguist, was also a master punster. Jesus loved to play with words in ways that elude us because of the language barrier. It is virtually impossible to translate into English the Hebrew puns and wordplay that you find in Isaiah 21:2 (a series of puns), or Genesis 3:20 (a simple wordplay that is missed in English): "And Adam called his wife's name Eve [*hawway*], because she was the mother of all living [*hay*]." As we saw in chapter 3, the Bible virtually begins with a pun in some of its earliest words, the micro creation account of Genesis 2:7: "And the LORD God formed man [*adam*] of the dust of the ground [*adamah*]."

In talking about hypocrites putting on a sad face, Jesus used a word that means "hide." Hypocrites hide their real faces behind the mask of sad expressions. In other words, hypocrites "hide to be seen." When Jesus was accusing the Pharisees of straining out a gnat but swallowing a camel (an impure animal), He was punning on the Aramaic words *galma* ("gnat") and *gamla* ("camel"). Jesus even founded the church on a pun in Matthew 16:18 (NIV): "I tell you that you are Peter [*Petras*], and on this

> *If life is really so formless that you cannot make head or tail of it, you cannot pull its tail; and you certainly cannot make it stand on its head.*
>
> —G. K. Chesterton[24]

rock [*petra*] I will build my church." For a church founded on a pun, the liturgical celebration of a "Holy Humor Sunday" or "Bright Sunday" seems especially fitting.

There is an ancient practice for the Sunday after Easter, or "low Sunday," to be a celebration of the joke God played on sin and death by raising Jesus from the dead. The choirs sing silly songs; the members dress weirdly; the preacher becomes a stand-up comic. There is so much playfulness, levity, and gospel joy in the Jesus movement that it makes it extremely difficult to be a real Jesus follower without a sense of humor.

MORE THAN "MEEK AND MILD"

Someone once said that Christianity is a mild-mannered religion preached by mild-mannered men who are trying to get others to be more mild-mannered. But the Gospels give us numerous glimpses into Jesus that cause us to question the portrayal of "gentle Jesus, meek and mild."[25]

We are told that Jesus is never harsh, yet consider His scathing rebukes to the Pharisees.[26] We are told that Jesus is never angry, let alone violent. Yet He made a whip of cords, overturned tables, and created a small riot in the temple.[27] We are told that Jesus is never impatient, and He never gets frustrated. But such a portrait of Christ doesn't square with the Gospels.[28] Yes, Jesus was tolerant to some but not to all.

The Gospels make abundantly clear that there are conflicting yet complementary aspects to His personality. As we have argued, Jesus always comes in surround sound. He is a man of sorrows and joys. He is blunt and strong, uttering stern commands and orders.[29] Yet at the same time, He is gracious, meek, and lowly of heart.[30] He is famous for eating and drinking,[31] especially with sinners.[32] Yet He speaks openly about a sin that cannot be forgiven.[33] He warns of the unspeakable consequences of misguiding children of faith[34] and speaks forthrightly about God's sobering judgment.[35] Yet He is easy to approach.

Jesus expresses anger. He weeps. He rejoices. He experiences sorrow and anguish. He sings. He is passionate. He is quiet. He preached a child-friendly faith. After all, Jesus was once a child, He said that the kingdom of God belongs to children, and children loved to be around Him.

We can also be sure that Jesus laughed—and contrary to the way most Hollywood films have depicted Him, Jesus had a sense of humor and razor-sharp wit. Because we don't understand ancient Hebrew culture, this is often missed. For instance, as we have seen, His remark that the Pharisees swallow camels but strain at gnats is a classic example of ancient wit and irony.[36] His remarks about casting pearls before swine, wiping the dust off your feet, and harlots entering the kingdom before the religious were jokes that jabbed.[37]

Irony, which Jesus often employed, is not sarcasm. Sarcasm, which means "to tear flesh," is designed to harm. Jesus' irony is marked by subtle insight and paradox, leading to comic self-discovery. His discourse in Matthew 6 about those who start a parade when they give alms and looking dismal when they fast—and His comical punch line in verses 2 and 5, "They have their reward"—is an example of such irony.

Jesus' conversation regarding John the Baptist in Luke 7:24–35 is full of irony and light teasing. Other examples of His humor abound.[38] When Jesus compared Herod to a fox,[39] He was not indicating a dislike of vulpines: "fox" is feminine in Greek. As we discussed in chapter 8, in His dialogue with the Canaanite woman, He even responded positively to her wit.[40]

The Gospels are clear that Jesus called forth the fury and bitter opposition of the religious authorities of His day. This was because He was perceived as a threat to the old order. But in the midst of such opposition, Jesus was a master at turning the tables on His opponents by using humor and paradox. Their reaction to this tactic is interesting. They marveled. They were silent. They dared not ask Him any more questions.[41] In all things, Jesus shows us what God is like, for He is the human face of God. Thus, humor and wit, as well as sorrow and agony, are in the heart of the Creator.

One of Jesus' greatest excitements in life was worship. He Himself admitted that He couldn't wait to worship with His disciples: "I have been very eager to eat this Passover meal with you."[42] Passover was a festive celebration. There was the singing of the four psalms called the "Great Hallel," which was supposed to "raise the roof" at the Passover feast.[43] It is hard to imagine Jesus and His disciples celebrating this freedom festival without singing and dancing, especially since dancing was a regular part of worship in ancient Israel.[44]

Jesus was no dry-eyed, "no-crying-He-makes" Messiah. Two times in the Bible, we are told that Jesus cried: once over a person, the other over a place.[45] The person was Lazarus, whom some believe was Jesus' best friend and one of three people He raised from the dead. The place was Jerusalem, a zip code Jesus knew well and loved enough to cry over it.

Lazarus was from Bethany. The small town of Bethany, nestled in the eastern slope of the Mount of Olives and two miles away from Jerusalem,[46] was a hideaway and haven for Jesus. It's where His best friend, Lazarus, lived along with Mary and Martha, and where Jesus was always welcome. It is probably where Jesus stayed when He went to Jerusalem at least three times a year for the pilgrimage feasts of Passover, Pentecost (the Feast of Weeks), and the Feast of Tabernacles. And it is where He spent the last week of His life. Bethany was supremely dear to the heart of Jesus.[47]

Jerusalem is where Jesus experienced His greatest rejection. Jesus gave us a sacrament of failure.[48] When people fail to receive you or take you seriously, Jesus said, shake the dust off your feet and move on. Jesus Himself had to take this sacrament in the towns of Chorazin and Bethsaida,[49] not to mention His hometown of Nazareth.

Then there was Jerusalem, the city Jesus loved enough to cry over but the city celebrated for being a "prophet killer." In one of the most memorable phrases of the Bible, Jesus "set His face to go to Jerusalem"[50] as He prepared to take the sacrament He could not escape. The people of Nineveh allegedly listened to the prophet Jonah, but that was unusual. Most cities didn't listen to their prophets, as Jesus must have pondered when He wept over the city.[51]

WHAT MAKES JESUS ANGRY?

Since Jesus was human "in every way that we are, except without sin,"[52] it is not surprising that He showed anger.[53] His anger never ran wild, however; and anger danger was never an issue with Him. But Jesus often got angry at His disciples, especially Peter. He got angry with the Pharisees. Jesus got angry with the priests and publicans of the temple. It is very revealing what ticked Jesus off. Of course, we are encoded beings, and human nature is *not* the same in all ages. If Jesus exhibited the seven basic facial expressions that correspond to seven basic emotions recognized by people from all cultures,[54] the emotion ascribed to that face would depend on the broader context in which it occurred. What sparks anger in particular can differ radically from one age to another.

The range of Jesus' ire is impressive. For example, within a very short period of time in Jesus' life, three things made Him see red, and each one reveals something important about the essence of the gospel.

Jesus' Anger at Unfruitfulness

The first anger episode occurred when Jesus was on His way to Jerusalem, and He was hungry. Off in the distance, He saw a fig tree, lush with leaves. That usually meant the tree bore figs, so Jesus walked up to the fig tree to feed off its bounty. Whether the tree was in season or out of season is debated, but when the Messiah beckons, we are to be "ready in season and out of season."[55] But this fig tree, lush with leaves, was barren of fruit. In other words, it had been hoarding all its resources for itself. Its mission had become to look good more than to feed a hungry world and a hungry Messiah. Jesus was so angry at the non–fruit-bearing tree that He cursed it.[56] After all, Jesus was on His way to the harvest festival (Feast of Sukkoth), which celebrates a messianic inauguration of a time of peace and prosperity when "everyone shall sit under his vine and under his fig tree."[57]

When God said, "Be fruitful and multiply,"[58] the Lord was only calling us to reflect God's nature. God is fruitful and multiplies. The fertility of the universe is amazing. The universe contains one hundred billion galaxies, each of which contains one hundred billion stars of incredible uniqueness and diversity.[59] When God commanded the first Adam to till and tend the garden and to "conserve and conceive,"[60] God was giving humans their prime directive. We were put here not to consume but to conceive. Jesus confronted a culture of consumption, reflected in that fruitless and unreproductive fig tree, with a culture of conception. "Every good tree bears good fruit, but a bad tree bears bad fruit," Jesus said.[61] Here was a tree that bore no fruit. "You will know them by their fruits. Do men gather grapes from thornbushes or figs from thistles?"[62] Jesus said things are most reliably known for what they are by examining their fruit. Jesus called His disciples to be more than faithful—He called them to be fruitful. Jesus wants to taste our fruit. The fruit of a tree is that tree come to consciousness. The fruit of a human life is that human coming to God consciousness. When there is nothing to taste, there is no consciousness in that life. And this does not make Jesus happy.

Jesus' Anger at Those Who Damage Children

If you want to really make Jesus mad, however, so mad that He could sound more like the Mafia than the Messiah, then damage a child. A wifeless and childless Jesus was the biggest patron and protector of children: "If you harm one of these little ones, better for you that a millstone be draped around your neck and you be dropped into the depths of the sea."[63] Or in the secret language of Omertà, "Better you sleep with the fish."

> *Many things are made holy by being turned upside down.*
>
> —G. K. Chesterton[64]

It is hard for us to imagine how low on the social scale children stood during Jesus' day. The ancient hierarchy of reverence, with father first, mother second, and child always last, was flipped on its head with Jesus and the Holy Family, where the story revolved around the child, then the mother, and the father somewhere to be found if you looked hard enough.

What made Jesus turn the social hierarchy upside down and place children at the pinnacle? Maybe it was Jesus' haunting realization that before He would die for us, a lot of children (firstborn sons) died for Him in

Herod's slaughter of the innocents.[65] Or maybe Jesus' tenderness toward those for whom culture had no room stemmed from His sensitivity to being born when there was no room for His mother to give birth to Him. In the parable of the good Samaritan,[66] there is a surprise ending based precisely on these lines. The innkeeper makes room for the distressed traveler and gives Him intensive care. Jesus knew from His mother's stories what it meant for people in need to have no place and no advocate.

When the disciples debated who among them was the greatest, Jesus took a page out of Isaiah 11:6 ("And a little child shall lead them") by plopping a little one in their midst and saying that the greatest reality was in front of them.[67] Jesus was not denying ambitions for greatness. He didn't rebuke the disciples for wanting to be "the best." But He reframed the nature of greatness and "the best" in terms of little ones' capacity to love, to live out of love, and to humble themselves out of graciousness. You want to aspire to true greatness, to being best? Then make yourself small. Become a "little one." The maximum is found in the minimum.[68]

Followers of Jesus are all "little ones." Childhood is not something you grow out of but grow into. "There will be no grown-ups in heaven" might be the best translation of Jesus' words in Matthew 19:14.[69] But even more than showcasing a child (not some adult scholar or soldier or priest or businessman) as His model disciple, Jesus made a child the primary metaphor for following Him and for holiness. The greatest gift of Jesus was the "right to become children of God."[70]

Jesus' Anger at Self-Righteous Judgmentalism

The third anger episode that makes Jesus' inner life less mysterious to us is His "temple tantrum." As He drove out the money changers from the spaces normally dedicated to prayer for Gentiles as well as Jews, overturning their tables and ATMs, He cried out the words of Isaiah: "My house shall be called a house of prayer for all nations."[71]

What is "My house"? The "house" is God's temple, and in the Hebrew tradition the temple and the garden are different ways of talking about the same reality. For Jesus, the "house" is the same, but the definition of the *temple* is more precise: the temple of the church, the body of Christ, and the temple of the person, as in "your body is the temple of the Holy Spirit."[72] Two of the most shocking events in the Second Testament, Jesus and the money changers and Peter and the money cheaters, are both cleansing rituals. When Jesus said, "Destroy this temple, and in three days I will raise it up,"[73] He was telegraphing the upcoming transition from the temple as a place, to the temple as a people. And just as there was a temple cleansing just before the closing of the placed temple, there was a temple cleansing (Ananias and Sapphira) just after the opening of the peopled temple.[74]

Something else made Jesus absolutely livid and was perhaps His greatest irritant: *self-righteous judgmentalism*. Survey those to whom Jesus directed His strongest, most severe words. It was the self-righteous, judgmental Pharisees and Sadducees—those who didn't see themselves as sinners but who leveled that charge against everyone else. He characterized such people as "blind guides," "hypocrites," "fools," "whitewashed tombs," a "brood of vipers," and children of the devil.[75] Not exactly kind words from a mild-mannered Messiah.

And to whom did Jesus show the most compassion? People who were involved in immorality of all types, such as prostitutes, adulterers, tax collectors, and thieves. It's easy for us today to acknowledge that Jesus treated the self-righteous more severely than the "real sinners" without applying this standard to our own context—or to ourselves.

> *I want to know this Jesus, though he scares me a little.*
>
> —John Eldredge[77]

But "Jesus Christ is the same yesterday, today, and forever."[76] What He deemed to be the severest of all sins (self-righteousness) is what many contemporary Christians view as a mere misdemeanor. And the sorts of sins toward which Jesus had great compassion and patience are what many Christians place at the top of the totem pole of "serious sins," deeming them to be felonies. Don't be deceived: the "odious complacency of the self-consciously pious" is what infuriated our Lord the most.[78] Philip Yancey was dead-on when he said that some Christians get very angry toward other Christians who sin differently than they do.[79]

JESUS' PRAYER LIFE

Prayer is breath, the breath that brings life to the temple and the breath that connects us to the God who created all temples. God breathed into a duvet of dust and the first temple, the first Adam, came to life. The last Adam, Jesus the Christ, breathed on the disciples, and a new temple, the church, was born. When the heartbeat of the church is something other than being a praying and inclusive church (whether it be missional, organic, seeker-sensitive, purpose-driven, or any number of good things), it arouses Jesus' ire.

Prayer was Jesus' most important spiritual practice. It appears that Jesus' custom was to lift up His eyes to heaven when He prayed.[80] As with all pious Jews, He may have prayed three times a day this psalm: "O Lord, open my lips, and my mouth shall show forth Your praise."[81] Sometimes Jesus may have sung His prayers, as His mother did when she sang a prayer of praise, known as the Magnificat, upon meeting her cousin Elizabeth in the land of Judah.[82] Jesus probably heard His mother sing this prayer song to Him throughout His growing up: "My soul magnifies the Lord . . . Princes he has dethroned and the poor he has uplifted."[83] Prayer songs may have often been on Jesus' lips: for example, at the end of His final meal, He and His disciples sang a song.[84] One of the psalms of Israel, a song, was on Jesus' lips when He died.[85]

Jesus made sure His disciples, then and now, knew they were at the receiving end of His prayers: "But I have prayed for you, that your faith should not fail."[86] What does it mean to be at the receiving end of a Jesus prayer? Ask Peter. He was at the receiving end of that just-cited prayer of Jesus. But you and I, as disciples of Jesus, are also at the receiving end of Jesus' prayers. Jesus is praying to the Father for us—for you, for me.[87] We tend to ask, "How should I pray?" We don't ask, "How should I receive prayer?" Yet we are here today because Jesus has prayed for us. And someone, somewhere, has been praying for you. This moment, right now, someone, somewhere is praying for you.

Jesus' major method of negotiating crises was prayer. In the morning, He was up early—"a long while before daylight"—to go to a "solitary place" to pray.[88] At end of the day, He would seek a quiet place to pray.[89] Sometimes when He went to prayer at dusk (late and light), Jesus spent the whole night in solitary prayer with His Father. His signs and wonders were often done through prayer, and sometimes only possible through prayer.[90] The disciples were so struck by Jesus' prayer life that they asked Him to teach them to pray as He did (hence the "Lord's Prayer" in Luke 11:1–4). Jesus was transfigured while in the act of prayer, which was in the presence of some of His disciples.[91] In crisis moments, Jesus prayed for strength and for discernment. Sometimes Jesus even fell on the ground and prayed. On the night of His betrayal and arrest, Jesus asked His disciples to keep watch and pray: three times He prayed, and each time He returned and found His disciples asleep.[92]

> ***I will lift up mine eyes unto the mountains: From whence shall my help come?***
>
> —A Song of Ascents[94]

Jesus made coming apart to pray a liturgy of life. It has been said He was always "coming apart" so He didn't "come apart."[93] But going off to a deserted place for some peace and solitude is different from isolation and aloneness. Jesus sought solitary communion with God, which was an expression of solidarity with the Creator and all creation, not isolation from God and the world.

JESUS' FOUR PRAYER LANDSCAPES

Jesus turned to the natural world as a source of ministration and inspiration. To delve deeper into His relationship with his Father, He conducted sacred pilgrimages to four landscapes of creation. His spirit soared toward heights, heat, water, and garden. Each prayer landscape provided a healing balm to the four broken relationships of human existence created by the first Adam's disobedience: mountains and God-awareness, deserts and self-awareness, water and others-awareness, and gardens and creation-awareness. The pulls of summit, wilderness, seascape, and garden were almost irresistible to Jesus' prayer life. The contrasting vistas of mountain, desert, water, and garden were some of Jesus' prime spiritual resources.

- Mountains are places of joy, revelation, awe, ecstasy.
- Deserts are places of spiritual discipline, introspection, inner struggle, insight.
- Waters are places of relationship, power, peace, connection, trust, nourishment.
- Gardens are places of wholeness, the presence of God, fulfillment, awareness, hope, growth, thriving, fruit.

Mountains: God-Awareness

The mountains are God's greatest architectural achievements, a temple not made with hands but where one can meet God firsthand if not face-to-face. Mountainness means a bond and bridge between earth and sky. You enter another world when you climb the world of the mountains and breathe the pure oxygen. That is why asceticism doesn't work in the mountains and woodlands.

Unlike the ancient Hebrew prophets, who regarded mountains as almost frightful places capable of settlement only by YHWH and assorted demons, Jesus loved the mountains. In the gospel of Matthew, Jesus made five treks up mountains, one for each book of the Torah, each mountain pilgrimage leading to a transformation: the bookend stories of the temptation[95] and transfiguration;[97] the Sermon on the Mount;[98] the feeding;[99] and the

We climb the mountain of revelation that we may gain a view of the shadowed valley in which we dwell and from the valley we look up again to the mountain. Each arduous journey brings new understanding, but also new wonder and surprise. This mountain is not one we climbed once upon a time; it is a well-known peak we never wholly know, which must be climbed again in every generation, on every new day.

—H. Richard Niebuhr[96]

commissioning.[100] Treks up mountains are steps up paths of purification and paradise.[101]

What has been called the "mountain effect" heals the soul in a couple of ways. First, it gives you humility. When you climb to the top of the mountain, you arrive only to see a host of other mountain peaks that invite climbing. The higher the mountain you climb, the more peaks you find.

But the mountains also have the opposite effect: a mountain gives you the confidence that comes from meaning and mission. Mountains are vistas of enlightenment, where you freshen your vision of the world with a godlike ability to "look down" and look farther.[102] And in looking down and looking farther, one looks deeper into oneself and God.

The climax of the book of Job is God speaking from the whirlwind, asking Job, "Who are you to inquire after meaning?" or "Where were you when I created the mountains?"[103] The mountains teach us that the quest for meaning falls short. Our mission in life is not so much to understand the "whys" of existence or suffering or death, but to live the mystery of existence and suffering and death and to please God.

Water: Others-Awareness

Jesus loved the lakeshore, so much so that He made Capernaum, a midsized fishing village on the border of a trading hub called the *Via Maris* (Latin for the "Way of the Sea"), His mission headquarters.[104] After the first miracle at Cana, the next place Jesus went, and the starting point for His preaching/teaching/healing mission, was the small fishing port of Capernaum, nestled on the west shore of the Sea of Galilee.[105] Some have even called Capernaum "the most important place in the history of Christianity," even the "cradle of Christianity."[106]

The Sea of Galilee was also known as Lake Tiberias or, since it was shaped like a harp, the Lake of Kinneret. It was thirteen miles long and eight miles wide. The fishing town of Capernaum, Jesus' base of operations, was also a bustling border town on an international trade route. Capernaum provided key access to the Jordan Valley, Jericho, and Jerusalem.

Of course, there were other reasons for Jesus' selection of mission central. Maybe as many as half of His disciples came from Capernaum or its nearby sister city of Bethsaida.[107] Most likely, Jesus stayed at the house of Simon and Andrew and their family when He was there, although there are some scholars who think Jesus may have had a house in Capernaum Himself.[108] It was always dangerous to have Jesus as a house guest. You entertained the possibility of getting your roof ripped off.[109]

But the biggest reason? Jesus' boyhood home of Nazareth was a day's walk away (about twenty miles). Seven hundred years earlier, Isaiah had prophesied about the coming Messiah: "The land of Zebulun and Naphtali [two of the twelve tribes of Israel located in Galilee] will be humbled, but there will be a time in the future when Galilee of the Gentiles, which lies along the road that runs between the Jordan and the sea, will be filled with glory. The people who walk in darkness will see a great light."[110] Nazareth was situated inside Zebulun's territory. Capernaum rested within Naphtali's borders. In one big respect, both Nazareth and Capernaum were alike: they gave Jesus a mixed reception.[111]

You go to the mountain to make a decision and to face the future with humble confidence. You go to the water for strength and recovery, especially from surmounting setbacks. Where Jesus liked to pray alone on the mountain or in the desert when He was facing a special trial or decision, He used the seashore to keep Him emotionally afloat and to nourish the human in His humanity.

> ***Jesus is the Word with God, the flesh with us, and the Word made flesh between us.***
>
> —Augustine[112]

While recovery of strength and healing are the primary gifts of the water, what has been called the "island effect" also teaches humility. The bigger an island gets, the bigger its shoreline becomes and the greater its exposure to the vast ocean beyond. The greater the amount of knowledge you accumulate, the bigger your island gets, but the greater the shoreline of the unknown becomes. In short, the more you know, the more you know you *don't* know.

Jesus didn't say, "You shall know the truth, and the truth shall make you know-it-alls." He said, "Learn from Me, for I am gentle and lowly in heart."[113] In every story He told, Jesus showcased His meek and humble heart, His salt-of-the-earth qualities. Jesus didn't use the language of the priests or the prophets or the intellectuals of His day (even though He was one). He used the language of the common people and told common stories. He didn't tell celebrity stories or treatises filled with theological jargon—only stories about sheep, grapes, stones, seeds, and weeds. Jesus was never so preoccupied with being the Messiah that He didn't see the littlest and least.

> *Though he was rich,*
> *yet for your sakes*
> *he became poor,*
> *so that by his*
> *poverty he could*
> *make you rich.*
>
> —The apostle Paul[114]

Interestingly, the Scriptures signal the possibility that demons do not like water. Jesus said that when a demon is cast out, it walks through "dry places," seeking rest.[115] When Jesus cast out a legion of demons, He cast the pigs that were housing them into water.[116] John the Revelator received his sublime revelation of Jesus Christ on the island of Patmos, a small spot of land surrounded by water.[117]

Water, the baptismal symbol of covenant, is the great connector and amplifier of human relationships. It is no accident that Jesus taught evangelism in the form of fishing lessons and faith in the form of sleeping in a storm.

Desert: Self-Awareness

The desert is the place where you go to find yourself . . . and to find something in yourself.

Jesus, the Son of God, knew a double *kenosis*, a double "emptying."[118] Once in the incarnation. Once on the cross. In the first *kenosis* Jesus came down, all the way down, even down to the point of washing His disciples' feet, which was as far down as any rabbi had ever gone in the history of Judaism.

In the second *kenosis*, on the cross, Jesus refused to come down.

He refused to come down from the cross, and on the crossbeams Jesus united us vertically to His Father and horizontally to one another and the world.

Jesus refused to come down from the deserts of pain, suffering, rejection, abandonment, and failure. He "humbled Himself . . . to the point of death," on a cross.[119]

Even after you find the right and righteous path, you will trip along the way. And sometimes you trip and fall to the point where you need to start over. We also need to learn how to start over, not replicate past success. Humility is needed to continually start over fresh. We need a proper humility about ourselves. We need a proper humility about each other. We need a proper humility about God. We need a proper humility about holy things: "We hold these truths in earthen vessels."[120]

> ***Behold, I establish My covenant with you and with your descendants after you, and with every living creature that is with you: the birds, the cattle, and every beast of the earth with you, of all that go out of the ark, every beast of the earth.***
>
> —God to Noah[121]

When you are starting afresh or starting over, you need the desert. The desert teaches humility: it is harsh, is barren, and covers a large part (one-fifth) of our planet. It also covers a large part of our souls.

When the Bible says Jesus sought a "deserted place," the phrase is sometimes used as a metaphor for the relational places of silence and solitude. But sometimes it means an actual desert, a wilderness.[122] In the story of the temptation of Jesus, the Greek word for "desert" is *heremon*, which can mean either a quiet place, a place apart, or a place in the Negev. The Judean desert is less like the Sahara desert and more like the South Dakota badlands, or the surface of Mars.

The most dangerous time in a person's life is when riding the crest of a wave. After He was baptized, Jesus went up into the desert, where He fasted for forty days and then was tempted by satan. He was with the wild animals, and angels attended Him.

Deserts impose asceticisms like fasting, and desert conditions enforce the rigors and restraints of solitude. Austerity is unique to the desert, affording the chance to wipe the slate clean and strip away the unnecessary. Deserts clarify (no waste of words, actions, or energy in the desert), purify (exposing our sins and detoxifying our souls), and sanctify (enabling us to be "called again" by God beyond the dark and doubt).

You sit and wait in the desert. Hence the frequent cries of "How long, O Lord?" The desert exposes as much as it is exposed.

Garden: Creation-Awareness

In the garden we are reminded, in the words of the psalmist, "Let everything that has breath praise the LORD."[123] Every living creature on the sea, on the land, and in the air God called "good,"[124] and God showed how "good" they were when saving them along with humans from the Flood.[125] The prophets used the metaphor of marriage to convey God's covenant with us, a covenant that extends not just to humans but to all of creation.[126] God gave specific instructions for the care of animals in the laws of Moses.[127] The animals participate with human beings in praising God[128] and are included in descriptions of the new heaven and the new earth.[129]

> ***If Israel behaved worthily, the Messiah would come in the clouds of heaven;***
> ***if otherwise, humbly riding on a donkey.***
>
> —TALMUDIC COMMENTARY ON DANIEL 7:13[130]

At every major juncture in the Jesus story, creation showed up—not just in His parables but at decisive moments in His mission. Jesus was born where livestock sheltered for the night. As if the baptismal appearance of a Noahlike dove showing God's pleasure weren't enough to contradict the famous Ogden Nash doggerel that "there is nothing in any religion, that forces us to love the pigeon,"[131] Jesus Himself likened the Spirit to a descending dove.[132] After His temptation in the wilderness, Jesus was ministered to by wild animals.[133] He is called the Lion of Judah as well as the Lamb of God.[134] In a world of wolves, Jesus taught His disciples to be "wise as serpents and harmless as doves"[135] while He reminded them of God's love for the sparrows of Jerusalem.[136] For His triumphal entry into Jerusalem, Jesus rode a young colt; not wanting to separate it from its mother, he brought her along.[137] A favorite etching on Christian gravestones has been "The Lord hath need of him," words originally spoken about an ass.[138] Jesus justified the law being broken to save animals in trouble,[139] and He picked up a rope used to tether one of the animals to flail over His head when He freed the caged animals and birds in the temple courtyard.[140]

As the heavens were awakened and split asunder at Jesus' baptism, so the earth awakened and split asunder at His crucifixion. All of creation, human and nonhuman, awaits the redemption of the body and will be delivered from corruption.[141]

CHAPTER 13

Jesus' Trial and Crucifixion

> *The cross is the greatest event in the history of salvation, greater even than the resurrection. The cross is the victory, the resurrection, the triumph; but the victory is more important than the triumph, although the latter necessarily follows from it. The resurrection is the public display of the victory, the triumph of the Crucified One. But the victory itself is complete. "It is finished" (John 19:30).*
>
> —Erich Sauer[1]

Jesus was crucified and buried in a garden. The garden of Golgotha was an old quarry that had been recycled into a garden.[2] But before the garden of Golgotha, where He was crucified, there was the Garden of Gethsemane, where Jesus underwent His greatest crisis of faith.

> [Jesus] went out with his disciples across the Kidron valley to a place where there was a garden, which he and his disciples entered.[3]

THE GARDEN OF GETHSEMANE

The garden entered by Jesus and His disciples was an "olive yard" called Gethsemane, a place where Jesus had often spent the night when He didn't avail Himself of the comforts of Bethany while visiting Jerusalem.[4]

Gethsemane was Jesus' most trying time:

> He took Peter, James and John along with him, and he began to be deeply distressed and troubled. "My soul is overwhelmed with sorrow to the point of death," he said to them.[5]

In this olive grove Jesus experienced the greatest agony of His life, recorded in Matthew 26:39: "My Father, if it is possible, let this cup pass from Me." Jesus communed with God but received no reply. "Abba, Father, for You all things are possible; remove this cup from Me." It was a request that received no response. But Jesus entered that silence and was obedient unto death, even death on a cross. Jesus emerged from Gethsemane's crisis of faith able to sum up His life: "Nevertheless not My will, but Yours, be done."[6]

In this episode, we discover the collision of two wills: the will of the human Jesus and the will of God the Father. In the end, as was His usual course, Jesus submitted His will to the will of His Father.[7]

The inner conflict of "Godforsakenness," and whether to climb down from the cross or bear the cross, did not take place in Golgotha but in Gethsemane. The degree of trauma involved in this crisis of faith is revealed in one tiny detail: Jesus sweat blood. This is called *hematidrosis*, a condition where the body pushes back on itself and protests its certain future.

Hematidrosis leaves the body extremely weak, dehydrated, and with skin so tissue-thin and tender that even a touching of the skin is excruciating. This makes almost unimaginable Jesus' searing anguish from the tearing and damage to the skin from repeated beatings, scourgings, and the crown of thorns.

In the "olive press" of Gethsemane, Jesus uttered these immortal words to His Father: "Father, if it is Your will, take this cup away from

Me; nevertheless not My will, but Yours, be done."[8] The cup has meaningful imagery throughout the First Testament. Scripture speaks of the cup of divine blessing and fellowship[9] and also the cup of divine wrath and judgment.[10]

Jesus, having the full favor of God, drank from the cup of God's blessing. We, who deserved death and judgment, were on course to drink the cup of divine wrath and judgment. In Gethsemane, Jesus Christ decided once and for all to do the unexpected. *He decided to switch cups with us!* At Gethsemane, Jesus resolved to drink the cup of wrath and judgment, which we deserved.[11] In turn, He would grant us the cup of blessing and fellowship, which we did not deserve.[12]

> ***Wherever the good news is proclaimed in the whole world, what she has done will be told in remembrance of her.***
>
> —JESUS[13]

The tragedy of the world began in a garden.[14] Jesus was betrayed by a kiss in a garden, sending Him to His death.[15] But the good news is that He was also resurrected in a garden, undoing both wrongs. Even so, in a world of pain, Gethsemane and the cross that followed show us that God is not immune to it. The olive grove called the Garden of Gethsemane is where the Savior of the world was trodden like green olives in an oil press, and from which there flows an ever-inexhaustible supply of healing, anointing, and blessing.

IN REMEMBRANCE OF HER

How do you remember Jesus? When you tell the "good news" of the gospel, what do you recall most vividly about the story of the Messiah? What message did Jesus want us to remember most about the story of His life and death?

Jesus connected His story to a woman's story to the point that He issued this injunction: "Whenever you remember Me, remember her." Jesus instructed us to eat a meal that included bread and wine "in remembrance of Me," and He also instructed us to tell a certain woman's contribution to His story in remembrance of her.[16]

Note exactly what Jesus did and did not say. He did not say, "When you tell the gospel story, remember Peter." Not, "When you tell the gospel story, remember John." Not, "When you tell the gospel story, remember James." But, "Remember *Me*—and you must not forget her."

Why did Jesus say that? Why did Jesus want a woman remembered for her act of faith wherever the gospel is proclaimed? What did she do that was so special to warrant the intermingling of His story and her story?[17]

The answer to these questions will take us through the whole Good Friday story. The answer also gives us a window into why the darkest day of Jesus' story reveals the brightest day of history.

Before we begin to explore why Jesus said what He did, we must first get a clear image of Calvary. Golgotha, Aramaic for "the Skull," was a place of infamy. And this was when "infamy" was not equated with celebrity. Golgotha was a small hill just outside the walls of ancient Jerusalem, near a well-traveled highway.[18] Everyone equated the name Golgotha with the termination zone for the wickedest and the worst, as judged by Roman law and society. In the Jewish mind, to be hung on a tree was to be cursed by God: "For anyone who is hung is cursed in the sight of God."[19]

When Jesus was crucified at Golgotha, He was one of three criminals executed that day. On either side of Him were two "bandits," or "criminals" (the same Greek word used earlier for Barabbas) sentenced to death for their crimes. It is a grievous theological mistake to leave out those two criminals from the Good Friday story. In fact, Karl Barth insisted that it was the height of theological incorrectness to portray Jesus on the cross by Himself, in pictures or in words, since it does violence to the story in which three criminals were crucified that day: one good and two bad, one of whom became good.[20] Jesus did not die alone. He died in company with others—two thieves (known extrabiblically as Dismas and Gestas), one of whom (Dismas) confessed his sins and became Jesus' first follower in heaven: "Today you will be with Me in Paradise."[21]

You might even say with Karl Barth that here was the first Christian community: three people, one good and two bad, one of whom became good. You could even say further that here was the first Christian "church": three people, one good and two bad, one of whom became good.[22]

The three crosses of Golgotha challenge every church. You call yourself "church"? Show me the bad people. If you are not living in company with bad people, what right do you have to call yourself church? Jesus died as He lived: in the company of "bad people." In fact, the gospel has been summarized as "Jesus ate good food with bad people." We live and die together, good and bad. And we never give up on anyone, no matter how bad. In fact, on the cross Jesus Himself converted only 50 percent, even when the "bad people" were in their dying moments. How much better do you think you can do?

Jesus was seen as one of those "bad people" by the establishment of His day. When Jesus was brought before Pilate by members of the Sanhedrin, Jesus first was accused of inciting civil unrest by urging people not to pay their taxes. He then was accused of proclaiming Himself "Christ [or Messiah], a king."[23] It was Pilate who restructured the accusers' testimony into his own question: "Are You the King of the Jews?" Jesus' response was enigmatic, an affirmation not of His identity but of the accuracy of Pilate's words: "You are saying it."[24]

Pilate finally crumpled under the pressure from the three-pronged demand for Jesus' blood: (1) from the Sanhedrin, (2) from Herod, and (3) from the mob. But he never veered from his original perception of Jesus as something other than one of those bad people. Pilate knew the accusations against Jesus were groundless. He knew the verdict of death was an injustice. And while the gruesome sentence was being carried out, Pilate managed to assert the truth about Jesus' identity as he knew it: "This is Jesus, the King of the Jews."

Pilate answered his own question of Jesus—"What is truth?"—in what would later become Christianity's first sermon and first creed.[25] In fact, Pilate was so confident of his answer that he had it translated into Greek, the language of trade and commerce; Latin, the lingua franca of the day; and Hebrew. Pilate put up a billboard announcing the truth in Hebrew to the Jews who condemned Jesus, the truth in Latin to the Roman authorities who sentenced Jesus, the truth in Greek to the learned citizens who demanded Jesus' blood. In other words, Pilate's answer to the question "What is truth?" was a global message preached multilingually that told the truth about the Truth: "THIS IS JESUS THE KING OF THE JEWS."[26]

No hand-washing ritual could sluice the truth from Pilate's heart.[27] The sign declaring the truth about Jesus inflamed the crowds.[28] Christianity's first sermon got a harsh review. The Jewish authorities complained about its message, chastising Pilate for writing it. Pilate's retort was as enigmatic as Jesus' own defense before His accusers: "What I have written, I have written."[29]

THE THIRD THIEF

Both Pilate and his critics were right: Jesus is King of kings and Lord of lords.

But the Romans were right too. There were three criminals on Golgotha that day. Jesus was as much a thief as those robbers on His left and His right.

Jesus was the Third Thief on Golgotha. The first two thieves stole money and objects from households. Jesus was a different kind of thief. The Third Thief, the one Pilate trumpeted as King of the Jews, pulled off the greatest heist in history . . . right in front of their eyes.

This Third Thief had a long criminal record. Jesus had already "robbed" the woman at the well, a woman with five husbands, of her shame and guilt. He had already robbed the cursed and ostracized lepers of their disease and disenfranchisement. Jesus had robbed the lame, the sick, and the poor of their disgraced places on the fringe, their dishonored seats at the table. He robbed two blind men of their muteness, and in giving them voice to praise, He gave them vision to see. Jesus had already robbed a crowd of five thousand of their complaints and self-pity, and He filled their bodies and souls with good things.

But Jesus, the greatest robber in history, pulled off still a greater caper. You might call it the "great soul robbery."

Jesus often contrasted the sanctimonious, self-righteous Pharisees and the contrite, confessing sinners (such as tax collectors and prostitutes).

He robbed all the smug, proud, and pious of their self-sufficiency. Self-reliance hung helpless on the cross with Jesus. Only God's grace and mercy can redeem our past and redream our future.

That was the Third Thief's most audacious theft. Through His sacrifice on the cross, in His descent into death and hell, Jesus showed just how weak self-sufficiency really was. And conversely He showed just how powerful dependency on God could be. Jesus, crucified among thieves, performed His greatest robbery after His execution. Jesus robbed satan of his power over sin and death. Jesus robbed death itself of its victory. Jesus ripped off the grave and stung the sting of death's futility and finality. The Third Thief on Golgotha committed His greatest robbery after He was cut down and buried. He robbed death of its power when He rose again to new life.

The most important decision every human being ever makes is this: Will you give Jesus the license to steal? Jesus wants to steal your heart. The story of Calvary asks each of us: In whom will you ultimately put your trust? Will you trust only in yourself—your powers, your strength, your goodness? Or will you give Jesus the license to steal? Will you confess that you are, at your most basic level of self, a sinner in need of God's mercy and utterly dependent on God's goodness?[30]

The Third Thief on the cross wants to rob every day . . .

the arrogant of their self-sufficiency;
the selfish of their self-centeredness;
the contented of their complacency;
the humorless of their solemnity;
the untouchables of their invulnerability;
the sick of their disease and doubts about the future;
the atheists of their skepticism;
the control freaks of their fears and obsessions.

But what is the biggest heist Jesus wants to commit on a daily basis? Jesus wants to rob satan of his power over you and to rob the grave of sin and death. To paraphrase an old gospel song that went global shortly after it was written in 1855, "What a thief we have in Jesus, all our sins and griefs to steal!" That Third Thief stole our grief and our sins and our hurts and our sorrows and all the things He bore on that cross. And as we shall soon see, He replaced them with, of all things, a song.

That's what it means that the Prince of Peace came bringing a sword. Jesus disturbs our peace before He distributes His peace, the peace that passes all understanding.[31]

JESUS' ACTIONS ON THE CROSS

We have mistakenly reduced Jesus' six hours on the cross to His "seven last words."[32] This formulation of Jesus' dying moments is really nothing more than a guesswork montage of Jesus' actions on the cross as presented variously from the four Gospels. But Jesus' time on the cross resists such neat, facile organization.

Jesus' first act on the cross was to preach forgiveness—"Father, forgive them, for they do not know what they do."[33] As thief of sin and death, Jesus removes impediments to healing, reconciliation, and life. Jesus not only forgave those who killed Him but also made excuses for them.[34] We aren't expected to make excuses for those who are hurting us. But we can at least forgive them, which Jesus made explicit in His first act following His resurrection. He commissioned His disciples to preach forgiveness: "Receive the Holy Spirit. If you forgive the sins of any, they are forgiven them; if you retain the sins of any, they are retained."[36] Henri Nouwen calls forgiveness "the well at the center of God's village."[37] At the heart of a godly life in the Jesus story is this grace of forgiveness.

> *The discoverer of the role of forgiveness in the realm of human history was Jesus of Nazareth.*
>
> —Hannah Arendt[35]

Jesus' next acts on the cross revolve around reconciling brokenness. As a thief in the night, Jesus removes the shackles that bind us down and instead binds up the broken pieces of our lives into wholeness and forms us anew. Even before the resurrection, Jesus was birthing and conceiving new life. At the moment He was in His body repairing and redeeming the four broken universals of human existence—our relationship with God, with ourselves, with each other, and with creation—Jesus also set about repairing and redeeming the particular brokenness that existed between His birth family and His disciples. Notice the change in terms: Jesus did not call Mary "Mother." He said, "Woman, behold your son!" Then to John the Beloved, "Behold your mother!"[38]

It is a major peephole into Jesus' first thirty years that He did not appear to choose anyone from that time to be a part of His team. Almost all of His disciples seem to have been chosen after Jesus' encounter with John the Baptist. None from Nazareth. Either Jesus did not confide in any friend the nature of His identity and mission and lived a life of sacred solitude, or that friend died before Jesus began His public ministry. You can sense Jesus' problems with His family, not only in His antifamily statements[39] but in what happened to Him when He returned home to Nazareth with His disciples. People in His hometown refused to recognize Jesus for who He was, and they even deemed His claims crazy, prompting some to want to conduct an honor killing to protect the reputation of the town.

Whether Mary and the apostle John wanted to be together or not, Jesus gave them to each other as family. And the feud between Jesus' two families was reconciled in that moment when John agreed to take care of Jesus' mother as his own and join her family, and Mary agreed to receive John as one of her own. Just as the first Adam's side was split and a bride was conceived, so the last Adam's side was split and a bride was conceived—the church, which was birthed when Jesus breathed on His disciples and came fully alive when the dove of the Holy Spirit descended at Pentecost.[40]

In the last hours of Jesus' life, He remembered a whole and healed body of Christ, reversing sin, misconceptions, preconceptions, and wrong perceptions, and initiating new life, a new order, and new perspectives. The "remembering" of the unknown woman who anointed Jesus before His death is a reversal that we still struggle with today. The in-remembrance-of-her story inaugurates the Triduum, which in Latin means "three days"—the Great Three Days or Three Holy Days of Maundy Thursday, Good Friday, and Holy Saturday, including Easter Vigil. The Triduum is regarded by many to be the holiest time of the Christian year. The story inaugurates Mark's account of the last hours of Jesus' life. For Mark, Jesus' Passion began with the story of the anointing woman and her deed of deep love and devotion. The Passion narratives in Mark that detail the last few days of Jesus' life feature one of the last kindnesses Jesus received while on this earth.

To give this story and the anointing woman the attention Jesus said they deserve, we have to keep some things in mind.

First, whenever Jesus was under stress or trying to discern God's will for Him, He headed for the hills, the water, or the desert. Unlike Freudian psychotherapy, which advises people in distress to go inward, Jesus went outward to go inward. Depending on where His soul was situated, Jesus advanced to three landscapes of the sacred: the mountains, the desert, or the water. In fact, the entire gospel of Mark is in many ways structured around these advances of Jesus.

Second, Mark loved reversals almost as much as he loved retreats. In a reversal of ancient storytelling, women are key to the Jesus story in Mark—from the healing of Simon's mother-in-law[41] to the appearance of the divine messenger, all the way to the three women at the very end of the gospel. The Passion story begins with a woman anointing Jesus' body, a woman who is presented as a model disciple. The Passion story ends with more women anointing Jesus' dead body for burial.[42]

A STUNNING REVERSAL—JESUS ANOINTED BY A WOMAN

One of the gospel's biggest reversals is stories of wonderful women and villainous men. Mark 14 is even framed by two sets of stories contrasting holy women and evil men. Men of rank and privilege conspire against Jesus and attack Him. Anonymous women and powerless others espouse Him, embrace Him, and care for Him. In contrast to the faithful women, there are a faithless Peter and the fearful Twelve. This anonymous woman is loyal; one among the innermost core of disciples is disloyal.[43]

There is another reversal deserving mention and attention. Have you ever noticed where this story took place? Jesus was reclining at the table with His own people "at the house of Simon the leper."[44] The religious establishment objected to Jesus' table manners. He ate with social outcasts and sinners. Once again, Jesus was found in the house of "Simon the leper," against the official banning of anyone with the disease of leprosy from worship in the temple and full participation in the community of Israel.[45]

> ***Ointment and perfume delight the heart.***
>
> —Proverb[46]

Picture the scene. The disciples were reclining on the floor, probably on mats, around a low table, eating from a common bowl, dipping chunks of bread into olive oil. Suddenly a woman crashed their party and crashed on Jesus' head a flask of perfume. She broke the expensive vial (or "snapped off the neck," meaning she used the entire flask) and poured out all the costly ointment. The magic of spikenard,[47] the pleasure of this perfume, is made clear in this simple phrase: "And the house was filled with the fragrance of the perfume."[48]

Given spikenard's high price tag, the reaction of Jesus' disciples to the alabaster jar being broken over Jesus' head is understandable: they were irate at Jesus and indignant with the woman.

Here was a woman who broke into the company of men, not carrying food from the kitchen, which was a woman's rightful place, but carrying the most expensive perfume of the ancient world. Here was a woman who took it upon herself to anoint Jesus during the meal—not before it.

It was the disciples' last straw.

Jesus had said, "Let the children come." So the disciples learned to share meals with children.

Jesus said, "Let the poor come." So the disciples learned to share meals with the least and the lowest.

Jesus had said, "Let the disabled come." So the disciples learned to share meals even with lepers.

But to let the woman come, to entertain the whim of this woman who disturbed their meal and mocked their frugality, was too much for the disciples. What was she thinking? What made her believe that the person of Jesus was more important than any principle of justice or practice of charity?

Here was a woman who believed Jesus, whereas the disciples didn't. On three prior occasions, Jesus tried to teach His disciples that there would be trouble ahead, even suffering and death. Each time, the Twelve dismissed His warnings and proved so clueless that they got into a squabble over the power structure of the church (who is going to sit at Jesus' right hand and His left?[49]).

Here was a woman who got what Jesus was saying when He called us to live incarnationally in the midst of pain, in the midst of poverty.

Here was a woman who knew she was living not in *chronos* time ("the poor you have with you always") but in *kairos* time ("Me you do not have always").[50] In a fallen world, there will always be the pains of life. Injustice, disease, prejudice, and despair we will always have with us. Opportunity to deal with issues of poverty will always be present. Not until God's kingdom comes will we have a perfect world with no social and economic disparity.

Here was a woman who understood that what is appropriate at one time and place may not be appropriate at another time and place. Jesus calls us to respond to the challenges of our day in ways that are appropriate to the time we are given. The right moment for doing certain things passes quickly. We must not miss our moment.

Here was the incarnate God in their midst in the flesh. Incarnations are fleeting. Can we not laugh and love, eat and dance, in the midst of the pain?

Here was a woman who, in the midst of plots by eight chief priests, empty promises from twelve chief disciples, guile and malice on the part of the scribes, and the betrayal of one key confidant, threw confidence to the wind, emptied her heart and voided her savings, and allowed herself to become a fool for love.

Any wonder the disciples were so mad? Any wonder, when Jesus rebuked the disciples, saying, "Let her alone . . . Why do you make trouble for her?" they almost lost it? One did lose it. Judas became so mad when Jesus defended this woman that he went out and betrayed Jesus. Judas traded in his silver-lined clouds about Jesus for thirty pieces of silver.[51]

"Messiah" literally means "Anointed One." There were diverse, even conflicting understandings and ideas of messiahship. But one thing was sure: when someone said "the Anointed One" in first-century Judaism, he or she was referring to the King of the Jews, whom God would raise up at the end of times. By pouring this perfume over Jesus' head, this unnamed woman was symbolically proclaiming Him to be the Messiah, the Anointed One of God.

Jesus was anointed Messiah, not by kings and potentates but by an unnamed woman. The anointing of Jesus as King was performed by a woman in the house of a leper (a Pharisee in Luke's account). Jesus was anointed Messiah, not in the Holy City but outside Jerusalem, in a place called Bethany. Jesus was anointed Messiah, not in the temple on Mount Zion but in a house, even the house of a leper. An unnamed woman branded Jesus as the Messiah—with spikenard.[53]

> *She did it so liberally and profusely that "the house was filled with the odour of the ointment." She did it under the influence of a heart full of love and gratitude. She thought nothing too great and good to bestow on the Savior. Sitting at His feet in days gone by, and hearing His words, she had found peace for her conscience, and pardon for her sins . . . Having freely received, she freely gave.*
>
> —J.C. Ryle[52]

At birth the mechanism of the nose is capable of detecting and identifying ten thousand different scents. The odor receptors of the nose are more sophisticated and complex than either the eye or ear. How much of this sensory capacity have we developed? Or how many of us are functionally "anosmic," functioning without a sense of smell? Some people are born anosmic; some people develop anosmia (often from head injuries)—people such as Ben Cohen, cofounder of Ben & Jerry's Homemade, Inc., which is why he says his ice cream has so many tactile and other sensory characteristics. Some people drill into anosmic states of being by repressing their senses of smell.

Of all our sense organs, the nose is the one that connects fastest to the brain. There is an immediate link between nose and brain. Odor information works on the brain directly, unlike the indirect route taken by auditory and visual. Olfactory neurons, unlike other nerve cells, regenerate. Each person has an odor-print that is as characteristic as a thumbprint or voiceprint.

> *Preaching without spiritual aroma is like a rose without fragrance. We can only get the perfume by getting more of Christ.*
>
> —A. B. Simpson[54]

How do sperm wend their way toward an egg? Smell.

How does an infant find its mother's nipple? Smell.

How does a mother pick out her newborn from other newborns? Smell.

How does a boy or girl pick out another boy or girl to date? Smell.

The psalmist said that God can smell a proud person from a long way away: "The proud He knows from afar."[55] Isaiah said explicitly that there is a stench to a proud person.[56] Different spirits have different smells. If you can smell in someone the aroma of arrogance and pride, what about the aroma of humility and obedience?

THE AROMA OF THE ALTAR

The ancient Hebrews believed they could smell God's presence in the incense. That's why an altar of incense was placed in front of the veil, and priests offered incense night and morning in the sacrifice of a lamb.[57]

We know two things about this least developed but most mysterious of all our senses. First, fragrances affect our moods. The sense of smell is wired in the brain to our emotions. Scientific research has demonstrated the power of smell or environmental fragrance to affect mental states. Things that smell good just may be good for you.

Second, the sense of smell is a trigger of memory. In fact, smell is the most powerful releaser of memory. The science of "olfactory-evoked recall" is the study of the ability of scents to transport people to pleasant faces and places. Smells are the presences that create absences. Smell chalk, and most people will recall schoolday memories. One whiff and an entire episode in one's past is brought back to mind. Whatever our pet smell, huge histories of time are relived within the microseconds of a sniff. Nothing can bring back a time, a place, or an emotion better than an aroma.

> *There is no*
> *odor so bad*
> *as that which arises*
> *from goodness tainted.*
>
> —HENRY DAVID THOREAU[58]

"Ivory Palaces" is an old gospel hymn that chronicles how Jesus came "out of the ivory palaces; into this world of woe."[59] Jesus left the smells of pearly gates, jasper walls, and streets of gold, for the smells of planet Earth.

Jesus entered this world smelling what? Barnyard smells of straw, stable dung, and smelly shepherds.

Jesus left this world smelling what? Perfume.

Ancient Israelites didn't take baths every day. They washed their hands frequently before every meal, but they washed their bodies even less frequently than the Egyptians did. In Jesus' day, wealthy Jewish aristocrats living in upper Jerusalem had in their houses baths for purification, called *mikvaot*. But Jesus' sense of purity and His reading of the Torah differed radically from those members of the Jerusalem establishment.

In short, the smell stayed with Him.

THE CRUELTY OF CRUCIFIXION

We tend to forget that crucifixion was the ultimate form of torture. The science of exquisite torture has never been equaled, much less exceeded, than in crucifixion. The crucifixion of Jesus of Nazareth was no exception. Crucifixion was more than an ugliness blotted out by Easter, more than a speed bump on the road to resurrection.

Part of the cruelty of crucifixion was the emotional as well as physical torture. Yes, Jesus' physical agonies were beyond imagining. But the emotional agonies were even worse—the humiliation of being stripped naked, with all bodily parts and functions exposed for the humiliating gaze of the public; the mixture of blood and sweat and urine and feces and refuse creating a nauseating stench, the smells of death that kept even the families of the crucified at a distance.

But what cut even deeper were the emotional agonies of Jesus' spirit. The Bible unabashedly testifies to Jesus' sense of total abandonment, defeat, rejection, and betrayal. In many ways, this was where Jesus was really crucified in spirit. Not on the cross but in the kiss. The cross crucified Him in body. The kiss crucified Him in soul. He was truly despised and rejected, a man of sorrows, acquainted with grief.

Jesus was really betrayed twice, first by the kiss of Judas, then by something that cut even deeper: the kiss-off of Peter. The disciple who stuck with Jesus the longest after Jesus' arrest, when accosted by a servant girl in the courtyard of the high priest, denied he knew Him. Before the barnyard cock crowed, the second betrayal took place.

Of Jesus' closest friends, one denied Him, all betrayed Him, and, save John, all ran away.

Now do you know why Jesus said to remember "her" (the woman who anointed His head with fragrant ointment)?

In the praetorium at Pilate's residence, the soldiers dressed Jesus in royal clothes, like some play doll. They draped over Him a scarlet robe, stuck a reed in His hands to mock a scepter, and then used that instrument to bludgeon Jesus on the head.

They beat Jesus' head with their hands, fracturing His nasal bones. They took turns spitting into the contusions of his blindfolded face and knelt before Him and taunted, "Hail, King of the Jews." Then they crushed onto His head that crown of thorns.

With blood, spit, and sweat running down His face, Jesus looked around.

Where were His disciples?

Where were all His faithful followers?

Where were all those whom He had healed?

Where were all those whose eyes He had opened, whose ears He had unstopped, whose mouths He had opened, whose limbs He had restored?

It was almost more than He could bear.

Then Jesus smelled the perfume . . . and He remembered the woman with the hemorrhage of twelve years who'd had the faith to reach out and touch the hem of His garment and be healed.

Jesus kept on.

And when the soldiers beat Him with a whip until the blood ran down His back like a waterfall, His skin already supersensitive from the effects of hematidrosis (sweating blood); when they marched Him 650 yards through the streets and made Him climb the Via Dolorosa, carrying the 150-pound patibulum on which His wrists were later to be nailed, reducing Him to a beast of burden being led to the slaughterhouse; and when the weight of the cross produced contusions on the right shoulder and back on that three-hour walk through the city of Jerusalem to Golgotha on the Way of the Cross—Jesus smelled the perfume.

And when He fell, causing more unnamed injuries; when He looked around for His most intimate friends, His disciples, and saw none but the four women and John at a distance; and when the agony was almost too much to bear—He smelled the perfume.

And He remembered the twelve-year-old daughter of Jairus, whom everyone thought was dead but whom God healed when He spoke these words: "Get up, My child."

Jesus kept on.

And when they stripped Him naked[60] and nailed Him to the crosspiece He had carried; when they took those six-inch spikes and lacerated the median nerves in His hands and feet; and when they lifted Him up on that cross, above the sinking garbage heap called Golgotha—Jesus smelled the perfume.

And He remembered the Syrophoenician woman and her daughter and the Galilean official and his son.

He kept on.

And when everyone who passed by mocked Him on the cross; when the chief priests and scribes, even those thieves who were crucified with

Him, taunted and teased Him in His agony; and when the loneliness became so severe He was about ready to call ten thousand angels to rescue Him, Jesus looked around. In the haze of hurt, He barely could make out the figures of the three Marys—His mother, Mary; His aunt Mary (wife of Cleopas); and Mary Magdalene—and then He smelled the perfume.

And He remembered the many children brought to Him by their mothers, children who jumped into His arms and lapped up His stories.

Jesus kept on.

And when His body, already in shock, hung from the wrists; and when He struggled for breath to chant two of His favorite psalms (31 and 22), unable to expel even small hiccups of sound without straightening His knees and raising Himself on the fulcrum of His nailed feet, the only thing the soldiers offered His parched throat ("I thirst!") so He could keep singing was a drink of vinegar, which only made singing more difficult. And when His crucifiers used Him for entertainment ("Let's see if He can call down the angels") and when He searched the landscape for signs of love and faithfulness and saw He was abandoned by virtually everyone He ever loved, leading Him to cry a prayer for His disciples as well as for those who crucified Him[61]—then Jesus smelled the perfume.

And He remembered the woman who had given all she had so He would remember God's love for Him, and in that smell He could even detect the odors that reminded Him that He was going home, from whence He had come.

He kept on.

The cross was the only footbridge that could get us across the chasm of sin into the true Promised Land. And that perfume kept Jesus on the cross.

The greatest honor a person can give anyone is to tell his or her story. Here was someone who "did what she could" (literally, "She used what she had"). She gave all that she had.

Love.

Now we know why Jesus said, "When you remember Me, remember her."

SONGS OF THE CROSS

There was one more activity of Jesus on the cross that went far beyond words. We have images of Jesus doing almost everything we do in worship—praying, preaching, teaching, and healing. But can you come up with an image of Jesus singing?

There are a couple of occasions where the Bible says clearly that Jesus sang. The first explicit reference was on Maundy Thursday, before Jesus and His disciples headed out into the darkness: "When they had sung a hymn, they went out to the Mount of Olives."[62] They sang the Hallel psalms (113–118), hymns that were (and are) standard fare on the first and last nights of Passover. Jesus would have sung these hymns His whole life. But we are reminded definitively by His disciples that Jesus sang at the Last Supper. At this "first Mass," Jesus even sang about His mother: "I am Your servant, the son of Your maidservant."[63]

The second time Jesus sang was on the cross. We have missed this song for many reasons, not the least of which is our acute versitis.[64] In fact, we have separated Jesus' final words ("My God, My God, why have You forsaken Me?" "I thirst!" "It is finished!") into separate phrases, but they are really parts of one song, the greatest song ever sung in the history of the world.

We have heard the cry of "My God, My God, why have You forsaken Me?" as a despairing scream from the depths of divine abandonment. Our secret shame is that we find it strangely consoling that Jesus said this since it makes us feel less special when we're feeling abandoned by God and alone in our anguish.

But the real story is very different.

First of all, these words—"My God, My God, why have You forsaken Me?"—are not Jesus' own words. They are famous as the opening line of Psalm 22.

Second, the Psalms are a hymnbook. They were meant to be chanted, not stated. In fact, a good Jew always sang the Psalms, never just spoke them. And they often came bundled. Psalms 22, 23, and 24 are examples of such a package. They are the "two mountains and a valley" song, with Psalm 22, the Psalm of the Cross, a song of tribulation and triumph; and Psalm 24, the Psalm of the Crown, a song of jubilation and exultation. Between these two great mountain peaks of human experience is the more famous rod-and-staff Psalm of the Valley.

Third, the question is not whether Jesus sang this Psalm of Tribulation and Triumph from the cross, but rather, how much of the psalm did Jesus sing? Even if He only lined out the first few stanzas, Jesus functionally sang the whole song in the same way we would be inviting others to inhabit the whole power of the song "Amazing Grace" if we only lined out the first few words. In times of trouble and uncertainty, we hum or sing. On the cross, Jesus sang Psalm 22.

It is the greatest song ever sung in the history of the world. And it behooves us to listen carefully to all the stanzas, because while Psalm 22 begins as a climb up the mountain of tribulation, it ends with a cheer and a view from the mountaintop of triumph.

My God, My God, why have You forsaken Me?
Why are You so far from helping Me,
And from the words of My groaning?
O My God, I cry in the daytime, but You do not hear;
And in the night season, and am not silent.

But You are holy,
Enthroned in the praises of Israel.
Our fathers trusted in You;
They trusted, and You delivered them.
They cried to You, and were delivered;
They trusted in You, and were not ashamed.

But I am a worm, and no man;
A reproach of men, and despised by the people.
All those who see Me ridicule Me;
They shoot out the lip, they shake the head, saying,
"He trusted in the LORD, let Him rescue Him;
Let Him deliver Him, since He delights in Him!"

But You are He who took Me out of the womb;
You made Me trust while on My mother's breasts.
I was cast upon You from birth.
From My mother's womb
You have been My God.
Be not far from Me,
For trouble is near;
For there is none to help.

Many bulls have surrounded Me;
Strong bulls of Bashan have encircled Me.
They gape at Me with their mouths,
Like a raging and roaring lion.

I am poured out like water,
And all My bones are out of joint;
My heart is like wax;
It has melted within Me.
My strength is dried up like a potsherd,
And My tongue clings to My jaws;
You have brought Me to the dust of death.

For dogs have surrounded Me;
The congregation of the wicked has enclosed Me.
They pierced My hands and My feet;
I can count all My bones.
They look and stare at Me.
They divide My garments among them,
And for My clothing they cast lots.

But You, O LORD, do not be far from Me;
O My Strength, hasten to help Me!
Deliver Me from the sword,
My precious life from the power of the dog.

Save Me from the lion's mouth
And from the horns of the wild oxen!

You have answered Me.

I will declare Your name to My brethren;
In the midst of the assembly I will praise You.
You who fear the LORD, praise Him!
All you descendants of Jacob, glorify Him,
And fear Him, all you offspring of Israel!
For He has not despised nor abhorred the affliction of the afflicted;
Nor has He hidden His face from Him;
But when He cried to Him, He heard.

My praise shall be of You in the great assembly;
I will pay My vows before those who fear Him.
The poor shall eat and be satisfied;
Those who seek Him will praise the LORD.
Let your heart live forever!

All the ends of the world
Shall remember and turn to the LORD,
And all the families of the nations
Shall worship before You.
For the kingdom is the LORD's,
And He rules over the nations.

All the prosperous of the earth
Shall eat and worship;
All those who go down to the dust
Shall bow before Him,
Even he who cannot keep himself alive.

A posterity shall serve Him.
It will be recounted of the Lord to the next generation,

They will come and declare His righteousness to a people who
will be born,
That He has done this.

Now do you know why we call it the greatest song ever sung? As the Roman "soldiers nailed him to the cross,"[65] Jesus was singing the fulfillment of biblical prophecy and transcending His tribulation and torture with a musical commentary on what everyone was doing. Once again, Jesus got there before everyone else, even at the point of His own death. Whether Jesus sang only Psalm 22 or sang different psalms that incorporated other features of His crucifixion,[66] He was connecting the dots for His disciples and for anyone else with ears to hear and eyes to see. Even the Roman soldiers went from maiming and mocking Him[67] to marveling and honoring Him: "Truly this was the Son of God!"[68]

The reason we are 99.99 percent sure that Jesus sang the whole song at least once? In the middle of the song, Jesus chanted with a loud voice, "I thirst!" ("My strength is dried up like a potsherd, and my tongue sticks to the roof of my mouth."[69]) And the very last line of the song is a shout of triumph: "[God] has done it."[70] The Hebrew words for the English translation "God has done it" are a bit different from the original Hebrew: "To a people that is born, that *He hath made*!" (תהילים). The people of God's new covenant have been newly born, made by Christ into a new church, for Jews and Gentiles. At the point of Jesus' death, the church was conceived, and Jesus' mission was completed. With that, Jesus' last words were heard: "It is finished!" In Hebrew, the word is *kalah*, the very word uttered by the temple priests after all the sacrificial lambs had been slaughtered. Jesus the Lamb of God had sung the final "amen" to His temple ritual, and the new Temple, the Garden of God, was born. In the Hebrew psalms, the word *selah* is used to denote a pause in the musical notation. With Jesus' last words, "It is finished," He uttered the final *selah*. But His psalm was a song of victory, for what was finished with a pause marked only the beginning of the resurrection promise.

As Jesus sang this victory song, the world resonated with the words. The earth quaked, and the most sacred temple curtain was ripped to shreds, the very curtain that once blocked the entrance to the temple's holiest room, the place that housed the ark of the covenant, God's earthly home. No longer could God be contained or controlled by space or time, clime or clergy. In the words of one of the church's earliest theologians,

> Christ has now become the High Priest . . . . He has entered that greater, more perfect Tabernacle in heaven, which was not made by human hands and is not part of this created world. With his own blood—not the blood of goats and calves—he entered the Most Holy Place once for all time and secured our redemption forever. . . . Therefore, brothers, since we have confidence to enter the Most Holy Place by the blood of Jesus, by a new and living way opened for us through the curtain, that is, his body.[71]

This is the good news of the Jesus story. The words *good news* are a literal translation of the Greek word *euangelion*, which was used at a specific time for a specific reason and at a specific place. The specific place was the village square where the community gathered. The specific time was after a battle had been finished. The specific reason was to cry out at the top of one's lungs: "Good news! The victory has been won!"

The greatest song ever sung in the history of the world was a victory song, sung by Jesus on the cross, announcing victory over the subjugation of sin. The entire universe echoed back that song in vibrations that shook the earth at its core.

CHAPTER 14

The Atonement and the Harrowing of Hell

There is redemptive power in Christ crucified unmatched anywhere else.

—F. F. Bruce[1]

The charges against Jesus were both political and religious: a threat to destroy the temple; blasphemy; being a false prophet; messianic claims that were a threat to the Roman officials. Most scholars agree that Jesus was put to death mainly because of His dramatic action in the temple.[2] When Jesus cleansed the temple, He was striking at its very existence and symbolizing its destruction. Since Jesus was challenging the most sacred symbol of Jewish life, the Jewish authorities had to act. Jesus, then, suffered the fate of countless prophets before Him.[3] Israel's true Messiah and the world's true Lord was executed by the state as a rebel ruler, a "king of the Jews."

LOOKING AT THE CROSS FROM A DIFFERENT MOUNTAIN

Let's now change the landscape and look at the Lord's crucifixion from the divine vantage point. We believe that the enormity of what Jesus did on the cross has been lost to us. But according to the Second Testament, what Jesus did on the cross is beyond what any of us can imagine.

- On that cross, He took upon Himself every sin that you and I would ever commit. He took upon Himself the accusation of the enemy against the whole human race. He paid the penalty for the transgressions that made us subject to decay and death.[4]
- On that cross, He took upon Himself the entire world system that is in rebellion to God.[5]
- On that cross, He took upon Himself the entire old creation, which is fallen and corrupt.[6]
- On that cross, He took upon Himself the condemnation of the Law.[7]
- On the cross, He took upon Himself our flesh—our old Adamic nature.[8]
- And on that cross, He took upon Himself the very power of satan himself . . . the dark personality that was behind every enemy of God's people. Spiritual wickedness now went head-to-head with the Son of God.[9]

In fact, satan fought Jesus on the cross all the way until the end. "And those who passed by blasphemed Him, wagging their heads and saying, 'You who destroy the temple and build it in three days, save Yourself! If You are the Son of God, come down from the cross.'"[10] The voice of the tempter is not hard to recognize: "Now when the tempter came to Him, he said, 'If You are the Son of God, command that these stones become bread.'"[11]

So Jesus took upon Himself the full weight of evil and the complete brunt of the curse. *And He crucified them all!*

Jesus became sin personified. He who was absolute righteousness became absolute sin.[12]

But beyond all that, He faced what the Bible calls "the last enemy"—God's greatest foe: death, the child of sin.[13]

Death, the antithesis of God. Death, the archenemy of God, darkened the wood of that cross, ready to take the Son of God into its hopeless domain.

And death won for a time. Behold the body of God's Son lying in a tomb. Death was victorious. But the fight wasn't over. Three days later God the Father stepped in. He got involved. And the greatest two powers of the universe squared off: death versus divine life. (We continue the story in chapter 15.)

What Jesus told His undiscerning disciples so many times finally came to pass. The Son of man would be handed over to the pagans and die a brutal death in order to fulfill the Scriptures. And there could be no kingdom without the cross. There could be no reigning without death. There could be no forgiveness without the shedding of holy blood. This stunned Jewish sensibilities. Most Jews thought the Messiah could not suffer, let alone die. The Messiah was supposed to inflict suffering, not receive it.

> *What God had done in his grace is to include us in Christ. In dealing with Christ he has dealt with the Christian; in dealing with the Head he has dealt with all the members.*
>
> —Watchman Nee[14]

In short, Jesus died with us (identification), instead of us (substitution), and for us (incorporation).[15] Jesus took the Roman instrument of torture and transformed it into an instrument of deliverance, salvation, and ultimately, peace—peace with God,[16] peace with others,[17] peace with oneself,[18] and peace with creation.[19]

THE ATONEMENT PROPHESIED

Whenever the Second Testament talks about a spiritual reality that is enormous in its significance and implications, it doesn't define it.

Instead, it uses a wide variety of images to capture and communicate its richness.

For example, Jesus Christ. Consider the many images of Christ presented in the Second Testament: Savior, Shepherd, Lord, Master, Teacher, Bridegroom, Foundation, Cornerstone, Lion, Lamb, King, Priest, Prince of Peace, the last Adam, and on and on.

Another example: the church, portrayed as the body, the bride, the building, the family, the vineyard, the temple, and on and on.

It's the same way with the atonement. The Second Testament gives various images to communicate the infinite richness of atonement. Why? Because the work of Jesus Christ at Calvary is too enormous in its scope and too rich in its meaning to be captured by a single image or definition.

> ***Jesus integrated into his self-consciousness themes which he drew from the context in which he ministered. He came as the fulfillment of the Old Testament hope that God would again act salvifically on behalf of his people, even on behalf of the entire world.***
>
> —Stanley Grenz[20]

Hence, the atonement was the ultimate sacrifice. It was the ultimate ransom. It was the ultimate satisfaction. It was the ultimate deliverance from the ultimate curse. It was the ultimate defeat of satan and the dethronement of the god of this world. It was the ultimate payment for the ultimate penalty. It was the ultimate victory over the forces of darkness. It was the ultimate mystery, and on and on and on. Consequently, the First Testament tells the story of Jesus' death and resurrection in various hues, shades, and colors.

Jesus said that the prophets testified of His sufferings and the glory that would follow.[21] Peter echoed the same.[22] Consequently, the sufferings and death of the Messiah, as well as His resurrection, were "according to the Scriptures."[23]

Here are some examples (Q indicates that the First Testament text is quoted in the Second Testament):

Shadow	Fulfillment	*His Sufferings*
Gen. 4:3–10	Heb. 11:4; 12:24	Abel's blood still speaks.
Gen. 37:11	Matt. 27:18	Joseph envied, just as Christ was
Gen. 37:18–20	Matt. 12:14	Joseph and Jesus targeted for murder
Gen. 37:28–29	Matt. 27:57–60	Joseph thrown into a pit, Christ put in a tomb
Ex. 12:5–14	1 Cor. 5:7	Christ our Passover sacrifice
Ex. 17:1–6	1 Cor. 10:4	Christ the smitten rock
Lev. 16:27–28	Heb. 13:11–13	Suffered without the gate
Num. 21:5–9	John 3:14–15	Serpent lifted up in wilderness
Ps. 22:1	Matt. 27:46	"Why have You forsaken Me?"
Ps. 22:6–8	Matt. 27:39–43	"Let Him [God] deliver Him."
Ps. 22:7	Matt. 27:35	His garments divided
Ps. 22:9–13	Matt. 27:33ff.	His sufferings on the cross
Ps. 22:14–15	John 19:34	Christ's heart "melting"
Ps. 22:16	John 19:18 (NLT)	Hands and feet pierced
Ps. 22:17	Luke 23:35	His enemies stared upon Him.
Ps. 22:18	Matt. 27:35Q	Enemies cast lots for His garment.
Ps. 31:5	Luke 23:46	"Into Your hands I commit My spirit."
Ps. 34:20	John 19:36Q	None of His bones broken
Ps. 35:11	Matt. 26:59–60	False witnesses rise up.
Ps. 35:19	John 15:25Q	Hated without cause
Ps. 38:7–14	Mark 14:43ff.	His sufferings and rejection
Ps. 38:11	Luke 23:49Q	His friends stood afar off.
Ps. 41:5–9	Matt. 26:20–25	Betrayed by a familiar friend
Ps. 69:1–4	John 15:25Q	"They hated Me without a cause."

Shadow	Fulfillment	*His Sufferings*
Ps. 69:7–8	John 7:5	A stranger to His brethren
Ps. 69:9	Rom. 15:3Q	Their reproaches fell on Me.
Ps. 69:21	John 19:28–29Q	They gave Him vinegar to drink.
Ps. 69:25	Acts 1:20Q	Let his [Judas's] habitation be desolate.
Ps. 88:1–18	Luke 23	His rejection, suffering, and death
Ps. 109:6–20	Matt. 26:24	Prophecy concerning Judas Iscariot
Ps. 109:8	Acts 1:20Q	Let another take His office.
Ps. 109:25	Mark 15:29	They wagged their heads.
Ps. 118:22	Acts 4:10–11Q	The stone the builders rejected
Isa. 50:6–7	Mark 14:65	Spat upon, buffeted, struck
Isa. 52:14–15	Matt. 27:26–35	His visage marred more than any man
Isa. 53:2–3	John 1:11	Despised and rejected of men
Isa. 53:4	Mark 8:16–17Q	Bore sickness and disease
Isa. 53:7	Matt. 27:12–14	"He opened not His mouth."
Isa. 53:9	Matt. 27:57–60	Buried in a rich man's tomb
Isa. 53:12	Mark 15:27–28Q	Numbered with the transgressors
Isa. 53:12	Luke 23:34	Made intercession for the transgressors
Micah 5:1	Luke 22:64	They smote Him on the cheek.
Zech. 11:12–13	Matt. 26:15	Thirty pieces of silver
Zech. 12:10	John 19:37Q	They look at Him whom they pierced.
Zech. 13:6	John 20:27	Hands pierced
Zech. 13:7	Matt. 26:31, 56Q	The sheep were scattered.
Jonah 1:17	Matt. 12:40Q	In hades three days and nights

Shadow	Fulfillment	*His Glory*
Gen. 2:7	1 Cor. 15:45	Adam made alive from the dust
Gen. 22:1–14	Heb. 11:17–19	Abraham receives back Isaac
Gen. 39:1–6	Phil. 2:7–9	Joseph exalted after suffering
Gen. 40:9–13, 22	1 Cor. 15:4	Chief butler restored on third day
Lev. 23:10–11	1 Cor. 15:20–23	The firstfruits of the resurrection
Num. 17:7–9	Heb. 9:1–5	Aaron's dead rod budded.
Ps. 2:7	Acts 13:33Q	"Today I have begotten You."
Ps. 16:8–11	Acts 2:25–32Q	He will not see corruption.
Ps. 30:3	Mark 16:9	"You brought my soul up from the grave."
Ps. 30:9–12	1 Cor. 15:17	What profit is My blood in death?
Ps. 41:10–12	Acts 2:25–30	"Be merciful to me and raise me up."
Ps. 49:15	Acts 2:25-30	Redeem My soul from the grave.
Ps. 68:18	Eph. 4:8Q	He ascended and gave gifts unto men.
Ps. 110:1	Acts 2:33–36Q	"Sit at My right hand."
Ps. 118:15–21	John 2:19–21	"I shall not die, but live."
Isa. 25:8	1 Cor. 15:54Q	He will swallow up death in victory.
Isa. 52:13	Phil. 2:9	He shall be exalted very high.
Isa. 53:10	2 Tim. 2:8	He will see His offspring and prolong His days.
Isa. 55:3	Acts 13:34Q	He will be given the sure mercies of David.
Hos. 6:1–2	Matt. 16:21	The third day He shall raise us up.

THE ATONEMENT FORESHADOWED

The First Testament gives many allusions to Jesus' death: the rejected prophet, the suffering righteous one, the stone the builders rejected, and so on. But beyond the direct prophecies about the Messiah's death and resurrection, the sacrifice of Jesus was foreshadowed in the actual events of Israel and her ancestors. For example, we meet the atonement in Genesis 3:15 when God announces that the seed of the woman will crush the head of the serpent.

We meet it again in Genesis 3:21 when God made coats of skins to clothe the nakedness of the first sinners. The making of coats out of animal skins required death. It was not sufficient for humans to make a covering out of leaves to cover their sin. No, their covering had to be made through the taking of a life.

Here we see a basic principle of redemption: without the shedding of blood there is no covering for sin.[24] A life must be taken in order for "the shame of [our] nakedness" to be covered.[25] This illustrates that the life of Christ had to be poured out for the forgiveness of our sins. The blood of our Lord Jesus had to be shed in order for the shame of our nakedness to be covered. For "without shedding of blood there is no remission."[26] For "the life of the flesh is in the blood."[27]

We see the atonement in its broader salvific aspect in Noah's day, when eight souls (the number of resurrection) were "saved" through an ark made of wood. The old world was destroyed, and the eight people were brought into a new creation where the dove could find a resting place.[28]

We meet the atonement in the Passover, where the blood of the Paschal Lamb protected the children of Israel from the death angel. Paul told us aptly that Jesus is our Passover.[29] According to Joseph Ratzinger, Jesus died at the same moment the Passover lambs were being slaughtered in the temple. He "dies as the real lamb, merely prefigured by those slain in the Temple."[30]

We meet the atonement again in the Red Sea, where the death waters buried the ungodly Egyptians and Israel passed onto dry ground.[31]

We find the cross of Christ again in the Jordan River, the river of death. The Jordan is the passageway between the wilderness and the land of promise, Canaan. The cross is the transition from one humanity into another, from one creation into another, from one kingdom into another.[32]

We meet the atonement again in the wilderness journey, when Moses struck the rock and out of it flowed rivers of living water. It is an apt picture of death (the striking of the rock) and resurrection life (the flowing waters). Paul wrote that the rock was Jesus Christ.[33] Interestingly, when Moses struck the rock a second time, he was barred from entering the land of promise. God had said to speak to the rock, but Moses struck it.[34] The striking of the rock a second time and the judgment that followed reminds us of the words of Hebrews, which speaks of crucifying "the Son of God afresh."[35]

We meet the atonement again when a certain tree was thrown into the bitter waters of Marah, and they were made sweet as a result.[36] We meet it again in the story of the brass serpent. In Numbers 21, many Israelites were bitten by poisonous serpents as a judgment. The people repented and Moses interceded. The Lord instructed Moses to create a serpent, put it on a pole, and lift it up for the Israelites to see. Everyone who was bitten by a snake would be healed if they looked upon the bronze serpent.

In John 3:14–15, Jesus said, "And as Moses lifted up the serpent in the wilderness, even so must the Son of Man be lifted up, that whoever believes in Him should not perish but have eternal life."

The serpent is the symbol of the enemy,[37] satan, the devil, the accuser. Through the First Testament, brass appears to represent judgment. In 2 Corinthians 5:21, Paul wrote that Jesus became sin—which is the nature of the enemy. Jesus *became* sin in order to defeat it. He tasted death in order to conquer it. He became the serpent of brass in order to destroy the power of the serpent.

We meet the atonement yet again when David, the shepherd boy anointed king of Israel, defeated an insurmountable Goliath. Bible students have long since pointed out that the Philistines, the enemies of the God of Israel and His people, have their analog in the "spiritual wickedness in high places."[38]

David's slaying of Goliath reminds us of the cross, wherein the new David slew the archenemy of God, satan,[39] triumphing and openly spoiling principalities and powers.[40] N. T. Wright has observed that David's five smooth stones correspond to the five wounds of Jesus on the cross—two hands, two feet, and the pierced side.[41]

So we come full circle. Jesus, the new David, was anointed to be King by the prophet (His baptism by John); He was hunted in the wilderness by Saul (His wilderness temptation); unpolished men joined Him in His mission at the cave of Adullam (the calling of the Twelve); He was a man after God's own heart (His life and ministry); He slew the chief enemy of God's people, Goliath (His defeat over satan on the cross); and He founded the city of Jerusalem and gathered and prepared materials for the building of God's temple (He produces "living stones" for the construction of God's house by His resurrection).[43]

> ***Christianity, in its purest form, is nothing more than seeing Jesus.***
>
> —Max Lucado[42]

But beyond all these images, perhaps the one that gives us the greatest insight into the profound fullness of the atonement is the five sacrifices unveiled in Leviticus—all of which speak of the different aspects of Christ's sacrifice.

- *The burnt offering* shows us how the sacrifice of Christ was for God's satisfaction.[44]
- *The meal offering* shows us that Christ's sacrifice was for the satisfaction of God's people.[45] Christ is the perfect grain of wheat, without the leaven of sin.[46]
- *The peace offering* shows us that Christ's sacrifice produces peace and reconciliation between God and those He has chosen.[47]
- *The sin offering* shows us that Christ's sacrifice has destroyed the old man (our old identity in Adam), which is the root of sin.[48]
- *The trespass (or guilt) offering* shows us that Christ's sacrifice not only puts the old self to death but also grants us forgiveness from all trespasses and cleanses our conscience.[49]

These five images demonstrate that the various models of the atonement presented by theologians (ransom, governmental, Christus

Victor, penal substitution, moral-exemplar, satisfaction, and so on) each give us a unique window into the fullness of Christ's atoning sacrifice.[50] So when it comes to the atonement of Jesus Christ, it's not either/or but both/and.

Richard Hays summarizes the point nicely, saying, "Heb 10:5–7 reads Ps 40:7–9 as words spoken by Christ . . . in place of burnt offerings and sin offerings, he offers himself in obedience as a sacrifice. 'See, I have come (in the scroll of the book it is written about me) to do your will, O God.'"[51]

JESUS' ENTRANCE INTO HELL

The story of Jesus' crucifixion and resurrection is a three-day story. But the middle day is hardly ever mentioned as part of the story. No theology of atonement and redemption is complete with an account of No-Name Saturday. But Holy Saturday is hard to celebrate, because it is based on the reality that Jesus died. For a while He actually entered into death and was swallowed by the grave. But there can be no resurrection without a death.

What did Jesus do when He lay dead in the tomb? He turned the tomb of death into the womb of life, and He planted in that womb the ticking time bomb of a new heaven and a new earth. The human One, the new Adam, returned to *adamah* to purify its soil with His spilt blood, to breathe resurrection breath into the dead of the earth, and to resurrect creation from within. This was the earth's baptism . . . as the last Adam went down into the earth to die and then rose as a new creation. All four broken relationships returned to fruition again.

While the details of what happened after Jesus died on the cross were not included in the Second Testament, Jesus' descent into hell has biblical warrant. Consider the following texts:

> For as Jonah was three days and three nights in the belly of a huge fish, so the Son of Man will be three days and three nights in the heart of the earth.[52]

> Because thou wilt not leave my soul in hell, neither wilt thou suffer thine Holy One to see corruption.[53]

> He seeing this before spake of the resurrection of Christ, that his soul was not left in hell, neither his flesh did see corruption.[54]

> For Christ died for sins once for all, the righteous for the unrighteous, to bring you to God. He was put to death in the body but made alive by the Spirit, through whom also he went and preached to the spirits in prison.[55]

> This is why it says: "When he ascended on high, he took many captives and gave gifts to his people." (What does "he ascended" mean except that he also descended to the lower, earthly regions?)[56]

Most of the Reformers and the majority of pre-Reformation theologians interpreted these passages to refer to Jesus' descent into hell. They regarded hades not to be the grave but to be the abode of the dead.[57]

Consider also Simon Peter's classic boast: "Lord, I would lay down my life for You." Peter asked Jesus, "Lord, where are You going?" Jesus replied, "Where I am going you cannot follow Me now, but you shall follow Me afterward."[58]

The obvious interpretation is Jesus means the cross. Indeed, most of the disciples did go on to martyrdom, a couple even being crucified. But there may be a deeper meaning of Jesus' words that refers to His impending descent into hell. Because of that harrowing, plundering, final pilgrimage, none of us need go there. Through His atoning work, Jesus made full provision to save us from God's judgment. Consequently, genuine disciples of Jesus cannot go through those doors, because Jesus has knocked them off their hinges. In a sense, the gates of hell are the reverse side of the gates of Eden. Jesus is the garden gateway, and in breaking down those gates, He reopens the garden, and binds all the sin and evil that inhibit the inhabitation of God in the Garden City called the New Jerusalem.[59]

JESUS' DESCENT INTO HELL DEPICTED IN CREED AND ART

In light of the biblical texts on the subject, the descent into hell is appropriately proclaimed in the Apostles' and Athanasian Creeds (Jesus "descended into hell").

While the Second Testament gives us little detail about the event, the story of the harrowing of hell has inspired some of the greatest Christian literature and art ever created. And the narrative of such literature and art harmonizes (in principle) with the pre-Reformation and Reformation church's understanding of the biblical texts on the subject. Orcadian poet George Mackay Brown, considered one of the greatest Scottish poets of the twentieth century, wrote a poem called "The Harrowing of Hell" about this day between Good Friday and Easter Sunday.[60]

The day between Jesus' crucifixion and His resurrection is known on the church calendar as Holy Saturday or No-Name Saturday. Also known as "the longest day," it is when Jesus' mission moved from the dark tomb into the womb of the earth and gate-crashed hell.

Every story needs a pause, and the pause in the Jesus story is the breathing space between the crucifixion and the resurrection, when Jesus was caught between earth and heaven. Sometimes all metaphors break down, and we sit voiceless in the presence of mystery. Sometimes "Let all Mortal Flesh Keep Silence."[61] One theologian calls it a "significant zero, a pregnant emptiness, a silent nothing which says everything."[62] Some religious traditions even prohibit the celebration of the Eucharist on Holy Saturday.[63]

The story of the "harrowing of hell" most often portrayed in Christian art and reenacted in liturgy goes like this: The condemned human race, from Adam to the time of the crucifixion, hears a voice calling out the psalmist's words: "Draw back, O princes, your gates, remove your everlasting doors. Christ the Lord the King of glory approaches to enter in."[65] Satan isn't worried because Jesus has

> *[Hell] is in an uproar, for it is now made captive.*
> *Hell took a body, and discovered God.*[64]
>
> —John Chrysostom

died on the cross. But hell warns satan against overconfidence. Then the voice is heard outside, demanding that the King of glory come in.

"Who is this King of glory?" satan and hell chant in unison.

"The LORD strong and mighty, the LORD mighty in battle," the psalmist responds.[66]

Then there appears a man with a cross on his back, knocking and demanding entrance. Since he is a robber, satan lets him into Sheol. But this robber is shining and bright, and as soon as satan stands at the gate, a voice outside the door is heard: "Open thou most foul one, thy gates, that the King of glory may come in." As the one who seeks and finds enters, He breaks down the gates of hell, in front of which He had founded His church,[67] binds satan in irons, and casts him down.

Then the last Adam, the Savior of all creation, greets the First Adam with kindness, saying to him, "Peace be to you, Adam, and unto your children unto everlasting ages. Amen."

> *If I ascend into heaven, You are there: if I make my bed in hell, behold, You are there.*
>
> —A PSALM OF DAVID[68]

Then the First Adam casts himself at the Lord's feet, rises up and kisses His hands, and sheds abundant tears, saying, "Behold the hands which formed me: testifying unto all." And he said to the Lord, "Thou art come, O King of glory, to set men free and gather them to Thine everlasting kingdom."

Then Mother Eve also in like manner casts herself at the feet of Jesus, rises up and kisses His hands, and sheds tears abundantly, and says, "Behold the hands that fashioned me: testifying unto all."

Jesus leads Adam and Eve into Paradise, with the penitent thief who shared His agony on Calvary, "testifying unto all" that the power of Jesus and the love of God are not confined by time and space.[69]

THE SEEDING OF THE ETERNAL GARDEN

But there is another significance to Holy Saturday that, if fully understood, would make it the true Earth Day, the greening of creation and the eruption of the eternal garden, filled with the Word of the Lord and the beauty of holiness. First Anastasis should be one of the most important liturgical celebrations of the Christian calendar. In the words of theologian Daniel O'Leary, who has elaborated on this aspect of Holy Saturday most powerfully, on the silent day between His crucifixion and resurrection, "Jesus was still accomplishing his most precarious mission."[70] It was this mission that expanded the horizons of Easter hope to include all creation.

Jesus' first action after His death was not to go up, but down, the Word sown. Jesus descended before He ascended. Before Jesus skyrocketed out of the universe, He sowed it with His divine life, seeds of expectation to germinate in the heart of creation so that one day it might be raised to glory as a restored creation. In short, before leaving the earth, Jesus completed the incarnation, the nonhuman as well as the human one. He went into the heart of the earth and seeded its core with His resurrection presence, with the Word of His Spirit. In this way He freed creation itself from its depravity. He restored its original beauty and goodness. He transformed the earth from the inside out, making possible that "all flesh shall see the salvation of God"[71] and the fulfillment one day of "a new heaven and a new earth."[72]

We are free to speculate on the prediction of Jesus in Matthew's gospel about spending three days in the heart of the world so as to inhabit it intensely and drive it forward from within. Maybe Jesus did not step out of the tomb and head for heaven. Maybe He went deeper into the broken reality of life, where death itself is so powerful, so as to redeem it from within. Having once become human in the body of His mother, Mary, He now actually becomes the whole world in a more comprehensive way than He ever could when He walked its roads and climbed its hills.

Jesus didn't so much leave this world behind Him as bring heaven to earth in our space and time, even the depths where the powers of death and the princes of darkness claim dominion. There is no place where heaven cannot break forth in the most promised manner.

Some theologians see the resurrection on the following day in the image of the first eruption of a volcano that reveals God's fire now burning in the innermost bowels of the earth. Jesus' resurrection was a real and cosmic rhythm of glory, dancing out the good news that this new world had already started turning, that the divine power of a transfigured earth was already leaping from the inner heart of the world—the world that Jesus had invaded to complete what His Father had begun.[73]

In terms of where we are in history and the backcloth against which we see time, we live on the other side of Easter Sunday. But it's still Holy Saturday. When we take on the resurrected Christ, we take on His mission in the world, a mission to carry that resurrection light into the darkest of places and to break down the gates of hell. As the resurrection of Christ is ongoing, our harrowing of hell is ongoing. The church conspires against the powers and principalities of this world who wage their last-ditch campaigns of crimes against humanity and sins against the Holy Spirit.

We live in the light of Easter Sunday but against the weight of Good Friday. Even as we row against the current, and strain from the errors and horrors of this no-name stream, we know that the wind and tide are in our favor. These harrowing times that often seem to be winning have already been defeated. The power of the resurrection overcomes all darkness. Those who walked in darkness have seen a great light—the light to the Gentiles and the glory to Israel. As best we can, we prophesy our way forward to that final, universal Easter Sunday.[74] Until that day, we are either "for" or "against." There are no noncombatants.

CHAPTER 15

The Resurrection, Ascension, and Pentecost

We are living in a time of great transition.

—EVE, TO ADAM, IN A CARTOON DEPICTING THEIR EXODUS FROM EDEN

THE GREAT DIVIDING LINE IN HISTORY, "THE MOMENT WHEN Before Turned into After,"[1] is not the BC/AD division, or the page that separates the First and Second Testament. The great dividing line in time is the BR/AR line of demarcation: Before Resurrection, After Resurrection. Resurrection is the theological singularity of all singularities, ushering in new realities that change everything. The resurrection isn't something that came about. The resurrection is something that opened up.

The richly diverse early church was united in one thing: an allegiance to Jesus and a belief in His death on the cross and His resurrection from the dead. Jesus Christ is the "center of gravity" in the story of the One who was, who is, and who is to come. The resurrection is not a doctrine about Jesus. The resurrection is an ongoing life with Jesus. The resurrection is our rejoicing in the voicing of the risen Messiah in our midst and our sharing in His resurrection life and love, the life of One we love. If Christ is alive, death is dead. The finality of death is finished. All life's undertakers are put out of business.

The story of Easter Sunday shocks us out of our No-Name Saturday sadness and fills our broken hearts with joy, our souls with hope, our mouths with praise. Even after two thousand years, Easter morning still packs a powerful punch of awe and astonishment every year we are privileged to celebrate the gift of resurrection.

> ***Anyone who does not believe in miracles is not a realist.***
>
> —David Ben-Gurion[2]

Try to imagine, then, how utterly mind-boggling and adrenaline-pumping that first Easter morning must have been for the women who suddenly found themselves confronting the most unexpected of scenes. The greatest story ever told rests its first case for the unbelievable on the eyewitness testimony of a group of women (Mary Magdalene; Mary, the mother of James; Joanna; and Salome) at a time when women's testimony was seen as "rash and frivolous," "irrational" and "untrustworthy."[3] Only two of the disciples (Peter and John) deemed the women's testimony worthy of checking out.

Mary Magdalene had trudged out to the barren, cold tomb of her Master even before daylight had managed to warm the ground or light her way. But in that dim first light of day, Mary saw well enough to discern a disaster: the stone had been rolled away from the mouth of Jesus' tomb.

For Mary, this was a sure sign that someone had tampered with the tomb, emptying it of all contents, including Jesus' body. Even without the presence of jewels or decorations, a dead body was well worth robbing. Thieves would find Jesus' body, wrapped in fine linen clothes that were filled with expensive spices, a valuable commodity.

A shattered Mary ran off to bring this final piece of bad news to Peter and John. Not only had Jesus' followers lost their living Master, but now they had lost His dead body and thus any chance to honor and tend His grave site. Everyone's terror was palpable.

Racing to the tomb to see for themselves, Peter and John had enough daylight to see into the gaping hole. John was the faster runner but balked at entering. Peter burst right in, bowing to gain entrance and intent upon seeing firsthand the extent of this tragedy.

The women had told the truth. Jesus' body was gone.

Strangely, both disciples noted a telling detail, even fixating on its particulars. They found the expensive linen wrappings and head shroud still there. What is more, they mentioned how these remnants were heaped in two separate locations. The head cloth was "rolled up" in the upper corner of the limestone slab, while the linen body wrappings lay tossed aside and crumpled in the bottom corner. Why, in the midst of the greatest story ever told, the resurrection of Jesus from the dead, are we reading verse after verse about dirty laundry? And why do we overlook this, as surely as we fail to recognize the depictions of fabric that cover oil painting canvases more than any other image from the Renaissance to the eighteenth century?

SWADDLING CLOTHES AND BURIAL LINENS

The story of Jesus begins and ends with swaddling clothes and burial linens. Priestly undergarments worn under no-longer-used robes were cut up for swaddling garments and burial clothes. Some considered them too holy to burn or throw away. Swaddling clothes were later used to wrap the scroll from which the child would read at the bar mitzvah.

Perhaps John, the "beloved disciple," had done more picking up after others in his life than Peter. He seems better able to read the laundry signs left in the tomb and come to the astonishing conclusion that these were signs of *life*, not death. He "saw and believed."[4] A head shroud, plucked off by a living hand, would be taken off first, then laid down by itself where the head had reclined. The linen wrappings, unwound, pulled and kicked off by living arms and legs, would end up in a heap somewhere down where the feet had rested. The living body was gone—only the telltale laundry remained to show its actions.

The disciples departed. But one wonders if John had to explain the joke to Peter: the first thing Jesus did after He was raised from the dead was to fold His clothes. Mary had taught Him well. But the eagerness that rushed in His veins of "being about His Father's business" was also there as well. One pile of dirty linen was neatly folded. The other was scattered, as if He were suddenly in a hurry. Note the difference in how Lazarus and Jesus emerged from the tomb. Lazarus came out still wrapped—signifying his continuing mortality and need to face death. Jesus emerged unwrapped. All three people Jesus resuscitated from the dead still died. Jesus was resurrected, not resuscitated. With Jesus there is no more death.

It was Mary Magdalene's turn to look into the tomb. But for Mary there were no piles of laundry. Instead, there were angels!

Where the disciples saw dirty linen, Mary saw angels.

Again, with great care, the narrative reports in detail the physical location of what was found in the tomb—two beings dressed in white. Like the laundry piles the two disciples saw, these angels were situated one at the head, one at the foot of where Jesus' body had rested. In the exact place where the disciples saw only discarded cloth, Mary saw heavenly messengers!

Mary at first didn't get it. The angels asked her, "Woman, why are you weeping?"[6] These messengers were not wondering *why* she was so overwhelmed with emotion. They were asking why *tears?* Why sorrow on such a joyful, miraculous day? Their very presence proclaimed Jesus' absence from the tomb: "He is not here; for He is risen."[7]

Adam's likeness,
Lord, efface,
Stamp thy image
in its place,
Second Adam
from above,
Reinstate us in
Thy love.

—Charles Wesley[5]

It's almost as if the gospel writer is asking us, "How many piles of your dirty laundry, sometimes even hidden in closets, are really angels unaware, wanting to deliver you Easter messages?" We know Christ is risen, not only because it is a verifiable fact but because it is a story that proves true and rings real in the deals of life.

ANGELS IN THE TOMB

Why did Mary see what was really there, angels at the head and at the feet where Jesus' body had lain, where Peter and John only saw stacks of dirty laundry? At a time when women were not credible witnesses, when their testimony was suspicious, what did Mary do differently that enabled her to become the first messenger of the resurrection, the "apostle to the apostles," as she is known in the Roman Catholic Church? There is no way this would have been part of the story if it hadn't happened that way, since no one would have written the story this way.[8]

Mary did two things differently that enabled her to see angels' robes rather than graveclothes. First, she stopped running and became still. She waded into the midst of the chaos and waited patiently for a clearing of the mist. Second, she cried. She entered the pain of her confusion and despair, and through the prism of her tears saw what was really there in the dimensions of the divine, not the plains of the physical.

But as with Simon Peter and Mary Magdalene, the only thing powerful enough to shake us free from our self-absorption and hopelessness is nothing less than the risen Christ Himself. Unawakened by angelic messengers, blinded to Jesus' presence before her, it was not until Mary heard Jesus call her

Sing, my tongue, how
glorious battle
Glorious victory
became;
And above the cross,
his trophy,
Tell the triumph
and the fame;
Tell how he, the
earth's Redeemer,
By his death for
man o'ercame.
His the nails, the
spear, the spitting,
Reed and vinegar
and gall;
From his patient
body pierced
Blood and water
streaming fall;
Earth and seas and
stars and mankind
By that stream are
cleansed all.

—Sixth-century hymn writer Venantius Fortunatus[9]

by name, like the Good Shepherd calling His sheep, that she snapped out of her gloom and awakened to the miracle of Easter morning.

In the death and resurrection of Jesus, the last Adam, we have been returned to the garden, restored to a right relationship with God, and the Fall has been reversed. How do we know that the mission of the last Adam is complete? On day one, as the light rose, Mary did not recognize Him. Why?

Because she thought He was the gardener. This one sign is a resurrection rocket, a Roman candle that flares over the temple-garden, and invites us to return to our prelapsarian relationship with God. All creation is made new.

One more time Jesus flipped the holiness code on its head and turned the world upside down by raising a scorned woman, looked down on by both men and women, and sometimes by the disciples, to a place of honor and preeminence. A woman was the first to behold Jesus after His resurrection and to speak the word "Rabboni" in a ceremony unseen by men. Just as those commissioned to be the first evangelists after Jesus' birth were lowly shepherds,[10] so Jesus commissioned a lowly woman to be the first evangelist after His resurrection.[11]

For the first disciples to hear described a tomb where two angels guarded the ends of where Jesus' body had been, their minds must have gone to the Holy of Holies, where the ark of the covenant was covered with a golden lid—the mercy seat, where an imageless God was enthroned, flanked by two golden cherubim.[12] The new Holy of Holies, where God's presence is found, is an empty tomb. It is a place of absence, for the body is gone, but it is a place of presence. For the AbsentPresence, Jesus Himself, is the mercy seat (*hilastērion*), whom God has enthroned: "the image of the invisible God."[13] The holiness of God is found not in a temple but in the world where the AbsentPresence is encountered.

Interestingly, the Scriptures never say that Jesus raised Himself from the dead. Instead, they tell us plainly that it was the Father who raised Him from the dead.[14] The resurrection, then, is something that *happened to* Jesus. It was the Father's vindication of His Son's life, message, and ministry.

THE GREATEST BATTLE IN HUMAN HISTORY

A rarely mentioned fact is that Resurrection Sunday marks the greatest battle in human history. It was the outcome of the battle of God's greatest enemy (death) versus divine life. It was where God the Father concentrated all of His infinite power, drawing all the powers of the heavens, bringing them straight toward a tomb. It was the greatest display of power since the visible creation.

On that day the earth shook. And the heavens shook. And the body of Jesus of Nazareth came to life. And death—the chief foe of the Almighty—*died*. For death could not hold the Son of God in its endless domain. Jesus Christ rose again from the grave, victorious over death, and He became "the firstborn from the dead."[15] Jesus shook off His chains, and He was no longer bound by space or time. He now lives on the other side of space, time, and history. And He became a "life-giving Spirit," as Paul called Him in 1 Corinthians 15:45. And He breathed His own life into His disciples.[16] The only begotten Son became the firstborn among many brethren—and they became the sons and daughters of God.[17] The grave turned into a garden. And we're back to Genesis 2. Jesus is the Tree of Life returned to earth again.

From the womb of death Christ brought forth an unprecedented creation—a new humanity. And in that new humanity, there is no Jew or Gentile . . . there is no male or female . . . there is no slave or free . . . there is no black or white . . . there is no Hispanic or Asian . . . and there is no rich or poor. All earthly barriers have been erased.[18] Behold, this is a new humanity . . . a new race . . . a new creation . . . a new kingdom from another realm, with the life of God beating within it. And Jesus Christ is the head of this new creation, and He alone is all in all.[19]

What is this? It's the *ekklesia* of God, the church. Bone of His bone and flesh of His flesh—kin to divinity—and you are part of her. What the disciples received in a closed room following Jesus' resurrection was soon experienced by thousands of Jews on the day of Pentecost some fifty days later:[20] the birth of the church; but it was rooted and grounded in the resurrection of Jesus.[21]

The resurrection of Christ was the ultimate vindication that He was this world's rightful King. It tells us that a new creation is now here, yet it is coming. In His resurrection, Jesus became something other than what He was before. He became one who had passed through death and is now untouchable by it. (And this is the life that we as Christians receive—divine life that has passed through death.) Through the cross, Jesus defeated the old king (satan); through His resurrection, He has been enthroned as the new King. He has been "vindicated by the Spirit"[22] to be the Messiah, God's true ruler over the earth, reclaiming for humanity its original intention: to rule for and with God.[23] In His resurrection, Jesus of Nazareth has been "declared" the Son of God.[24]

THE RESURRECTION FORESHADOWED

As is the case with each stage of His life, the resurrection of Jesus is sufficiently foreshadowed in the First Testament. Knowing that Jesus is the New David, Peter said of Him,

> But God raised him from the dead, freeing him from the agony of death, because it was impossible for death to keep its hold on him. David said about him: "I saw the Lord always before me. Because he is at my right hand, I will not be shaken. Therefore my heart is glad and my tongue rejoices; my body also will live in hope, because you will not abandon me to the grave, nor will you let your Holy One see decay. You have made known to me the paths of life; you will fill me with joy in your presence."[25]

Peter went on to say, "Seeing what was ahead, he [David] spoke of the resurrection of the Christ."[26]

We meet the foreshadowing of Jesus' resurrection on the third day of creation, when the first sign of life emerged out of the receding waters of death.[27] We meet it again in Noah's ark, when it rested on the top of Mount Ararat and eight souls (the number of resurrection) stepped into a new world.[28] We meet it again in Isaac, of whom the book of Hebrews says, "Abraham reasoned that God could raise the dead, and figuratively speaking, he did receive back Isaac from death."[29] We meet it again in the budding of Aaron's dead rod. Aaron's dead stick was placed in the tabernacle for a long, dark night. And in the morning, it brought forth life.[30] We meet it again in the feast of the firstfruits of the harvest.[31] God will eventually do for the whole creation what He has done with Jesus' body as the firstfruits of the resurrection.[32] There are many other examples of where the First Testament foretells the resurrection of Jesus "according to the Scriptures."[33]

> Come, and let us return unto the LORD: for he hath torn, and he will heal us; he hath smitten, and he will bind us up. After two days will he revive us: in the third day he will raise us up, and we shall live in his sight.[34]

THE FORTY DAYS

In the book of Acts, Luke wrote that Jesus remained on the earth for forty days following His resurrection.[35] And according to John, those days were full. Referring to His postresurrection appearances, John said that "Jesus did many other signs in the presence of His disciples."[36] We've already seen the significance of the number forty. Moses remained on Sinai for forty days. Elijah fasted before God for forty days. The rains from the flood during Noah's day lasted forty days. The Israelite spies searched the land of Canaan for forty days. Goliath presented himself to Israel for forty days. During the days of Jonah, God gave the people of Nineveh forty days to repent. Jesus was proved in the wilderness for forty days just as Israel was proved in the wilderness for forty years. The number forty represents testing or proving.

So why the forty days after Jesus' resurrection? Well, the church's very existence depended on it. The apostles' work depended on it. The future of Christ's work on earth depended on it. Those forty days were the basis for the apostles' ability to endure the most severe suffering. How? *Because in those forty days Jesus proved Himself to be a resurrected human being.* Not a ghost. Not a delusion. Not a figment of their imaginations. But a real, living person who had pierced the veil of death and come out on the other side victorious. Luke wrote, "After his suffering, he showed himself to these men and gave many convincing proofs that he was alive. He appeared to them over a period of forty days and spoke about the kingdom of God."[37]

Note the words, "he showed himself to these men and gave many convincing proofs." Had it not been for those forty days, faith in Jesus' resurrection would have had a weak foundation. Had it not been for those forty days, the disciples would have continued to misunderstand the Scriptures. During those forty days, Jesus opened up their understanding as He spoke of Himself from Genesis to Malachi, expounding the kingdom of God.[38]

Had it not been for those forty days, Paul couldn't have written in such detail what he did in 1 Corinthians 15 about the resurrected body. (No doubt, Paul received his information about the glorified body from the apostles who spent time with Jesus during those forty days.) During those forty days, Jesus appeared to the Twelve and then quickly disappeared.[39] Being free of space and time, Jesus showed Himself to more than five hundred disciples at the same time.[40] In this way, the Lord was proving to His followers that He had no bounds, no limitations, no restrictions. He was free to "presence" Himself wherever and whenever He wished. That includes through physical walls and through your physical body.[41]

The forty days also established a new way of knowing Christ, a way that was not after the flesh but after the Spirit.[42] Recall that when the disciples first saw Jesus in His resurrected state, "some doubted."[43] But in the course of those forty days, Jesus revealed to His followers a new way of knowing Him—a way that would carry forward after His ascension, where believing without seeing became the norm.[44]

JESUS' ASCENSION

The return journey of Jesus to the Father, known as the ascension or sometimes as the ascending, culminated in Pentecost. Jesus' exaltation followed the resurrection, but a final departure scene didn't come until forty days after the resurrection.[45] At the beginning of His ministry, Jesus prepared Himself for His mission for forty days. At the end of His ministry, He prepared His disciples for their mission for forty days.

The Holy Spirit was given to the disciples when the Son was

glorified, when Jesus was present with the Father, as He said, "with the glory which I had with You before the world was."[46] Of all the Jewish ascension stories (Enoch, Elijah, Ezra, Moses), the Jesus ascension is strikingly parallel with the Elijah rapture. When Elijah ascended, the mantle came down.[47] When Jesus ascended, the Holy Spirit came down. It is the Holy Spirit, the overflow of the Father-Son relationship, who enables Jesus to be two places at once: with and in us at all times and everywhere, and seated at the right hand of the Father,[48] in the language of the most quoted First Testament text in the Second Testament.

> Therefore being exalted to the right hand of God, and having received from the Father the promise of the Holy Spirit, He poured out this which you now see and hear.[49]

> But this He spoke concerning the Spirit, whom those believing in Him would receive; for the Holy Spirit was not yet given, because Jesus was not yet glorified.[50]

A risen, regnant Jesus "seated at the right hand" is not offhand, hands-off imagery. The image of the "right hand" means that Jesus occupies the seat of honor with the Father. The image of a "seated" Jesus means that the work of atonement and reconciliation is completed.[51] It was done once, for all time, and does not need to be repeated, though He continually intercedes for us, a word in Greek (*entynchano*) that means He looks after our interests and purposes our betterment.[52]

Our Easter faith is that we really do encounter Jesus himself; not a message from him, or a doctrine inspired by him, or an ethics of love, or a new idea of human destiny, or a picture of him, but Jesus himself.

—Herbert McCabe[53]

But as Jacob found out at Jabbok, happy endings cost us something. His happy ending left him with a limp. Every one of us carries a scar that reminds us of who we are and where we have come from. Jacob's wound never fully healed, and Jesus took His wounds with Him into eternity. Do His wounds still bleed there? Is that part of how He continually intercedes for us? The scarred hands of Jesus—is that how God carved our names in the palms of Jesus' hands? "See, I have engraved you on the palms of my hands," the prophet Isaiah heard God say.[54] Are you wearing the brand of Jesus? The wounded side of our Lord, out of which the church came forth on the day of Pentecost—this was the womb for the bride of Christ. She, the bride, is perfect, holy, and without blemish. But He, the Bridegroom, is flawed; for He will take those scars into eternity.

Once Jesus was seated, "the last days" (also known as "the age of the Spirit") began, when the true Israel, which now includes Gentiles, gathered to form the body of Christ on earth, "the church of God."[55] To live as a member of the body of Christ is a participative reality. There is always an element of DIY ("Do It Yourself") in the incarnation story. The greatest gift ever given is not a prepackaged story where the Messiah suddenly plops down on the scene. The Gift comes in parts and spurts, stages and pieces, needing us to open up the Gift and put it all together. When the church gathers, the incarnation Gift is received again, and the whole body of Christ becomes "gifted." When the church scatters, the incarnation Gift is given again, and the parts of the body of Christ become a gift.

> *We are not defenders of the Jesus story, but participants with him in his story.*
>
> —Novelist/professor Mike McNichols[56]

From the ascension on, three things became indissoluble in God's mission in the world: the Scriptures, the Holy Spirit, and Jesus. Of course, the Scriptures were there from the beginning: "Christ died for our sins *according to the Scriptures* . . . He rose again the third day *according to the Scriptures*."[57] Jesus Himself did not separate the Scriptures from the Spirit, as He showed when He referred to Psalm 110:1 as "David, speaking by the Spirit."[58] But after the ascension, the Spirit opened up the Scriptures so we can see Jesus.

The Holy Spirit is the universalization of Jesus. The activity of the Holy Spirit, directed by the ascended Lord of the church and the transcendent reign of Christ in heaven, is to rebirth Himself on earth within and among us until He shall return in final glory and create a new heaven and a new earth. Theology is nothing more than the Holy Spirit making His way through our brains, as the Scriptures make their way through our hearts.

THE EMMAUS ROAD

The most famous event in the ascending is another on-the-road story, where all roads lead to Jesus. The Emmaus road story is about the play of memory and imagination. The real story is why these disciples failed to recognize Jesus in the first place—and the need for memory and imagination to link. This road story[59] describes the transition of the disciples from road rage ("we thought He was the One") and disbelief to a more informed understanding of Jesus' identity, and a newly re-formed community of faith. The journey from Jerusalem to Emmaus and back again may have been only a short distance for the legs. But it was a life journey for the disciples into newer and deeper dimensions of discipleship.

The trip to Emmaus took place on "that same day"; that is, that same third day in which the empty tomb was discovered and the women reported the messages from the two angels. Instead of believing the report, however, the women's words were apparently judged as idle talk in accordance with the custom of the day regarding women's words. The disciples hadn't bothered to go to the tomb themselves. They left that to the women. They spent their time in Jerusalem hiding, afraid of being picked up by the police. Not just one disciple betrayed Jesus. Or two. They all did.

They could find no way to harmonize Jesus' life and teachings with His horrible death on the cross, or with the strange discovery of an empty tomb. Here was a theological transition that left the disciples in the throes of their own form of PTSD: posttraumatic shock disorder. The women's report was dismissed. The remaining disciples began to scatter. Peter went back to the tomb. Just how close the entire group was to breaking up was demonstrated by these two other disciples as they left Jerusalem to travel to Emmaus. Jesus' disciple-community was on the verge of disbanding.

As these two people—one named Cleopas, who may have been Jesus' uncle or Joseph's brother[60]—set out on the road to Emmaus, they were joined by Jesus, but "they were kept from recognizing him."[61] The first problem the disciples had after the resurrection was a recognition problem. They had a problem recognizing Jesus in their midst. Some things haven't changed. Our problem is the same as the first disciples' problem.

When the stranger asked what they were talking about, they "stood still" on the road, like deer in headlights, frozen by the bone-chilling sadness of it all. Cleopas's answer was unknowingly ironic: he accused Jesus of being "out of it," though He was the only one who truly *did* know about all "the things" that had happened in Jerusalem and the only one who held all the answers to their questions about "the things."[62]

Now comes the most astonishing line in all of history, much less all of literature. "What things?" Jesus said.[63]

When the feigning Jesus pressed them to tell Him "What things?" they told the shorthand version of the Jesus story, framed in simple honesty about their confusion and depression. First these disciples described Jesus as a prophet, "mighty in deed and word before God and all the people."[64] This image of Jesus recalls that of other great prophets, most especially of Moses. But this understanding of their prophet-teacher Jesus was marred by the terrible events that had occurred. The disciples recounted how their chief priests and leaders had handed over Jesus to be crucified. The disciples and others in Jerusalem had hoped Jesus was the One who would "redeem Israel." Jesus' death on the cross had crushed all their messianic expectations.

Coupled with this great disappointment was the confusion that the women's report of the empty tomb had brought. Still focused on a prophetic Jesus who was "mighty in deed and word," the disciple-community failed to remember one telling aspect of all prophets' mission: the suffering and rejection that go hand in hand with living a prophetic life.

Jesus went gently with these two "foolish" disciples,[65] even though they had forgotten all His previous warnings about a suffering, dying Messiah who would bring redemption to the world.

A JOURNEY TOWARD NEW UNDERSTANDING

Walking this Emmaus road now became a journey toward a new state of comprehension. Jesus walked those two disciples through the Scriptures,[66] using the Torah itself to testify to a tradition of a "suffering Messiah." Jesus showcased on this Emmaus road the SERT (Scripture, Experience, Reason, Tradition)[67] journey that all future followers would have to take: finding reasoned validation for faith from biblical texts and traditions as well as from personal experiences of the resurrected Christ.

As the travelers approached Emmaus, the narrative tension heightened when Jesus walked ahead of them as though He were going on. But the story continues because there was an invitation to fellowship. "Stay with us," the two disciples urged their new friend, the unrecognized risen Jesus.

The slender thread that held the three travelers together was suddenly strengthened by being woven into a tablecloth. The invitation to "table" together kept Jesus in their midst. Perhaps these two disciples had retained some of what Jesus had earlier spread before them after all.

The Eucharistic "Last Supper" comes quickly to mind.[68] While it became the central celebration of the church community, what happened next is most similar to the feeding of the multitude.[69] Before that miraculous meal there was hazy comprehension of who Jesus was, among both His followers and the uneasy civil authorities.[70] Immediately afterward Peter recognized and confessed Jesus as "the Christ of God."[71]

Similarly, at this evening meal, Jesus morphed before their eyes from invited guest to host: offering the blessing for the bread, breaking it, and distributing it. His closed-eyed tablemates now had their eyes pried open, and they instantly recognized the One before them.[72] Truth is recognition. Jesus surprises us with what we already know.

But as suddenly as recognition came, the recognized vanished, leaving two stunned disciples at the table, staring at one another. The paradox of knowing and not knowing, of particularity and universality, was once again demonstrated in Jesus' postresurrection appearances. Jesus revealed Himself to the disciples, then vanished from their sight almost in the same moment. In a mysterious way, by Jesus' physical absence—by not clinging to Him,[73] as Jesus instructed Mary Magdalene and here as He disappears just when He appears—we are able to enter into a deeper presence of Him that holds on to us and draws us into His resurrection life. There is a breathlessness to it all, as we are always catching up to Jesus. He is always ahead of us. He always goes before us.

A simple loaf of bread, broken at a roadside table after a dusty day on the road, becomes a miraculous feast when it is shared with the risen Christ. The Emmaus road disciples were the first to experience the postresurrection transformation of bread at the table to the bread of life. But every time any disciple of the risen Lord breaks bread with loved ones, that same miracle occurs. Where two or three are in relation with Me, Jesus promised, there am I also.[74] In fact, until we live out what we are talking about, we stumble through life in confusion and uncertainty.

> *We must keep the soul terribly surprised.*
>
> —Widely attributed to Emily Dickinson

Until we live out of redemptive and reconciling relationships and not merely theorize about them, our eyes won't be open: "He was known to them in the breaking of bread."[75] Jesus is discovered in acts of relationship and reconciliation. The resurrection gives us not so much new insights and a Christian worldview as it does new relationships and a Christian "world life." Enacted truth through embodied relations is what gives life and power to previous experiences of God.

The story of the risen Christ in Luke 24 throws us back to Genesis 3 immediately after Adam and Eve fell. Notice the wording in Genesis 3:7: "Then *the eyes of both of them were opened, and they knew* that they were naked." Compare it with Luke 24:31: "Then *their eyes were opened and they knew* Him."[76] A reasonable allusion: Jesus, in His resurrected state, has reversed the Fall.

Note also that the disciples didn't say, "Did not our heart burn within us when He broke the bread and ate with us?" Rather they said, "Did not our heart burn within us while He talked with us on the road, and while He opened the Scriptures to us?"[77] In our own personal narratives, we tend to remember more what we anticipate than what we actually experience. Childhood memories are *not* of the ripped-off wrapping paper or the too-stuffed belly. They are of the pile of pristine packages awaiting Christmas morning, or of the heavy-laden table decked out with favorite foods and goodies. The Emmaus disciples—like all disciples since—recalled best those moments just *before* their eyes were opened to the truth and their spirits recognized Jesus.

Jesus mandated that they return to Jerusalem, and then He left. The action was no longer around the table, but back in Jerusalem. Yet even then, the action was not theirs, but God's—and it is not ours, but God's. The action is not initiating something for God but becoming part of God's initiatives in the world. We're on the road again.

On the road back to Jerusalem from Emmaus. On the road from Jerusalem unto the uttermost ends of the earth. On the road of resurrection faith, where being faithful means trusting and obeying without being told things; and being road-ready, even when you're living in transition, moving in the shadows of understanding, and walking in dark valleys of despair and uncertainty; where time spent on the road with Jesus is not actualizing ourselves but releasing and unleashing His resurrection energies.

MOVING UPWARD AND FORWARD

The Emmaus disciples left "that same hour" on that enchanting "third day." The two travelers hustled off to where the disciples and their companions were hiding out—once again excitedly discussing events all along the way. But instead of "sadness," there was ecstasy. They recalled how their hearts had been "burning within"[78] as they listened as Jesus "opened the Scriptures" to them.[79] They remembered how their "slow" hearts[80] had beat faster with a cadence of hope as they began to hear a song of new possibilities and dreams. When they arrived at their destination, they found a galvanized group of disciples celebrating a truth corroborated in cobblestone: "The Lord is risen indeed, and has appeared to Simon!"[81]

Paul said Jesus appeared to more than five hundred of His followers[82] before He left His marching orders on the hilltop to go (missional) into all the world and make disciples (relational) of all cultures (incarnational), baptizing in His name and teaching His story.[83]

Both the journey (the way) and the journey's end at table talk with Jesus (the truth) were necessary for the risen Jesus to be revealed to His missionizing disciples (the life). The ascension chapter in the Jesus story moves Jesus not just upward but forward, toward a new heaven and a new earth and God's kingdom come on earth, as it is in heaven.[84] No-Name Saturday and the ascension teach us that heaven is not just a reality outside of creation.

When Jesus said, "I have been given all authority in heaven and on earth,"[85] He was referencing the prophecy of Daniel: "I saw someone like a son of man. . . . He was given authority, honor, and sovereignty over all the nations of the world."[86] So He told them to return to Jerusalem and stay there until there was a baptism of wind and fire to go with the baptism of water.[87] For even "cradle Christians," there comes a time when the "baptism of water" must turn into the "baptism of spirit," when conversion through the involuntary coercion of parental loins turns into the leonine conviction of personal choice.

John the Evangelist said there were three witnesses to Jesus on earth: the water, the blood, and the wind.[88] Water for cleansing, blood for drinking, wind for resurrecting.[89] Next, we'll look at Acts to see the story of what happens when the wind mixes with the water and blood.

PENTECOST

While Jesus ascended into heaven in bodily form, He descended from heaven in the Spirit on the day of Pentecost.[90] The Emmaus walk is the journey that conveyed the disciple-community into its new identity as the body of Christ. The bride conceived on the cross when the last Adam's side was split, then quickened in the Upper Room when the resurrected Christ breathed on the disciples, was brought fully to life on Whit Sunday, the seventh Sunday after Easter, also called Pentecost, from the Greek for "fiftieth." As Joshua continued Moses' work in leading the people into the promised land,[91] so the Holy Spirit continues Christ's mission in the life of the church. The Spirit is the ultimate egalitarian—knowing no age, gender, geography, or social class,[92] poured out on everyone who "calls on the name of the LORD."[93] In the New Jerusalem of Revelation, all divisions are obliterated . . . whether it be Hebrew and Gentile, holy and unholy, male or female, light or dark.[94]

Jesus was taken up into a cloud on the Mount of Olives. But He made it clear that His physical absence means a spiritual presence that takes on a physical form: the church. The church isn't divine, of course. But it's united with Christ as His body, sharing His life. And His body, empowered and emboldened by the Spirit, would be able to do things that Jesus didn't do and harness energies of holiness that we didn't know existed. Jesus is the "Son of God with power according to the Spirit of holiness, by the resurrection from the dead."[95]

The private experience in the house became public, a reversal of Babel, where everyone heard each other in their own native tongue. The coming of the Spirit is a multisensory experience, replete with features that often show up with God's self-revelation—wind and fire.[96]

Jesus' spirit constructed a new creation of humanity. In the beginning, God breathed the divine spirit into Adam and created humans in God's image. By breathing His Spirit into this new community, Jesus re-created humanity afresh in His image. In John 20:22, Jesus breathed on His disciples, an allusion to God breathing into Adam in Genesis 2:7.[97] This new humanity would be a community with a particular kind of spirit, the spirit of Jesus Christ. The church is Jesus' continued presence in the world, tongued with fire and driven by wind.

The church does not exist for itself but exists for four major purposes:

1. to be a *bride* who loves Jesus Christ as He loves her
2. to be a *house* for God the Father to dwell in and find rest
3. to be a *body* through which Jesus Christ may express Himself visibly in the universe
4. to be a *family* for the Father's pleasure and enjoyment

This is the narrative we find in Genesis 1 and 2 (before the Fall occurred), and it is consummated in Revelation 21 and 22 (after the Fall is erased). It is the storyline of God's neglected and forgotten "eternal purpose," wherein Jesus Christ is the Bridegroom for the bride; the foundation, cornerstone, and capstone of the house; the head of the body; and the firstborn of the family. To obtain a bride for the Son, a house for the Father, a body for the Son, and a family for the Father is the grand mission of God—and it is fulfilled in His church. And the Holy Spirit of God has come to make it all a reality.

> *We can say where the Church is, but not where she is not.*
>
> —Russian theologian Paul Evdokimov[98]

When the Spirit descended, the disciples were gathered to keep the Jewish feast of Shavuot, commemorating the bestowal of Torah on Moses. Fifty days after hiding in fear while Jesus was hanging in agony, these same disciples fearlessly proclaimed the gospel to Jewish pilgrims visiting Jerusalem for the annual Shavuot festival. Threatened with death by the same people who killed Jesus, the disciples preached on, and on, and on. James was the first to be killed, slain with a sword by King Herod Agrippa.[99] Except for John, they all would be persecuted or martyred, most in other countries (in keeping with the Great Commission).

From the middle of the second century there has been an early baptismal creed that concludes with these words: "I believe in the Holy Spirit, and the church." You can't separate the Spirit and the church: when you get the Bridegroom you get the bride. You can't adequately follow Jesus without being part of a shared-life community that lives and gathers under the headship of Christ. The Christian life was never meant to be lived in isolated individualism; following Jesus has always been a corporate experience. And it always will be.[100]

THE JESUS COMMUNITY

"Do not call anyone on earth your father," Jesus said.[101] At Pentecost Jesus gave us a new and better bonding than conventional family: *koinonia.*

Koinonia is like a patchwork quilt—every patch is different, but they are all sewn together into an artistic pattern. *Koinonia* is community, not conformity. *Koinonia* is anathema to individualism, but advancing of individuality. Evangelism is not *convincing* people that Jesus is the way, the truth, and the life. One does not become a Christian because one is convinced. One becomes a Christian because one is convicted to change (repent and believe in Jesus) and to connect to a community. This community (*koinonia*) is held together by the power of the Spirit, not by the agreement or even agreeableness of its members.

To be "in the body" (*koinonia*) is to be more than "in touch." To be "in the body" is to be in sync because we are in Christ . . . even though we are all different members of the same body. By being members of the body of Christ—"as the body is one and has many members . . . so it is with Christ"[102]—we participate in the temple ownership, since Christ is Himself the fulfillment of the temple and therefore the restoration of our fallen state and the fractured relationship between Creator and creature.

> ***I will give you a new heart and put a new spirit within you; I will take the heart of stone out of your flesh and give you a heart of flesh.***
>
> —THE LORD GOD[104]

The new covenant is more than a Jesus veneer to the old covenant. People want stone tablets they can cling to and brandish, but Jesus wants to be written and beat in our hearts. Which will it be? A heart-of-stone Jesus or a heart-of-flesh Jesus? A stone-tablet Jesus or a living-stone Jesus?[103] When Jesus cuts a covenant in our hearts, He carves a new channel through which God's energies flow.[105] The cutting of the new covenant on the cross is symbolized by the curtain rent in two. Jesus is now the new High Priest who can enter the temple at any time, and He has pulled down the curtain separating us from the presence of God.

A free church, like a free nation, is bound to be full of things and people we don't like. The right hand and left hand may be going in opposite directions at the same time, but we share the same mind and mission of Christ.

We love the church. And so does our Lord. In fact, the church is His chief passion. For that reason, the Scriptures say that Christ "gave Himself for" her,[106] "purchas[ing]" her "with His own blood."[107] We are living in a day when God is seeking to restore her glory, making the Son preeminent in and through her. The will of God, we believe, is that every expression of the body of Christ on earth today would become a spiritual "Bethany," where Jesus is welcomed, received, and is running the show . . . a place where He can lay His head and find rest.[108]

CHAPTER 16

The Return of the King

Behold, your King is coming,

Sitting on a donkey's colt.

—John 12:15

Many Christians, especially those who live in America, are obsessed with the second coming of Christ. Various interpretations surrounding the when, where, and how of this incredible event have spawned endless divisions among Jesus' followers. In fact, some Christians are so fixated on the second coming of Christ that they haven't given sufficient time to understand His first coming.

In this chapter, we will explore the return of Christ in a way that transcends classic interpretations. Rather than enter into the eschatological wars that have raged over the last two hundred years, we will focus our attention on how the First and Second Testaments harmonize in telling us what God has in store for the future as it concerns His Son.

GOD'S PLAN FOR PLANET EARTH

As we saw in the beginning of this book, God's intention from the beginning was to bring heaven and earth together. It was to expand the garden of Eden to the rest of the world. Consequently, God's intention is centered upon earth. God loves the earth and regards it highly. After God created the earth, the Bible says, "God saw everything that He had made, and indeed it was very good."[1] Contrary to what many believe, Scripture teaches that the earth will exist forever.[2]

Although the Bible speaks of a new heaven and a new earth,[3] the foundation of the earth will never pass away. The Lord is not going to do away with the world of space, time, and matter. Instead, God is going to *renovate* the earth, judge all things by fire, and burn up certain of its elements.[4]

Some have mistakenly embraced the notion that God hates this dirty little planet and has promised to rescue His people out of it before He trashes it. But Scripture teaches no such thing. Indeed, Scripture repeatedly warns that "the world" is evil.[5] But the Greek words translated "world" in these passages do not refer to the earth, but to the world system (*kosmos*) or the present age (*aion*) that is marked by the corruptions of sin.

The Bible makes clear that this present *age* is evil,[6] that the world system is headed up by satan,[7] and that God will judge the world system in the end.[8] But it teaches with equal force that the earth itself is precious to God, who has wonderful plans for it.

Because the world presently stands under the defilement of sin, God's people are strangers and pilgrims to it.[9] We are told that our citizenship is in the heavens,[10] and we are not to be attached to that which is earthly.[11] This present age and the world system are temporal and will pass away.[12]

At the same time, the new creation has arrived with the resurrection of Jesus. While we are not *from* this world,[13] we are certainly *for* the world—just as Jesus was not *from* this world but *for* it.[14]

The kingdom of God is certainly for the world, as Jesus prayed: "Your kingdom come. Your will be done on earth as it is in heaven."[15]

Although we do not belong to this present world, God's people will dwell on the renewed earth in the age to come. The New Jerusalem (God's eternal habitation in the glorified church) will descend from heaven *to* earth.[16]

Scripture portrays a God who is very much in love with His creation.[17]

The earth was created primarily for Jesus Christ.[18] Therefore, God does not despise the earth. He loves it and has created humans to be trustees of this estate that He loves.[19] In fact, God has sworn by Himself that He will redeem the earth, deliver it from its corruption, and fill it with His glory:

> The creation waits in eager expectation for the sons of God to be revealed. For the creation was subjected to frustration, not by its own choice, but by the will of the one who subjected it, in hope that the creation itself will be liberated from its bondage to decay and brought into the glorious freedom of the children of God. We know that the whole creation has been groaning as in the pains of childbirth right up to the present time. Not only so, but we ourselves, who have the first-fruits of the Spirit, groan inwardly as we wait eagerly for our adoption as sons, the redemption of our bodies.[20]

> But as truly as I live, all the earth shall be filled with the glory of the LORD.[21]

> For the earth shall be filled with the knowledge of the glory of the LORD, as the waters cover the sea.[22]

> The wolf also shall dwell with the lamb, and the leopard shall lie down with the kid; and the calf and the young lion and the fatling together; and a little child shall lead them. And the cow and the bear shall feed; their young ones shall lie down together: and the lion shall eat straw like the ox. And the sucking child shall play on the hole of the asp, and the weaned child shall put his hand on the cockatrice' den. They shall not hurt nor destroy in all my holy mountain: for the earth shall be full of the knowledge of the LORD, as the waters cover the sea.[23]

> He will judge between the nations and will settle disputes for many peoples. They will beat their swords into plowshares and their spears into pruning hooks. Nation will not take up sword against nation, nor will they train for war anymore.[24]

THE CENTRAL ISSUE OF THE UNIVERSE

The ultimate issue in the universe is over who will be worshipped. The eternal purpose of God is to make Christ preeminent over all things.[25] From the very beginning, satan has sought to dethrone the Lord Jesus Christ from His rightful place. This is the essence of the battle that has raged through the ages. The controversy over the universe is over who will have the authority. Therefore, in an attempt to seize the authority of Christ, satan has influenced the nations to oppose His lordship.

Psalm 2:1–2 says, "Why do the heathen rage and the people imagine a vain thing? The kings of the earth set themselves, and the rulers take counsel together, against the LORD, and against his anointed [Christ]."[26] Similarly, because Christ is united with His church, and because Christ's sovereignty will be realized through the church, satan's attack is not only against the Lord Jesus (the Anointed One), but against His people (the anointed ones).

Thankfully, however, this battle has already been won. Jesus Christ has triumphed through the cross, and His church has entered into His victory. As a result, we are more than conquerors through Him who loves us.[27] Jesus Christ shall indeed reign over the universe, satan will be cast out, and God's eternal purpose will be realized. However, in the interim, the battle over the earth continues to rage.

THE PRESENT YET FUTURE OF THE KINGDOM

As we have seen, one of Jesus' core messages was the kingdom of God. The Bible never *defines* the kingdom; it only *describes* it. The kingdom is the manifestation of God's ruling presence. As we established in our book *Jesus Manifesto*, the kingdom is embodied in Jesus Himself.

Consequently, wherever a group of people recognize the sovereignty of Christ and submit to His lordship, the kingdom of God is present in that place. In addition, wherever the kingdom of God is being expressed, satan has no ground or power in that place. His occupancy is destroyed. At the same time, wherever Christ's authority is not recognized, the kingdom of God is not present and satan is in control—for

Christ and satan cannot dwell together.[28] So wherever the King is present and practically enthroned, His kingdom is also present.[29]

In the 1994 Disney animation *The Lion King*, the king named Mufasa shows the vast expanse of the Pride Lands to his son, Simba. He then says that their kingdom is wherever the light hits. Exactly. Wherever the Light of the World falls, there is the kingdom. To live in the kingdom is to live in Jesus' light.

Scripture reveals that there are two aspects of the kingdom of God that are closely related. The first aspect of the kingdom is what we may call the *spiritual reality* of the kingdom. In this aspect, the kingdom of God does not come with visible observation. It is not physical, but is here in mystery. You can't see it or touch it. Rather, it is perceived spiritually.[30]

Since Christ is reigning on His throne right now (since His ascension), those who submit to His headship are in the kingdom and partake of its blessings. This includes the authority of the kingdom.[31] Therefore, in this present evil age, one can experience the righteousness, peace, and joy that are part of God's kingdom by submitting to Jesus Christ as the world's rightful Lord.

> *The first generation of Christians was fired by hopes for the kingdom. The second wave of Christianity built the church as an interim device while waiting for the kingdom. Later generations identified the two. Today the task is to reactivate the Christian hope by pointing to the Kingdom of God whose biblical images have been blurred in the history of Christianity.*
>
> —Norwegian theologian Carl Braaten[32]

The second aspect of the kingdom is what we might call the *physical reality* of the kingdom. The physical reality of the kingdom will become manifest when the King physically appears. At that time, Jesus the King will return to planet Earth in visible form, and all things will be submitted to His rulership.

The first time Jesus appeared, He came as the Lamb. The second time He appears, He shall come as the Lion from the tribe of Judah. That is, He will come to judge the world.[33] This means that He will set all things right. He will straighten the crooked. The world is severely out of joint, but Jesus will rejoin the disjointed. Jesus, as Judge and King, will exercise His complete rule over all things.[34] Jesus of Nazareth is ruling from the heavens now until He makes His enemies a footstool for His feet.[35]

While the spiritual reality and the physical reality are two distinct aspects of the kingdom, they are not separate. The physical reality is the "outward manifestation" of the spiritual reality. There is only one kingdom, and it possesses both an inward reality and an outward manifestation. In this age, we partake of the kingdom *spiritually*, while in the age to come we will partake of it *physically*.

This explains why the Bible says that we now taste "the powers of the age to come."[36] As believers we may taste (partially or minimally partake) of the power of the coming kingdom age. This is a reference to the spiritual reality of the kingdom that is now available to all who submit to Jesus.[37] It explains why some are healed and delivered (the kingdom is here). But it also explains why some get sick and are never healed (the kingdom is not yet).

> ***Heaven will be recognized as a country we have already entered, and in whose light and warmth we have already lived.***
>
> —British monk Harry Williams[38]

To put it in a sentence, those who follow Jesus live in the presence of the future. Instead of thinking of God as "up above," why not think of God as "up ahead," drawing the world upward toward Christ? While God draws the world toward unity from "up ahead" and the full manifestation of God's kingdom is yet future (awaiting Christ's return), today the church can live in the beauty and power of that kingdom and infect the earth with God's healing salvation.[39] With Jesus, heaven begins now. In fact, heaven begins now or never.

What we do in this age has an effect on the age to come. Those who are last in this life will be first in the coming age. Those who suffer today will reign tomorrow.[40] Jesus gained His victory through suffering. His followers will gain it by sharing His sufferings.[41] Paul closed his long thesis of the resurrection of the believer by urging God's people to always abound in the work of the Lord because it "is not in vain."[42] There is a connection between our lives in the present and our future destiny.

THE SABBATH AND THE LAND

Aside from the temple (which we've explored in previous chapters), the land and the Sabbath are two images that take up a lot of ink in the First Testament. Temple, land, and Sabbath were closely tied with the unique identity of God's people, Israel.

We've already seen how the temple was a shadow of Jesus Christ (chapter 2). The same is true with the land and the Sabbath. In fact, both the Sabbath and the land teach us a great deal about the already-but-not-yet nature of the kingdom of God.

God's plan for Israel was to rescue them from Egypt (a symbol of the world system),[43] bring them through the wilderness of testing, and bring them into Canaan—the land that "flows with milk and honey."[44]

Some Bible students regard the land of Canaan as representing the afterlife in heaven. We do not agree. The land was full of God's enemies, seven Canaanite nations in all. And God's word to Israel was to defeat them. So there was a great deal of war in the land. And Israel had to "press in" to occupy it.

We believe the Second Testament parallel to the land is the kingdom of God. In Hebrews, we are told to "labor" or "make every effort" to enter into the land:

> Now we who have believed enter that rest, just as God has said, "So I declared on oath in my anger, 'They shall never enter my rest.'" And yet his work has been finished since the creation of the world. For somewhere he has spoken about the seventh day in these words: "And on the seventh day God rested from all his work." And again in the passage above he says, "They shall never enter my rest." It still remains

> that some will enter that rest, and those who formerly had the gospel preached to them did not go in, because of their disobedience. Therefore God again set a certain day, calling it Today, when a long time later he spoke through David, as was said before: "Today, if you hear his voice, do not harden your hearts." For if Joshua had given them rest, God would not have spoken later about another day. There remains, then, a Sabbath-rest for the people of God; for anyone who enters God's rest also rests from his own work, just as God did from his. Let us, therefore, make every effort [labor] to enter that rest, so that no one will fall by following their example of disobedience.[45]

In this text, the writer of Hebrews coupled the land of Canaan with the rest of God, the Sabbath. God's plan was that Israel defeat the enemies who occupied the land and "possess" it for herself. By doing so, she would enjoy rest.

Paul told us that Jesus Christ is the rest of God, our true Sabbath.[46] Only in Him do we find rest. Jesus is also the reality of the promised land. He is the kingdom embodied: the manifestation of God's ruling presence. But there's something else, something more.

The First Testament repeats over and over again how "rich" the land was. In this regard, the land corresponds not only to the kingdom of God, where there is "righteousness and peace and joy in the Holy Spirit,"[47] but also to what Paul called "the unsearchable riches of Christ"[48] and "every spiritual blessing in the heavenly realms because we are united with Chirst."[49]

Consider what was in the land and how it reminds us of the inexhaustible riches that are in Christ Jesus: It was spacious.[50] It was good.[51] It contained water.[52] It had valleys and hills.[53] It contained wheat,[54] barley,[55] vines,[56] figs,[57] olive oil,[58] milk,[59] bread,[60] mountains,[61] and so on.[62]

When Paul penned Ephesians and Colossians, it seems that he had the land in mind when he spoke about the unsearchable riches of Christ. He talked about the "breadth, and length, and depth, and height" of Christ's love.[63] He spoke about being "grounded" in Christ, "rooted" in Christ, "built up" in Christ, and to "so walk" in Christ.[64] All of this language conjures up images found in the book of Joshua when describing the land. It also contains echoes of the temple, which was to be built and grounded on the land.

The spiritual blessings that are in Christ are located in "heavenly realms."[65] The heavenly realms do not speak of heaven after we die. For the heavenly realms are also the location of our spiritual warfare.[66] So just as the Israelites had to labor to possess the land, believers must labor, possess, press into the spiritual blessings and riches of Christ that are ours by standing against principalities and powers who would seek to rob them from us. The seven Canaanite nations—which foreshadow the "principalities," "powers," and "spiritual wickedness in high places"[67]—sought to rob God's people of the land that God gave them as their inheritance. So they had to possess it by faith.

> *The coming of Christ will also be an* apokalypsis, *an "unveiling" or "disclosure." The power and glory that are now his by virtue of his exaltation and heavenly session must be disclosed to the world.*
>
> —GEORGE E. LADD[68]

Jesus is the new Joshua who leads His people into His kingdom to possess the riches that are theirs in Him.[69] Yet we enter that kingdom through "many tribulations."[70] So in one way the land is ours now. We can enter into the rest of Christ today. We can enjoy the riches and blessings that are in Him now. This is the "already" of the kingdom.

Yet in another way our rest will not be complete until all of God's enemies are defeated and there is no more war. This is the "not yet" of the kingdom. Jesus is the reality of temple, Sabbath, and land. He is also the reality of the new creation. And all of these elements have already-but-not-yet dimensions.

THE APPEARANCE OF JESUS

Some scholars believe that Jesus never talked about His second coming. For them texts like Mark 13, Matthew 24, Luke 17, and Luke 21 all speak about Jesus' vindication in AD 70 when the temple of Jerusalem was destroyed.[71] Other scholars believe these texts have a dual meaning.[72] One layer of prophecy speaks of what happened in AD 70, while another layer speaks of what will happen in the future when Jesus returns to earth.[73]

We are not going to weigh in on this debate. It is both technical and complicated, and if properly treated, it would demand an entire book of its own. Instead, we will list some of what the First and Second Testaments have to say about the Lord's return with great consistency—when the personal presence of Jesus Christ within God's new creation will occur:

- God will remake heaven and earth completely, affirming the goodness of the original creation and ending its corruption and finality.[74]
- Jesus will reappear and usher in the age to come.[75]
- When Jesus appears, those Christians who are still alive will be changed, transformed, so that their mortal bodies will become incorruptible, like Christ's glorified, resurrected body.[76]
- When Jesus appears, the resurrection will occur. All who have died in Christ will rise again from the dead and take on a body of immortality, just like Jesus' glorified, resurrected body.[77]
- The day the resurrection occurs is also called "the last day" (or "the latter day)[78] and "the day of the Lord,"[79] and it will come unexpectedly.[80]
- The coming of Christ in glory, which will usher forth the resurrected, glorified bodies of the redeemed, is the Christian's hope.[81]
- The resurrection will occur on the "day of redemption" when our bodies will be redeemed, as well as the earth itself.[82]
- Both the "just" and the "unjust" will rise again. And Jesus will judge both.[83]
- The Lord will be revealed from heaven and return with thousands of His holy ones to judge the earth and show Himself to be King over all.[84]
- In texts such as 1 Thessalonians 4, Paul used imagery from the story of Moses coming down from Mount Sinai with the

Law. The trumpet sounds and a loud voice is heard. Paul also drew on the imagery of Daniel 7, in which God's people were vindicated over their pagan enemies by being raised up to sit with God in glory.

- Jesus Christ is the omega point of creation. Upon His return, Jesus will defeat the last enemy, death. He will transform the world as the Judge. He will sum up and subdue all things to Himself. Finally, He will hand the kingdom back over to His Father, and God will become all and all.[85]

C. S. Lewis has summed it up this way: "Unlike His first coming, Jesus' second coming will be with power and splendour. The Bible states that everyone will see Him, and everyone will appear before Him in judgement. Simply put, He will confront every person and pronounce his or her destiny."[86]

The return of Christ is presented by the Second Testament authors with various rich metaphors. One is the new creation being born from the womb of the old creation.[87] Another is the marriage of the new heavens and the new earth.[88] Another is the kingdom of God triumphing over and swallowing up all other kingdoms.[89]

Still another is drawn from the Roman imperial world of Caesar. The Greek word *parousia* is one example. When Caesar was away on a journey and he returned, his royal appearing—his imperial return to the city—was called the *parousia*. Caesar's followers would go out to meet him and welcome him back to the city.

Paul used this exact language and imagery when he spoke of Christ's return in 1 Thessalonians 4. Paul talked about meeting the Lord in the air, and how God will bring with Jesus those who have died with Him.[90] Putting all of the texts together on the subject, the scenario of Christ's return perfectly fits how the Romans and Greeks understood the word *parousia*. Jesus will appear, the resurrection will occur, and those Christians who are alive will be transformed "in the twinkling of an eye"[91] and meet Jesus in the air. They will then escort Him down from heaven to the newly recreated earth.[92]

The *parousia* ("bodily presence," "appearance," "revelation," or

> *God's eternal community has dawned, is dawning, and will one day arrive in its fullness. The God who has reconciled us to himself through Christ will one day bring us into full participation in the grand eschatological community of his divine reign.*
>
> —Stanley Grenz[94]

"unveiling") of Jesus on earth draws all of the promises, prophecies, and unfulfilled events in both First and Second Testaments into a whole. They all come rushing together in this amazing event—an event that Luke called the "restoration of all things"—and "heaven must receive" Jesus until it occurs.[93]

In this connection, the First Testament writers would often prophesy an event in the space of a few paragraphs, all of which have elements in them that occur thousands of years apart. So the two-part coming of Jesus, His appearance in the first century and His second coming (which hasn't occurred yet) are stated as if they are a single event.

THE FEASTS OF ISRAEL

The First Testament prophecies all find their climax in Christ. This includes the feasts (or festivals) of Israel.

> Therefore do not let anyone judge you by what you eat or drink, or with regard to a religious festival, a New Moon celebration or a Sabbath day. These are a shadow of the things that were to come; the reality, however, is found in Christ.[95]

While an entire book could be written on how Jesus fulfills all of Israel's ancient feasts, here is a brief survey:

- *The Feast of Passover*[96] was fulfilled in Jesus' sacrifice on the cross. (Many scholars believe that Jesus was put to death on Passover.) Paul called Him our "Passover lamb."[97]

- *The Feast of Unleavened Bread*[98] was fulfilled in the burial of Jesus, which marks the transition between the old creation and the new creation—a creation that is marked by truth and sincerity. Our union with Christ in His burial is experienced in water baptism.[99]
- *The Feast of Firstfruits*[100] was fulfilled in the resurrection of Jesus. He is, as Paul calls Him, "the firstfruits" of those who will be resurrected to life.[101]
- *The Feast of Pentecost* (or the Feast of Weeks)[102] was fulfilled in the descent of Jesus in the Holy Spirit on the day of Pentecost.[103] At Pentecost, Jesus came in the Spirit to live His life in and through His people.[104]
- *The Feast of Trumpets*[105] seems to find its fulfillment at the second coming of Jesus Christ, wherein the trumpet of God is mentioned.[106]
- *The Day of Atonement*[107] seems to find its fulfillment when the church will be glorified with Christ, the glory of God will fill the earth, and the universe will be saved from the curse.[108] While the Passover represents the salvation of God's people (based on the cross of Christ), the Day of Atonement represents the salvation of the entire cosmos (also based on the cross of Christ).
- *The Feast of Tabernacles*[109] seems to find its fulfillment in the resurrection of the holy ones (God's people), which will occur at Christ's return, when the kingdom comes in its fullness and Jesus judges the world. This is the final harvest.[110]
- *The Year of Jubilee*[111] finds its initial fulfillment in the earthly ministry of Jesus Christ to set the captives free.[112] But it will find its complete fulfillment at Christ's return, when the earth will be set free from the curse of sin and returned back to its rightful owner.[113]

While all Israel's feasts are presented close together in Leviticus 23, the first three feasts are separated in time from the last three feasts. The first three feasts occur during the first month (Nisan), while the last three feasts occur during the seventh month (Tishri). Interestingly, the first three have to do with the Lord's first coming; the last three have to do with His second coming.

In biblical prophecy, the coming of Jesus is viewed as one event separated by parentheses that stretch from the ascension to His royal appearing at the end of the age. We are now living in the parentheses, wherein we look back to His first coming and anticipate His second coming. Put another way, the kingdom has come and will come. Jesus' first coming inaugurated the kingdom of God; His second coming will consummate it. So the coming of the Messiah is one event separated by two moments: Bethlehem and the end of the age. The writer of Hebrews included both moments, saying, "So Christ was sacrificed once to take away the sins of many people; and he will appear a second time, not to bear sin, but to bring salvation to those who are waiting for him."[114]

Indeed, "He who is coming will come."[115]

JESUS' SECOND COMING

In Scripture, the word *salvation* means "deliverance" and includes three tenses: we *were* saved (justification = salvation from the penalty of sin); we *are being* saved (sanctification = salvation from the power of sin); and we *will be* saved (glorification = salvation from the presence of sin). Salvation, then, is Jesus Christ: Christ as our righteousness (past); Christ as our sanctification (present); Christ as our hope of glory (future).[116] The latter will occur when Jesus "will appear a second time."[117]

In this way, Jesus will complete what He began at His first appearing. He will end the exile. He will complete the exodus. He will bring His people and His good creation into its full rest. He will bring forth peace, justice, and prosperity to the entire world.

If we know nothing else about biblical prophecy, we know this: the fulfillment fleshes out the details. Christ's first coming contained many surprises, even among those who studied the prophecies of the First Testament. We believe the same will be true for His second coming. It will contain surprises for even the most learned biblical scholars. In this regard, we agree with Karl Barth, who said, "We can't fathom the Second Advent of Jesus Christ, and we stammer when we try to speak of it."[118]

In Philippians 3:20, Paul told the believers in Philippi that their "citizenship is in heaven." The meaning is not that their destination was heaven. Philippi was a Roman colony. Most of the Philippians were Roman citizens. Their destiny, therefore, was not Rome. The function of a Roman colony was to bring the culture of Rome to the city of Philippi. Thus Paul's word to the Philippian Christians was this: "Bring the culture of the heavens to earth."

So our calling as disciples is to labor for the kingdom of God by announcing in the power of the Holy Spirit that Jesus of Nazareth is Savior and Lord in both word and deed, praying and living that God's will be done on earth as it is in heaven, and holding in our hearts the words of Paul and John: "Maranatha . . . Come, Lord Jesus!"[119]

CONCLUSION

The Jesus Spirit

"HAVE THIS ATTITUDE IN YOURSELVES WHICH WAS ALSO IN CHRIST Jesus," Paul exhorted the church in Philippi.[1] So what is the attitude of Christ Jesus, the very Son of God, that Paul was talking about? What is a Jesus spirit? What is a Christ attitude?

It's the attitude of thinking of others more than and above oneself. Paul was reflecting from prison on how Jesus' spirit was of such humility that He thought of you and me as more important than Himself.

Whoa! Now, that's humility.

At the same time, Jesus exudes an air of assurance. Throughout this theography we have seen how confident Jesus is of His identity—the Son of God. To pick almost at random one more such incident: Jesus and the disciples took a shortcut through some grain fields one Sabbath. The disciples were hungry, so Jesus plucked some ears of grain and began

> *He lay in the crib*
> *so that you might*
> *stand at the altar.*
>
> —SAINT AMBROSE[2]

passing them around. Some Pharisees saw what He did and recoiled in horror. Here is Jesus' response:

> [Jesus] said to them, "Have you not read what David did when he was hungry, he and those who were with him: how he entered the house of God and ate the showbread which was not lawful for him to eat? . . . Or have you not read in the law that on the Sabbath the priests in the temple profane the Sabbath, and are blameless? Yet I say to you that in this place there is One greater than the temple. But if you had known what this means, 'I desire mercy and not sacrifice,' you would not have condemned the guiltless. For the Son of Man is Lord even of the Sabbath."[3]

"Greater than the temple"? "Lord" of the Sabbath? Another "David"? You can't get more confident than that. Yet unlike the Pharisees, Jesus gave no sense that He breathed purer air than the rest of us.

Humble confidence.

You can feel this Jesus spirit in His invitation, "Learn from me, because I am meek and humble in heart."[4] A humble and meek Messiah? Talk about the ultimate oxymoron. So strange and foreign to Jesus' hearers that some scholars have argued that the first followers of Jesus invented the concept of humility. The Greeks and Romans did not have a word for *humility* and despised the very concept.

> *What a chimera then is man. What a novelty. What a monster, what a chaos, what a contradiction, what a prodigy! Judge of all things, imbecile worm of the earth; depository of truth, a sink of uncertainty and error, the pride and refuse of the universe.*
>
> —Blaise Pascal[5]

John Calvin's commentary on Psalm 127 presents the model disciple as someone in motion with a "composed and tranquil mind."[6] The key to a Jesus spirit from a biblical perspective is the embodiment of paradoxical qualities: simultaneity of strength and vulnerability, innocence and experience, singularity and typicality, confidence and humility. Humility is what keeps confidence from going off the rails and becoming arrogance.

JESUS' GROWING AWARENESS OF HIS MESSIAHSHIP

Our theography ends with a brief exploration of Jesus' self-awareness as it relates to His messiahship and divine sonship. Contrary to the opinions of some, Jesus did not immediately know that He was "the Messiah, the Son of the living God," as Peter declared Him to be. He did, however, grow into that awareness, and He was not confused about it.

By the age of twelve, Jesus knew that God was His Father.[7] The gospel of John makes clear that Jesus didn't see Himself as a "Son of God" in the general sense that all children of the Creator are sons and daughters of God. Instead, He understood Himself to be the Son of God in a unique and decisive way. Calling Himself "the only begotten" (or "one and only") Son as well as habitually calling God "Abba" (a term that children used to address their fathers) are examples.[8]

When Luke wrote that "Jesus increased in wisdom and stature, and in favor with God and men,"[9] the first part ("grew in wisdom and stature") means that Jesus grew in age and height. In other words, He developed as all humans develop. This, of course, would include His memory and self-awareness. Part of that awareness was the consciousness that He was the incarnation of the second person of the triune God.[10] His words, "Before Abraham was, I AM,"[11] are just one example. By age thirty, Jesus had a high self-awareness and a clear Messianic self-understanding.[12]

Jesus' favorite term for Himself is an odd expression: "Son of man" or "Son of Adam" or "the human one." This phrase occurs eighty-two times in the Gospels. Jesus used it in two ways. It means "I'm one of you," or "I'm a man just as you are" or "I'm human too." But then it can also mean something much more glorified. The Son of man is also the One who looks like a man but who will come in the clouds in glory and wisdom and power. The very phrase is an oxymoron of humility and confidence, effacement and exaltation.[13]

The statements Jesus made about Himself are so lofty that they have given rise to the "trilemma" best summarized by C. S. Lewis in a BBC radio talk: Jesus was either "Lunatic, Liar, or Lord." Other people have defined the trilemma as "Mad, Bad, or God."

THE JESUS STORY REVEALED THROUGHOUT SCRIPTURE

The claims of Jesus give us insight into the humble confidence, the lowly certainty, the quiet resolve that marks the life of a perfect man whose life is given over to God. They also reveal how the Jesus story recapitulates and replays the major biblical dramas and narratives of the Hebrew Scriptures. The Jesus story is a tightly bound sequence of actions that move toward a climax and resolution. But each twist and turn of the story is scripted by the Hebrew story. The history of Israel is His story. Or as R. T. France has put it:

All Scripture testifies of me.

—JESUS[14]

> Thus he [Jesus] uses *persons* in the Old Testament as types of himself (David, Solomon, Elijah, Elisha, Isaiah, Jonah) or of John the Baptist (Elijah); he refers to Old Testament *institutions* as types of himself and his work (the priesthood and the covenant); he sees in the *experiences* of Israel foreshadowings of his own; he finds the *hopes* of Israel fulfilled in himself and his disciples; and sees his disciples as assuming the *status* of Israel; in Israel's deliverance by God he sees a type of the gathering of men into the church. . . . In all these aspects of the Old Testament people of God Jesus sees foreshadowings of himself and his work. . . . Jesus saw his mission as the fulfillment of the Old Testament Scriptures; not just of those which predicted a coming redeemer, but of the whole sweep of Old Testament ideas.[15]

In sum, what Torah is to Judaism, and the Qur'an is to Islam, Jesus is to Christianity.

David

Let's start with the story of King David, warlord and wordsmith—the one whom Bono calls "the Elvis of the Bible."[16] Jesus' story replayed David's story.[17] Born of David's earthly lineage, born in "the city of David" (Bethlehem), Jesus was promised the throne of David.[18] Others called Jesus "the son of David"—a Messianic title.[19] In the Hebraic mind, the son of a person was the reappearance or continuation of that person. Thus when Jesus was called the "son of David," it meant that David was present in and through Jesus. He was, in effect, David in another person.[20]

Jesus understood His connection with David when He invoked David's "unlawful" eating of the showbread in His sharp reply to the Pharisees.[21] Jesus was the full embodiment of the "man after God's heart" whom the Father chose to rule Israel. David wished to build God a house, and God in turn promised He would make a house for David—meaning a "family."[22] The Jews believed that God would establish His kingdom through David and His royal lineage. All of this is exactly what came to pass in Jesus, the true David. (We have sketched many other allusions to David in Jesus' life throughout this book.)

Adam

Jesus was also aware that He was "Son of man." This is a direct reference to Daniel 7, but the title means "son of Adam." Thus Jesus also saw Himself as the new Adam, which is how Paul portrayed Him (see chapter 4). Craig Keener points out that "Son of man" can be translated "the human one."[23] Jesus knew that as the Son of man, He who would suffer, die, and rise again.[25] In addition, Jesus saw Himself as the reality of the temple (see chapter 2), the reality of the Sabbath, (see chapter 2), the reality of creation (see chapter 2), and the reality of Israel (see chapter 7).[26]

> *The living Christ*
> *still has two hands,*
> *one to point the way,*
> *and the other held*
> *out to help us along.*
>
> —Thomas Walter Manson[24]

On top of all this, Jesus saw Himself as the manna that came down from heaven to feed Israel in the wilderness.[27] He saw Himself as the Lamb of God, which gave the people of God the strength to leave Egypt by eating it and saved them from death by the shedding of its blood.[28] He saw Himself as the Tree of Life and the flowing river in the garden of Eden.[29] He saw Himself as the new Solomon,[30] the new Moses,[31] and the new Elijah.[32] He also saw Himself in some of Jonah's story.[33]

From the lips of our Lord Himself:

- "For the Son of Man is Lord even of the Sabbath."[34]
- "Someone greater than Jonah is here."[35]
- "Someone greater than Solomon is here."[36]
- "There is one here who is even greater than the Temple!"[37]

The book of Hebrews makes clear that Jesus is the reality of the priestly king Melchizedek—"having neither beginning . . . nor end of life"—who gave Abraham bread and wine.[38] He is also the new Aaron, the real High Priest.[39] He's also the new Joshua, who brings God's people into the rest of God.[40]

Moses

In addition, Jesus is the new Moses, the one who delivers Israel out of Egypt and builds God's tabernacle.[41]

Matthew best connected the dots from Moses to Jesus. Here are some examples:

- Pharaoh tried to kill all the Hebrew baby boys, and only Moses was saved. Herod tried to kill all the Jewish baby boys, and only Jesus was saved.[42]
- When Moses' life was in danger, he fled Egypt to Midian and returned to Egypt later. When Jesus' life was in danger, He fled Israel to Egypt and returned to Israel later.[43]
- Moses was rejected by his own people ("Who made you a

ruler . . . over us?") and so was Jesus ("His own did not receive Him." And "Who made Me a judge . . . over you?")[44]
- Moses ascended a mountain to receive the Law; Jesus ascended a mountain to give a new "Law."[45]
- Moses was the mediator of the old covenant through blood. Jesus is the Mediator of the new covenant through His blood.[46]
- Moses fasted for forty days and forty nights; Jesus did also.[47]
- Moses led the exodus, bringing God's people out of Egypt. Jesus led the new exodus, bringing His people out of the world system.[48]

The First Testament calls Moses a prophet, a priest, a shepherd, and a ruler. The Second Testament does the same with Jesus.[49] Some of the Jews of Jesus' day believed (rightly) that Jesus was the fulfillment of this well-known prophecy concerning Moses: "I will raise up for them a Prophet like you [Moses] from among their brethren, and will put My words in His mouth, and He shall speak to them all that I command Him. And it shall be that whoever will not hear My words, which He speaks in My name, I will require it of him."[50]

During the transfiguration, which was a preview of the future glorification of Jesus at His resurrection, Jesus appeared in glory with Moses and Elijah. The Father spoke and said, "This is My beloved Son. Hear Him!"[51] These words echo the prophecy concerning the coming Messiah in Deuteronomy 18. The message seems to be that Jesus supersedes both the Law (represented by Moses) and the Prophets (represented by Elijah). Jesus is God's best and final word, as Hebrews 1 puts it. Peter, who was one of the "eyewitnesses of His majesty" on the Mount of Transfiguration, rehearsed the story in one of his letters.[52] The writer of Hebrews summed it up nicely:

> He was faithful to the one who appointed him, just as Moses was faithful in all God's house. Jesus has been found worthy of greater honor than Moses, just as the builder of a house has greater honor than the house itself. For every house is built by someone, but God is

> the builder of everything. Moses was faithful as a servant in all God's house, testifying to what would be said in the future. But Christ is faithful as a son over God's house. And we are his house, if we hold on to our courage and the hope of which we boast.[53]

Joseph

The Scriptures also portray Jesus as the new Joseph. Here are some examples:

- Both are firstborn.[54]
- Both are the most loved of their fathers.[55]
- Both were prophesied to be rulers.[56]
- Both Joseph's and Jesus' brothers were jealous of them and did not believe them.[57]
- Both were betrayed with pieces of silver.[58]
- Joseph was apparently put to death (and Jesus truly was) by his own people to get him out of the way.[59]
- Reuben wanted to rescue Joseph. Pilate wanted to rescue Jesus.[60]
- Both ended up in Egypt.[61]
- Both were made slaves.[62]
- Joseph was exalted and became a ruler; Jesus was exalted and became a ruler.[63]
- All knees bowed to Joseph. All knees will bow to Jesus.[64]
- Joseph's brothers did not recognize him. Jesus' own people didn't recognize Him.[65]
- Joseph was finally revealed to his brothers. Jesus will finally be revealed to Israel.[66]
- The evil that Joseph's brothers intended was used by God to save them. The same is true with Jesus.[67]
- Both were Saviors.[68]

Isaac

For another exercise in reading Jesus' life as the fulfillment of who and what came before, here are a few examples from the story of Isaac:

- Jesus and Isaac are the only two people in the entire Scripture who are referred to as "the only begotten son."[69]
- Isaac was a promised seed. Jesus Christ was the promised seed.[70]
- Isaac's birth was a miracle, as it was physically impossible for him to be conceived.[71] Jesus Christ's birth was miraculous as well.[72]
- Abraham was instructed to sacrifice his son Isaac.[73] God the Father spared not His only Son, Jesus Christ.[74]
- The sacrifice of Isaac was on Mount Moriah.[75] Moriah was located on a hill in what would later be called Jerusalem. Jesus Christ died on a hill outside of Jerusalem.[76]
- Isaac was obedient to his father unto death.[77] Jesus Christ was obedient to His Father unto death.[78]
- For three days Abraham considered that his son Isaac would be dead.[79] Jesus Christ was dead for three days.[80]
- Isaac carried wood for his own sacrifice.[81] Jesus Christ bore His own cross, which was made of wood.[82]
- After the obedience of Isaac, his mother, Sarah, died.[83] After the death of Christ, the nation of Israel was set aside.[84]
- Abraham gave all things to Isaac.[85] God has given all things to Jesus Christ.[86]

JESUS' SELF-UNDERSTANDING

Since Jesus saw Himself as the new Adam, the new David, the new Solomon, the new Temple, the new Israel, and the new Elijah, it's not a stretch to assume that He also saw Himself as the new Moses, the new Joseph, the new Isaac, and even the new Boaz (our kinsman-redeemer).[87] In the words of Ben Witherington,

> Jesus' way of expressing His transcendent self-understanding was by using metaphorical language, symbolic gestures, and actions that, in the light of the Old Testament, had messianic overtones . . . (1) he interpreted his exorcisms as the inbreaking of God's dominion, and (2) he interpreted his other healings in light of the Isaianic vision of

> future eschatological restoration. It is in Jesus' interpretation of these deeds that we found at least an implicit christological claim.[88]

As Jesus spent time listening to His Father and learning the Scriptures, He connected the biblical dots to realize that all Scripture witnesses to Him.[89] He came to understand that the Law, the Prophets, and the Writings (the wisdom literature)—all three parts of the Hebrew Bible—were His biography.

It is clear that Jesus knew He was uniquely God's Son and the promised Messiah. Beyond all of the evidence that we have given so far, it is confirmed by the following facts: He chose His disciples (instead of having them choose Him); He told His disciples that they would never surpass or equal Him;[90] He used the Jewish *amen* before He spoke ("Truly I say to you"), indicating that His words carried divine authority (the *amen* was never used this way throughout Jewish literature), and that He understood Himself to supersede the temple.[91]

Jesus' identity also has a corporate element to it. All who repent and trust in Jesus become united with Him. And as we argued in *Jesus Manifesto*, His history becomes our destiny—His story our story.[92]

RETHINKING THE GOSPEL

All of this throws new light on the word *gospel*. As young Christians, both of us were taught that the gospel is a plan—"the plan of salvation." Some Bible teachers used to frame that plan into "Four Spiritual Laws" and "The Romans Road."

In the first-century Roman world, however, the word *gospel* was used to describe the announcement that a new emperor had taken the throne. Heralds would be sent throughout the Roman empire to announce this good news. Their message was, "We have a new emperor. His name is Tiberius Caesar; adjust your life and bow the knee." Interestingly, the Roman emperor was also called "Savior" and "Lord" and was regarded as the one who would establish peace in the empire.[93]

Consequently when the apostles ("sent ones") used the term *gospel* and declared that Jesus was now the Lord and Savior of the world, it was a direct affront to the Roman hierarchy, especially Caesar.[94] The believing Jews no doubt connected the gospel-preaching of the apostles to Isaiah's prophecy—a proclamation that God Himself was now reigning in the person of Jesus.[95]

If you examine everywhere the term *gospel* is used throughout the Second Testament, you will discover that it's always bound up with the person of Jesus. (His work is united with His person. While people regularly separate His work from His person, you can't separate His person from His work. The same is true with His teachings.) In His preaching and teaching Jesus consistently pointed to Himself.

Read the four Gospels carefully sometime and count the number of times Jesus spoke about Himself. You will have no doubt that His message—His gospel—was Himself. Paul, Peter, John, and all the apostles preached the same gospel as did Jesus. Their message was also Christ.

In short, the message of the gospel is this: Jesus Christ is Lord (world ruler), Savior, the fulfillment of the entire First Testament (including the Adamic commission, the prophets, the priests, the kings, the sages, the temple, the sacrifices, the land, the Law, the promises, and the entire story of Israel), and the Resurrection and the Life.[97]

I have called Christ the "first instance" of the new man. But of course He is something much more than that. He is not merely a new man, one specimen of the species, but the new man. He is the origin and centre and life of all the new men. He came into the created universe, of His own will, bringing with Him the Zoe, the new life. (I mean new to us, of course: in its own place Zoe has existed for ever and ever.) And He transmits it not by heredity but by what I have called "good infection." Everyone who gets it gets it by personal contact with Him. Other men become "new" by being "in Him."

—C. S. Lewis[96]

The gospel, then, isn't a postulate; it's a person. Of course, without

> *[Word made flesh] Here the impossible union of spheres of existence is actual.*
>
> —T. S. Eliot[98]

postulating others cannot tell which person you are referring to. Without postulates one cannot say why this person is special and what he has done that makes a difference for people. But, properly conceived, the gospel is the proclamation of Jesus—His life, story, and work—reaching back from the First Testament story of Adam, the patriarchs, and Israel to the Second Testament, which announces His first and second appearances.

Jesus of Nazareth is the good news.

For this reason, the four Gospels were regarded as "the gospel" by the early church. And what story do the four Gospels tell? *They tell the story of Jesus. He is the gospel incarnate.*[99] The story found in the Gospels is the same story that is told in the First Testament.

Likewise, the Jesus of the history (the Jesus of the Gospels) and the Christ of faith are the same person. Consequently, we want to repeat what we find to be one of the striking realities about our Lord: *His character never changes*. If Jesus was tender toward children when He was on earth, He's tender toward children today. If He was playful, humorous, and witty in the days of His flesh, He is playful, humorous, and witty today. If He had little tolerance for self-righteous people who put the sins of others above their own sins,[100] He has little tolerance for it today. If He extended love, mercy, tenderness, and forgiveness when He walked this planet, He extends the same today.

Indeed, Jesus Christ is "the same yesterday, today, and forever."[101] Yet the Bread of Life must become fresh every morning, a living and daily presence in your life and ours as we struggle with the reality that each one of us is made in the image of God—a colossus with feet of clay.

BACK TO THE BEGINNING

This brings us back to the original thesis of this book. The Bible is the narrative of Jesus—the Christ, the Savior, the living Lord, and our All. On every page of the First Testament, God poured out His heart. He bled with His people long and hard before He entered earth through the womb of a young virgin girl in Bethlehem. In the ocean of words that many call "the Hebrew Bible," God revealed His character to us. He dispassionately enumerated His heart's desire—and with fiery passion, He laid out His plan. The cry of God in Jesus bled through every page from Genesis to Malachi. And in Matthew, YHWH took on human flesh and broke into planet Earth. The living Word of God clothed Himself with mortality and became one of us. And in so doing, He fulfilled every promise. Jesus, therefore, is God's best and final word.[102]

This explains why God wanted His people to learn His ways all throughout the First Testament. The First Testament is the historical grid by which we can understand the ways of God in Christ. Jesus repeats, embodies, fulfills, and completes the story of Israel in Himself. But more, Jesus came to bring the story of humanity to conclusion and correction, to resolve the human dilemma for both Jew and Gentile. Thus Jesus is not only the new Israel but also the new Adam, bringing humanity back to God's original design. N. T. Wright states it with dead-on simplicity:

> Scripture—the Old and New Testaments—is the story of creation and new creation. Within that, it is the story of covenant and new covenant. When we read scripture as Christians, we read it precisely as people of the new covenant and of the new creation. We do not read it, in other words, as a flat, uniform list of regulations or doctrines. We read it as the narrative in which we ourselves are now called to partake. We read it to discover "the story so far" and also "how it's supposed to end." To put it another way, we live somewhere between the end of Acts and the closing scene of Revelation. If we want to understand scripture and to find it doing its proper work in and through us, we must learn to read and understand it in the light of that overall story.[103]

May you live in that story for the glory of God, which remains in the face of the glorious One whom we affectionately call Lord Jesus.[104]

To the architect, He is the chief cornerstone.
(1 Peter 2:6)

To the bride, He is the bridegroom.
(Matt. 25:1)

To the carpenter, He is the door.
(John 10:9)

To the engineer, He is the new and living way.
(Heb. 10:20)

To the farmer, He is the Lord of the harvest.
(Matt. 9:38)

To the horticulturist, He is the true vine.
(John 15:1)

To the jurist, He is the righteous judge.
(2 Tim. 4:8)

To the lawyer, He is the advocate.
(1 John 2:1)

To the philanthropist, He is
the unspeakable gift.
(2 Cor. 9:15)

To the philosopher, He is the wisdom of God.
(1 Cor. 1:24)

To the preacher, He is the Word of God.
(Rev. 19:13)

To the soldier, He is the
captain of his salvation.
(Heb. 2:10)

To the statesman, He is the
desire of the nations.
(Hag. 2:7)

To the sinner, He is the Lamb of God
that taketh away the sins of the world.
(John 1:29)

—HENRIETTA MEARS (1890–1963)

APPENDIX

Post-Apostolic Witnesses

Justin Martyr (ca. 103–165)

"'But if you knew, Trypho,' continued I, 'who He is that is called at one time the Angel of great counsel, and a Man by Ezekiel, and like the Son of man by Daniel, and a Child by Isaiah, and Christ and God to be worshipped by David, and Christ and a Stone by many, and Wisdom by Solomon, and Joseph and Judah and a Star by Moses, and the East by Zechariah, and the Suffering One and Jacob and Israel by Isaiah again, and a Rod, and Flower, and Corner-Stone, and Son of God, you would not have blasphemed Him who has now come, and been born, and suffered, and ascended to heaven; who shall also come again, and then your twelve tribes shall mourn. For if you had understood what has been written by the prophets, you would not have denied that He was God, Son of the only, unbegotten, unutterable God.'"[1]

Tertullian (ca. 160–225)

"In the person of Moses there is a prefiguring of Christ, who intercedes with the Father, and offers his own soul for the saving of the people."[2]

Augustine (ca. 354–430)

"These hidden meanings of inspired Scripture we track down as best we can, with varying degrees of success; and yet we all hold confidently to the firm belief that these historical events and the narrative of them have always some foreshadowing of things to come, and are always to be interpreted with reference to Christ and his Church, which is the City of God."

"He opened unto them the Scripture, and showed them that it behooved the Christ to suffer, and all things to be fulfilled that were written concerning him in the law of Moses and the prophets and the psalms—so embracing the whole of the Old Testament. Everything in those Scriptures speaks of Christ, but only to him that has ears. He opened their minds to understand the Scriptures; and so let us pray that he will open our own."[3]

Irenaeus (d. ca. 202)

"If any one, therefore, reads the Scriptures with attention, he will find in them an account of Christ, and a foreshadowing of the new calling. For Christ is the treasure which was hid in the field, that is, in this world (for 'the field is the world'); but the treasure hid in the Scriptures is Christ, since He was pointed out by means of types and parables."[4]

John Chrysostom (ca. 347–407)

"What then is the shadow (*skia*) what then is the truth (*aletheia*)? . . . You have often seen an Emperor's portrait which is prepared on a dark background, then the artist by drawing white lines all around it, makes an emperor, an imperial throne, and horses standing nearby, and body guards, and bound prisoners of war lying down. Now when you see these things merely sketched out you neither know everything nor are you totally ignorant of everything, but you know that a man and a horse are drawn there, though they are indistinct. But you don't accurately [or fully] know what sort of emperor or what sort of prisoner it is until the truth of the colors comes and makes the face distinct and clear. For just as you don't ask everything of that image / portrait before the truth of the colors, but if you receive some indistinct knowledge of what is there, you consider the sketch to be sufficiently ready, in just that same way consider with me the Old and New Testaments, and don't demand from me the whole fullness of the truth in the [Old Testament] type . . . for as in the painting, until someone draws in colors it is a shadowy sketch."[5]

Ambrose (ca. 337–397)

"*In the volume of the book it is written of Me.* Yes, it is written of Christ in the beginning of the Old Testament that He should come, to do the will of God the Father in the redemption of mankind; since it is written that He formed Eve, in the likeness of the Church, to be a help to man."[6]

John Cassian (ca. 359–440)

"Revelation is linked to allegory insofar as it explains in a spiritual sense the truths hidden under the historical account. For example, suppose we wished to discover how 'our fathers were all beneath the cloud and all were baptized in Moses in the cloud and in the sea and [how] all ate the same spiritual food and drank the same spiritual drink from the rock and that rock was Christ.' (1 Cor. 10:1–4)."[7]

Thomas Aquinas (1225–1274)

"For the ceremonies of the Old Law foreshadowed Christ. But this was done only by the sacrifices, which foreshadowed the sacrifice in which Christ *delivered Himself an oblation and a sacrifice to God* (Ephes. v. 2). Again, in this respect, it also fulfils what the Old Law foreshadowed. Hence it is written (Coloss. ii. 17) concerning the ceremonial precepts that they were 'a shadow of things to come, but the body is of Christ'; in other words, the reality is found in Christ. Therefore the

New Law is called the law of reality; whereas the Old Law is called the law of shadow or of figure."[8]

John Calvin (1509–1564)

"We ought to read the Scriptures with the express design of finding Christ in them . . . "

"By *the Scriptures*, it is well known, is here meant the Old Testament; for it was not in the Gospel that Christ first began to be manifested, but, having received testimony from the Law and the Prophets, he was openly exhibited in the Gospel."

"This is what we should in short seek in the whole of Scripture: truly to know Jesus Christ, and the infinite riches that are comprised in him and are offered to us by him from God the Father."[9]

Martin Luther (1483–1546)

"Whoever would study well in the Bible . . . should refer everything to the Lord Christ."

"In the whole Scripture, there is nothing but Christ, either in plain words or involved words. . . . The whole Scripture is about Christ alone everywhere, if we look to its inner meaning, though superficially it may sound different. . . . It is beyond question that all Scriptures point to Christ alone. . . . The entire Old Testament refers to Christ and agrees with Him. . . . The New Testament is not more than a revelation of the Old, just as when a man had first a closed letter and afterwards broke it open. So the Old Testament is an epistle of Christ, which after His death He opened and caused to be read through the Gospel and proclaimed everywhere."[10]

George Whitefield (1714–1770)

"There are very few that ever gave this book of God, the grand charter of salvation, one fair reading through: though we profess to have assented to the truth of scripture, as our Lord said, 'In them we think we have eternal life,' yet most read them as they would a proclamation, a romance, a play, or novels, that help only to bring them to the devil, but choose not to read God's book, which is to be our guide to glory; 'they are they (says Christ) which testify of me: "Lord God, convert and change our hearts."' However, this was spoken in reference to the Old Testament, and certainly shews us, that Christ is the treasure hid in that field, yet, as there are equal proofs of the divinity of the New Testament, the word Holy Scriptures include both, especially as Christ is the antitype of all the types, the Alpha and Omega, the beginning and the end, of all divine revelation."

"He bade many; the eternal God took the Jews for his peculiar people, under the Mosaic dispensation; and by types, shadows, and prophesies of the Old Testament, invited them to partake of the glorious privileges of the gospel."[11]

John Wesley (1703–1791)

"There are more types of Christ in this book [Exodus] than perhaps in any other book of the Old Testament. The way of man's reconciliation to God, and coming into covenant and communion with him by a Mediator, is here variously represented; and it is of great use to us for the illustration of the New Testament. . . . [Exodus 2] begins the story of Moses, the most remarkable type of Christ as prophet, saviour, lawgiver, and mediator, in all the Old Testament."[12]

Jonathan Edwards (1703–1758)

"Jesus of Nazareth is indeed the Son of God, and the Saviour of the world; and so that the Christian religion is the true religion, seeing that Christ is the very person so evidently pointed at, in all the great dispensations of Divine Providence from the very fall of man, and was so undoubtedly in so many instances foretold from age to age, and shadowed forth in a vast variety of types and figures. . . . What has been said, affords a strong argument for the divine authority of the books of the Old Testament, from that admirable harmony there is in them, whereby they all point to the same thing. For we may see by what has been said, how all the parts of the Old Testament, though written by so many different penmen, and in ages so distant, harmonize one with another. All agree in one, and centre in the same event; which it was impossible for any one of them to know, but by divine revelation."[13]

J. C. Ryle (1816–1900)

"In every part of both Testaments, Christ is to be found—dimly and indistinctly at the beginning—more clearly and plainly in the middle—fully and completely at the end—but really and substantially everywhere. Christ's sacrifice and death for sinners, and Christ's kingdom and future glory, are the light we must bring to bear on any book of Scripture we read . . . Christ is the only key that will unlock many of the dark places of the Word. Some people complain that they do not understand the Bible. And the reason is very simple. They do not use the key. To them the Bible is like the hieroglyphics in Egypt. It is a mystery, just because they do not know and employ the key."

"In the last place, *read the Bible with Christ continually in view*. The grand primary object of all Scripture is to testify to Jesus. Old Testament ceremonies are shadows of Christ. Old Testament judges and deliverers are types of Christ. Old Testament history shows the world's need of Christ. Old Testament prophecies are full of Christ's sufferings, and of Christ's glory yet to come. The first advent and the second, the Lord's humiliation and the Lord's kingdom, the cross and the crown, shine forth everywhere in the Bible. Keep fast hold on this clue, if you would read the Bible aright."[14]

Charles Spurgeon (1834–1892)

"But there is no fear of any tautologies in Christ; you may look at Christ a thousand times, and you shall have, if you please, a thousand different aspects. If you choose to turn to one book of the Old Testament you shall see him in a vast variety of aspects. You shall see him as a Paschal Lamb; you shall see him as the scapegoat; you shall see him at one time as the bullock, strong to labor, and then you shall see him as the lamb, patient to endure; you shall behold him as the dove, full of innocence; you shall see him in the blood sprinkled, in the incense burning, in the laver filled with water; you shall see him in Aaron's rod that budded, and in the golden pot that was full of manna; you shall see him *in* the ark; you shall see him *over* the ark; *in* the ark you shall see him having the law within his heart, and over the ark you shall see the golden light and the mercy-seat, and say, 'Christ is here.' In every type you shall see Christ—in so many different shapes, too, that you shall say, 'Turn this whichever way I like, there is something fresh.'"

"For every text in Scripture, there is a road to the metropolis of the Scriptures, that is Christ. And my dear brother, your business is, when you get to a text, to say, 'Now what is the road to Christ?' . . . I have never yet found a text that had not got a road to Christ in it."[15]

John Newton (1725–1807)

"The types of Christ in the Old Testament may be considered as twofold, personal and relative. The former describing under the veil of history, his character and offices as considered in himself; the latter teaching under a variety of metaphors, the advantages those who believe in him should receive from him. Thus Adam, Enoch, Melchizedek, Isaac, Joseph, Moses, Aaron, Joshua, Sampson, David, Solomon, and others, were in different respects types or figures of Christ. Some more immediately represented his person; others prefigured his humiliation; others referred to his exaltation, dominion, and glory. So, in the latter sense, the ark of Noah, the rainbow, the manna, the brazen serpent, the cities of refuge, were so many emblems pointing out the nature, necessity, means and security of that salvation which the Messiah was to establish for his people. Nor are these fanciful allusions of our own making, but warranted and taught in scripture, and easily proved from thence, would time permit; for indeed, there is not one of these persons or things which I have named, but would furnish matter for a long discourse, if closely considered in this view, as typical of the promised Redeemer . . . The New Testament shows that all these characters and circumstances were actually fulfilled in Jesus of Nazareth; and that it was he of whom 'Moses in the law, and the prophets did write;' and that we are not to look for another."[16]

A. B. Simpson (1843–1919)

"The Tabernacle is the grandest of all the Old Testament types of Christ. It was all one great object lesson of spiritual truth. In its wonderful furniture, priesthood, and worship, we see, with a vividness that we find nowhere else, the glory and grace of Jesus, and the privileges of His redeemed people. And as in the architect's plan we can understand the future building better, even, than by looking at the building without the plan; so, in this pattern from the mount, we can understand as nowhere else, that glorious temple of which Christ is the corner-stone and we also, as living stones, are built up in Him a spiritual house, an holy priesthood, to 'offer sacrifices acceptable to God through Jesus Christ.'"[17]

Sinclair B. Ferguson (1948–)

"In discussing the pre-Christ revelation of God as Trinity, B. B. Warfield describes the Old Testament as a richly furnished but dimly lit room. Only when the light is turned on do the contents become clear. That light has been switched on in Christ and in the New Testament's testimony to him. Now the triune personal being of God becomes clear. To read the Old Testament with the light switched off would be to deny the historical reality of our own context. On the other hand, we would be denying the historical reality of the text and its context if we were to read and preach it as though that same light had already been switched on within its own pages."[18]

A. W. Pink (1886–1952)

"The Old Testament Scriptures are fundamentally a stage on which is shown forth in vivid symbolism and ritualism the whole plan of redemption. The events recorded in the Old Testament were actual occurrences, yet they were also typical remigrations. Throughout the Old Testament dispensations God caused to be shadowed forth in parabolic representation the whole work of redemption by means of a constant and vivid appeal to the senses. This was in full accord with a fundamental law in the economy of God."

"Concerning the Person and work of the Lord Jesus, God first gave a series of pictorial representations, later a large number of specific prophecies, and last of all, when the fullness of time was come, God sent forth His own Son. . . . Let the reader constantly bear in mind this important principle and fact, namely, that everything in the Old Testament Scriptures typified or represented Gospel or Eternal realities."[19]

Dietrich Bonhoeffer (1906–1945)

"Therefore it [the Church] reads the whole of Holy Scripture as the book of the end, of the new [*vom Neuen*], of Christ. Where Holy Scripture, upon which the church of Christ stands, speaks of creation, of the beginning, what else can it say other than that it is only from Christ that we can know what the beginning is? The Bible is after all nothing other than the book of the church. It is this in its very essence, or it is nothing. . . . In the church, therefore, the story of creation must be read in a way that begins with Christ and only then moves on toward him as its goal; indeed one can read it as a book that moves toward Christ only when one knows that Christ is the beginning, the new, the end of our whole world. Theological exposition takes the Bible as the book of the church and interprets it as such."

"The Old Testament must be read in the light of the incarnation and crucifixion, that is, the revelation which has taken place for us. Otherwise, we are left with the Jewish or heathen understanding of the Old Testament."

"The God of the Old Testament is the Father of Jesus Christ. The God who appears in Jesus Christ is the God of the Old Testament. He is the triune God."[20]

Karl Barth (1886–1968)

"As regards the handling of Old Testament texts, we maintain that for us the Old Testament is valid only in relation to the New. If the church has declared itself to be the lawful successor of the synagogue, this means that the Old Testament is witness to Christ, before Christ but not without Christ. Each sentence in the Old Testament must be seen in this context. . . . Even in a sermon on Judges 6:3 it is possible both to insist on the literal sense and also to set one's sights on Christ. As a wholly Jewish book, the Old Testament is a pointer to Christ. . . . The Old Testament points forward, the New Testament points backward, and both point to Christ."

"Christ has risen from the dead, and has revealed the fulfillment of Scripture and therefore its real meaning. In the light of this, how can the Church understand the Old Testament witnesses except as witnesses to Christ? A religio-historical understanding of the Old Testament in abstraction from the revelation of the risen Christ is simply an abandonment of the New Testament and of the sphere of the Church in favour of that of the Synagogue, and therefore in favour of an Old Testament which is understood apart from its true object and content."[21]

F. F. Bruce (1910–1990)

"To the early Christians Jesus was the central theme of the Old Testament revelation, which indeed reached its fulfillment in him as the Messiah."

"The books of the Old Covenant then, tell how God made the necessary preparation for the sending of His Son to inaugurate the new covenant. The books of the New Covenant tell how the Son of God came to do this and set forth the implications of this New Covenant. Both collections alike speak of Christ; it is He who gives unity to each and to both together."

"These words, 'it is they that bear witness to me' [Jn. v. 39] are crucial for our inquiry. The Christian approach to the Old Testament is bound up with its witness to Christ. Christ is the goal of the Old Testament. To change the figure, He is the key to the Old Testament; the Old Testament, that is to say, cannot be properly understood apart from Him. . . . The two Testaments are like two parts of one sentence;

both are necessary to complete the sense; either is imperfect without the other. And when we listen to the whole sentence pronounced by the two Testaments together, it is the sentence which proclaims God's saving grace in Christ."[22]

Erich Sauer (1898–1959)

"The Old Testament exists for the New Testament. Christ Himself is the goal and soul of the pre-Christian historical revelation. He is the Goal of Old Testament history; the meaning of Old Testament worship to God; the fulfillment of Old Testament Messianic prophecy."[23]

E. E. Ellis (1926–2010)

"'The law and the prophets' represent here [Matt. 5:17f.], as elsewhere, the whole OT. Jesus is revealed not only as the proclaimer of God's word but also as the proclaimer of himself as the one in whom the OT word is to find fulfillment. Jesus fulfills the OT in two ways. By his interpretation of it he unveils its true and final (eschatological) meaning. In his person and work he fulfills the true intention of its prophecies and the goal of its history of salvation."[24]

Stanley Grenz (1950–2005)

"In short, for Barth the revelatory nature of the Bible is dependent on its function as a witness to the revelation of God in Jesus Christ. Although we may resist his inordinate emphasis on the event character of revelation, Barth was surely correct in his delineation of the relationship between Scripture and Christ. As G. C. Berkouwer asserted, 'Every word about the God-breathed character of Scripture is meaningless if Holy Scripture is not understood as the witness concerning Christ.'"[25]

Wilhelm Vischer (1895–1988)

"The hallmark of Christian theology is that it is Christology; a theology that can affirm nothing of God except in and through Jesus Christ. . . . From that it is clear that all the knowledge of God which resides in the Old Testament scriptures is mediated through Jesus Christ.

Consequently, the theological exposition of these writings within the Church can be nothing other than Christology.

"The two main words of the Christian confession 'Jesus is the Christ'—the personal name 'Jesus' and the vocational name 'Christ'—correspond to the two parts of the Holy Scriptures: the New and the Old Testament. The Old Testament tells us *what* the Christ is; the New, *who* he is.

"The Christian Church stands and falls with the recognition of the unity of the two Testaments. A 'Church' which disparages the value of the Old Testament in face of the New disbelieves the decisive element in the apostolic teaching, and ceases to be 'Christian.'"[26]

Brevard Childs (1923–2007)

"One of the earliest crises of the Church came in the middle of the 2nd century when it became increasingly evident that the scriptures of the Old Testament, even when read as the Law of Christ, were not adequate or complete without being supplemented by a written evangelical witness, that is by a New Testament.

"What finally emerged was a Christian Bible consisting of both an Old Testament and a New Testament both witnessing to Jesus Christ, the one testifying in terms of prophecy, the other of fulfillment, yet both speaking of the future eschatological rule of God. The Christian Bible was formed from two different collections, each having its discrete traditional history, yet together comprising the one unified testimony to God in Jesus Christ . . . the Old and New Testaments together comprise the Christian Bible. The voice of Israel and the voice of the evangelists constitute a single narrative of God's redemptive actions spanning prophecy and fulfillment. The two testaments are neither to be fused, nor separated."[27]

Richard Longenecker (20th–21st century)

"There is little indication in the New Testament that the authors themselves were conscious of varieties of exegetical genre or of following particular modes of interpretation. . . . What the New Testament writers are conscious of, however, is interpreting the Old Testament

(1) from a Christocentric perspective, (2) in conformity with a Christian tradition, and (3) along Christological lines."[28]

R. T. France (1938–2012)

"The idea of fulfillment inherent in New Testament typology derives not from a belief that the events so understood were explicitly predicted, but from the conviction that in the coming and work of Jesus the principles of God's working, already imperfectly embodied in the Old Testament, were more perfectly re-embodied, and thus brought to completion. In that sense, the Old Testament history pointed to Jesus. For the Old Testament prophets the antitypes were future; for the New Testament writers they have already come. . . .

"Jesus' types are drawn from a wide range of aspects of Israel seen in the Old Testament; they are not restricted to any one period or single class. Thus he uses *persons* in the Old Testament as types of himself (David, Solomon, Elijah, Elisha, Isaiah, Jonah) . . . he refers to Old Testament *institutions* as types of himself and his work (the priesthood and the covenant); he finds the *hopes* of Israel fulfilled in himself and his disciples and sees his disciples as assuming the *status* of Israel; in Israel's *deliverance* by God he sees a type of the gathering of men into his church. . . . In all these aspects of the Old Testament people of God Jesus sees foreshadowings of himself and his work."[29]

John Goldingay (1942–)

"The Old Testament is Act I to the New Testament's Act II. And, as in any story, you understand the final scene aright only in the light of the ones that preceded it. For this reason, a Christian is interested in understanding the whole Old Testament story, in order that he can see as fully as possible its implications for understanding Christ. The converse is also true. As well as understanding Christ in the light of the Old Testament story, Matthew understands the Old Testament story in the light of the Christ event. Matthew's claim is that the story from Abraham to David and from the exile on into the post-exilic period comes to its climax with the coming of Christ, and needs to be understood in the light of this denouement. Now this is not the only way to read the history of Israel.

A non-Christian Jew will understand it very differently. Whether you read Israel's story in this way will depend on what you make of Jesus. If you believe he is the Christ, then you will believe that he is the climax of Old Testament history. If you do not, you won't."[30]

N. T. Wright (1948–)

"The Old Testament must be seen as part of the Christian scripture. I respect those who call the Old Testament the Hebrew scriptures to acknowledge that they are still the scriptures of a living faith community different from Christianity. But Luke insists that since Jesus really was raised from the dead, the ancient scriptures of Israel must be read as a story that reaches its climax in Jesus and will then produce its proper fruit not only in Israel but also in Jesus' followers and, through them, in all the world."

"When Luke says that Jesus interpreted to them all the things about Himself, throughout the Bible, he doesn't mean that Jesus collected a few, or even a half dozen, isolated texts, verses chosen at random. He means that the whole *story*, from Genesis to Chronicles (the last book of the Hebrew Bible; the prophets came earlier), pointed forwards to a fulfillment which could only be found when God's anointed took Israel's suffering, and hence the world's suffering, to himself, died under its weight, and rose again as the beginning of God's new creation, God's new people. This is what had to happen; and now it just had."

"God has, as it were, written the story of Messiah into larger history as the story of 'the Messiah's people according to the flesh' (Rom. 9:5). The only way Paul knows how to understand what has happened to Israel is the pattern of Jesus the Messiah, the one in whom all God's secret wisdom is now revealed."[31]

James D. G. Dunn (1939–)

"The first thing to be said is that the choice of the OT text as a rule was not arbitrary. The NT writers did not simply seize on *any* text, or create texts *ex nihilo.* There was a *givenenss* in the passages they quote. They are for the most part passages which had already been accepted as messianic (Ps. 110:1), or which in light of Jesus' actual life have a *prima facie* claim to be messianic (like Ps. 22 and Isa. 53). . . . Second, the interpretation was achieved again and again by reading the Old Testament passage or incident quoted *in the light of the event of Christ*, by viewing it from the standpoint of the new situation brought about by Jesus and of the redemption effected by Jesus.

"Jesus again stands at the centre—the traditions about him and the Christians' present relation to him through the Spirit. The OT therefore does not rival Jesus as the foundation of Christian unity, for the first Christians read it only from the perspective of the Jesus revelation."[32]

Donald Bloesch (1928–2010)

"The christological hermeneutic that I propose is in accord with the deepest insights of both Luther and Calvin. Both Reformers saw Christ as the ground and center of Scripture. Both sought to relate the Old Testament, as well as the New, to the person and work of Christ. Their position, which was basically reaffirmed by Barth and Vischer, was that the hidden Christ is in the Old Testament and the manifest Christ in the New Testament. Luther likened Christ to the 'star and kernel' of Scripture, describing him as 'the center part of the circle' about which everything else revolves. On one occasion he compared certain texts to 'hard nuts' which resisted cracking and confessed that he had to throw these texts against the rock (Christ) so that they would yield their 'delicious kernel.' . . . Christological exegesis, when applied to the Old Testament, often takes the form of typological exegesis in which the acts of God in Old Testament history as well as the prophecies of his servants are seen to have their fulfillment in Jesus Christ. Such an approach was already discernible in the New Testament where, for example, the manna given to the children of Israel in the wilderness was regarded as a type of the bread of life (John 6:31, 32, 49–50, 58). Typological exegesis differs from allegorical and anagogical exegesis in that it is controlled by the analogy of faith, which views the events and discourses of the Old Testament in indissoluble relation to Jesus Christ, to the mystery of his incarnation and the miracle of his saving work (cf. Acts 26:22; I Peter 1:10–12)."[33]

Joseph Ratzinger (Pope Benedict XVI) (1927–)

"The Old and New Testament belong together. This Christological hermeneutic, which sees Jesus Christ as the key to the whole and learns from him how to understand the Bible as a unity, presupposes a prior act of faith."[34]

Norman Geisler (1932–)

"In the Law we find the foundation for Christ. In History we find the preparation for Christ. In Poetry we find the aspiration for Christ. In the Prophets we find the expectation of Christ. In the Gospels we find the manifestation of Christ. In Acts we find the propagation of Christ. In the Epistles we find the interpretation of Christ. In Revelation we find the consummation in Christ."[35]

John Stott (1921–2011)

"Jesus is the focus of Scripture. The Bible is not a random collection of religious documents. As Jesus himself said, 'The Scriptures . . . bear witness of me' (John 5:39, RSV). And Christian scholars have always recognized this. For example, Jerome, the great church father of the fourth and fifth centuries, wrote that 'ignorance of the Scriptures is ignorance of Christ' . . . Luther similarly, in his *Lectures on Romans,* was clear that Christ is the key to Scripture."[36]

J. Todd Billings (20th–21st century)

"The Son fulfilled such divergent Old Testament passages, because even though 'our ancestors' did not recognize it in their day, the Son is the Creator who is also the 'heir of all things' and has been made known in history in Jesus Christ. This means that spiritual readings of the Old Testament should not annihilate the Old Testament narrative. When the risen Jesus opened the minds of his companions on the Emmaus road 'to understand the Scriptures,' he did not suggest that the 'law of Moses, the Prophets, and the Psalms' had been displaced;

rather, they had been 'fulfilled' in himself (Luke 24:44–45). In the words of Wheaton College theologian Daniel Treier, reading Scripture in a 'Christ-centered' way 'makes possible spiritual participation in the realities of which Scripture speaks.'"[37]

J. I. Packer (1926–)

"Biblical theology is the umbrella-name for those disciplines that explore the unity of the Bible, delving into the contents of the books, showing the links between them, and pointing to the ongoing flow of the revelatory and redemptive process that reached its climax in Jesus Christ. Historical exegesis, which explores what the text meant and implied for its original readership, is one of these disciplines. Typology, which looks into the Old Testament patterns of divine action, agency, and instruction that found final fulfillment in Christ, is another . . . The importance of this theme—the Old Testament pointing to Christ—is great, although for half a century Bible teachers, possibly embarrassed by the memory of too-fanciful ventures into typology in the past, have not made much of it. (Its abiding importance, we might say, is commensurate with its current neglect!)"[38]

Christopher J. H. Wright (1947–)

"So, when we look back on the original historical exodus in light of the end of the story in Christ, it is filled with rich significance in view of what it points to.

"The New Testament presents him to us as the *Messiah*, Jesus the *Christ*. And the Messiah 'was' Israel. That is, the Messiah was Israel representatively and personified. The Messiah was the completion of all that Israel had been put in the world for—i.e., God's self-revelation and his work of human redemption.

"Israel was unique because God had a universal goal through them. Jesus embodied that uniqueness and achieved that universal goal. As the Messiah of Israel he could be the saviour of the world. Or as Paul reflected, going further back, by fulfilling God's purpose in choosing Abraham, Jesus became a second Adam, the head of a new humanity (Rom. 4–5; Gal. 3).

"Matthew clearly wants his readers to see that Jesus was not only the *completion* of the Old Testament story at a historical level, as his genealogy portrays, but also that he was in a deeper sense its *fulfillment*. This gives us another way of looking at the Old Testament in relation to Jesus. Not only does the Old Testament *tell the story which Jesus completes*, it also *declares the promise which Jesus fulfills* . . . the more you understand the Old Testament, the closer you will come to the heart of Jesus."[39]

Edmund Clowney (1917–2005)

"The Bible is the greatest storybook, not just because it is full of wonderful stories but because it tells one *great* story, the story of Jesus.

"Both the tablets of the law and the tabernacle were given by God at Sinai. Both point to Christ, who is the fulfillment of the law to all who believe and who is the heavenly Priest, the Lamb of God, and true Tabernacle."[40]

Albert Mohler (1959–)

"You cannot read the law without reading me [Jesus]. You cannot read the history without reading me. You cannot read the psalms without reading me. You cannot read the prophets without reading me. These are they that testify of me. . . . I've actually heard some preachers state as a matter of principle that they preach from the New Testament because it is the Christian book. . . . How they are robbing their people of the knowledge of Christ from the scriptures. How impoverished is that preaching. How undernourished are those congregations. . . . And we also should look to the Old Testament and find a constant, continual, cumulative, consistent testimony of Christ. . . . We do not look back to the Old Testament merely to find the background of Christ and his ministry, nor merely for reference and anticipation of Christ. We are to look to the Old Testament and find Christ. Not here and there, [but] everywhere. . . . Let's admit it, a good many evangelical preachers and Bible teachers simply have no idea what to do with the Old Testament. . . . To many Christians, to many pastors, to many preachers, and to all too many Christians, the Old Testament is a foreign book."[41]

Jon Zens (1945–)

"The heart-throb of the N.T. reveals the O.T. is 'the book of Christ.' Jesus Himself 'explained to them the things concerning Himself in all the Scriptures' (Luke 24:27, 44). A veil remains over one's eyes if he reads the O.T. apart from Christ (2 Cor. 3:14–15). Our ethical use of the O.T. must be done in light of the final revelation of God in Jesus Christ (Heb. 1:1). The O.T. must always be 'interpreted' from the perspective of the new age and new humanity created in Christ Jesus (1 Cor. 10:11; 1 Pet. 1:12)."[42]

D. A. Carson (1946–)

"The point is that however much the Old Testament points to Jesus, much of this prophecy is in veiled terms—in types and shadows and structures of thought. The sacrificial system prepares the way for the supreme sacrifice; the office of high priest anticipates the supreme intermediary between God and sinful human beings, the man Christ Jesus, the passover displays God's wrath and provides a picture of the ultimate passover lamb whose blood averts that wrath; the announcement of a new covenant (Jer. 31) and a new priesthood (Ps. 110) pronounce obsolescence in principle of the old covenant and priesthood."[43]

Eugene Peterson (1932–)

"Luther said that we should read the entire Bible in terms of what drives toward Christ. Everything has to be interpreted through Christ."[44]

John Piper (1946–)

"The glory of Jesus Christ shines more clearly when we see him in his proper relation to the Old Testament. He has a magnificent relation to all that was written. It is not surprising that this is the case, because he is called the Word of God incarnate (*John 1:14*). Would not the Word of God incarnate be the sum and consummation of the Word of God written? Consider these summary statements and the texts that support them. All the Scriptures bear witness to Christ. Moses wrote about Christ. *John 5:39, 46* . . . All the Scriptures are about Jesus Christ, even where there is no explicit prediction. That is, there is a fullness of implication in all Scriptures that points to Christ and is satisfied only when he has come and done his work. 'The meaning of all the Scriptures is unlocked by the death and resurrection of Jesus.'"[45]

Tim Keller (1950–)

"There are two ways to read the Bible. The one way to read the Bible is that it's basically about you: what you have to do in order to be right with God, in which case you'll never have a sure and certain hope, because you'll always know you're not quite living up. You'll never be sure about that future. Or you can read it as all about Jesus. Every single thing is not about what you must do in order to make yourself right with God, but what he has done to make you absolutely right with God. And Jesus Christ is saying, 'Unless you can read the Bible right, unless you can understand salvation by grace, you'll never have a sure and certain hope. But once you understand it's all about me, Jesus Christ, then you can know that you have peace. You can know that you have this future guaranteed, and you can face anything.'"[46]

Graeme Goldsworthy (20th century)

"The hermeneutical question about the whole Bible correlates with the question, 'What do you think of Christ?' . . . The hermeneutical center of the Bible is therefore Jesus in his being and in his saving acts—the Jesus of the gospel. . . . We can say that, while not all Scripture is the gospel, all Scripture is related to the gospel that is its centre. . . . The Bible makes a very radical idea inescapable: not only is the gospel the interpretive norm for the whole Bible, but there is an important sense in which Jesus Christ is the mediator of the meaning of everything that exists. In other words, *the gospel is the hermeneutical norm for the whole of reality.*"[47]

Scot McKnight (20th–21st century)

"Paul explicitly cites the Old Testament more than one hundred times, and the number of implicit allusions and echoes in his letters boggles the mind. . . . The Story of Jesus Christ is locked into one people, one history, and one Scripture: it makes sense only as it follows and completes the Story of Israel . . . the 'gospel' is the Story of Jesus that fulfills, completes, and resolves Israel's Story."[48]

Richard Hays (1948–)

"For Paul, Scripture, rightly read, prefigures the formation of the eschatological community of the church.

"Christ's death as Passover lamb marks the community's deliverance from bondage and passage to freedom. The community, then, is metaphorically portrayed not only as the unleavened bread but also as the journey people of the exodus, called to celebrate the feast and to live in ways appropriate to their identity as people rescued by God from the power of evil and death.

"Abraham serves for Paul not just as an exemplar of Christian living but also as a typological foreshadowing of Christ, the 'one man' (Rom. 5:19) through whose obedience 'the many were constituted righteous.'"[49]

G. K. Beale (1949–)

"There is unity to the Bible because it is all God's word. Therefore, there is legitimacy in attempting to trace common themes between testaments.

"We may say that the authorial intentions of the Old Testament writers were not as comprehensive as the simultaneous divine intentions, which became progressively unpacked as the history of revelation progresses until they climax in Christ. The Old Testament writers prophesied events to occur not only distant in time from them but in another world, a new world, which Jesus inaugurated . . . our contention is that Christ not only fulfills the Old Testament temple and all that its prophecies represent, but that he is the unpacked meaning for which the temple existed all along. . . . Typology is not mere analogy of something in the New Testament with something in the Old. Typology indicates fulfillment of the Old Testament's indirect prophetic foreshadowing of people, institutional and events in Christ, who is the ultimate climactic expression of everything God completely intended in the older revelation—whether it be the Law, temple and its rituals, various prophets, priests, and kings, and so on."[50]

Christian Smith (20th–21st century)

"The purpose, center, and interpretive key to scripture is Jesus Christ. It is embarrassing to have to write this, for it should be obvious to all Christians. But I am afraid that this is not always so obvious in practice in biblicist circles. At least the profound *implications* of this fact *for reading Scripture* are not always obvious to many evangelicals. Truly believing that Jesus Christ is the real purpose, center, and interpretative key to scripture causes one to read the Bible in a way that is very different than believing the Bible to be an instruction manual containing universally applicable divine oracles concerning every possible subject it seems to address. . . . We do not read scripture as detached historians trying to judge its technical accuracy in recounting events. We do not read scripture as a vast collection of infallible propositions whose meanings and implications can be understood on their own particular terms. We only, always, and everywhere read scripture in view of its real subject matter: Jesus Christ. This means that we always read scripture Christocentrically, christologically, and christotelically, as those who *really* believe what the Nicene and Chalcedonian creeds say. That is, for Christians, Christ is the center, the inner reason, and the end of all Scripture."[51]

C. S. Lewis (1898–1963)

"It is Christ Himself, not the Bible, who is the true word of God. The Bible, read in the right spirit, and with the guidance of good teachers, will bring us to Him."[52]

Robert D. Brinsmead (1933–)

"The purpose of all Scripture is to bear witness to Christ (John 5:39; 20:31). The Bible in itself is not the Word of God. The Word of God is a person (John 1:1). Neither does the Bible have life, power or light in itself any more than did the Jewish Torah. These attributes may be ascribed to the Bible only by virtue of its relationship to Him who *is* Word, Life, Power and Light. Life is not in the book, as the Pharisees supposed, but only in the Man of the book (John 5:39)."[53]

Dallas Theological Seminary

"We believe all Scriptures center about the Lord Jesus Christ in His person and work in His first and second coming, and hence that no portion, even of the Old Testament, is properly read, or understood, until it leads to Him."[54]

Notes

Introduction: The Jesus Story

1. References to "salvation history" to describe the Bible's main theme did not arise until the seventeenth century. See H. W. Frei, "The 'Literal Reading' of Biblical Narrative in the Christian Tradition: Does It Stretch or Will It Break?" in Frank McConnell, ed., *The Bible and the Narrative Tradition* (New York: Oxford University Press, 1986), 37–38. The Bible isn't about salvation; it's about Jesus Christ. Salvation is one of the things Christ does. But Jesus is far more than Savior. See our book *Jesus Manifesto: Restoring the Supremacy and Sovereignty of Jesus Christ* (Nashville: Thomas Nelson, 2010) for an unfolding of that statement.
2. In this regard, this book is really an expansion of chapter 1 of *Jesus Manifesto.* In that chapter, we point out that Jesus is the occupation of the entire biblical canon, both First and Second Testaments. *Jesus* blows that point up into an entire volume.
3. For the history of the First, Second, and Third "Jesus Quests" as well as some of the most influential works in historical Jesus studies, see Craig Evans's *Life of Jesus Research: An Annotated Bibliography* (Leiden: E. J. Brill, 1989) and *Fabricating Jesus: How Modern Scholars Distort the Gospels* (Downers Grove, IL: IVP Books, 2006); Martin Hengel's *The Charismatic Leader and His Followers* (New York: Crossword, 1981) and *Studies in Early Christology* (Edinburgh: T. & T. Clark, 1995); Dale Allison's *The Historical Christ and the Theological Jesus* (Grand Rapids: Eerdmans, 2009); Ben Witherington's *The Jesus Quest: The Third Search for the Jew of Nazareth* (Downers Grove, IL: InterVarsity Press, 1995), *The Christology of Jesus* (Minneapolis, MN: Fortress, 1990), and *Jesus the Sage: The Pilgrimage of Wisdom* (Minneapolis, MN: Fortress, 1994); Scot McKnight's *Jesus and His Death: Historiography, the Historical Jesus, and Atonement Theory* (Waco, TX: Baylor University Press, 2005); Craig Keener's *The Historical Jesus of the Gospels* (Grand Rapids: Eerdmans, 2009); N. T. Wright's *The Original Jesus: The Life and Vision of a Revolutionary* (Grand Rapids: Eerdmans, 1996), *Who Was Jesus?* (Grand Rapids: Eerdmans, 1992), *The Challenge of Jesus: Rediscovering Who Jesus Was and Is* (Downers Grove, IL:

InterVarsity Press, 1999), *The New Testament and the People of God*, vol. 1 of *Christian Origins and the Question of God* (Minneapolis: Fortress, 1992), and *Jesus and the Victory of God*, vol. 2 of *Christian Origins and the Question of God* (Minneapolis: Fortress, 1996); Darrell Bock and Robert Webb's *Key Events in the Life of the Historical Jesus: A Collaborative Exploration of Context and Coherence* (Grand Rapids: Eerdmans, 2010); Darrell Bock's *Studying the Historical Jesus: A Guide to Sources and Methods* (Grand Rapids: Baker Academic, 2002); Gregory Boyd and Paul Eddy's *Jesus Legend: A Case for the Historical Reliability of the Synoptic Jesus Tradition* (Grand Rapids: Baker, 2007); Beverly Roberts Goventa and Richard Hays's *Seeking the Identity of Jesus* (Grand Rapids: Baker Academic, 2007); James Beilby and Robert Price's *The Historical Jesus: Five Views* (Downers Grove, IL: IVP Press, 2009); H. J. Cadbury's *The Peril of Modernizing Jesus* (New York: Macmillan, 1937); Richard Bauckham's *Jesus and the God of Israel: God Crucified and Other Studies on the New Testament's Christology of Divine Identity* (Grand Rapids: Eerdmans, 2009); Nicholas Perrin and Richard Hays's *Jesus, Paul, and the People of God: A Theological Dialogue with N. T. Wright* (Downers Grove, IL: IVP Academia, 2011); John Meier's *A Marginal Jew: Rethinking the Historical Jesus* (New York: Doubleday, 2001); Stephen Barton's *The Spirituality of the Gospels* (Peabody, MA: Hendrickson, 1992); Otto Betz's *What Do We Know About Jesus?* (Philadelphia: Westminster, 1968); Raymond Brown's *The Death of the Messiah: From Gethsemane to the Grave: A Commentary on the Passion Narratives in the Four Gospels* (New York: Doubleday, 1994); G. B. Caird's *Jesus and the Jewish Nation* (London: Athlone Press, 1965); James D. G. Dunn's *A New Perspective on Jesus: What the Quest for the Historical Jesus Missed* (Grand Rapids: Baker Academic, 2005), *Christology in the Making: A New Testament Inquiry into the Origins of the Doctrine of the Incarnation*, 2nd ed. (Grand Rapids: Eerdmans, 1996), *Evidence for Jesus* (Philadelphia: Westminster, 1985), and "Faith and the Historical Jesus," in *Jesus Remembered* (Grand Rapids: Eerdmans, 2003); Bruce Chilton's *The Temple of Jesus: His Sacrificial Program Within a Cultural History of Sacrifice* (University Park, PA: Pennsylvania State University Press, 1992); Stephen Davis's *Risen Indeed: Making Sense of the Resurrection* (Grand Rapids: Eerdmans, 1993); W. R. Farmer's *Jesus and the Gospel: Tradition, Scripture, and Canon* (Philadelphia: Fortress, 1982); C. F. D. Moule's *The Origin of Christology* (New York: Cambridge University Press, 1977); E. P. Sanders's *Jesus and Judaism* (Philadelphia: Fortress, 1985) and *The Historical Figure of Jesus* (New York: Penguin, 1995); Craig Blomberg's *Jesus and the Gospels: An Introduction and Survey* (Nashville: Broadman and Holman, 1997); Gerd Theissen's *The Shadow of the Galilean: The Quest of the Historical Jesus in Narrative Form* (Philadelphia: Fortress, 1987); Albert Schweitzer's *The Quest of the Historical Jesus* (first published London: A. and C. Black, 1911); and Luke T. Johnson's *The Real Jesus: The Misguided Quest for the Historical Jesus and the Truth of the Traditional Gospels* (San Francisco: HarperSanFrancisco, 1996).

4. Paul Johnson's *Jesus: A Biography from a Believer* (New York: Viking, 2010), 1–2.
5. Some scholars, like Scot McKnight, believe that writing a biography of Jesus is not possible because we do not have enough information about His early life. Ben Witherington, on the other hand, discusses the difference between a modern biography and an ancient biography in his book

The Gospel of Mark (Grand Rapids: Eerdmans, 2001), 3–9. Mark's gospel, Witherington argues, possesses all the marks of ancient biography. In like manner, Craig Keener argues that the four Gospels are *ancient* biographies in contrast with the genre of modern biography (*The Historical Jesus of the Gospels*, 78–83). See also Richard Burridge's *What Are the Gospels?* and *Four Gospels, One Jesus?* (Grand Rapids: Eerdmans, 2005), as well as N. T. Wright's *Who Was Jesus? A Comparison with Greco-Roman Biography* (Grand Rapids: Eerdmans, 2004, 73–74) and *How God Became King* (New York: HarperOne, 2012), 62–64; and James D. G. Dunn's *Jesus Remembered*, 184–86. We believe that *The First Quest for the Historical Jesus* went wrong in trying to write a full-fledged modern biography of Jesus of Nazareth. History simply doesn't furnish us with enough material about Jesus' early life (from birth to age twelve, and age twelve to thirty). In addition, *The First Quest* was based on looking at Jesus purely as a human being with a human biography. We believe with the council of Chalcedon that a purely human Jesus never existed. The Jesus that existed was the One who was God's self-knowledge in-fleshed. Thus His Deity cannot be ignored. For this reason, we will begin the Lord's life before time in His preincarnate state as the eternal Son (see chapter 2).

6. Some of the most helpful books in this genre are James D. G. Dunn's *Jesus Remembered*; Darrell Bock's *Jesus According to the Scripture: Restoring the Portrait from the Gospels* (Grand Rapids: Baker Academic, 2002); Joseph Ratzinger's *Jesus of Nazareth* (two vol.) (New York: Doubleday, 2007; San Francisco: Ignatius Press, 2011); John Meier's *A Marginal Jew: Rethinking the Historical Jesus* (New York: Doubleday, 1991); Ben Meyer's *The Aims of Jesus* (San Jose, CA: Pickwick Publications, 2002); N. T. Wright's *Simply Jesus: A New Vision of Who He Was, What He Did, and Why He Matters* (New York: HarperCollins, 2011); *Jesus and the Victory of God*, vol. 2 of *Christian Origins and the Question of God*; and *Who Was Jesus?* (Grand Rapids: Eerdmans, 1993); Ethelbert Stauffer's *Jesus and His Story* (London: SCM, 1960); C. H. Dodd's *The Founder of Christianity* (London: Macmillan, 1970); Dale Allison's *Constructing Jesus: Memory, Imagination, and History* (Grand Rapids: Baker Academic, 2010) and *Jesus of Nazareth: Millenarian Prophet* (Minneapolis: Fortress, 1998); F. F. Bruce's *Jesus, Lord and Savior* (Downers Grove, IL: InterVarsity, 1986) and *Jesus Past, Present, and Future: The Work of Christ* (Downers Grove, IL: InterVarsity, 1998); Craig Keener's *The Historical Jesus of the Gospels*; G. B. Caird's *New Testament Theology* (New York: Oxford University Press, 1994); A. F. Kirkpatrick's "Christ the Goal of History," lecture 18 in his *The Doctrine of the Prophets: The Warburtonian Lectures for 1886–1890* (London: Macmillan, 1901); Joachim Jeremias's *New Testament Theology* (New York: Scribner, 1971); William Willimon's *Why Jesus?* (Nashville: Abingdon, 2010); Scot McKnight's *The Story of the Christ* (Grand Rapids: Baker Academic, 2006); and Arnold Fruchtenbaum's *Jesus Was a Jew* (Nashville: Broadman, 1974).
7. Gen. 1:1; John 1:1.
8. John 1:1.
9. At least what Scripture tells us will happen after Jesus returns.
10. Some people believe that the main subject of the biblical narrative is God. But reading the Bible as a book about God misses the point. It is a book

about God-in-Christ. The biblical understanding of God is the God we know in Christ. The biblical understanding of humanity is the humanity we know in Christ. Christ is the true humanity, and Christ is the true God. Jesus reveals the very nature and character of God. Therefore, the theological interpretation of Scripture must be a christological interpretation of Scripture. As we point out in *Jesus Manifesto*, the Father and the Spirit both continually point to the Son. We cannot contemplate God apart from Jesus. So all theology is christology, and the Scriptures are a book about Christ—God's revelation of Himself in and through Jesus. This point will be made abundantly clear throughout this book. For further reading on how Jesus is the content of the biblical narrative, see Hans Frei, *The Identity of Jesus Christ*.

11. Col. 1:16.
12. For those who would argue that we shouldn't call the Savior "Jesus" but "Yeshua," we are following the example of the Second Testament writers themselves, who called Him Iesous, not Yahshua. In fact, God is never called YHWH in the Second Testament. In this connection, the Judaism of Jesus' day and locale was Hellenized. For this reason, many of the apostles (who were Jewish) took Greek names (as did most of their Hasmonean rulers). And many of them spoke at least some Greek. Simon, Philip, and John, among others, were not exactly Hebrew names.
13. This touches on the debate between grammatical-historical criticism and canonical criticism, which we will discuss later in the endnotes. We are not against historical Jesus research. We are against historical Jesus research that somehow thinks it has a privileged theological status over canonical criticism and biblical theology. Historical Jesus studies, while helpful, are limited. And they should never control biblical theology.
14. One of the things we will be demonstrating in this book is how to interpret the Old Testament within the context of the entire biblical canon. We will be interpreting the Old Testament with Jesus, Paul, Peter, John, Mark, Luke, and Matthew at our side. When we read about Adam, for instance, we will be reading how Jesus and Paul understood Adam. So in essence, this book is a canonical approach to the life of Jesus. In it, we are asking and answering the question, what does the entire canon teach us about the life of Jesus?
15. We've observed that many Christians find little relevance or application for their lives in the Old Testament. They approach it as if they are reading someone else's mail. We trust that after you read this book, you will no longer see the Old Testament as a mere historical document, but rather as a living, breathing account of your Lord.
16. In the year 170, Melito, bishop of Sardis, called the First Testament (Hebrew canon) the *palaia diatheke* (old covenant) and the Second Testament the *kaine diatheke* (new covenant). Tertullian in the West rendered *diatheke* to be *testmentum* in Latin, thereby calling each section of the Bible "the Old Testament" and "the New Testament." This coinage survived despite the fact that neither part of the Bible is a "testament" in the common sense of the word. See J. D. Douglas and H. Hillyer, et al., eds., *The New Bible Dictionary*, 2nd ed. (Downers Grove, IL: InterVarsity, 1986), 138, and "What Is the New Testament?" http://www.catholicapologetics.info/scripture/newtestament/ntestament.htm.

17. John 5:39 NLT.
18. In 1 Corinthians 15:2–4, Paul described the gospel in three verses. And twice he said that it was "according to the Scriptures." See also Acts 26:22–23, where Paul tells King Agrippa that Moses and the prophets spoke of Christ's suffering and resurrection from the dead.
19. "When Luke says that Jesus interpreted to them all the things about himself, throughout the Bible, he doesn't mean that Jesus collected a few, or even a half dozen, isolated texts, verses chosen at random. He means that the whole *story*, from Genesis to Chronicles (the last book of the Hebrew Bible; the prophets came earlier), pointed forwards to a fulfillment which could only be found when God's anointed took Israel's suffering, and hence the world's suffering, to himself, died under its weight, and rose again as the beginning of God's new creation, God's new people. This is what had to happen; and now it just had" (Tom Wright, *Luke for Everyone* [Louisville: Westminster John Knox, 2004], 294–95). James D. G. Dunn agrees that the Second Testament authors did not use random proof-texting to make their points (Dunn, *Unity and Diversity in the New Testament: An Inquiry into the Character of Earliest Christianity* [London: SCM, 2006], 94ff.). In another place, N. T. Wright states, "'Beginning with Moses and all the prophets, he interpreted to them in all the Scriptures the things concerning himself.' This could never be a matter of so-called 'messianic' proof-texts alone. It was the entire narrative, the complete story-line" (*The Challenge of Jesus: Rediscovering Who Jesus Was and Is* [Downers Grove, IL: InterVarsity, 2011], 162). In short, the Second Testament authors never use the First Testament out of context. The context is always in mind. But they understood the context as being fulfilled in Christ.
20. For specific examples, see C. H. Dodd's *According to the Scriptures: The Sub-Structure of New Testament Theology* (London: Nisbet, 1952), 61–110. Dodd writes, "The method included, first, the *selection* of certain large sections of the Old Testament scriptures. . . . These sections were understood as *wholes*, and particular verses or sentences were quoted from them rather as pointers to the whole context than as constituting testimonies in and for themselves."
21. With painstaking detail, C. H. Dodd in *According to the Scriptures* demonstrates that the Second Testament writers consistently drew from the same portions of First Testament Scriptures and interpreted them the same way, independent of one another (ibid., 28–60).
22. After tracing in detail how the Second Testament authors consistently (yet independently) interpreted the First Testament texts in light of Jesus Christ, Dodd comes to this conclusion as well (ibid., 108–10). Eminent New Testament scholar F. F. Bruce has this to say about Dodd's book: "Analogy, apart from anything else, might suggest that the scheme of biblical interpretation which pervades the New Testament was similarly derived from the Founder of Christianity. The New Testament biblical exegesis is not the same as attested in the Qumran documents; both resemblances and disparities are readily recognized. But the one scheme bespeaks the influence of one powerful mind. When we observe that the main features of primitive Christian exegesis recur independently in the works of several New Testament writers, we have to look behind them for this powerful mind, and (as C. H. Dodd has remarked in his classic treatment of this subject),

we are not compelled to reject the New Testament evidence which points unmistakably to the mind of Jesus Himself" (F. F. Bruce, foreword to R. T. France, *Jesus and the Old Testament* [Vancouver, BC: Regent College Pub., 1998], v).

23. Luke 24:27 NASB.
24. Luke 24:32 NASB.
25. Luke 24:44–45 NASB.
26. TNK (*Tanakh*) is an acronym derived from the three sections of the Hebrew Bible: Torah, Nevi'im, and Ketuvim.
27. In his book *Jesus and the Old Testament,* R. T. France analyzes exactly how Jesus interpreted the Old Testament.
28. Ibid., 223.
29. Ibid., 225.
30. It should be noted that the phrase "the Law and the Prophets" is often shorthand for the entire First Testament. See Romans 3:21 with 4:7. The "law" sometimes refers to the entire Hebrew canon (Rom. 3:19 with 3:10–18; 1 Cor. 14:21). The same is true for the "prophets" (Acts 13:27; 26:27).
31. John 5:46.
32. Matt. 5:17.
33. Jesus believed the Hebrew Scriptures were the revelation of God and that He was the true embodiment and fulfillment of them. See E. E. Ellis, "How Jesus Interpreted His Bible," *Criswell Theological Review* 3 (1989): 341–51.
34. France, *Jesus and the Old Testament*, 79–90.
35. "As Christians standing within the light of New Testament revelation and looking back on the Old Testament, Christ himself acts as a hermeneutical prism. Looking back through him, we see the white light of the unity of the truth of Jesus Christ broken down into its constituent colours in the pages of the Old Testament. Then, looking forwards we see how the multi-coloured strands of Old Testament revelation converge in him. When we appreciate this we begin to see how the constituent colours unite in Christ and are related both to each other and to him. In this way we see how the Old Testament points forward to him. We see how sometimes one 'colour,' sometimes another, or perhaps a combination of them, points forward to Jesus Christ, is related to Jesus Christ, and is fulfilled by Jesus Christ" (Sinclair Ferguson, "Preaching Christ from the Old Testament," PT Media Paper, vol. 2., http://www.proctrust.org.uk/dls/christ_paper.pdf).
36. Because Jesus Christ and His church are united, the Bible is not only Christocentric; it's also ecclesiocentric. To find Christ in the Bible is to find His house, His bride, His family—the church. This will become clear throughout this book. In this regard, we agree with Augustine's first rule of biblical interpretation, *totus christus*: the whole Christ, Head and Body. Richard Hays unfolds what he calls Paul's "ecclesiocentric hermeneutics" in *Echoes of Scripture in the Letters of Paul* (New Haven, CT: Yale University Press, 1989), 84.
37. Karl Barth was one such theologian.
38. Martin Luther, as quoted in Emil Brunner, *The Word of God and Modern Man* (Richmond, VA: John Knox, 1964), 30.
39. Scot McKnight, *The King Jesus Gospel: The Original Good News Revisited* (Grand Rapids: Zondervan, 2011), 153.

40. In scholarly circles, this method of interpretation is known as "historical criticism" or the "historical-critical method" because it uses modern tools to critique the text in its historical setting. Historical criticism is essentially scientific exegesis that came into prominence in the eighteenth century onward. (The original sense of the word *reductionist* is *re ducere*, which means "to lead back.") It's a modern invention.
41. In scholarly circles, this holistic method is called "canonical criticism" because it interprets the entire biblical canon as a unified whole. It's also called "theological interpretation" because it utilizes theology as the interpretive key to exegete the Bible. As an approach, canonical criticism says that nothing less than the whole biblical canon is adequate to properly interpret each of its parts. Theological interpretation is often associated with Karl Barth's *Der Romerbrief*, 1919. As a method of biblical interpretation, theological exegesis is rooted in the Scripture itself. It is also known as the "christological hermeneutic." Donald Bloesch wrote, "This approach, which is associated with Karl Barth, Jacques Ellul, and Wilhelm Vischer, among others, and which also has certain affinities with the confessional stances of Gerhard van Rad and Brevard Childs, seeks to supplement the historical-critical method by theological exegesis in which the innermost intentions of the author are related to the center and culmination of sacred history mirrored in the Bible, namely, the advent of Jesus Christ. It is believed that the fragmentary insights of both Old and New Testament writers are fulfilled in God's dramatic incursion into human history which we see in the incarnation and atoning sacrifice of Jesus Christ, in his life, death, and resurrection" (Donald Bloesch, "A Christological Hermeneutic: Crisis and Conflict in Hermeneutics" in *The Use of the Bible in Theology: Evangelical Options*, ed. Robert K. Johnston [Atlanta: John Knox Press, 1985], 81. Also available as "A Christological Hermeneutic," http://www.religion-online.org/showarticle.asp?title=0). See also Werner G. Jeanrond, "After Hermeneutics: The Relationship Between Theology and Biblical Studies," in *The Open Text: New Directions for Biblical Studies?*, ed. Francis Watson (London: SCM, 1993), 85–102; John Goldingay, "Biblical Narrative and Systematic Theology," in *Between Two Horizons: Spanning New Testament Studies and Systematic Theology*, eds. Joel B. Green and Max Turner (Grand Rapids: Eerdmans, 2000), 123–42 (138); Joel B. Green, "The Bible, Theology, and Theological Interpretation," *SBL Forum*, n.p. [cited Sept 2004], http://sbl-site.org/Article.aspx?ArticleID=308; J. Todd Billings, *The Word of God for the People of God: An Entryway to the Theological Interpretation of Scriptures* (Grand Rapids: Eerdmans, 2010); Stephen Fowl, *Theological Interpretation of Scripture* (Eugene, OR: Cascade Books, 2009); Daniel Treier, *Introducing Theological Interpretation of Scripture: Recovering a Christian Practice* (Grand Rapids: Baker Academic, 2008); and Kevin Vanhoozer, *Dictionary for Theological Interpretation* (Grand Rapids: Baker Academic, 2008).
42. We agree with Brevard Childs when he said, "Many insights from the last 150 years made by historical-critical study also can be of great exegetical value if correctly used within a proper theological context. In a word, the hermeneutical issue is not between a critical and a non-critical reading, but rather how one makes use of all available insights in order to illuminate the

canonical scriptures without destroying the confessional context" ("The One Gospel in Four Witnesses" in *The Rule of Faith* by Ephraim Radner and George Sumner [Harrisburg, PA: Morehouse Publishing, 1998], 55). In the same vein, Joseph Ratzinger (Pope Benedict XVI) makes a case for the need to use *both* historical-criticism and canonical exegesis in understanding the life of Jesus (*Jesus of Nazareth*, xvi–xxiv [see n. 6]). Two twentieth-century professors at Yale, Brevard Childs and Hans Frei, championed the holistic way of viewing Scripture. Their work marked a new shift for returning to the christological way of interpreting Scripture that predates modern hermeneutics and grammatical-historical exegesis. They both pointed out that a christological reading of the First Testament is indispensable if we are to understand history as the story of God revealing Himself in Christ. They argued that the church's understanding of Scripture is essentially found in Jesus. Therein lies the charter for christological interpretation. The holistic approach, also known as "canonical criticism," basically says that every part of the Bible must be interpreted in its relationship to the entire canon. Therefore, when the Second Testament was created and the canon expanded, the meaning of the First Testament changed from our perspective. It became fuller because it could be completely interpreted from the standpoint of Christ. Both Frei and Childs accept historical criticism. However, their position is that historical criticism is a good beginning but a bad stopping place. We must go on to see the fullness of the canon. Consequently, reductionism (historical criticism) and holism (canonical criticism) do not constitute an *either/or* choice. It's a *both/and* choice. We regard them as complementary. In short, historical study of the biblical text must be inserted into the larger and richer context—the existing canon of Scripture that contains a revelation of Jesus Christ. For further reading see Hans Frei, "The 'Literal Reading' of Biblical Narrative in the Christian Tradition" (see n. 1) and *The Eclipse of Biblical Narrative* (New Haven, CT: Yale University Press, 1980); Brevard Childs, *Old Testament Theology in a Canonical Context* (Philadelphia: Fortress, 1985), *Biblical Theology: A Proposal* (Minneapolis: Fortress, 2002), and *Introduction to the Old Testament as Scripture* (Philadelphia: Fortress, 1979); Karl Barth, *Der Romerbfrief* (Munich: Chr. Kaiser, 1922) and *Epistle to the Romans* (New York: Oxford University Press, 1977); Willem Van Gemeren, *The Progress of Redemption: The Story of Salvation from Creation to the New Jerusalem* (Grand Rapids: Academie Books, 1988) and "Jesus Christ the Lord and the Scriptures of the Church," "The Nature of the Christian Bible: One Book, Two Testaments," and "The One Gospel in Four Witnesses" in Radner and Sumner, *The Rule of Faith*.

43. Joseph Ratzinger describes the Bible's hermeneutic thusly: "This Christological hermeneutic, which sees Jesus Christ as the key to the whole and learns from him how to understand the Bible as a unity, presupposes a prior act of faith . . . 'Canonical exegesis'—reading the individual texts of the Bible in the context of the whole—is an essential dimension of exegesis. It does not contradict historical-critical interpretation, but carries it forward in an organic way toward becoming theology in the proper sense" (*Jesus of Nazareth*, vol. 1, xix). In this connection, we believe the modern historical reconstruction is both legitimate and important. But we do not believe that the historian's interpretation should have some sort of primacy over

the theologian's interpretation. Consequently, we do not embrace the dominance of modern empirical epistemology in theology. The church does not have to submit its theology to the judgment of supposed neutral disciplines in modern evangelical or liberal theology. Some theologians have called this submission "the Babylonian captivity of Christian theology." We believe that modern critical study of the Scripture—linguistic inquiry and historical investigation—though important, do not exhaust the content of Scripture. To properly understand the Bible, it must be interpreted not only as a historical, literary document but also as a source of divine revelation. Both the theological unity and the historical unity of Scripture must be held together as a cohesive narrative about Jesus. Thus we cannot understand the First Testament without the Second Testament, nor the Second without the First. The historical-critical approach, when held to exclusively, seems to imply that Genesis through Malachi are not Christian books. Therefore, when Christians read them, they are reading someone else's mail. Historical-criticism by itself rejects the concept of a unified canon and turns advocates into near Marcionites. This was a charge that Dietrich Bonhoeffer leveled against this method. For Bonhoeffer, rejecting the authority of the First Testament was part of the way of thinking that prepared the way to anti-Semitism.

44. *Reply to Faustus the Manichean*, 12, 14. http://enlargingtheheart.wordpress.com/2010/02/23/augustine–of–hippo–christ–in–the–old–testament (no longer accessible). Luther said likewise: "There is no word in the New Testament which does not look back on the Old, where it has already been proclaimed in advance. . . . For the New Testament is nothing more than a revelation of the Old" (quoted in Sidney Greidanus, *Preaching Christ from the Old Testament: A Contemporary Hermeneutical Method* [Grand Rapids: Eerdmans, 1999], 116).
45. Andrea Fernandez coined the term *sensus plenior*, or "the fuller sense," to describe this fact. The *sensus plenior*, as developed by Raymond E. Brown in *The Sensus Plenior of Sacred Scripture* (Baltimore: St Mary's University, 1955), 92, refers to "the deeper meaning, intended by God, but not clearly intended by the human author, which is seen to exist in the words of a biblical text . . . when they are studied in the light of further revelation or development in the understanding of revelation." See also David Puckett's *John Calvin's Exegesis of the Old Testament* (Louisville: Westminster John Knox, 1995). One of the things that modern interpreters assume is that the only safe way to understand a text is to assert it has only one true meaning. All other meanings are either false or secondary. We do not believe this. The text has many possible but harmonious meanings, all of which can be legitimized from the Bible. Each meaning harmonizes with each other; none contradicts another. That richness is why the Scriptures can continue to speak to people in different places and at different times just as powerfully as they did for their original hearers. The notion that there is only one true interpretation of the text is a modern construction. Throughout most of church history, Christians believed that there are various interpretations of a single text. Yet we will always locate their fullest meaning in Christ. In fact, a good chunk of the Second Testament, in substance, is a christological reading of the First

Testament. Geerhardus Vos said that biblical theology draws a line while systematic theology draws a circle. That is, biblical theology is diachronic; systematic theology is synchronic. Diachronic reading treats the Bible as a historical book. And the historical context is preeminent in interpreting a biblical text. Synchronic reading treats the Bible as a complete and unified whole. Context, therefore, becomes the key to biblical interpretation. A diachronic reading of Scripture reads the Second Testament in light of the First. A synchronic reading looks at the First in light of the Second. The diachronic reading regards the First Testament as a pre-Christian book that prepares the way for the coming of the Anointed One. The synchronic reading treats the First Testament as a Christian book that prefigures Christ. We believe that the diachronic and the synchronic approach to the Bible must be taken together.

46. Dodd, *According to the Scriptures*, 130. Dodd adds, "It would not be true of any literature which deserves to be called great, that its meaning is restricted to that which was explicitly in the mind of the author when he wrote. On the contrary, it is a part of what constitutes the quality of greatness in literature that it perpetuates itself by unfolding ever new richness of unsuspected meaning as time goes on. The ultimate significance of prophecy is not only what it meant for its author, but what it came to mean for those who stood within the tradition which he founded or promoted, and who lived under the impact of the truth declared" (131–32). Some modern scholars are still stuck in '70s and '80s "neoevangelicalism." The neoevangelical school did a valuable service in helping us see the benefits that historical study could bring to our understanding of Scripture. But it missed the heart of the Bible by limiting one's understanding to modern historical methodology. Medieval allegorization failed because of its tendency to dehistoricize the biblical text. But neoevangelicalism also failed because of its tendency to detextualize the history behind the text. Neoevangelicalism argued that the only meaning of the text is what was in the brain of the writer at the time that he wrote it. Neoevangelicals put the primacy on history as being the "real stuff" and the canonical text as simply being a witness to it. In his book *Truth and Method* (New York: Seabury, 1975), Hans Georg-Gadamer looks at the question of hermeneutics and argues for the necessity of bringing together two horizons to accurately interpret a text. Gadamer's thesis is that we cannot understand texts by the methods of natural science alone. They require a different sort of approach. The author of a given text was operating in his own historical horizon (of the past). We, the readers, are operating within our own historical horizon (the present). In order to understand a text, the past historical horizon of the text must be brought together with the present historical horizon of the reader. The act of interpretation is the act of bringing those two horizons together. Allegorization failed to take into account the past horizon of the original writers and readers. But neoevangelicalism also failed because it didn't connect the past historical horizon together with the message of the entire biblical canon and the historical horizon of present readers.

47. See 1 Peter 1:10–12.

48. There is a significant difference between typology and allegory. Typological exegesis (of the "essential correspondence" school) is a legitimate

interpretation of the text, and it was used profusely by the Second Testament authors. A type is an event, object, or person that finds a parallel and deeper realization in Jesus Christ, His people, or His work. Typology "is grounded in history, and does not lose sight of the actual historical character of the events with which it is concerned. Typology may be described as 'the theological interpretation of the Old Testament history.' Allegory, on the other hand, has little concern with the historical character of the Old Testament words" (France, *Jesus and the Old Testament*, 40). Typology, unlike allegory, does not dehistoricize the text. Allegorical interpretations are highly subjective and are based on the interpreter's imagination. Patristic allegorizing and post-Reformation spiritualizing both leapfrog over the historical realities of the First Testament text, acting as if the Hebrew Scriptures have no historical significance in their own context. To learn more about the legitimate use of typological interpretation and how it differs from allegorical exegesis, see Patrick Fairbaim, *The Typology of Scripture: Two Volumes in One* (Philadelphia: Smith & English, 1854); A. Berkeley Mickelsen's *Understanding Scripture: How to Read and Study the Bible* (Hendrickson, 2005), where "essential correspondence" posits guidlines to keep the typology from slipping into allegorism; Leonhard Goppelt's *Typos*; R. T. France's *Jesus and the Old Testament*, 38–79; J. Danielou's *From Shadows to Reality*; G. W. H. Lampe's "Typological Exegesis," *Theology* 56, 201–8; E. E. Ellis's *Paul's Use of the Old Testament*; "How the New Testament Uses the Old," in *New Testament Interpretation*, ed. I. Howard Marshall (Grand Rapids: Wm. B. Eerdmans Publishing Co., 1977), 201–8, "Biblical Interpretation in the New Testament Church," *Compendia Rerum Judaicarum ad Novum Testamentum*, eds. S. Safrai et al., and "How Jesus Interpreted the Old Testament," *Criswell Theological Review* 3:2, 1989, 341–51; Richard M. Davidson's *Typology in Scripture* (Berrien Springs, MI: Andrews University Seminary Dissertation Series, 1981), 115–90; G. W. H. Lampe and K. J. Woollcombe's *Essays on Typology*; Graeme Goldsworthy's *Preaching the Whole Bible as Christian Scripture and According to Plan*; A. T. Hanson's *Jesus Christ in the Old Testament*; F. Foulkes, *The Acts of God*; James Preus's *From Shadow to Promise*; Paul Heinisch's *Christ in Prophecy*; Richard Longenecker's *Biblical Exegesis in the Apostolic Period*; Sidney Greidanus's *Preaching Christ from the Old Testament*, 111–278; F. F. Bruce's *New Testament Development of Old Testament Themes* and *The Time Is Fulfilled*; Nathan Pitchford's *Images of the Savior from the Pentateuch*; Edmond Clowney's *Preaching and Biblical Theology* and *The Unfolding Mystery*; H. Wheeler Robinson's *The Cross in the Old Testament*; D. A. Carson's "Current Issues in Biblical Theology," *Bulletin for Biblical Research* (1995), 27; G. K. Beale's *The Temple and the Church's Mission*, 376ff., and *A New Testament Biblical Theology*; Sinclair Ferguson's "Preaching Christ from the Old Testament"; Walter Wilson's *A Dictionary of Bible Types*; Ada Habershon's *The Study of Types*; E. W. Bullinger's *Numbers in Scripture*; A. B. Simpson's *The Christ in the Bible* (4 volumes) and *Christ in the Tabernacle*; Stephen Kaung's *God Has Spoken* (8 volumes) and *Seeing Christ in the New Testament* (6 volumes); and InterVarsity Press's *Dictionary of Biblical Imagery*. For older works, see C. H. Mackintosh's *Notes on the Pentateuch* and C. H. Spurgeon's *Christ in the Old Testament*. D. L. Moody once stated that if his entire library were to be burned and his Bible and C. H. Mackintosh's *Notes on the Pentateuch* were to remain, those would be sufficient. See also "Index of Allusions and Verbal Parallels" printed in the corrected third edition of *The Greek New Testament*, ed. K. Aland et al. (United Bible Societies, 1983), 901–11; and Peter Enns's "Apostolic Hermeneutics and an Evangelical Doctrine of Scripture: Moving Beyond a Modernist Impasse," *Westminster Theological Journal* (Fall 2003). In the latter, Enns persuasively argues for a Christoletic hermeneutic for interpreting the Bible. Dave Moser is a blogger who has written a helpful book on Christ-centered Bible study that he offers at no charge in PDF: http://armchair-theology.net/Christ-Centered-Bible-Study.pdf.

49. Interpretations that stress only the historical-grammatical elements of the text miss the heart and spirit of Holy Scripture. They cause us to lose the grand narrative of the biblical canon. Interpretations that stress only the spiritual element of the text lead to "subjective hermeneutics" that spawn fanciful and erroneous interpretations. In this book, we are marrying the historical-grammatical approach with the theological/spiritual approach. The linchpin that brings them both together is the way in which the Second Testament authors consistently interpreted the First Testament. The mammoth volume *Commentary on the New Testament Use of the Old Testament*, edited by G. K. Beale and D. A. Carson (Grand Rapids: Baker Academic, 2007), explores the different ways the Second Testament cites and alludes to the First Testament. (This commentary is 1,239 pages long.) The various ways that the Second Testament makes use of the First Testament can be understood using these different models: Promise and Fulfillment; Type and Antitype; Shadow and Reality; Beginning and Completion; History and Application; Part and Fullness. We believe each of these models is divinely intended. However, if taken by themselves, each could be misleading. But when we allow them all to be present, they complement one another and present us with a full-fledged portrait of Jesus. What we are doing in this book, in effect, is putting into action what C. H. Dodd and R. T. France have uncovered in their classic volumes *According to the Scriptures* and *Jesus and the Old Testament* (respectively). Dodd traces how the Second Testament authors interpreted the First Testament while France traces how Jesus interpreted it. As previously stated, both used the same method of interpretation. See also Hays, *Echoes of Scripture in the Letters of Paul* and *The Conversion of Imagination: Paul as Interpreter of Israel's Scriptures*, as well as Darrell L. Bock's *Recovering the Real Lost Gospel: Reclaiming the Gospel as Good News* (Nashville: B&H Academic, 2010), 7–21.

50. Because the historical-critical method has become so prominent today, the relationship between the First and Second Testaments has been largely lost. We agree with Henry Vander Goot's observation: "It is not out of proportion to the reality of the situation to speak today of a crisis in Biblical theology that is owing to the fact that much Christian reflection fails to view the Scriptures as a single narrative whole. Modern Biblical theology seems unable to hold together in a positive, comprehensive, and coherent unity the Old and New Testaments" (Henry Vander Goot, "*Tota Scriptura*: The Old Testament in the Christian Faith and Tradition," in *Life Is Religion: Essays in Honor of H. Evan Runner*, ed. Henry Vander Goot [St. Catherines, ON: Paideia, 1981], 97). In like manner, Walther Eichrodt says, "All the ever so brilliant results of historical research cannot seriously offer any substitute

for a grasp of the essential connexion between the Old Testament and the New Testament" (Walther Eichrodt, *Theologie des Alten Testament* [Berlin, Germany: Evangelische Verlagsanstalt, 1933], 1:4). We agree with Brevard Childs that historical and canonical criticism can live and work together. But priority must be accorded to the entire biblical canon.

51. "The Nature of the Christian Bible: One Book, Two Testaments," in Radner and Sumner, *The Rule of Faith*, 120–21.
52. We, along with most Christian scholars, strongly disagree with Reinhold Niebuhr's opinion that reading Jesus into the Hebrew canon is somehow anti-Semitic. The whole notion that Christianity is simply a second story built on Judaism is incorrect. Renowned Jewish scholar Jacob Neusner eloquently pointed this out. According to Neusner, Christianity is a Judaism. But it's a *different* Judaism than rabbinic Judaism. Both Christians and Jews interpret the *Tanakh* from a certain interpretive lens. For the rabbinic Jew, the interpretative lens is the discussion among the rabbis through the centuries—the rabbinic line of interpreters. For the Christian, it is not the rabbinic tradition of interpreters but Jesus who gives meaning to the ancient Hebrew text. So Jesus plays the role for Christians what the rabbinic tradition plays for the Jews.
53. The theological phrase for this is "grounded christologically." The story of Jesus is the deep structure that lies underneath all of what Paul and the other Second Testament writers wrote. They were working from the Jesus story, presupposing it and basing everything on it. Yet they did not dehistoricize the First Testament.
54. Matt. 2:15.
55. Matt. 2:14–15. See also Matthew 4:15–16; 8:16–17; 12:18–21; 13:35 for some examples. "Matthew has shown us how the Old Testament tells the story which Jesus completed. Then he showed us how the Old Testament declares the promise which Jesus fulfilled. Now he opens up the Old Testament as a store house which provides images, precedents, patterns and ideas to help us understand who Jesus is" (Christopher J. H. Wright, *Knowing Jesus Through the Old Testament* [Downers Grove, IL: InterVarsity, 1995], 108). Craig Keener rightly points out that the context of Hosea 11:1 speaks of a new exodus and a new era of salvation (Craig Keener, *The Gospel of Matthew: A Socio-Rhetorical Commentary* (Grand Rapids: Eerdmans, 2009, 108–9). Like Matthew, all the writers of the Second Testament highlight the narrative patterns of the First Testament, which are larger than the individual books that make up the Hebrew canon but which ultimately point to the Author behind it all.
56. John 1:45.
57. John 12:38.
58. For instance, Jesus is the Lamb slain for the sins of the people (John 1). He is the reality of the tabernacle and the temple (John 2–3). He is the serpent in the wilderness who brings healing (John 3). He is the new Jacob (John 1 and 4). He is the manna sent from heaven (John 6), etc.
59. 2 Cor. 3:14–16. According to E. E. Ellis, Paul quoted the First Testament ninety-three times in his writings. See E. E. Ellis, *Paul's Use of the Old Testament* (Grand Rapids: Baker, 1981), 11.
60. Rom. 5:14.
61. Col. 2:16–17.

62. 1 Cor. 10:1–4.
63. Heb. 7:21–24.
64. Heb. 10:1.
65. 1 Peter 1:10–11.
66. 1 Peter 2:4–7.
67. F. F. Bruce, *New Testament Development of Old Testament Themes* (Grand Rapids: Eerdmans, 1969), 21.
68. In his book *The Bible Made Impossible: Why Biblicism Is Not a Truly Evangelical Reading of Scripture* (Grand Rapids: Brazos, 2011), sociologist Christian Smith compares what he calls "biblicism" with reading Scripture Christotelically. Smith makes a compelling case that the answer to interpretative pluralism, which discounts the approach of biblicism, is reading the Scripture through the lens of Jesus Christ. See especially p. 97ff.
69. YHWH (also Yahweh) is the ancient Israelite name for God, at least from the time of the exodus (Ex. 3:14). By Jesus' day, it was considered unholy to speak this name out loud (except for the high priest once a year).
70. YHWH is the Hebrew word that is most frequently used for God in the First Testament. In chapter 5 of *The Challenge of Jesus: Rediscovering Who Jesus Was and Is* (2011), Wright argues at length that "the Old Testament portrait of YHWH fits Jesus like a glove" (121). Bonhoeffer argues that "the name of Jesus Christ is the name of the very One who in Genesis is named Yahweh" (*Creation and Fall: A Theological Exposition of Genesis 13* [Minneapolis: Fortress Press, 2004], 173). Scot McKnight points out that the name "Jesus" translates the Hebrew *Yeshua*, which means "YHWH is salvation." YHWH-is-salvation has become "God-in-flesh-salvation" and "Jesus-is-salvation" (Scot McKnight, *The King Jesus,* 87). See also Jeremiah 23:5–6, where the prophet declares that a righteous Branch and a prospering King will be raised up. And He shall be called "YHWH our righteousness." This text is clearly a reference to Jesus. See also Richard Bauckham's *God Crucified: Monotheism and Christology in the New Testament* (Grand Rapids: Eerdmans), 1998.
71. Some may think that the Trinity—Father, Son, and Spirit—is the subject of the Bible. But the reality is that both Father and the Spirit point to Jesus, and Jesus points to Himself as the content of all Scripture. Jesus, Paul tells us in Colossians 2:9, is "the fullness of the Godhead [in] bodily [form]." As Miroslav Volf once put it, "We worship one undivided, divine being who comes to us in three persons" (Mark Galli, "Do Muslims and Christians Worship the Same God?" *Christianity Today*, April 15, 2011; available at Virtue Online, http://www.virtueonline.org/portal/modules/news/article.php?storyid=14283). And we can only know this one undivided, divine being in and through Jesus Christ (John 1:18). For details, see *Jesus Manifesto*, 161–63; Erich Sauer's *From Eternity to Eternity: An Outline of the Divine Purposes* (Grand Rapids: Eerdmans, 1954), 14ff; David Fitch's *The End of Evangelicalism: Discerning a New Faithfulness for Mission; Towards an Evangelical Political Theology* (Eugene, OR: Cascade Books, 2011), xxvff; and Fred Sanders's *The Deep Things of God: How the Trinity Changes Everything* (Wheaton, IL: Crossway, 2010), 175ff.
72. See the important work by Mary Douglas, *Thinking in Circles: An Essay on Ring Composition* (New Haven, CT: Yale University Press, 2010). This genre reached its height between the eighth and the fifth centuries BC.

73. To those who would question the reliability of the First Testament and the Gospel accounts therein, we recommend *The New Testament Documents: Are They Reliable?* by F. F. Bruce (Downers Grove, IL: InterVarsity, 1960); *The Canon of Scripture* by F. F. Bruce (Downers Grove, IL: InterVarsity, 1988); *The Historical Reliability of the Gospels* by Craig Blomberg (Downers Grove, IL: InterVarsity, 1987); *Jesus and the Eyewitnesses: The Gospels as Eyewitness Testimony* by Richard Bauckham (Grand Rapids: Eerdmans, 2006); *The Historical Jesus of the Gospels* by Craig Keener; *Jesus, Paul, and the Gospels* by James D. G. Dunn (Grand Rapids: Eerdmans, 2011); *Memory, Jesus, and Synoptic Gospels* by Robert McIver (Atlanta: Society of Biblical Literature, 2011); *Jesus Legend: A Case for the Historical Reliability of the Synoptic Jesus Tradition* by Gregory Boyd and Paul Eddy (see n. 3); *Seeking the Identity of Jesus: A Pilgrimage* by Beverly Roberts Gaventa and Richard Hays; *The Case for the Real Jesus: A Journalist Investigates Current Attacks on the Identity of Christ* (Grand Rapids: Zondervan, 2007) and *The Case for Christ: A Journalist's Personal Investigation of the Evidence for Jesus* (Grand Rapids: Zondervan, 1998) by Lee Strobel; and *Gospel Perspectives* (6 volumes), eds. R. T. France, David Wenham, and Craig Blomberg (Sheffield, UK: JSOT Press, 1980–1986). See also *The Art of Reading Scripture* by Ellen David and Richard Hays (Grand Rapids: Eerdmans, 2003); *Scripture and the Authority of God: How to Read the Bible Today*, rev. and exp. ed. by N. T. Wright (New York: HarperOne, 2011); *The Blue Parakeet: Rethinking How You Read the Bible* by Scot McKnight (Bloomington, IN: AuthorHouse, 2006); *Inspiration and Authority: Nature and Function of Christian Scripture* by Paul Achtemeir (Peabody, MA: Hendrickson, 1999); and *The Bible Made Impossible* (see intro., n. 68).
74. In Greek, the word used in 2 Timothy 3:16 is *theopneustos*—literally, "God-breathed."
75. 2 Tim. 3:16.
76. 1 Cor. 2:14.
77. John 1:1. This passage climaxes by contrasting Jesus with the Torah given through Moses (John 1:17–18). Consequently, Jesus is the Word in the fullest ancient Jewish sense—the embodiment of God's revelation in the Torah.
78. For an explanation of the "extended meaning" of a text, see G. K. Beale's *The Temple and the Church's Mission: A Biblical Theology of the Dwelling Place of God* (Downers Grove, IL: InterVarsity Press, 2004), 376ff.
79. See Robert Mounce's groundbreaking book *Jesus, In His Own Words* (Nashville: B & H Pub. Group, 2010).
80. Frank Viola has done the same with Acts and the Epistles, putting the story found therein in chronological order in his book *The Untold Story of the New Testament Church: An Extraordinary Guide to Understanding the New Testament* (Shippensburg, PA: Destiny Image, 2004).
81. Irenaeus called this principle "recapitulation." See also Dodd, *According to the Scriptures*, 103. R. T. France wrote about God's dealings, saying, "Thus his acts in the Old Testament will present a pattern which can be seen to be repeated in the New Testament events . . . New Testament typology is thus essentially the tracing of constant principles of God's working in history, revealing 'a recurring rhythm in past history which is taken up more fully and perfectly in the Gospel events'" (France, *Jesus and the Old Testament*, 39).

82. Edmund Clowney, *Preaching Christ in All the Scriptures* (Wheaton, IL: Crossway Books, 2003), 31.
83. Also see John 21:25.
84. Robert Farrar Capon wrote a book, *Genesis, the Movie* (Grand Rapids: Eerdmans, 2003), in which he argues that the Bible is best approached as a movie, one whole movie, with a main character named Jesus. "You have to see the Bible as one complete story, with redemption in Christ as the underlying theme and plot, the whole point of the story from the first scene. You know what's fun? When you watch a movie, try to identify the Christ figure. I mean the figure who makes the plot work. It doesn't even have to be a human character. It's the one who does for the plot of that particular film what Jesus Christ does for the world." See Tim Brassell, "Interview with Robert F. Capon," Grace Communion International, http://www.gci.org/gospel/capon.

Chapter 1: Christ Before Time

1. G. C. Berkouwer, *Holy Scripture*, trans. and ed. Jack B. Rogers (Grand Rapids: Eerdmans, 1975), 166.
2. There are two major views among Christians regarding time and eternity. Augustine's view sees eternity to be timeless and nonlinear. Newton's view sees eternity as being marked by linear time that never ends in either direction. In Augustine's view, which was championed by C. S. Lewis and others, God is outside of and transcends time. In Newton's view, which was championed by Oscar Cullmann and others, God's actions are accomplished in real time before, during, and after creation. Time is infinite and never had a beginning. We agree with Augustine and Lewis that God is timeless. We agree with Einstein that time began with creation. God, therefore, is at the beginning and the end of creation at the same moment. He lives in the eternal now. Yet we also agree with the great theologian Karl Barth, who taught that God can move into time and act there, even though He stands outside of time as well (*Church Dogmatics,* vol. 2, part 1). Barth believed that eternity surrounds time on all sides. Eternity accompanies time and contains all of time's fullness simultaneously. Because we are temporal beings, we experience events in bits and pieces in a linear fashion. So rather than seeing God's eternity as a sort of lack of temporality, it's more accurate to see that God is present in His fullness in all time. Does God know it's today? Yes. He knows it's today, but He also knows it is yesterday and tomorrow. C. S. Lewis put it this way: How can God be incarnate and the man who lives in time also be God who lives outside of time? The answer is that the incarnation is not something we work our way toward intellectually. As Bonheoffer said, you have to begin with the incarnation. We understand God and humanity in terms of the incarnation. If we begin with a set notion of God and man and time and eternity, and try to fit God into it, it becomes impossible to resolve all the paradoxes. We must always begin with the incarnate Christ. For more on the subject of time and eternity, see *Mere Christianity* by C. S. Lewis (San Francisco: HarperSanFrancisco, 2001); *Time and Eternity: Exploring God's Relationship to Time* by William Lane Craig (New York: Oxford University

Press, 1998); *Eternal God* by Paul Helm; *God and Time: Essays on the Divine Nature*, edited by Gregory Ganssle (New York: Oxford University Press, 2002); *Time and Eternity* by Brian Leftow; *Christ and Time: The Primitive Christian Conception of Time and History* by Oscar Cullmann (Philadelphia: Westminster, 1950); and *Predestination & Free Will: Four Views of Divine Sovereignty & Human Freedom*, edited by David Basinger and Randall Basinger (Downers Grove, IL: InterVarsity, 1986), especially "Norman Geisler's Response," 132–33.

3. Phrases such as "before creation" and "before the foundation of the world" are *facons de parlers*, or figures of speech. The reason is because God is eternal. He does not exist temporally prior to creation. Thus there is no moment or time before creation. God exists beyond, or without, creation. Time, space, and matter are in Him. We don't see God in temporal terms. Instead, we see the coming of Christ as being the in-breaking of God into time. And that is the kingdom.
4. See, for example, Ephesians 1:4; 1 Peter 1:20; Revelation 13:8.
5. Ps. 90:2.
6. Jude 25.
7. 2 Cor. 4:18 NIV.
8. John 17:24 NIV.
9. Gen. 1:3.
10. C. S. Lewis discussed this eternal love affair in *Mere Christianity*, 176ff. See Stanley Grenz's *Created for Community: Connecting Christian Belief with Christian Living*, 2nd ed. (Grand Rapids: Baker Academic, 1998), 47–49; Leonardo Boff's *Holy Trinity, Perfect Community* (Maryknoll, NY: Orbis, 2000); Milt Rodriguez's *The Community Life of God: Seeing the Godhead as the Model for All Relationships* (Box Elder, SD: Rebuilders, 2009); and C. Baxter Kruger's *The Great Dance: The Christian Vision Revisited* (Vancouver, BC: Regent College Pub., 2005).
11. Some examples are found in John 17:24; 14:31; 1 Corinthians 15:28.
12. 1 John 4:8, 16.
13. John 14:9; 10:30.
14. See Bill Freeman's *The Triune God in Experience: The Testimony of Church History* (Scottsdale, AZ: Ministry Publications, 1994).
15. According to Karl Barth, "this pretime is the pure time of the Father and the Son in the fellowship of the Holy Spirit" (*The Doctrine of God*, vol. 2, pt. 1 of his *Church Dogmatics*, eds. G. W. Bromiley and T. F. Torrance, 4 vols. [Edinburgh: T. & T. Clark, 1957], 622ff.). Barth saw the incarnation—God becoming human and joining humanity—as the purpose for the creation. God's intent in eternity was to be with humans even if they hadn't sinned.
16. Proverbs 8:22–31; John 1:1–3, 18; 15:26; 17:5; and John 17:24; 14:31 give us a peek into the fellowship in the Godhead. The theological term for this is *perichoresis*, which contains the ideas of interpenetration and interpermeation. The metaphor that has been commonly used for it is that of a dance.
17. Frank Viola's *Reimagining Church: Pursuing the Dream of Organic Christianity* (Colorado Springs: David C. Cook, 2008) and *Finding Organic Church: A Comprehensive Guide to Starting and Sustaining Authentic Christian Communities*

(Colorado Springs: David C. Cook, 2009) explore how the church, God's mission, and the Christian life all find their roots in the eternal Godhead.

18. Phil. 2:6–11.
19. Phil. 2:8. An entire book can be written on the *kenosis* (self–emptying) of Jesus mentioned in Philippians 2:6–8. When Jesus emptied Himself, His divinity didn't pass out of existence. The incarnation didn't cause Him to cease from being divine. As a man, Jesus never ceased from being divine, but He ceased to subjectively experience that divinity. He does not call upon it as His own. What Jesus did in the way of miraculous power was an operation of Him being a human anointed by the Holy Spirit (Acts 10:38). For this reason, the apostles (who weren't divine beings) repeated the same works that Jesus performed, including knowing people's thoughts, raising the dead, healing the sick, and discerning and casting out demons. Christ continued to receive as a human being power from His Father as He always had and always will as the second person of the triune God.
20. For details, see T. F. Torrance, *Incarnation: The Person and Life of Christ* (Downers Grove, IL: IVP Academic, 2008). Also see Karl Barth's treatment on the incarnation and how it connects with the Trinity in "The Incarnation of the Word," *Church Dogmatics*, vol. 1, pt. 2 (New York: T. & T. Clark International, 2004), 1–202.
21. John 17:5 NIV.
22. Before creation, the Father continually poured His fullness into the Son. And the Son continually emptied Himself in order to receive that fullness. And the Spirit is the bond of love that joins Father and Son together in oneness.
23. We don't put the event first and try to fit our doctrinal God into the event. We look at the incarnate Son, and that incarnate Son is both divine and human. And from the standpoint of the Son as the divine Son, as the person with a divine nature, there is no before or after for Him. If there were, He would not be eternal. He would be temporal. In the incarnation, the action of *kenosis*, of pouring out the divine glory, which happens in the Godhead eternally, is transposed into a relationship between the divine and human natures in the one person, Jesus. There's a transposition that goes on so that what we see in that human person historically is that which is true in God eternally. The incarnation is a divine person assuming a human nature. There's only one person in the incarnation, and that person is divine. And in the incarnation, that person has two natures. That divine person in that divine nature, which is His own proper nature, existed eternally. It was present during the time of Abraham.
24. The Father as the source of the Son's life can be found in such texts as John 5:19–20, 26–27, 30; 6:46, 57; 7:16, 28–29; 8:28, 42; 13:3; 14:10; 16:27; 17:8. The Eastern church preferred to speak of the Father as the source of the triune God. The Father is the fountainhead of the trinitarian community. All things flow from Him. The Western church preferred to speak of the mutual equality and reciprocity of the members as they share the one divine nature. In his book *Holy Trinity, Perfect Community*, Leonardo Boff correctly points out that these two views are not in contradiction. Rather, the Eastern church *begins* with the Father as source while the Western church *begins* with the one divine nature of Father, Son, and Spirit. The Father is the Father only because

He begot the Son. Without the begetting of the Son, there is no Father. The same is true with the procession of the Spirit. All the members are dependent on the existence of the others. The Father as source doesn't imply that the Son is inferior. All the members of the triune God are dependent upon one another. For details, see Kevin Giles, *The Trinity & Subordinationism* (Downers Grove: InterVarsity Press, 2002) and *Jesus and the Father* (Grand Rapids: Zondervan, 2006); Thomas F. Torrance, *Christian Doctrine of God, One Being, Three Persons* (London: T. & T. Clark, 2001) and *Trinitarian Faith: The Evangelical Theology of the Ancient Catholic Faith* (London: T&T Clark, 2000); Gilbert Bilezekian, *Community 101* (Grand Rapids: Zondervan, 1997); Miroslav Volf, *After Our Likeness: The Church as the Image of Trinity* (Grand Rapids: Eerdmans, 1998) and *God's Life in Trinity* (Minneapolis: Fortress Press, 2006); Stanley Grenz, *Theology for the Community of God* (Grand Rapids: Eerdmans, 1994); Ted Peters, *God Is Trinity* (Louisville: Westminster Press, 1993); Baxter Kruger, *The Great Dance* (see n. 11, above); and Fred Sanders, *The Deep Things of God*, 86ff (see intro., n. 71).

25. Paul Fiddes, *Participating in God: A Pastoral Doctrine of the Trinity* (Louisville: Westminster John Knox, 2000), 40.
26. Gen. 1:3.
27. 1 John 4:8, 16.
28. John 17:5.
29. Ibid.
30. Heb. 1:3 NASB.
31. Heb. 9:23.
32. John 8:56 NIV; 8:58.
33. Isa. 6:1.
34. John 12:41 NIV.
35. Along this line, Justin Martyr regarded Jesus as the Angel of Great Counsel in Isaiah (9:6); as a Man in Ezekiel (40:3); as the Son of Man in Daniel (7:13); as wisdom in Solomon (Prov. 8:22ff.); as a star in the books of Moses (Gen. 49; Num. 24:17); as the Branch in Zechariah (6:12); and as a child, the suffering One, Jacob, Israel, a Rod, the Flower, the Cornerstone, and the Son of God throughout Isaiah (9:6; 42; 43; 52–53; 8:14; 28:16; 11:1) (*Dialogue with Trypho*, 126). According to Justin, it was Christ as the preexistent Logos who shut Noah in the ark (Gen. 7:16), who came down to see the tower of Babel (Gen. 11:5), who spoke to Abraham (Gen. 18), who wrestled with Jacob (Gen. 32), and who spoke to Moses from the burning bush (Ex. 3) (*Dialogue*, 61–62, 126ff.). In like manner, some of the early church fathers saw references to Jesus in the Pentateuch. They argued that the divine name *Elohiym* in Genesis 1:26 points to the plurality of persons in the Godhead, since *Elohiym* is a compound plural word and comports with God's complex unity. They also saw Christ in various "theophanies" in the Old Testament, such as in the Angel of the Lord. For further discussion, see *The Divinity of Our Lord and Savior Jesus Christ* by H. P. Liddon (London: Pickering & Inglis, 1864), 29–37.
36. Ex. 16:10; 40:38.
37. 1 Cor. 10:3–4. In a very real sense, Jesus was present in the First Testament. So Paul could say that Christ was the Rock that followed Israel around, which does not mean that Jesus became a geological formation. But it does

mean that all of God's work is a work that is understandable only in Christ. Jesus is the Logos, the sheer intelligibility of God. Therefore, wherever God reveals Himself, He reveals Himself in Logos. There is no revelation outside of the Logos. The Logos is God's revelation of Himself. So whatever reveals God in the First Testament is inherently a place in which the Logos, the divine person who was incarnate in Christ, is present and at work.

38. See F. F. Bruce, *Jesus: Past, Present and Future: The Work of Christ* (Downers Grove, IL: InterVarsity, 1998), chap. 8, "Before the Incarnation."
39. Ex. 33:20 NASB. For the full story, see Ex. 33:12–23.
40. 2 Cor. 4:6.
41. John 1:18.
42. Ex. 40:34.
43. See John 1:14.
44. God revealed His "goodness" to Moses, "full of grace and truth" (see Ex. 34:5–6; John 1:14), but Moses could see only part of God's glory. In Jesus, however, God is fully unveiled (John 1:18). Therefore, the law came through Moses, but "grace and truth came through Jesus Christ" (1:17).
45. Luke 2:9.
46. John 1:1; authors' paraphrase.
47. Luke 9:32. See also Matthew 17:2; Luke 9:29; 2 Peter 1:18.
48. Luke 9:34 NIV.
49. Eph. 3:8–11 NASB.
50. Luke 9:35.
51. In 1 Corinthians 15, Paul wrote about the glory of various things, including the sun, the moon, etc. When an object is at its highest visible expression, it is glorified.
52. Just as the Son receives from the Father the gloriousness of the divine life, so we through Christ become participants of that same divine life, and therefore, we share His glory (2 Peter 1:4; John 17:22). Glory is the full and outward expression of an inner excellence. I've defined *glory* to be the highest expression of a life. A flower is glorified when it is in full bloom. The inner excellence of the flower is the seed. In eternity, there was no visible, physical expression. But in the eyes of the Godhead, there was an expression as they beheld one another.
53. See Romans 3:25 YLT.
54. 1 Kings 8:6–7; Ex. 25:18–19; cf. Heb. 7–10.
55. Rev. 21:9–11.
56. Rev. 21:22–23 NIV.
57. Rom. 3:23; 8:18–21.
58. Frank's book *From Eternity to Here: Rediscovering the Ageless Purpose of God* (Colorado Springs: David C. Cook, 2009) is an unfolding of the eternal purpose. See also DeVern Fromke's *Ultimate Intention* (Mount Vernon, MO: Sure Foundation, 1963) and T. Austin-Sparks's *The Stewardship of the Mystery* (Shippensburg, PA: MercyPlace Ministries, 2002).
59. C. Baxter Kruger expounds on this idea in *The Great Dance*, 24ff. John R. W. Stott puts it crisply in his *God's New Society: The Message of Ephesians* (Downers Grove, IL: InterVarsity, 1986), 36.
60. C. S. Lewis, *Mere Christianity*, rev. and amplified ed., 176.

61. Eph. 3:2–6, 8–11; 1:9; Eph. 5:25–32.
62. Eph. 3:8 NASB, footnote a.
63. Eph. 1:4.
64. Eph. 2:19–22.
65. Heb. 4:3 NASB.
66. Col. 1:17 NIV.
67. F. F. Bruce translates Colossians 1:16 to say "all things were created *in* Him." The same Greek term can mean either "in" or "through," but Bruce argues for "in" (F. F. Bruce, *The Epistles to the Colossians, to Philemon, and to the Ephesians* [Grand Rapids: Eerdmans, 1984], 61).
68. Stanley Grenz, *Created for Community*, 56–57 (see n. 11 above).
69. Lewis, *Mere Christianity*, 166–71.
70. Grenz, *Created for Community*, 57.
71. Rev. 1:8; 2:8; 21:6, 13.
72. John 7:34.
73. Rev. 1:4, 8. The name of God, I AM, is susceptible to multiple interpretations in terms of tense. Therefore, it can be translated "I am that I will be," "I am what I was," "I will be what I am." All those are possible ways of translating. You put all those things together and see them as different slices of the same reality. What they are saying is that God is, in all times and at all places, simply who God is. God will be always what He was, and is, and will be. His being takes in all the different verb tenses and concentrates them into one eternal act, the act of the divine being. Therein lies the identity of Jesus Christ.
74. Ex. 6:7; Isa. 43:10. We are aware that until John 8:58, Jesus is using wordplay that His hearers within the narrative wouldn't necessarily catch. "I AM" is an acceptable way to say, "I am He," as in John 9:9. But Jesus is taking the meaning somewhere else.
75. John 8:24.
76. John 8:28.
77. John 8:58.
78. John 13:19. See Raymond Brown, *An Introduction to New Testament Christology* (Mahwah, NJ: Paulist, 1994), appendix 4, "Features of John's Christology," 205–10.
79. Isa. 11:10; Jer. 23:5; 33:15; Zech. 3:8; 6:12; Isa. 11:1; 4:2.
80. Rev. 22:16.
81. Rom. 8:30.
82. The divine life in our mortal bodies is simply a partial participation in the reality of resurrection life. This is one of Paul's arguments in Romans 8. The resurrection in that sense has already begun. But more than that, as Paul put it in Romans 8:30, He has already "glorified" us.
83. Rom. 8:28–30.
84. Rev. 13:8; see also 1 Peter 1:19–20.The slaying of the Lamb of God that took place at one time in one place was a revelation of an eternal reality within God Himself. The sacrifice of the Son to the Father, the self-emptying of the Son for the Father, is an eternal reality. And this was true at the foundation of the world and has been true since the foundation of the world. It has now been revealed for our sakes in the actual historical event. It's been brought

down to a human level. A divine reality has been joined to history and to the human experience. Calvary brought an eternal reality to the highest human point. Because God doesn't live in time, Jesus' historical event—His dying for the sins of the world—from the viewpoint of God had already happened before He created. That's the reason why God could pass over sins when the animal sacrifices were made, because the historical gap between the animal sacrifices and the cross did not exist at a divine level. At a divine level, the sacrifices in their own way not just picture but partially participate in the reality that they picture.

85. Karl Barth taught that Christ is the basis for and the fulfillment of the covenant made within the Godhead before creation. Consequently, the "eternal covenant" mentioned in Hebrews may have in view the first covenant that forms the basis for all subsequent covenants: the covenant between the Father and the Son. Implicit in their relationship with one another was a promise to one another—a commitment. The eternal covenant is another way of talking about God's life. The covenants in history—the Abrahamic covenant, the Mosaic covenant, etc.—are what we mortals experience in our relationship with God as historical expressions of the covenant that lies at the heart of the trinitarian life—the eternal covenant.
86. Acts 4:27–28; 2:23; Eph. 3:9–11; 1 Peter 1:20; Rom. 8:29–30; 11:2.
87. Eph. 1:4–9; 2 Tim. 1:9; 1 Peter 1:2; 2 Thess. 2:13.
88. Rev. 17:8; Luke 10:20. The Book of Life is obviously metaphorical, as a book couldn't exist before the visible creation. It's rather a way of talking about the mind of God.
89. Gen. 1:3.
90. Titus 1:2; Matt. 25:34; 1 Cor. 2:7–9; Eph. 1:11.
91. Matt. 13:35; 1 Cor. 2:7.
92. Eph. 1:4; Jer. 1:5; Rom. 8:29; 11:2; 1 Peter 1:2; 2 Tim. 1:9. Regarding the question of election and predestination, we agree with Karl Barth, who said that Christ is the elect man, and we are elect in Him. We are corporately elect in the Son. So whatever ends up in the Son, ends up in the sphere of God's election. We, along with Barth, are unconcerned with the old classic arguments on this question. The two prevailing paradigms of election versus free will that have raged throughout church history have solid uses as well as deficiencies. One of the deficiencies is that both paradigms put the question on a purely individualistic horizon. The other deficiency is that neither grasps the fact that God is outside of time, and time is within Him. So He is at the end at the same moment that He is at the beginning. In short, our election is incomprehensible apart from a lot of other eternal realities. Thus we rather view election and predestination christologically. See also Ben Witherington's *The Letters to Philemon, the Colossians, and the Ephesians: A Socio-Rhetorical Commentary on the Captivity Epistles* (Grand Rapids: Eerdmans, 2007), 234, where he says of Ephesians 1:3–4, "The concept of election and destining here is corporate. If one is in Christ, one is elect and destined."
93. Leonard Sweet and Frank Viola, *Jesus Manifesto* (see intro., n. 1).
94. Eph. 3:9 NASB.
95. Rev. 13:8.

96. Col. 1:20.
97. Acts 10:40.
98. Rom. 16:25–27 NIV.
99. C. S. Lewis discusses this cogently in *Mere Christianity*, 157ff. So does Erich Sauer in his *The Dawn of World Redemption: A Survey of the History of Salvation in the Old Testament* (Grand Rapids: Eerdmans, 1994), 15–22.
100. Col. 1:15–18.
101. Eph. 1:10.
102. Col. 1:16.
103. John 20:28.
104. T. Austin-Sparks, *Words of Wisdom and Revelation* (Corinna, ME: Three Brothers, 2000), 6.
105. John 1:1–3.
106. John 1:14; see also 1 John 1:1.
107. Jer. 10:12; 51:15.
108. Ps. 33:6 ESV.
109. 1 Cor. 1:24.
110. The "Word" in the First Testament was especially God's message (the Law and the Prophets). See Craig Keener, *The Gospel of John: A Commentary* (Grand Rapids: Baker Academic/Peabody: Hendrickson, 2003), 341–63 (esp. 361) and 405–26 (esp. 419–23).
111. Robert Jenson draws much on the theology of Karl Barth. He has authored *Alpha and Omega: A Study in the Theology of Karl Barth* (New York: Nelson, 1963); *God After God: The God of the Past and the God of the Future, Seen in the Work of Karl Barth* (Indianapolis: Bobbs-Merrill, 1969); *The Knowledge of Things Hoped For: The Sense of Theological Discourse* (New York: Oxford University Press, 1969); and *Systematic Theology* (2 volumes) (New York: Oxford University Press, 1997–1999), among other volumes.
112. A.W. Tozer, *The Knowledge of the Holy* (New York: HarperOne, 1961), 39.
113. The word *firstborn* in this text has to do with rank, primacy, and heirship. Some translations say "the firstborn before creation."
114. Heb. 1:2.
115. Col. 1:16–17.

Chapter 2: Christ in Creation: The Macro Version

1. Michael Horton, *The Gospel Commission* (Grand Rapids: Baker Books, 2011), Kindle ed., 25. Horton is summarizing Christopher J. H. Wright's idea from *The Mission of God: Unlocking the Bible's Grand Narrative* (Downers Grove, IL: InterVarsity Academic, 2006).
2. Heb. 1:1–2 NIV.
3. Matt. 12:34.
4. John 1:1.
5. Frank's book *From Eternity to Here* (see chap. 1, n. 59) traces the themes contained from Genesis 1–2 to Revelation 21–22.
6. John 1:3. See also 1 Corinthians 8:6; Hebrews 1:2.
7. Heb. 11:3.
8. 2 Cor. 4:4–6.

9. NIV.
10. 1 Cor. 1:24.
11. Col. 2:9.
12. Ps. 19:1–5 NIV.
13. Heb. 1:3. See also Colossians 1:15.
14. For a comparison of the same wording in John 1 and Genesis 1, see *From Eternity to Here*, 116ff.
15. John 1:23.
16. John 1:32.
17. Karl Rahner, *Foundations of Christian Faith: An Introduction to the Idea of Christianity* (New York: Seabury, 1978), 213.
18. Isa. 57:20.
19. Gen. 1:3.
20. 1 Peter 1:23; James 1:18.
21. John 1:4–9ff.; Luke 1:79; 2:32.
22. John 1:4–5.
23. John 1:9. See also John 8:12; 9:15; 12:46; Revelation 21:23.
24. John 3:5–6; 1 Peter 1:23; James 1:18.
25. Gen. 1:2.
26. Gen. 1:3; John 1:4–5.
27. 2 Cor. 4:6.
28. Col. 1:13; John 3:3ff; 1 Cor. 2:9–16.
29. 2 Peter 3:6.
30. 1 Peter 1:20–21.
31. Rom. 6:6.
32. Gen. 8:11; John 14:17; 2 Cor. 5:17.
33. Luke 12:51; John 7:43.
34. Rom. 6:6; Gal. 2:20; Col. 2:20.
35. Col. 3:8–9; Eph. 4:22; Col. 3:5.
36. John 8:23; James 1:17; 3:15, 17; Col. 3:1–2.
37. Acts 2:38–40.
38. Rom. 6:4; 1 Peter 3:21.
39. Gal. 5:24; 6:14.
40. Heb. 4:12.
41. Rom. 6:6ff.; 2 Cor. 6:17ff.
42. Matt. 16:21; 17:23; 20:19; Luke 24:46; Acts 10:40; 1 Cor. 15:4. According to *Dictionary of Biblical Imagery* (Downers Grove: InterVarsity Press, 1998), the third-day motif "reaches its sacral climax in the third-day resurrection of Jesus" (864).
43. Hos. 6:1–2.
44. Ex. 14:21ff.
45. 1 Cor. 10:1–2.
46. Ex. 14:30; Rev. 20:13; Matt. 8:32; Mark 11:23.
47. Rom. 6:3–4; Col. 2:12.
48. Rev. 21:1, 4.
49. Gen. 1:11.
50. John 12:23–24 NIV.
51. John 15:1; 6:57.

52. 1 Kings 4:33.
53. See John 12:24. Barley is the first to come up during the spring harvest.
54. Rom. 7:4 NIV.
55. See chapter 19 of Frank Viola's *From Eternity to Here* for details.
56. Ps. 104:15.
57. Col. 2:12; 3:1; Rom. 6:4–5; Eph. 2:5.
58. Luke 1:78; John 8:12; Ps. 19:4–6; Col. 2:9.
59. Mal. 4:2.
60. Luke 1:78 NIV.
61. Rev. 22:16 NIV; see also 2 Peter 1:19.
62. John 15:5.
63. Ps. 89:36–37; Matt. 5:14–15; John 12:36; Eph. 5:8.
64. Phil. 2:15; Dan. 12:3; Rev. 1:20.
65. Eph. 2:6.
66. Eph. 1:20–22.
67. Matt. 13:43.
68. Song 6:10 NIV.
69. John 17:22–24.
70. Isa. 60:19–20.
71. 2 Cor. 6:14 NIV.
72. Rev. 21:25; 22:5.
73. Gen. 1:14 NIV.
74. Col. 2:16–17 NIV.
75. God destroyed all life on earth in Noah's day by salt water (Gen. 6–8), except the eight who lived in the ark.
76. Dan. 7:1–12; Rev. 13:1.
77. John 11:26; 1 Cor. 15:55–57.
78. See "Tertullian on Necessity of Baptism," http://www.piney.com/Tertullian-Baptism.html.
79. Phil. 3:20; Eph. 2:6.
80. John 17:16.
81. Isa. 40:31.
82. Luke 13:34.
83. Mark 1:10; see also Gen. 8.
84. 2 Cor. 3:17; Rom. 8:9–11.
85. John 14:16–18.
86. 1 Cor. 15:47.
87. John 16:33; 1 John 5:4.
88. John 1:29, 36; 1 Cor. 5:7.
89. Rev. 5:5.
90. Heb. 9:13.
91. Eph. 5:2; Heb. 7–10.
92. 1 John 3:2.
93. Phil. 3:21.
94. 1 Cor. 15:20–58.
95. NLT. Other translations say that Adam was "a type, a prototype, a figure, a pattern, an image" of the One who was to come, meaning Jesus. In Romans 5 and 1 Corinthians 15, Paul compared and contrasted Jesus with Adam.

96. For an insightful treatment on Jesus as the true human, see Stanley Grenz's *Theology for the Community of God*, chaps. 10 and 11 (see chap. 1, n. 25).
97. Karl Barth, *The Doctrine of Creation*, vol. 3, pt. 2, of his *Church Dogmatics*, trans. G. W. Bromiley (London: T. & T. Clark, 2004), 3.
98. John 14:9.
99. Gen. 1:28.
100. 1 John 1:3; Acts 10:38.
101. Luke 10:19.
102. 2 Tim. 4:1; Jude 14–15.
103. 2 Tim. 2:12; 1 Cor. 6:3.
104. 1 Cor. 15:45.
105. 1 Cor. 15:25.
106. Rev. 5:10.
107. Wright, *Simply Jesus*, 4 (see intro., n. 6).
108. Heb. 6:5.
109. Phil. 2:10.
110. 2 Tim. 2:12; Rev. 11:15; 22:5.
111. Rev. 21–22.
112. Rev. 21:9.
113. 1 Cor. 15:28. See also Ephesians 1:10.
114. N. T. Wright, *Scripture and the Authority of God: How to Read the Bible Today*, rev. and expanded ed. (New York: HarperOne, 2011), 160.
115. Heb. 4:9–10.
116. John 19:30.
117. Col. 2:17.
118. Isa. 11:7–9; Hab. 2:14.
119. Psalm 104 retells the creation story in poetic language, and Psalm 8 rehearses the creation of humanity.
120. Donald Joy, professor at Asbury Theological Seminary, says, "It is clear that Adam in Genesis 1 and in Genesis 5 includes both the male and the female: 'They' are Adam" (Donald Joy, *Bonding: Relationships in the Image of God* [Nappanee, IN: Evangel Publishing, 1999], 21). In chapter 2 of the same book, Joy goes into detail on how Eve's formation foreshadows the formation of the church. A. B. Simpson echoes these thoughts, saying, "Man was created male and female. This does not mean, as it would seem at first from the language, that he created the male and the female at the same time, but He created male and female in one person. The woman was included in the man physically and psychically, and afterwards was taken out of the man and constituted in her own individuality" (A. B. Simpson, *The Christ in the Bible Commentary, Book 1* [Camp Hill, PA: WingSpread Publishers, 2009], 25). Also C. H. Mackintosh: "Eve received all her blessings in Adam: in him, too, she got her dignity. Though not yet called into actual existence, she was, in the purpose of God, looked at as part of the man" (C. H. Mackintosh, *Notes on the Book of Genesis* [New York: Loizeaux, 1880], 12). A similar view prevails in later Jewish (Tannaitic) tradition (Midrash Rabbah Gen. 8:1).
121. See E. W. Bullinger, *Number in Scripture* (Grand Rapids: Kregel, 1967), p. 196ff.
122. 2 Peter 2:5; 1 Peter 3:20.
123. Gen. 17:12; Col. 2:11; Rom. 2:29.

124. Ex. 22:29–30.
125. 1 Sam. 17:12.
126. *The Epistle of Barnabas* is one of the earliest Christian documents to state that Jesus was raised from the dead on the eighth day.
127. Wright, *The Scriptures and the Authority of God*, 161. Revelation 1:10 uses the phrase "the Lord's Day." Some of the first-century churches met on the first day of the week, i.e., the eighth day (1 Cor. 16:2; Acts 20:7). Wright points out that Hebrews 3:7–4:11 is really an exposition of Psalm 95:7–11, which speaks of Joshua leading God's people into the promised land of rest.
128. 1 Cor. 15:45; Rom. 5:14.
129. Eph. 5:25–32.
130. Eve doesn't make her appearance until Genesis 2, after creation has ended. In Genesis 1:27 and 5:2, the implication is that the female was created inside the male at the time that Adam was created. Later, God "split the Adam" and took the woman out of the man. But before that, "they" were Adam.
131. Viola, *From Eternity to Here*, 30–31.
132. John 19:5.
133. We give credit to N. T. Wright for this insight. This statement also parallels the words, "Behold your King!" in John 19:14, which echoes 1 Samuel 12:13 and Zechariah 9:9, quoted in John 12:15.
134. John 19:30.
135. John 20.
136. John 20:15. The garden also seems to have connections to Jesus as the true vine in John 15.
137. John 20:22.
138. 1 Cor. 15:45.
139. John 20:1, 19 NLT.
140. Eph. 1:4.
141. In the Second Testament, the death of God's own is referred to as sleep—John 11:11; Acts 7:60; 1 Corinthians 15:6, 18, 20, 51; 1 Thessalonians 4:13–15. Furthermore, death as "sleep" was a common idiom. It appears widely on ancient tomb inscriptions, both Greek and Jewish, and elsewhere, including in earlier Greek mythology.
142. John 19:34. This brings John's water motif—e.g., John 2:6; 3:5; 4:1–30; 7:37–39—to a climax. It has symbolic import in John's gospel. Jesus' death on the cross glorified Him so that He gave the Spirit (John 20:22). We give credit to Craig Keener for this insight.
143. Ex. 17:6.
144. 1 Cor. 10:4.
145. Eph. 5:26; John 17:17; 1 John 5:6–8.
146. F. F. Bruce, *Jesus, Lord & Savior* (Downers Grove, IL: InterVarsity, 1986), 207.
147. Col. 1:26; see also Eph. 5:32.
148. Col. 1:27; 2:2.
149. Eph. 3:3–9.
150. Eph. 5:29–32.
151. Num. 3:7–8.
152. Gen. 3:8.
153. Deut. 23:14; 2 Sam. 7:6.

154. Isa. 51:3.
155. Ezek. 28:13.
156. Gen 2:8; 3:24.
157. Ex. 27:9–18; Num. 2:1–34; Ezek. 40:6.
158. Ezek. 28:13–16.
159. Ex. 15:17; 2 Chron. 3:1; see also Rev. 21:10.
160. Gen. 2:9.
161. Ps. 27:4; 96:6.
162. 1 Kings 6:14–18, 29, 32; 7:18–26, 42.
163. Ex. 26:31–34.
164. Gen. 3:24; Ex. 25:10–22.
165. 1 Sam. 4:4; 2 Kings 19:15; 1 Chron. 13:6; Ps. 80:1.
166. 2 Chron. 3:6; 1 Chron. 29:4; 1 Kings 6:20–22; 5:17; 7:9–10.
167. Some translations have bdellium, or aromatic resin. However, some scholars believe the reference in Genesis 2:12 is to pearl. The margin note in the New International Version has "pearls." Either way, bdellium is a resin that hardens like a pearl.
168. 1 Chron. 29:2; Gen. 2:12.
169. Ex. 30:11–16; Zech. 11:12–13; 1 Peter 1:18–20.
170. Gen. 2:12.
171. Rev. 21:21.
172. See the Book of Jubilees 3:27; 4:23–25; 8:19; Midrash Rabbah Genesis 21:8; The Testament of Levi 18:6–10; 1 Enoch 24–27.
173. For more details on the parallels between the garden and the temple, see Beale, *The Temple and the Church's Mission* (see intro., n. 78).
174. Compare the seven days of Genesis 1 with Exodus 25:1; 30:11, 17, 22, 34; 31:1, 12.
175. 1 Kings 6:38.
176. 1 Kings 8:2.
177. Compare Genesis 1:31; 2:2–3 with Exodus 39:32, 43; 40:33.
178. Ps. 132:7–8, 13–14; 1 Chron. 28:2; Isa. 66:1.
179. Ps. 78:69. This thought is echoed by Josephus (*Antiquitates Judaicae* 3:180ff; 3:123) and Philo (*De Vita Mosis* 2:71–145), among other early Jewish writers. Other scholars who have pointed out the parallels between the temple and creation include John Walton, Michael Fishbane, and G. K. Beale.
180. John 15:1; John 6:57.
181. John 7:38.
182. Col. 1:15; 3:11; Gal. 6:15.
183. Watchman Nee, *A Table in the Wilderness: Daily Meditations* (Wheaton, IL: Tyndale, 1978), January 26; words in all caps appear in original.
184. Ezek. 40–43.
185. Rev. 21:16.
186. Among other things, gold represents the divine nature of God (Job 22:25). For the significance of each element from a spiritual perspective, see *From Eternity to Here* by Frank Viola, chap. 20.
187. 2 Cor. 4:7; Rom. 9:21.
188. John 15:5; John 6:57; Gal. 2:20; Col. 3:4.

189. Rev. 21–22.
190. 1 Cor. 3:16–17; Eph. 2:19–22; 1 Peter 2:5.
191. Wright, *Simply Jesus*, 148.
192. John 5:46. See also Hebrews 10:7.
193. For a full discussion, see the first volume of Augustine's *The Literal Meaning of Genesis,* trans. John Hammond Taylor, *Ancient Christian Writers*, 41, (New York: Newman Press, 1982).

Chapter 3: Christ in Creation: The Micro Version

1. From a Sonnet by Michelangelo, as quoted by Ralph Waldo Emerson, "Michel Angelo," in *Emerson's Complete Works* (Cambridge, MA: Riverside Press, 1993), 12: 132.
2. Jesus as "Morning Star" is found in Revelation 22:16.
3. Isa. 9:2, 6 NASB.
4. "Dirt as matter out of place" is the famous line of anthropologist Mary Douglas. See her *Purity and Danger: An Analysis of Concepts of Pollution and Taboo* (London: Routledge, 2002), 44–50.
5. Eccl. 3:20.
6. Maybe we shouldn't be so surprised that the soil contains friendly bacteria that affect the brain in a similar way to antidepressants. UK scientists were the first to discover that bacteria commonly found in soil activated brain cells to produce the chemical serotonin, which acts as an antidepressant. Low levels of serotonin are linked with a number of disorders, including aggression, anxiety, depression, obsessive compulsive disorder (OCD), bipolar disorder, irritable bowel syndrome, and fibromyalgia. The lead author of the study, Dr. Chris Lowry from Bristol University, suggests that their research "leaves us wondering if we shouldn't all be spending more time playing in the dirt." It also makes one wonder if this isn't one reason why many pregnant women crave clay and dirt. For the research, see C. A. Lowry et al., "Identification of an Immune-Responsive Mesolimbocortical Serotonergic System: Potential Role in Regulation of Emotional Behaviour," *Neuroscience* 146 (May 11, 2007): 756–72.
7. Gen. 2:7; see also 2 Tim. 3:16.
8. See G. K. Beale's magisterial *The Temple and the Church's Mission* (see intro., n. 78).
9. Gen. 2:15.
10. Lancelot Andrewes, Easter Sermon 1620, "Sermons of the Resurrection" (Full text of "Works"), http://archive.org/stream/worksninetysix03andruoft/worksninetysix03andruoft_djvu.txt.
11. To "conserve" and "conceive" the earth are gentler translations of the Genesis 1:28 command to "have dominion over" and "subdue" the earth.
12. See Revelation 11:18. For more on this, see Leonard Sweet, *The Jesus Prescription for a Healthy Life* (Nashville: Abingdon Press, 1996), 159–60.
13. E. Y. Harburg, Fred Saidy, and Burton Lane, *Finian's Rainbow: A Musical Satire* (New York: Random House, 1947), 117. Of course, this is a pun on Cole Porter's song of twelve years earlier, "Begin the Beguine."
14. Sub-creation and being a sub-creator were favorite themes of J. R. R. Tolkien's. See, for example, his "On Fairy-Stories," in his *Poems and Stories* (Boston: Houghton Mifflin, 1994), 133, 146.

15. Isa. 43:19; 2 Cor. 5:17.
16. Gen. 2:9.
17. Ibid.
18. Paul Evdokimov, *The Art of the Icon: A Theology of Beauty* (Redondo Beach, CA: Oakwood Publications, 1990), 299.
19. Gen. 2:9.
20. As quoted by Douglas Burton-Christie, "Beauty," *Spiritus* 7 (Spring 2007): ix.
21. Gen. 2:16.
22. Gen. 2:17.
23. So Paul calls Jesus in 2 Corinthians 1:18–20.
24. Rev. 22:17 NLT.
25. Rev. 2:7.
26. Thanks to Professor Robert Stallman of Northwest University for this insight. At Westminster Theological Seminary, Stallman wrote his 1999 dissertation on the "banquet of the Bible," with a focus on this first command and last command.
27. Matt. 26:26–28; John 1:29 [John speaking]; 4:10; 6:35, 53–57; 12:24; 1 Cor. 5:7; 10:3–4 [Paul speaking].
28. Matt. 4:4; 15:26–27; 26:29; Luke 12:37; 15:23; 22:30; John 4:32; 7:37.
29. John 1:4; 14:6.
30. John 1:4; 8:12.
31. John 20:22.
32. John 6:35.
33. John 4:14; 7:37–39.
34. John 15:5.
35. *Confessions*, VII.16. This wording is found in Robert E. Meagher, *Augustine: An Introduction* (New York: Harper & Row, 1979), 49.
36. Gen. 2:18.
37. Note the plural used in Genesis 1:26: "Let *Us* make man [*adam*] in *Our* image" (emphasis added).
38. Gen. 2:21.
39. Matt. 10:8.
40. Gen. 2:22.
41. Gen. 2:23.
42. Gen. 2:24.
43. See Jeremiah 1:16; 2:13; Deuteronomy 4:4 WEB; 10:20 NLT.
44. Gen. 2:23 NLT.
45. Gen. 3:8; "In the Garden," words and music by C. Austin Miles, 1912.
46. As quoted in *The Sermon of All Creation: Christians on Nature*, eds. Judith Fitzgerald and Michael Oren (Bloomington, IN: World Wisdom, 2005), 117.
47. Byoungo Zoh, *The Rise and Fall of the Five Empires of the Bible*, Kindle ed. (Amazon Digital Services, 2011).
48. Gen. 9:16.
49. Ex. 10:26.
50. Acts 3:15 NIV.
51. We expound this point scripturally in our book *Jesus Manifesto*.

52. See Irenaeus, *Against Heresies*, bk. 5, chap. 19, at http://wesley.nnu.edu/sermons-essays-books/noncanonical-literature/noncanonical-literature-the-fathers-of-the-church/irenaeus-against-heresies-book-v.
53. Col. 3:10.
54. "I determined not to know anything among you except Jesus Christ and Him crucified," Paul said (1 Cor. 2:2).
55. See John 14:7–10.

Chapter 4: Jesus' Birth and Boyhood

1. See Ben Witherington, "The Birth of Jesus," *Dictionary of Jesus and the Gospels* (Downers Grove, IL: InterVarsity, 1992); and Raymond Brown's magisterial work, *The Birth of the Messiah* (New Haven, CT: Yale University Press, 2007). As for His birthday being December 25, this is unlikely. For the church's first three centuries, the Lord's birth wasn't celebrated in December. If it was observed at all, it was lumped in with Epiphany on January 6. While it's possible that Jesus was born in the winter, this is uncertain. Because shepherds were watching over their flocks by night, winter seems less likely than spring. At least, this is what scholars often argue. In short, the exact day of Jesus' birth is unknown. It is for this reason that the early Christians ended up confiscating a pagan holiday to celebrate the Lord's birth, thus redeeming the day—December 25—for Christ. The early writers of the church disagreed on the Lord's birth date. Some, like Clement of Alexandria, argued that He was born on May 20. Others, like Hippolytus, argued that He was born on January 12. Other proposed dates were March 21, March 25, April 18, April 19, May 29, November 17, and November 20. The eventual selection of December 25 was chosen as early as AD 273. Finally, because of the infants "two years and under" killed by Herod and his death in 4 BC, some scholars suggest that Jesus was maybe born around 7 or 6 BC.
2. Luke 2:7.
3. Luke 2:10–11 NLT.
4. See Luke 22:11. Jesus sent out Peter and John to secure this space, telling them to ask their would-be host for him, "Where is the guest room (*katalyma*) where I may eat the Passover with My disciples?" The *katalyma* Peter and John were shown was "a large room upstairs, furnished [with carpets and with couches]" (Luke 22:12 AMP).
5. See Isaiah 1:3. "And on the third day after the birth of our Lord Jesus Christ, Mary went out of the cave, and, entering a stable, placed the child in a manger, and an ox and an ass adored him. Then was fulfilled that which was said by Isaiah the prophet, 'The ox knows his owner, and the ass his master's crib.' Therefore, the animals, the ox and the ass, with him in their midst incessantly adored him. Then was fulfilled that which was said by Habakkuk the prophet, saying, 'Between two animals you are made manifest'" (*The Oxford Bible Commentary*, ed. John Barton and John Muddiman [New York: Oxford University Press, 2001], 1319). See Laura Hobgood-Oster, *Holy Dogs and Asses: Animals in the Christian Tradition* (Champaign, IL: University of Illinois Press, 2008). Another source for the tradition may be the extracanonical text the Gospel of Pseudo-Matthew of the seventh century. (The translation in this text of Habakkuk 3:2 is not taken from the Septuagint.)

6. Emil Brunner, *Philosophy of Religion*, 2nd ed. (London: James Clarke and Company, 1958), 55.
7. G. K. Chesterton, *Autobiography of G. K. Chesterton* (San Francisco: Ignatius, 2006), 220.
8. Matt. 22:37–40.
9. John 1:1, 14.
10. Zech. 4:2–3 NIV.
11. John 6:35, 41, 48–51.
12. Luke 2:4–6.
13. John 8:12; 9:5.
14. Matt. 2:1–12.
15. John 10:7, 9.
16. Luke 2:7.
17. John 10:11, 14.
18. Luke 2:8–20.
19. John 11:25.
20. Matt. 2:13–16.
21. John 14:6.
22. Matt. 2:1–12.
23. John 15:1, 5.
24. Mic. 5:2; Matt. 2:5–6.
25. Or what Dwight Friesen calls more memorably, "orthoparadoxy." See Dwight J. Friesen, "Orthoparadoxy: Emerging Hope for Embracing Difference," in *Emergent Manifesto of Hope*, eds. Doug Pagitt and Tony Jones (Grand Rapids: Baker Books, 2007), 201–12.
26. James Buchan, *Frozen Desire: The Meaning of Money* (New York: Farrar Straus Giroux, 1997), 40.
27. Luke 14:27.
28. Heb. 7:3.
29. Matthew traced Joseph's genealogy, and Luke traced Mary's. The rabbinic way of counting lineage through the mother was a later development. In the first century, Jesus' lineage would have been counted through Joseph, even though Joseph was not His biological father.
30. See Matthew's list, divided into three groups of fourteen, which is the sum of David's name *DVD,* where D equals 4 and V equals 6.
31. This is one reason Luke's genealogy is different from Matthew's. Luke, a Gentile, wanted to highlight Jesus' pedigree before His connection to the Jews through Abraham. Luke also traced Jesus' blood connection to David through Mary while Matthew traced it through Joseph's adoption.
32. Luke 3:38.
33. Some scholars question whether the term used for Rahab was not just a term for innkeepers rather than prostitutes. But other scholars argue that it was *applied* to inn workers because many of them doubled as prostitutes back then.
34. Heb. 2:11.
35. Interestingly, the number of generations in the book of Matthew is forty-two, and Matthew grouped the generations into three units of fourteen. In the Bible, forty-two seems to indicate human opposition to God. There were forty-two

stations from Egypt to Canaan whereby Israel tried and tested the Lord (Num. 33:5–48). There were forty-two young men who mocked Elijah's ascension (2 Kings 2:23–24). Revelation predicted that the Gentiles would oppose the temple for forty-two months (Rev. 11:2; 13:5). So the history of Abraham to Jesus is one of rebellion against the Lord, a fitting introduction to the Saviorhood of Jesus Christ. New Testament scholar Scot McKnight (University of Illinois) goes further and observes that because Matthew organized his genealogy into three groups of fourteen, he was demonstrating that all of Israel's story has a Davidic shape, and the Davidic story is completed in Jesus. See page 86 of Scot McKnight's *The King Jesus Gospel* (see intro., n. 39), where he argues that Matthew was using the Jewish method called *gematria*, whereby the number fourteen points to King David. In a single page, Matthew summed up Israel's history, ending with Jesus as its climax. In like manner, Mark opened His gospel with prophecies from Isaiah and Malachi, both of which refer to the end of Israel's exile. Luke began His gospel in the temple, where God promised to meet His people, and with John the Baptist, the last and final prophet of the old covenant era. And John began his, "In the beginning," posturing his gospel as the new Genesis. See Wright, *The Original Jesus*. In short, the genealogies present Jesus as the Davidic Messiah (setting Him into the history of Israel) as well as the Son of Man (setting Him into the history of the world).

36. Gen. 3:15.
37. Luke 2:21–24.
38. For Jesus Christ born of a virgin, see Matt. 1:18–22; Luke 1:34. For details on this question, see Donald A. Hagner, *World Biblical Commentary*, vol. 33A, *Matthew 1–13* (Grand Rapids: Eerdmans, 1993), 21; Craig Keener, *A Commentary on Matthew* (Grand Rapids: Eerdmans, 1999), 81–95; Craig Blomberg, *New American Commentary*, vol. 22, *Matthew* (Nashville: Broadman, 1992), 56–61. For a great treatment on Jesus' birth, see Witherington, "The Birth of Jesus," *Dictionary of Jesus and the Gospels*.
39. 1 Tim. 3:16.
40. The Son of God was also regarded as a title for Israel and later for the true Messiah. See N. T. Wright's *Who Was Jesus?* (London: SPCK, 1992), 79.
41. Heb. 4:15.
42. George MacDonald, "That Holy Thing," in *The Poetical Works of George MacDonald* (London: Chatto & Windus, 1893), 2: 323.
43. Max Lucado, *God Came Near* (Portland, OR: Multnomah, 1987), 25.
44. Josh. 19:15.
45. Bethlehem would also be the area where the events of the book of Ruth take place, replete with the kinsman-redeemer and Ruth's connection in Jesus' genealogy. Bethlehem is located on the Wadi el Hrobbe (from Jerusalem to Hebron), with the land of Moab visible immediately to the southeast. Thanks to David Wahlstedt for reminding us of this.
46. Dunn, *Jesus Remembered*, 293–96 (see intro., n. 3).
47. Isa. 9:1–2; 42:6–7; Matt. 4:15–16.
48. John 1:46.
49. Cornelia Horn and John W. Martens, *Let the Little Children Come to Me: Childhood and Children in Early Christianity* (Washington, DC: Catholic University of America Press, 2009), 21.

50. John 6:35, 48; 1 Chron. 2:12–15; Matt. 1:5–6.
51. Syriac is most similar to Aramaic.
52. Lev. 3:11.
53. Isa. 1:3.
54. Num. 28:1–8.
55. Ex. 12:6, 13.
56. John 21:15. See Martin Barrack, *Second Exodus* (Houston: Magnificat Institute, 1999).
57. John 10:18.
58. Ex. 12:5.
59. It is the same word used as "perfect," describing Noah in Genesis 6:9, and used as "blameless" by YHWH to Abraham in Genesis 17:1.
60. *Migdal Eder* was a watchtower located in the northern part of Bethlehem built to protect the temple flocks. During lambing season the sheep were brought there from the fields, and the lower level served as the birthing room for sacrificial lambs.
61. Mic. 4:8.
62. John 1:29.
63. Num. 22–24.
64. Joseph O'Hanlon, "Slow Steps to Bethlehem," *The Tablet*, November 12, 2011; http://content.yudu.com/A1umhp/TheTablet/resources/15.htm.
65. John 10:14–15.
66. Heb. 13:20.
67. 1 Peter 5:4.
68. Steve Mason, updated by Basil Bactawar, " Lamb Mortality," http://www.agf.gov.bc.ca/sheep/publications/documents/lamb_mortality.pdf.
69. John 10:1–21.
70. Matt. 27:46; Mark 15:34.
71. John Donne, "Wilt thou love God, as he thee? Then digest," in *The Poetical Works of Dr. John Donne, with a Memoir* (Boston: Little, Brown, 1955), 163.
72. It is mostly ignored that the "Magi" or "wise men" could possibly have been Jewish, not pagan. Jewish healers who were well versed in the "powers" of ancient herbs, metals, ointments, rocks, and the alignment of the stars were also called "Magi." For example, Daniel was the chief "magus" in Nebuchadnezzer's court. These Magi were sometimes called in by royalty or someone with means to facilitate a birth or provide rituals for the newborn.
73. First Timothy 4:10 says that Jesus is "the Savior of all people, and especially of those who believe" (UPDATED NIV).
74. As horrible as infanticide sounds to us today, the Romans practiced child abandonment routinely. The prophet Ezekiel described the practice: "On the day you were born, no one cared about you. Your umbilical cord was not cut, and you were never washed, rubbed with salt, and wrapped in cloth. No one had the slightest interest in you; no one pitied you or cared for you. On the day you were born, you were unwanted, dumped in a field and left to die" (16:4–5 NLT). The Jews were different. In the words of Tacitus, "Jews regard it as a crime to kill any late-born children" (Tacitus, *The Histories*, vol. 2 [London: William Heinemann, 1931], 183). Jeremiah prophesied of Herod's slaughtering of innocents during Jesus' day (Jer. 31:15).

75. Angelus Silesius, "It Depends on You," in *The Enlightened Heart*, ed. Stephen Mitchell (New York: HarperPerennial, 1993), 88.
76. Teri Hyrkas, posted on the Facebook page of Leonard Sweet. Used with permission.
77. Isa. 7:14; Matt. 1:23.
78. Josh. 3–4; Matt. 1:21. Jesus' name is "Joshua" in the Greek.
79. Mic. 5:1–3; Matt. 2:5.
80. Mic. 5:2 NIV.
81. Mic. 5:4–5 NIV.
82. Job 19:27 NLT.
83. Luke 2:22–39.
84. Hos. 11:1.
85. Lev. 5:11.
86. John J. Parsons, "Pidyon HaBen: Redemption of the Firstborn Son," Hebrew for Christians, http://www.hebrew4christians.com/Life_Cycle/Pidyon_Haben/pidyon_haben.html.
87. The Jewish birthright is passed by the mother of the family.
88. Luke 2:32.
89. Parsons, ibid.
90. Matt. 2:11.
91. Josephus, *Antiquities*, 17:7:4.
92. See Job 22:25 NIV. Watchman Nee, T. Austin-Sparks, C. H. Mackintosh, H. W. Soltau, and Kevin J. Conner are just some examples of respected teachers who viewed gold in the Bible as an allusion to the divine nature (among other things). Gold is relatively scarce, it doesn't decay, and it can endure just about anything.
93. Mark 15:23.
94. Luke 4:18.
95. While myrrh deadens pain, wine makes the heart glad (Psalm 104:15).
96. 2 Cor. 2:14.
97. Mic. 5:2.
98. Isa. 7:14.
99. Gen. 3:15; Matt. 16:18; Rom. 16:20.
100. Gen. 22:18; Gal. 3:16.
101. 2 Sam. 7:12ff; Acts 2:30; 2 Tim. 2:8.
102. Gen. 49:10; Rev. 5:5.
103. Isa. 9:6–7.
104. Hos. 11:1; Matt. 2:13–18.
105. John 1:46; 7:52; Matt. 2:23. Nazareth was a tiny village, probably around four acres, containing roughly fifty homes.
106. Luke 2:40.

Chapter 5: Jesus' Missing Years

1. Luke 19:40.
2. Margaret Mitchell, *Gone with the Wind* (New York: Warner Books, 1993; originally published 1936).
3. John Wesley's notes on the passage in Habakkuk 2:11, which is often associated with Luke 19:40, agree with this rendering: [this] "confirms the

charge against thee!" (John Wesley, *Explanatory Notes Upon the Old Testament* [Salem, OR: Schmul, 1975], 3: 2559). The words were used to testify or accuse, particularly in reference to the covenant.

4. Hab. 2:11.
5. Gen. 4:10.
6. Prov. 8:29–30.
7. "My house will be called a house of prayer *for all nations*" (Mark 11:17 NIV; emphasis added). John Dominic Crossan accepts that Jesus caused a disturbance in the temple, but Paula Fredriksen argues that the money changers occupied an isolated spot within the huge temple plaza, and knocking over the tables would have been noticed by at most a few dozen people.
8. Josh. 24:27.
9. Isa. 28:16.
10. 2 Sam. 23:3.
11. Isa. 51:1.
12. Gen. 49:24.
13. Dan. 2:44–45.
14. Those showing faithfulness and loyalty to God are stones. See Kirsten Nielsen, "Metaphors and Biblical Theology," in *Metaphor in the Hebrew Bible*, ed. P. van Hecke (Dudley, MA: Peeters, 2005), 272.
15. 1 Peter 2:5 NIV.
16. 1 Cor. 3:9–10.
17. Eph. 2:21–22.
18. The word in Hebrew for "to dig into the garden" is *pardes*. This is the same word for the fourfold exegetical method in the Hebrew language for layered meaning. And it is the same root of the noun for the word *garden* and for *paradise*. The messianic tradition is strongly connected to the garden of Eden, the temple construction, the Torah and its meaning, and also to the Messiah, the covenant, the apocalyptic City of God, the resurrection, and the way, truth, and life of Jesus. This interconnectedness of meaning is like an entangled root mass within the garden of symbolism and signs within the Hebrew tradition, a tradition that Jesus was well acquainted with, and which he employed symbolically and linguistically extremely well. Jesus, the rabbi and the Messiah, was master of not only the architecture of stones but the architecture of the Scriptures, the parable, the messianic message, and Himself the living Word and covenant of God.
19. Luke 8:10.
20. Luke 8:10–11.
21. Matt. 16:2–3; Mark 4:9, 23; authors' paraphrase. See also John 9:39.
22. PaRDeS is an acronym that includes all four methods of interpreting the Torah: *p'shat* (literal), *remez* (allusive), *drush* (homiletic, hermeneutic), and *sod* (secret, esoteric).
23. Ex. 25:31–40.
24. Isa. 42:6.
25. Num. 17:5.
26. Isa. 11:1.
27. Rev. 22:2.

28. 1 Kings 6:29.
29. John 14:6.
30. John 20:15.
31. Luke 23:43.
32. John 20:16.
33. Rev. 2:7.
34. Gen. 4:7.
35. Rev. 3:20.
36. Heb. 10:19–20 UPDATED NIV.
37. John 14:6 UPDATED NIV.
38. See the chapter with that name in Eduard Schweitzer, *Jesus*, trans. David Green (Richmond, VA: John Knox, 1971), 13ff.
39. N. T. Wright, *Simply Jesus*, 176 (see intro., n. 6).
40. T. Austin-Sparks, *The Octave of Redemption* (Tulsa, OK: Emmanual Church, 2000), chap. 3; http://www.austin-sparks.net/english/books/001611.html.
41. Matt 2:23.
42. Luke 2:51–52.
43. See his discussion with Adam Bradford at www.premierradio.org/uk.
44. Luke has let us know that at age twelve, Jesus was extremely bright (Luke 2:41ff.).
45. Heb. 2:17 NRSV.
46. If Jesus had received formal theological training, for instance, these statements would be unintelligible. If He was a student of some respected rabbinic school, the words "Where did this man get this wisdom?" and "Is this not Joseph's son?" would make little sense. These people knew Jesus' family. If Jesus had been officially trained as a "chief rabbi" or "doctor of the Law," they would have known and not been surprised by His knowledge and wisdom.
47. Luke 4:22 NASB.
48. Matt. 13:54–56 NASB.
49. Mark 6:2–3 NASB.
50. John 7:14–16.
51. Ben Witherington says, "There is, however, no evidence of Jesus' pursuing higher learning at an urban center like Jerusalem (compare Luke 2:47 to Mark 6:2–3)" (Ben Witherington, *The Jesus Quest: The Third Search for the Jew of Nazareth*, 2nd ed. [Downers Grove, IL: InterVarsity, 1997], 38). Scholars like Witherington have pointed out that it is anachronistic to call Jesus a "rabbi" in any formal sense. Doing so is reading later Jewish writings back into the first century. Francis Moloney interprets the challenge of the Jews, saying, "Jesus can lay claim to no authoritative teacher and therefore there can be no authority in what he has to teach (v. 15b)" (Francis J. Moloney, *Sacra Pagina: The Gospel of John* [Collegeville, MN: Liturgical Press, 1998], 242). Arguments such as "Jesus would have been arrested by the temple guard when He taught in the temple courts if He wasn't rabbinically authorized to teach" don't hold water. According to David Instone-Brewer, who is an expert on rabbinic Judaism, the so-called *unauthorized* rabbis often taught in the temple courts without being arrested (see his discussion with Adam Bradford on www.premierradio.org/uk and his *Traditions of the Rabbis from the Era of the New Testament*, 2 vols. [Grand

Rapids: Eerdmans, 2004, 2011]). The temple guards existed to keep order and peace. They didn't care if someone was a "rabbi" or not; they cared only about riots. The temple guards wanted to arrest Jesus (especially when He cleansed the temple), but they couldn't because He was too popular with the people and an uncontrollable riot would have ensued (John 26:3–5; Luke 19:47–48; Mark 11:18). Robert Mounce, in his chronological arrangement of the Gospels (*Jesus, In His Own Words*; see intro., n. 79), confirms this on page 193, placing Mark 11:18–19 and Luke 19:47–48 immediately after the cleansing of the temple. The Pharisees did send officers to arrest Jesus on several occasions, but their attempts failed (John 7:25–32, 44–47; see also 8:59 and 10:39).

52. N. T. Wright, *John for Everyone* (London: SPCK, 2002), 1:97–98. The renowned Jewish scholar Jacob Neusner has soundly established that during Jesus' day, there was no normative expression of Judaism. New Testament scholars like N. T. Wright, Ben Witherington, Scot McKnight, and James D. G. Dunn agree. See also Dunn, *Jesus Remembered*, 256ff (see intro., n. 3). What later became an official school of rabbis didn't exist in the first century. New Testament scholars such as Dunn, Witherington, Wright, and McKnight point out that *rabbi* simply meant teacher. (*A Greek-English Lexicon of the New Testament and Other Early Christian Literature,* 3rd ed., by Walter Bauer and Frederick William Danker [BDAG] [University of Chicago Press, January 15, 2001]: "master, sir, rabbi, a term for an outstanding teacher." *Thayer's Greek-English Lexicon of the New Testament* by Carl Ludwig Wilibald Grimm [Hendrickson Publishers; Rei Sub ed., June 1, 1996]: "my great one, my honorable sir. A title with which Jews called their teachers.") Witherington, McKnight, and Dunn were of personal help to me in sorting through some of the historical data related to this subject. It was a term very similar to the way we use *Reverend* today; some people who hold that title are theologically educated. Others are not. David Instone-Brewer argues that *rabbi* didn't become an official title until AD 80. See his discussion with Adam Bradford on www.premierradio.org/uk and his *Traditions of the Rabbis from the Era of the New Testament*. Before AD 70, *rabbi* was not an official or technical term. (Both Pharisees and Sadducees were called *rabbi* if they taught. It was simply a respectful title for a teacher.) The word took on a technical, official meaning years later with the emergence of rabbinic Judaism. Jacob Neusner has effectively proven that theories that make Jesus an officially trained rabbi are the result of reading later Jewish documents back into the first century. See Jacob Neusner's *Judaism When Christianity Begun: A Survey of Belief and Practice* (Louisville: Westminster John Knox, 2002); *Introduction to Rabbinical Literature* (New York: Doubleday, 1994); *In Quest of the Historical Pharisees*, eds. Jacob Neusner and Bruce D. Chilton (Waco, TX: Baylor University, 2007). Also see *Eerdmans Dictionary of Early Judaism*, eds. John Collins and Daniel Harlow (Grand Rapids: Eerdmans, 2010).

53. For a discussion on the difference between upper and lower Galilee, see Keener, *The Historical Jesus of the Gospels*, 178ff.
54. Isa. 11:1; 53:2 NIV.
55. John 1:46 NIV.
56. There is a tradition that says that *Sepphoris* was the home of Joachim and Anna, the parents of Mary, the mother of Jesus.
57. Dunn, *Jesus Remembered*, 313 (see intro., n. 3).

58. Ben Witherington, *What Have They Done With Jesus? Beyond Strange Theories and Bad History—Why We Can Trust the Bible* (San Francisco: HarperSanFrancisco, 2006), 170. Witherington points out that artisans were used to bartering. And first-century Jews didn't like handling or dealing with money, particularly Roman coins ("The Royal Line of Jesus?" 13 April 2006, http://benwitherington.blogspot.com/2006/04/did-jesus-found-dynasty-ja_114493136136345584.html).
59. 2 Cor. 8:9.
60. They could only offer two doves as a sacrifice when bringing Jesus into the world, a clear sign that the family wasn't well-to-do (Luke 2:24; Lev. 12:8). Some would argue that this was before Jesus received gifts from the Magi. See the next note, which addresses that objection. In addition, Scot McKnight points out that Mary belonged to a class of Jews called *Anawim* ("the pious poor"), which were noted for being socially destitute, gathering around the temple to express their frustration and hope, and yearning for justice with the coming Messiah. Simeon and Anna were examples of the *Anawim.* Mary's Magnificat illustrates liberation for the poor (Luke 1:46–55). McKnight says, "It is this 'hand that rocked Jesus' crib'—and it is from Mary that Jesus developed a vision of the kingdom that meant justice for the poor. *Shalom* cannot exist when people are marginalized" (McKnight, *The Story of the Christ*, 41 [see intro., n. 6]).
61. Some prosperity preachers who have projected their wealthy statuses upon Jesus have taken 2 Corinthians 8:9 to mean that Jesus was materially wealthy and that He has promised to make His followers materially wealthy. They argue that the Magi's gifts of gold, frankincense, and myrrh given to Jesus at His birth set Him up for life. But most scholars believe that Mary and Joseph used these gifts to get to and from Egypt. It is highly doubtful they would have lasted a lifetime; there is no evidence to suggest it, and the Gospels contradict it. For instance, why would Jesus need to be taken care of financially by some of the women (Luke 8:1–3), and why would He say that He had no place to lay His head (Luke 9:58)? Also, to say that Jesus was rich because the soldiers bargained over His seamless robe is a stretch. Perhaps one of His well-to-do followers gave Him the garment as a gift. We just don't know.
62. N. T. Wright, *Paul for Everyone: 2 Corinthians* (Louisville: Westminster John Knox, 2004), 90.
63. Jerome Murphy O'Connor, *Holy Land: An Archaeological Guide from Earliest Times to 1700*, 5th ed. (New York: Oxford University Press, 2008), 468; http://www.itsgila.com/highlightssepphoris.htm.
64. Some scholars believe that Jesus would not have worked in Sepphoris. They argue that since Jesus was a pious Jew, and Sepphoris was a profoundly pagan city, He would have stayed clear of it, especially because it was the special turf of Herod, whom Jesus called "that fox" (Luke 13:32).
65. Luke 4:16ff. Consider also His often-asked question, "Have you not read?" While He did say this to the learned scribes (who were literate), Luke 4 makes clear that He could read Himself.
66. Josephus, *The Life Against Apion*, trans. H. St. J. Thackeray, The Loeb Classical Library (Cambridge, MA: Harvard University Press, 1997), 187, 375.

67. Baum's book is presently only in German: *Der Mündliche Faktor und Seine Bedeutung für die Synoptische Frage* (Tübingen: Francke, 2008). Its English title would be *The Orality Factor and Its Meaning for the Synoptic Question*. Reading in the ancient world was normally done aloud.
68. Not all scholars agree with this point. See R. A. Horsley and J. A. Draper, *Whoever Hears You Hears Me: Prophets, Performance, and Tradition in Q* (Harrisburg, PA: Trinity Press International, 1999); and W. V. Harris, *Ancient Literacy* (Cambridge, MA: Harvard University Press, 1989). For a full-length contextual study of education in ancient Israel, see James Crenshaw, *Education in Ancient Israel: Across the Deadening Silence* (New Haven, CT: Yale University Press, 2007).
69. See the discussion by James D. G. Dunn in *Jesus Remembered*, 314–16, and Thomas Rausch in *Who Is Jesus? An Introduction to Christology* (Collegeville, MN: Liturgical Press, 2003), 65. Also see Ben Witherington, *The Christology of Jesus* (Minneapolis: Fortress, 1990), 236. David Flusser believes that Jesus spoke and even taught in Hebrew, not Aramaic (David Flusser and R. Steven Notley, *The Sage of Galilee* [Grand Rapids: Eerdmans, 2007], 111). Few scholars would agree with him.
70. See R. Riesner, *Jesus als Lehrer* (Tübingen: Mohr, 1984), 228–32.
71. Luke 4:16ff.; Josephus, *Antiquities*, 4:212; Dunn, *Jesus Remembered*, 316.
72. Mark 9:20; Luke 8:44; Mark 6:56; Matt. 14:36; see also Num. 15:38–40 and Deut. 22:12. Luke says it was Mary and Joseph's custom to observe the Passover feast each year (Luke 2:41). Although the Torah commanded a trip to Jerusalem three times a year, in the first century, it was regarded as common to make the trip once a year from Galilee (Darrell Bock, *Jesus According to Scripture: Restoring the Portrait from the Gospels* [Grand Rapids: Baker Academic, 2002], 74).
73. Luke 2:21–24, 27, 39, 41; 1:28; Matt. 1:19. Ben Witherington confirms all of the above in his book *The Jesus Quest: The Third Search for the Jew of Nazareth*, 2nd ed., 38. N. T. Wright concurs, saying, "His later life indicates that, like many Jewish boys, he was from an early age taught to read Israel's ancient scriptures, and that by adulthood he knew them inside out and had drawn his own conclusions as to what they meant" (*Simply Jesus*, 6).
74. Luke 2:49 NIV. The Greek could also be translated "my Father's affairs" or "my Father's business."
75. Luke 2:51 NIV.
76. Luke 2:46; 24:7.
77. Luke 2:49.
78. John 20:15 MSG.
79. Luke 2:51.
80. Luke 24:8.
81. Luke 2:48–9; emphasis added.
82. Luke 2:52.
83. Isaiah prophesied that the Messiah would be endowed with divine wisdom (Isa. 11:1–2 NIV).
84. Isa. 53:2 NLT.
85. Ps. 45:2 NLT.
86. 1 Sam. 16:6–7 NIV.

87. John 1:14.
88. An entire book could be written expounding each part of the tabernacle of Moses, showing how it all points to Christ. The book of Hebrews alludes to some of it. See also *Dictionary of Biblical Imagery*, 837–39.
89. Fredrick Buechner, *The Life of Jesus* (New York: Harper & Row, 1989), 14.
90. 1 Cor. 11:14 NLT.
91. Matt. 6:17–18 NIV.

Chapter 6: Jesus' Preparation for Ministry

1. C. H. Spurgeon, "Sermons—Their Matter," in *Lectures to My Students: A Selection from Addresses Delivered to the Students of the Pastor's College*, Metropolitan Tabernacle, 1st series (London: Passmore and Alabaster, 1875), 82.
2. Wright, *Simply Jesus*, 21 (see intro., n. 6). Albert Schweitzer (*The Quest for the Historical Jesus* [1906, English 1910]) made the explosive observation that the inherent danger in doing historical Jesus research is to unwittingly create a Jesus in our own image. This, of course, must be guarded against whenever one tries to reconstruct the life of Christ, as it's always a realistic trap into which to fall.
3. Wright, *Simply Jesus*, 64.
4. Num. 4:3, 34–35, 47.
5. In Jesus' day, students applied to study with teachers. Teachers did not select students.
6. Acts 22:3.
7. And if God the Father so chose, Jesus could have been born into a Levitical family and become a priest.
8. A blue-collar worker is defined as someone who is part of the working class and performs manual labor. Blue-collar work may involve skilled or unskilled construction. The image of Jesus as a blue-collar worker, in contrast to a religious professional in occupation and training, was inspired by a speech, given many years ago, by Gene Edwards that one of us heard.
9. *A Greek-English Lexicon of the New Testament and Other Early Christian Literature*, 3rd ed., by Walter Bauer and Frederick William Danker [BDAG] (University Of Chicago Press, January 15, 2001): "one who constructs, builds, a carpenter." Most scholars suggest that Jesus would have worked with both wood and stone. Ben Witherington says that Jesus and Joseph would have used both stone and wood to build houses, "since stones were the normal main material used to construct a house in Galilee (see Luke 6:48)" ("The Royal Line of Jesus?" www.benwitherington.blogspot.com). See also Robert L. Webb, "Jesus's Baptism by John: Its Historicity and Significance," in Bock and Webb, eds., *Key Events in the Life of the Historical Jesus*, 133n128 (see intro., n. 3).
10. Joseph isn't mentioned alive during the ministry of Jesus, and whenever the family is mentioned, only Mary and the children are referred to (John 2:1–15; 7:1–10; Mark 3:31–34; 6:1–3). We do not know how Joseph died, but it's possible that he died from a deadly illness, such as tuberculosis or malaria, both of which plagued Galilee. There is no evidence that Jesus began His healing ministry until age thirty, when He was anointed upon being baptized by water by John the Baptist.

11. Luke 2:7; Matt. 1:25.
12. See Mark 6:2–3. Also see J. P. Meier, *A Marginal Jew: Rethinking the Historical Jesus* (New York: Doubleday, 1991), 1:316–32, arguing that these were true siblings to Jesus. Eusebius mentions Jesus' brothers and sisters "after the flesh" (*Ecclesiastical History* 2.23; 3.19). Mary and Joseph probably named their four boys after the Patriarchs (Jacob and Joseph) and the Maccabean heroes (Simon and Judas).
13. Heb. 4:15.
14. Lucado, *God Came Near*, 26 (see chap. 4, n. 43).
15. John 1:1–3.
16. Acts 5:30; 10:39; 13:29; Gal. 3:13; 1 Peter 2:24.
17. Col. 1:16.
18. Heb. 4:15.
19. Heb. 5:8.
20. 1 Cor. 10:13.
21. See Matthew 10:39—which speaks of self-denial and cross-bearing—for the principle of losing one's life. Jesus' self-denial is a mark of the divine life.
22. 1 Cor. 10:31.
23. John 5:30 NIV.
24. John 6:57 KJV.
25. John 7:16–17 NIV.
26. John 8:28 NIV.
27. John 12:49 NIV.
28. John 14:10 NIV.
29. John 14:24 NIV.
30. Frank's summarizing paraphrase after putting together all of the above texts.
31. Isa. 50:4–5.
32. John 11:41–42.
33. This is clear from texts like Luke 24 and John 5. Virtually every time Jesus quoted the First Testament, He revealed something specific about Himself. We know that Jesus understood something of who He was at age twelve (Luke 2:41–52).
34. John 8:56–58 NIV.
35. Matt. 6:25–33 NIV.
36. John 6:42.
37. Mark 6:6; Luke 13:22.
38. N. T. Wright, *Who Was Jesus?* (London: SPCK, 1992), 98.
39. Luke 5:17.
40. See McIver, *Memory, Jesus, and Synoptic Gospels* (see intro., n. 73).
41. Matt. 21:23 NIV.
42. Mark 6:4; John 7:16.
43. Witherington, *The Christology of Jesus*, 80.
44. George MacDonald, *Wisdom to Live By* (Eureka, CA: Sunrise Books, 2001), 179.
45. See Ben Witherington, "The Sage from Galilee" at www.patheos.com/blogs/bibleandculture. See also the work of Jacob Neusner and David Instone-Brewer. The oral tradition existed, but Jesus repudiated "the tradition of the elders." The Mishnah is the eight-hundred-page Jewish

sequel to the Torah that spans the time after the birth of Jesus to AD 200. It contains thousands of opinions among different rabbis.

46. Ben Witherington, *Jesus the Sage: The Pilgrimage of Wisdom* (Minneapolis: Fortress Press, 2000).
47. Matt. 12:42; 1 Cor. 1:24; John 1:1, 14.
48. See John 8:41. The people in His village called Him "Mary's son," not Joseph's (Mark 6:3 NIV).
49. See Matthew 9:3.
50. See Matthew 27:63; John 7:12.
51. See Matthew 11:19. Scot McKnight argues that the accusation of being a "drunkard and a glutton" is a throwback to Deuteronomy 21:20. It is the equivalent of a rebellious son worthy of being stoned. Scot McKnight, *The Story of the Christ*, 46.
52. See Luke 7:39.
53. See Matthew 12:24.
54. I (Frank) wrote the dedication of my book *Pagan Christianity* (Carol Stream, IL: BarnaBooks, 2008) to such individuals. See also *The Reformers and Their Stepchildren* by Leonard Verduin (Grand Rapids: Eerdmans, 1964).
55. John 15:20 NIV.
56. Matt. 27:18 NIV.
57. Acts 5:16–18 NIV.
58. Acts 13:45 NIV.
59. Acts 17:4–5 NIV.
60. From his discussion with Adam Bradford on www.premierradio.org/uk.

Chapter 7: Jesus' Baptism and Temptation

1. Cyril of Jerusalem, Gregory Nazianzen, *A Select Library of Nicene and Post-Nicene Fathers of the Christian Church*, vol. 7, *The Cathetical Lectures*, ed. Philip Schaff (Grand Rapids: William B. Eerdmans, 1978), 15.
2. For a thorough discussion on the historicity of John and his baptism, see Robert L. Webb, "Jesus's Baptism by John: Its Historicity and Significance," in Bock and Webb, eds., *Key Events in the Life of the Historical Jesus*, chap. 3, pp. 95–150 (see intro., n. 3). See also Keener, *The Historical Jesus of the Gospels*, chap. 11.
3. Num. 4:3, 34–35, 47.
4. Some scholars believe John received part of his spiritual formation in the Qumran community.
5. Matt. 11:11.
6. Isa. 40:3.
7. Mal. 3:1; see also Mal. 4:5; Luke 1:17; Mark 9:13.
8. We agree with those scholars who suggest that baptism means immersion.
9. 2 Kings 2:6–14.
10. At a very transitional time in Israel's past, a dramatic sign was given that speaks prophetically of a sign that will be given in the near future. It is both the Bride Theft and the baptism of the 144,000 sons of Israel. The setting was a showdown on Mount Carmel between Elijah's God and Baal. The 950 prophets of Baal and Asherah and the one prophet of the God of Israel faced off in prayer. The God who was to win was the God who would answer by

fire. The stakes were high—winner take all—all the hearts of Israel. See 1 Kings 18:30–39.

11. Scot McKnight says that Zechariah was likely a Sadducee, or at least sympathetic to their concerns, which was the maintenance of the temple system (McKnight, *The Story of the Christ*, 16).
12. Luke 1:36–37.
13. Some scholars (like Joseph Ratzinger and David Flusser) believe it's reasonable to assume that John was part of the Qumran community (near the northeast corner of the Dead Sea) known as the Essenes. The Essenes lived in the foot of a cliff very close to where John was baptizing. They were known for their ritual baths, isolation, study of the Torah, and prayer. They were "the Pharisee's Pharisees." They believed that the Pharisees didn't go far enough in being pure and separate, so they left Jerusalem and civilization to study Scripture and observe the laws of cleanliness in the desert.

    Other scholars believe John probably wasn't an Essene. Ben Witherington says John may have spent some time at Qumran and used the same prophetic texts that the Essenes did, but he interpreted those texts differently than they interpreted them. The Essenes were more introverted and exclusive while John (and Jesus) were more extroverted and inclusive (*What Have They Done With Jesus?*, 300). N. T. Wright doesn't think John was an Essene, but it's highly likely that he drew support from the original Essenes (from N. T. Wright's interview with John Ankerberg, "Who Were the Essenes and Were Jesus and John the Baptist Essenes?" posted on YouTube, November 3, 2009). It is from the Essenes that we have the Dead Sea scrolls; the Essenes were prolific copyists.
14. Isa. 40:3–5; Mal. 3:1; 4:5 with Matt. 3:3; 11:10–14; 17:10–12; Mark 1:2–4; 9:11–13; Luke 1:76; 3:4–6; 7:27; John 1:23.
15. See Leonard Sweet, *Nudge: Awakening Each Other to the God Who's Already There* (Colorado Springs: David C. Cook, 2010), 171–203.
16. Recall Jesus' words about John: "What did you go out into the wilderness to see?" (Matt. 11:7).
17. Some scholars believe that John deliberately selected the location of Aenon near Salim, just south of the Sea of Galilee (John 3:23), because it was near Tishbe, the home of Elijah ("The Royal Line of Jesus?" www.benwitherington.blogspot.com).
18. Joseph Ratzinger, *Jesus of Nazareth: From the Baptism in the Jordan to the Transfiguration* (New York: Doubleday, 2007), chap. 1.
19. Matt. 3:7.
20. Bruce, *Jesus, Lord & Savior*, 21.
21. John 3:28–29.
22. Josh. 3.
23. Josh. 4:1–11.
24. Mark 1:9.
25. James D. G. Dunn says that it's quite possible that Jesus apprenticed to John (*Jesus Remembered*, 350) (see intro., n. 3). He states that "this point is widely recognized."
26. Mark 10:38; Luke 12:50.
27. Jonah 1:12.

28. Joseph Ratzinger, *Jesus of Nazareth*, vol. 1, chap. 1.
29. Luke 3:21.
30. Luke 3:22.
31. Isa. 42:1 NIV.
32. John 1:23.
33. Gen. 1:2.
34. The Spirit anointed Jesus, but John baptized Him in water. The two are connected.
35. Ps. 110:4; Heb. 2–7. The high priestly ministry of Jesus was prefigured by both Melchizedek (in Genesis) and Aaron (in Exodus).
36. 2 Sam. 5:4.
37. Acts 2:29–30.
38. Acts 10:38 NIV.
39. Acts 2:22 NIV.
40. Luke 24:49 NIV. See also Acts 2.
41. Acts 2–12.
42. Acts 13–20.
43. Luke 4:18–19 NIV.
44. Isa. 11:1–2; 45:7; 61:1.
45. Ex. 30:23ff.; 29:21ff.; Luke 4:18ff.
46. Matt. 21:23ff.; Mark 11:27ff.
47. Ps. 72:1–8; Isa. 9, 11, 42.
48. Matt. 3:17.
49. Eph. 1:6 KJV.
50. Acts 13:33; Rom. 1:4.
51. John 1:29.
52. Willimon, *Why Jesus?*, ix (see intro., n. 6).
53. 1 Cor. 5:7.
54. John 19:36.
55. 1 Peter 1:19.
56. Rev. 5:6; 17:14; 21:14.
57. Isa. 53:7ff.
58. Matt. 4:1; Luke 4:2.
59. Ps. 115:16.
60. 2 Cor. 4:4 KJV.
61. Eph. 2:2.
62. John 12:31; 14:30; 16:11.
63. Nee, *A Table in the Wilderness*, April 19 (see ch. 2, n. 183).
64. John 14:30.
65. It should be noted that satan quoted the Psalms out of context. In like manner, he twisted God's words when he tempted Eve.
66. Matt. 8:29 NIV; see also Luke 8:28 NIV.
67. Luke 4:34 NIV.
68. Gen. 1:26; Luke 10:19.
69. Gen. 1:26ff.
70. Gen. 2:15.
71. Luke 8:28 ESV.
72. 1 John 4:1–3.

73. John 12:24.
74. Matt. 4:3; authors' paraphrase. Satan was questioning what God had just said to Jesus: "You are My beloved Son." See Matthew 3:16–17.
75. Matt. 4:4; authors' paraphrase.
76. Phil. 2:7.
77. Ps. 8:4–5.
78. Matt. 4:8; John 6:15.
79. Matt. 4:4.
80. Matt. 4:5–6; authors' paraphrase.
81. Matt. 4:7.
82. Matt. 4:9.
83. John 12:31; 14:30; 16:11.
84. Matt. 4:10.
85. John 5:26–27.
86. Luke 4:8.
87. James 4:7.
88. Mark 1:13.
89. Jesus rebuked satan by name on two occasions in the Gospels (see Matt. 4:10; Luke 4:8 and Matt. 16:23; Mark 8:33).
90. Heb. 4:15.
91. Heb. 2:17–18.
92. Eugene Peterson, from the foreword to Mark Galli, *Jesus Mean and Wild: The Unexpected Love of an Untamable God* (Grand Rapids: Baker Books, 2006), 11.
93. See Mark 3:11–12, 22–27; 5:1–20; Luke 10:18; 13:16; 22:31; John 13:2, 27.
94. 1 John 2:16.
95. Gen. 3:6.
96. Matt. 4:4; John 4:32.
97. Luke 4:8.
98. Rom. 8:29; Heb. 2:10 KJV.
99. John 12:24.
100. Dodd, *According to the Scriptures*, 133 (see intro., n. 20).
101. Deut. 8:3, paraphrased.
102. Deut. 6:16.
103. Deut. 6:13, paraphrased.
104. Deut. 8:2–3 NIV.
105. Matt. 4:1–4 NIV.
106. N. T. Wright, *The Challenge of Jesus: Rediscovering Who Jesus Was and Is* (2011), 41 (see intro., n. 19).
107. Gen. 32:28.
108. C. H. Dodd further makes the case that Jesus is the New Israel in *The Founder of Christianity*, chap. 6 (see intro., n. 6).
109. Gen. 28:12.
110. Joseph Ratzinger, *Jesus of Nazareth*, vol. 1, xviii (see chap. 7, n. 18).
111. Rom. 5:19 NIV.
112. Luke 11:4 NRSV.
113. Malcolm Guite, *What Do Christians Believe? Belonging and Belief in Modern Christianity* (New York: Walker, 2002), 70.
114. Matt. 4:13; Isa. 9:1–2.

115. J. L. Reed, *Archaeology and the Galilean Jesus: A Re-examination of the Evidence* (Harrisburg, PA: Trinity Press International, 2002), 149–52.
116. Ibid., 152.
117. Matt. 4:17.
118. Matt. 9:1.
119. Mark 1:21; Luke 4:31.
120. Jesus would later denounce Capernaum along with Chorazin and Bethsaida, two towns near Capernaum (Matt. 11:21; Luke 10:13).
121. Dunn, *Jesus Remembered*, 319. Scholars are not agreed on whether the house mentioned in the gospel of Mark (2:1; 3:20; 7:17) belonged to Jesus or Peter.
122. Reed, *Archaeology and the Galilean Jesus*, 166. Dunn observes that Mark made a point of recording Jesus' crisscrossing of the lake (Mark 4:35–5:43; 6:30–56; 8:1–26) (Dunn, *Jesus Remembered*, 319, footnote 316).
123. Mark 1:39; Matt. 4:23; Mark 6:6; Matt. 9:35; Luke 8:1.
124. Mark 6:1–6.
125. R. A. Horsley, *Galilee: History, Politics, People* (Valley Forge, PA: Trinity Press International, 1995), 190–193.
126. Jesus promised Nathanael an open heaven also (John 1:51). The best discussion of the meaning of an open heaven that we know of is T. Austin-Sparks's remarkable little book *The School of Christ* (Lindale, TX: David Wilkerson Ministries, 2000), 199ff.

Chapter 8: Jesus Chooses His Disciples

1. Stephen M. Miller, *The Jesus of the Bible* (Ulrichsville, OH: Barbour, 2009), 127.
2. For more on this, see Leonard Sweet, *I Am a Follower: The Way, Truth, and Life of Following Jesus* (Nashville: Thomas Nelson, 2012).
3. Mark 6:34.
4. Mark 2:15–16; 3:7–9; Matt. 8:19, 21; John 2:2; 19:38; Luke 24:13ff; Acts 1:21–23.
5. Luke 8:1–3; John 11:1ff.
6. Luke 6:12–13.
7. Mark 3:13–15 NIV.
8. 1 Kings 12:31; 13:33.
9. Pirkei Avot 1:16.
10. John 15:16.
11. Richard Lamb, *The Pursuit of God in the Company of Friends* (Downers Grove, IL: InterVarsity, 2003), 17.
12. Luke 6:12–13 NLT.
13. John 5:19–20; 8:28.
14. Luke 8:1; 9:12; 22:47; Acts 6:2.
15. See Meyer, *The Aims of Jesus* (see intro., n. 6).
16. Matt. 19:28.
17. John 1:51.
18. John 1:47; emphasis added.
19. Hos. 11:1.
20. Matt. 2:15.
21. Isa. 49:6.

22. John 8:12.
23. Matt. 5:14.
24. Compare Isaiah 49:8 with 2 Corinthians 6:2, for example. The servant songs were first identified by Bernhard Dhum in his 1892 commentary on Isaiah. The songs are four psalms written about the servant of YHWH: servant song 1: Psalm 42:1–4; servant song 2: Psalm 49:1–6; servant song 3: Psalm 50:4–9; servant song 4: Psalm 52:13–53:12. Some scholars regard Isaiah 61:1–3 to be a fifth servant song.
25. Gal. 3:16.
26. 2 Cor. 1:20.
27. Christopher J. H. Wright, *Knowing Jesus Through the Old Testament*, 44 (see intro., n. 55).
28. N. T. Wright, *The Challenge of Jesus: Rediscovering Who Jesus Was and Is* (2011), 184 (see intro., n. 19).
29. From "The Temple and the Church's Mission," part 1 of an interview with Keith Giles, www.subversive1.com. Beale's book *The Temple and the Church's Mission* takes more than 450 pages to demonstrate that Jesus is the reality of the temple, the garden of Eden, and creation itself. See also R. T. France's discussion on Jesus as the new Israel in *Jesus and the Old Testament*, 50–52 (see intro., n. 22).
30. Ex. 19:6.
31. Sparks, *Words of Wisdom and Revelation*, 38 (see chap. 1, n. 105).
32. Matt. 10:2–4; Mark 3:14–19; Luke 6:13–16.
33. Mark 3:17; Luke 9:49, 54.
34. Some scholars believe James and his brother John were from a family of some wealth and influence possibly derived from their fishing trade. After all, their father owned his own boat, maybe even a small fleet (*Dictionary of Jesus and the Gospels*, eds. Joel B. Green, Scot McKnight, and I. Howard Marshall [Downers Grove, IL: InterVarsity, 1992], 179). Fishing was a major industry in Galilee. Darrell Bock points out that fishermen were the closest thing to our middle class in the West. They even had hired servants (Mark 1:20) (Darrell Bock, *Jesus According to the Scripture*, 98 [see intro., n. 6]). Peter's mother-in-law had enough wealth to own a home. Matthew was a tax collector, which was a lucrative Roman government job. The point of all this? There was economic diversity as well as other kinds of diversity among the disciples.
35. John 1:35–37.
36. Acts 1:26.
37. Acts 1:22.
38. Luke 5:10.
39. John 1:43–44.
40. Acts 4:13.
41. F. F. Bruce, *Jesus Lord & Savior* (Downers Grove, IL: InterVarsity, 1986), 51.
42. Craig Keener, *The Historical Jesus of the Gospels* (Grand Rapids: Eerdmans, 2009), 182ff.
43. Matt. 9:14–17 NIV.
44. Rev. 21:14.
45. Some scholars, like J. D. Crossan, believe that the life expectancy of Jewish males in the Jewish state in the first century was twenty-nine. Others put it higher, as this figure may include infancy death rates. (Of all the humans born

in the first-century Roman empire, half died before age five. And 25 percent of babies did not survive their first year.) Other scholars put the life expectancy of males in the Roman empire at forty-five.

46. Keener, *The Historical Jesus of the Gospels*, 246ff.
47. See Jesus' prayer in John 17.
48. See Matthew 11:19.
49. Teri Hyrkas, posted on the Facebook page of Leonard Sweet. Used with permission.
50. 1 Cor. 15:45.
51. We talk a good bit about living by the life of Christ in our book *Jesus Manifesto*.
52. Acts 1:21.
53. 1 John 1:1–3.
54. See Viola, *Finding Organic Church*, chap. 3 (see chap. 1, n. 18); A. B. Bruce's *The Training of The Twelve, or Passages Out of the Gospels* (New York: Armstrong, 1889); and Robert Coleman's *The Master Plan of Evangelism*, 2nd ed. (Grand Rapids: Revell, 2010).
55. 1 Sam. 22.
56. 1 Chron. 12:8.
57. Rev. 21:2; Gal. 4:26.
58. See Matthew 19:28. For a thorough discussion on the historicity of the Twelve and their missional significance, see Scot McKnight, "Jesus and the Twelve," in Bock and Webb, eds., *Key Events in the Life of the Historical Jesus*, 181–214 (see intro., n. 3).
59. For a detailed discussion showing how Jesus' leadership paradigm was radically different from both the Jewish and Gentile paradigms, see Frank Viola's *Reimagining Church*, chaps. 8–13 (see chap. 1, n. 18), and Leonard Sweet's *I Am a Follower*.
60. Acts 2:17–18 NIV.
61. Matt. 23:10–12 NASB.
62. Matt. 18:1.
63. Matt. 20:20–21.
64. Besides lifting up a child as the model of leadership, Jesus told His disciples that they would never equal Him (John 13:16; Matt. 10:25). He was fully conscious that He was the Messiah and the Son of God.
65. This section is taken from Frank's spoken message, "God's View of a Woman," http://www.ptmin.org/view.htm.
66. For an excellent treatment on this subject, see *Jewish Women in Greco-Roman Palestine: An Inquiry into Image and Status* by Tal Ilan (Peabody, MA: Hendrickson Publishers, 1996).
67. One hundred women are worth only two men, says Berakoth 45b. See *The Babylonian Talmud: Tractate Berakot*, trans. A. Cohen (Cambridge, UK: Cambridge University Press, 1921), 293.
68. Tosefta Berakhot, Vilna Shas 6:23, states that these three blessings should be recited each day, as quoted in Hayim Halevy Donin, *To Pray as a Jew: A Guide to the Prayer Book and the Synagogue Service* (New York: Basic Books, 1980), 194.
69. Luke 7:36ff.
70. Luke 10:38–42.

71. Luke 10:41–42; authors' paraphrase.
72. John 11:27.
73. Luke 8:1–3; authors' paraphrase.
74. Luke 23:55; emphasis added.
75. Acts 1:14; emphasis added.
76. The wording of Luke 8:1–2 indicates that these women were followers of Jesus just as much as the Twelve were. The phrase "with Him" (*syn auto*) is terminology used for discipleship in Luke (Luke 8:38; 9:18 NIV; 22:56). See the discussion in Green, McKnight, and Marshall, *Dictionary of Jesus and the Gospels*, 178 (see chap. 4, n. 1).
77. Willimon, *Why Jesus?*, 69 (see intro., n. 6).
78. Luke 8:1–3.
79. Some manuscripts say seventy-two.
80. Gen. 10; Deut. 32:8; Ex. 1:5.
81. Matt. 15:24.
82. Num. 11:16.
83. Luke 14:26; Matt. 10:35–37; Luke 9:60; Matt. 8:22; Mark 3:33–35.
84. Mark 3:33–35.
85. Luke 14:26; Mark 10:29.
86. Mark 2:14; Mark 1:16–17.
87. Mark 10:30.
88. Matt. 23:8.
89. See Sweet and Viola, *Jesus Manifesto*, chap. 9.
90. Mark 5:37; 9:2; Matt. 26:37.
91. Mark 3:16; Luke 6:14; Matt. 10:2; Acts 1:13; 1 Cor. 15:5–8 NIV.
92. Matt. 26:69ff.
93. John 21:15ff.
94. Acts 2:14ff.
95. For a discussion on Peter's ten failures and the Lord's unexpected response to each of them, see Frank Viola's "Remember Peter: Rethinking the Love of Christ" (audio): http://ptmin.podbean.com/?s=remember+peter.
96. Matt. 12:48–49.
97. John 1:18; Rom. 8:29.
98. Heb. 2:11.
99. Matt. 28:10.
100. John 19:26–27.
101. Viola, *Finding Organic Church*. Some scholars call the Twelve "the eschatological people of God."
102. See Frank Viola, *Reimagining Church*, chap. 5.
103. For a detailed unfolding of the eternal purpose of God, see Frank Viola, *From Eternity to Here* (see chap. 1, n. 59); and DeVern F. Fromke, *Ultimate Intention*, rev. ed. (Indianapolis, IN: Sure Foundation, 1998).

Chapter 9: Jesus' Mission Statement

1. 1 John 3:8.
2. Matt. 25:31–46.
3. See John 14:23.

4. Mark 15:17; John 19:2.
5. John 19:19.
6. Matt. 23:27.
7. Matt. 25:31–46.
8. Bill Hull, *Straight Talk on Spiritual Power* (Grand Rapids: Baker Books, 2002), 86.
9. Friedrich Nietzsche, *On the Genealogy of Morals* (1887).
10. Matt. 28:19.
11. Mark 16:15.
12. Luke 4:18–21 NIV.
13. 1 Chron. 23:30 NLT.
14. Mark 1:35.
15. Mark 6:46.
16. Compare Job 38:1 with Genesis 3:8.
17. Matt. 4:23–24 NIV.
18. Luke 7:19.
19. Luke 7:22.
20. *The Babylonian Talmud: Tractate Berakot*, trans. Cohen, 182 (see chap. 8, n. 67).
21. Jer. 31:33 NIV.
22. Luke 6:43–44.
23. Matt. 25:40.
24. See John 5:19, 30 (paraphrased); 15:5.
25. E. Stanley Jones, *The Unshakable Kingdom and the Unchanging Person* (Nashville: Abingdon, 1972), 11.
26. Matt. 25:40.
27. Luke 11:20 NASB.
28. Matt. 6:10.
29. Matt. 28:18.
30. Pss. 10; 10:16–18; 11–13; 22:2–28; 44:4–5; 74:12–13; 93:1–2; 95:3–7; 96; 99:1–5; 145:1–13; 147–49; Isa. 40:10–11; 52:7–10; Jer. 31:10–12; Ezek. 34:2–31; Zech. 14:5–9.
31. Ps. 2:1–9; see also Pss. 22; 72.
32. Ezek. 10–11; 43:1–5; Zech. 8:3–8; Mal. 3:1–5; Dan. 7.
33. Zech. 9:9–11.
34. Isa. 53; Zech. 13:7.
35. Isa. 54.
36. Isa. 55.
37. Isa. 59:16 NIV.
38. Isa. 53:1–2 NIV.
39. Luke 4:19.
40. Rev. 5:10.
41. 1 Peter 2:9.
42. Gen. 1:26–28.
43. Read the wording of Acts 1:1 carefully. There, Luke indicated that the book of Acts was the *continuation* of Jesus' acting and teaching through His church, as it proclaims that "there is another King—Jesus" (Acts 17:7).

Chapter 10: Jesus: Healer and Miracle-Worker

1. John 1:14.
2. Matt. 17:1.
3. Ex. 24:16.
4. Isa. 4:5 NIV.
5. Note that the first action on this mountaintop is focused on Jesus, not on any other heavenly or divine presence. The text simply states that "he was transfigured" (*metamorphote*). The Greek suggests a change in form but does not specify what exactly is transformed. Obviously there are some physical manifestations of this change. Matthew's description echoes several other biblical images that appear when heavenly beings made themselves known to humans (Ps. 104:2; Dan. 10:5–6; Matt. 28:3; Luke 24:4). Matthew noted that Jesus' face "shone like the sun," a detail that would also remind Jewish readers of Moses' experience on Sinai, where Moses' own face shone with the reflection of the glory he had witnessed on the mountain (Ex. 34:29–35). Unlike Moses, however, Jesus' facial illumination was not a reflection. It was a revelation of His divinity and glory. Likewise there was no other heavenly being around who "bedazzled" Jesus' clothes. The dazzling whiteness came from Jesus Himself.
6. For David Martin's "The Restored Face" see "The Transfiguration: The Restored Face," in his *Christian Language in the Secular City* (Aldershot, UK: Ashgatem, 2002), 77–78.
7. Malachi 4:5 explicitly states that Elijah will return before the final day of judgment. Deuteronomy 18:15–19 makes the less precise promise of the return of a prophet like Moses.
8. Matt. 17:4.
9. Matt. 17:5.
10. Ex. 13:21–22; 33:9–10; 40:34–38; 1 Kings 8:10–11.
11. Matt. 17:5.
12. Matt. 3:17.
13. Deut. 18:15.
14. Ex. 20:18–21; Deut. 4:33; Heb. 12:18–21.
15. Matt. 17:7.
16. Matt. 17:9.
17. Josh. 4:1–7.
18. Josh. 4:7.
19. 2 Cor. 3:18.
20. Matt. 17:15.
21. Matt. 4:23–24 NIV.
22. Johann Wolfgang von Goethe, *Italian Journey* [December 1787], trans. Robert R. Heitner (New York: Suhrkamp, 1989), 364.
23. Luke 4:39.
24. Luke 13:10–17; Matt. 12:22–32; 17:14–21; Mark 9:17–26. For a detailed discussion on this point, see John Christopher Thomas's *The Devil, Disease and Deliverance: Origins of Illness in New Testament Thought* (Cleveland, TN: CPT Press, 2010).
25. Acts 10:38; emphasis added.
26. 1 John 3:8; emphasis added.

27. Granted, Galatians 3:14 is explicit about which part of the promise believers receive now (as opposed to the time of eschatological consummation). It is the Spirit. Yet believers live in the presence of the future. Thus the Holy Spirit, whom Paul elsewhere identifies as the down payment on our future inheritance in the kingdom, is given to us now. And the Spirit still heals today, though He doesn't always cure, as we will see later.
28. Deut. 7:15.
29. Ex. 15:26.
30. Ps. 103:2–3.
31. Prov. 3:7–8.
32. Prov. 4:20–22.
33. John 5:14; 9:1–2.
34. Luke 13:10–16.
35. Interestingly, healing and forgiveness are often coupled together in Scripture (2 Chron. 7:14; Ps. 103:3; Mark 2:9–11).
36. Witherington, *The Christology of Jesus*, 94. N. T. Wright notes that "there was no single monolithic and uniform 'messianic expectation' among first-century Jews" (*The New Testament and the People of God*, vol. 1 of *Christian Origins and the Question of God*, 307).
37. Luke 7:21–22 NIV.
38. John 7:31 NIV.
39. This teaching comes from Dr. Arnold Fruchtenbaum in *The Life of the Messiah from a Jewish Perspective: Complete Series Recorded Live at Chafer Theological Seminary* (DVD) (San Antonio: Ariel Ministries, 2008).
40. Matt. 12:22–23.
41. Luke 5:17 NLT.
42. Interestingly, the Jews who rejected Jesus' claims to messiahship couldn't deny His miracles. So the rabbinic tradition alleges that He was a magician and a false prophet.
43. For a technical discussion on the relationship between Jesus' exorcisms, His battle against satan, and the kingdom of God, see Craig A. Evans, "Exorcisms and the Kingdom: Inaugurating the Kingdom of God and Defeating the Kingdom of Satan," in Bock and Webb, eds., *Key Events in the Life of the Historical Jesus*, chap. 4, 151–79 (see intro., n. 3).
44. Acts 9:34.
45. John 14:12; Mark 16:15ff (though some scholars question if this text is part of the original). We see examples of Jesus' ministry of healing through the disciples all throughout the book of Acts.
46. Isa. 53:3–5 NIV.
47. Matt. 8:16–17.
48. 1 Peter 2:24.
49. Matt. 12:28 NIV.
50. Luke 4:24–27; Matt. 4:23–24; Mark 1:15; Luke 11:20.
51. Acts 2:22 NIV.
52. The best volume on miracles is the two-volume treatment by Craig Keener, *Miracles: The Credibility of the New Testament Accounts* (Grand Rapids: Baker Academic, 2011).

53. John Wimber, *Power Evangelism* (New York: Harper & Row, 1986), 91.
54. In *Jesus Manifesto* we demonstrated that eternal life does not simply point to longevity but to a certain kind of life. It means divine life, which is Christ (1 John 5:20).
55. John 1:4.
56. John 3:15.
57. John 4:14.
58. John 5:40.
59. John 6:35, 48.
60. John 8:12.
61. John 10:10.
62. John 11:25.
63. John 14:6.
64. John 17:3.
65. John 20:31.
66. For details on the spiritual meaning of the temple of God from Genesis to Revelation, see Viola, *From Eternity to Here*, pt. 2 (see chap. 1, n. 59).
67. John 1:14; Ex. 40:34.
68. John 20:22–23.
69. Mark 14:58 NIV.
70. 1 Cor. 3:6–17; 2 Cor. 6:16; Eph. 2:19–22; 1 Peter 2:4–9.
71. 2 Chron. 7:1–3.
72. Acts 17:24; Heb. 8:2; Dan. 2; Isa. 66; Heb. 9.
73. Matt. 6:10.
74. N. T. Wright, *The New Testament and the People of God*, vol. 1 of *Christian Origins and the Question of God*, 299ff.; *Simply Jesus*, chap. 12 (see intro., n. 6).
75. Witherington, *The Christology of Jesus*, 94; *Psalms of Solomon* 17 in *Psalms of Solomon: A New Transaction and Introduction*, by Heerak Christian Kim (Highland Park, NJ: Hermit Kingdom Press, 2008), 18–21. In addition to these signs, as I have learned from Arnold Fruchtenbaum, many rabbis believed that the Messiah would return the urim and thummim, the ark of the covenant, and the shekinah glory. While this represents later rabbinic tradition, some scholars believe it reflects first-century Jewish thinking as well.
76. Frank developed this thought in his book *From Eternity to Here* (see chap. 1, n. 59), saying, "From the very beginning, a battle has raged over the land of Canaan. Satan's intention has always been to rid God's people from the Promised Land. The reason is simple. In the Bible, Canaan represents the building site for God's house. If the Enemy could keep God's people out of the land, God cannot have His home. On the other hand, if God can bring His people into the Land of Promise (Canaan), then God has His building site. And in a sense, He possesses the whole earth. The Scriptures are fairly clear on this. Throughout the Bible, whenever God's people were standing on the building site (Canaan), God was called the 'God of heaven *and earth*.' But whenever God's people were taken out of the building site, He was simply called 'the God of heaven' (Gen. 14:1–19; Josh. 3:11–13; Ezra 1:2; 7:12, 21, 23; Neh. 1:4–5; 2:4; Dan. 2:18, 28; Matt. 11:25)" (181–82).
77. N. T. Wright develops this idea in his books *Jesus and the Victory of God*, vol. 2 of *Christian Origins and the Question of God*; *The Challenge of Jesus:*

Rediscovering Who Jesus Was and Is (2011) (see intro., n. 19); and *Simply Jesus* (see intro., n. 6).
78. Matt. 9:6.
79. Matt. 23:37ff.; Luke 13:34ff.; John 1:11.
80. Jeremiah had long before prophesied that this would happen (Jer. 7:3–15).
81. Rev. 21–22.
82. Zech. 3:8; 6:12–13.
83. Zech. 8:18–19; Mark 2:18–20.
84. Andrew Murray, *The Spirit of Christ* (New Kingsington, PA: Whitaker House, n.d.), 17.
85. Mark 6:48–51.
86. For more on this, see Leonard Sweet, *Health and Medicine in the Evangelical Tradition* (Valley Forge, PA: Trinity Press International, 1994) and *The Jesus Prescription for a Healthy Life* (see chap. 3, n. 12).
87. This story comes from Nels Ferré's son, Fred Ferré, who spoke to a group of theology students about his father. With thanks to Wayne Brouwer and Schuyler Rhodes for Fred Ferré's story. See "The Road Ahead," SermonSuite, January 8, 2012, http://sermonsuite.com/content.php?i=778028410&key=S1xyzSsxogdm0pai.

Chapter 11: Jesus: Teacher and Preacher

1. Blaise Pascal, *The Thoughts of Blaise Pascal*, trans. from the text of Auguste Molinier by C. Kegan Paul (London: George Bell and Sons, 1905), 224–25.
2. Luke 8:1–3.
3. Matt. 4:17.
4. Luke 10:38–42.
5. Mark 4:1–2.
6. Matt. 4:17; Luke 8:1.
7. Heb. 4:4 NIV.
8. 1 Cor. 15:3–9.
9. Or as a modern translation puts it, "Christ was a historical person whose biography was already determined before he was born" (Friedrich von Schelling, *The Philosophy of Art*, ed. and trans. Douglas W. Stott [Minneapolis: University of Minnesota Press, 1989], 59).
10. Mark 6:35.
11. 2 Kings 4:43.
12. Matt. 5:1–12.
13. Psalm 49:4 ESV.
14. Thanks to Christine Sine for first making this connection.
15. Luke 22:20 NLT.
16. John 7:22–23.
17. Hyam Maccoby, "The Leper and the Pharisee," in his *Jesus the Pharisee* (London: SCM, 2003), 40–42.
18. Mark 2:27.
19. Matt. 7:29; Mark 1:22.
20. See, for instance, the NIV renderings of Matthew 5:18, 26; 6:2, 16; 8:10; 10:15, 23, 42, et al. See especially Matthew 5:21–48 (NKJV). Also in John, Jesus

used, "Amen, amen, I tell you" (two amens instead of the one found often in the Synoptic)—see, for example, the NAB renderings of John 1:5; 3:3, 5, 11; 5:19, 24, 25.

21. John 14:9.
22. John 14:11.
23. John 8:28.
24. John 5:43.
25. Matt. 7:29; Mark 1:22.
26. Jose A. Pagola, *Jesus: An Historical Approximation* (Miami: Convivium Press, 2011), 233.
27. Matt. 12:11–12.
28. Mark 6:3.
29. Mark 6:1; Luke 4:16.
30. Luke 4:21.
31. The people in Jesus' hometown were so astounded that they remarked, "Isn't this Mary's son and the brother of James, Joseph, Judas and Simon? Aren't his sisters here with us?" (Mark 6:3 NIV).
32. Matt. 12:7 NLT.
33. Luke 4:29.
34. John 7:5.
35. Mark 15:43–46.
36. Acts 1:13–14.
37. Mark 7:7 NIV; Matt. 15:9 NIV.
38. Matt. 23:2.
39. See Frank Viola's "Diary of a Desperate Woman" (audio), April 2009, http://ptmin.podbean.com/?s=Diary+of+a+Desperate+Woman, for a novelized version of the Samaritan woman's encounter with Jesus in John 4.
40. 1 John 3:23; 4:2–3; 5:1.
41. Gal. 2:20.
42. Luke 10:29.
43. Ralph Lewis, "The Triple Brain Test of a Sermon," *Preaching* 1 (September/October 1985): 11.
44. Jonathan Sacks, *The Great Partnership: God, Science and the Search for Meaning* (London: Hodder & Stoughton, 2011), 253.
45. Luke 17:21. Some translations render this "among you" or "in your midst."
46. 1 Cor. 15:21–28; Matt. 16:28.
47. Leslie Houlden mentions this in *Companion Encyclopedia of Theology*, eds. Peter Byrne and Leslie Houlden (New York: Routledge, 1995), 178.
48. Mishnah, Tohoroth 7:6.
49. See Luke 14:15–24.
50. John 10.
51. Brennan Manning, *Abba's Child: The Cry of the Heart for Intimate Belonging*, rev. ed. (Colorado Springs: Navpress, 2002), 109. Manning continues: "God *pazzo d'amore* and *ebro d'amore* ('crazed with love' and 'drunk with love'—Catherine of Siena) is embodied in Jesus dwelling within us."
52. Mark 1:40–45.
53. Luke 11:37–38.
54. Compare Mark 6:30–44 with Mark 8:1–10.

55. See Mark 8:17–21.
56. "Midrash Pesher" refers to a way of interpreting biblical stories. Many of the ancient types of teaching were passed down to modern times. The major example is that of the acronym PaRDeS, representing the first letter of the four basic types of Jewish exegesis used during the first century. These methods were Peshat (simple), Remez (hinting, intuitive), Derash (complex), and Sod (secret). You can see all of these somewhere in Jesus' teaching. For example, in remez, or hint, a teacher would use part of a Scripture passage, assuming the audience knew enough of the story to deduce for themselves fuller meaning. Jesus liked this technique and used it often, letting those in authority fill in the blanks. When the children sang Hosanna to him in the temple and the Sadducees demanded Jesus quiet them, He quoted Psalm 8:2 (NIV): "From the lips of children and infants you have ordained praise." We wonder why they got so angry at Jesus, but the next phrase in the psalm that is only hinted at in Jesus' response gives the reason why children and infants would praise—because the enemies of God would be silenced (Ps. 8:2). In other words, Jesus didn't say it directly, but in citing this text Jesus hinted that the chief priests were God's enemies.
57. For Ben Witherington's marvelous portrayal of Jesus as a "sage," see his *Jesus the Sage* (see chap. 6, n. 46). See also Craig Keener's superb book *The Historical Jesus of the Gospels*.
58. John 1:38.
59. John 11:25.
60. Ralph L. Lewis with Gregg Lewis, *Learning to Preach Like Jesus* (Westchester, IL: Crossway Books, 1989), 23: "For all practical purposes, with most of His listeners, Jesus had to start from scratch."
61. John 1:14, 18.
62. Archibald Thomas Robertson, *Word Pictures in the New Testament* (Nashville: Broadman Press, 1932), 5:18.
63. Mark 14:61.
64. Mark 2:23–28; Matt. 12:1–8; Luke 6:1–5.
65. Mark 8:27 NIV.
66. Matt. 5:47 NIV.
67. Matt. 16:26 NIV.
68. Mark 2:8 NIV.
69. Matt. 17:25 NIV.
70. Luke 10:26 NIV.
71. Conrad Gempf, *Jesus Asked: What He Wanted to Know* (Grand Rapids: Zondervan, 2003).
72. Lewis, *Learning to Preach Like Jesus*, 28.
73. Jesus was asked 183 questions in the Gospels, and He answered just 3 of them.
74. Tom Hughes, as quoted in Don Everts and Doug Schaupp, *I Once Was Lost: What Postmodern Skeptics Taught Us About Their Path to Jesus* (Downers Grove, IL: InterVarsity, 2008), 54.
75. Mark 8:29.
76. See Eberhard Jüngel's thesis in *God as the Mystery of the World: On the Foundation of the Theology of the Crucified One in the Dispute between Theism*

and Atheism, trans. Darrell L. Guder (Grand Rapids: Eerdmans, 1983), 10–11, where he wrote, "The art of speaking does not result in something different from itself; instead, its effect consists of the fact that the person addressed and the result of what is said are both drawn into the act of speaking." Jüngel calls this a "perlocutionary-attractive act."

77. Mark 4:34.
78. Matt. 13:35.
79. John 6:26.
80. Mark 4:34 NLT.
81. Mark 4:10.
82. Marc Bregman, quoted by David Halperin, "Talmud and Taekwando," *Journal of a UFO Investigator*, January 11, 2011, http://www.davidhalperin.net/tag/sugya.
83. Mark 7:17, 20–23.
84. Matt. 13:51.
85. Luci Shaw, "Reversing Entropy," *Image* 41 (Winter 2003): 96.
86. Matt. 13:11–12 NLT.
87. Robert Johnston's dissertation on Tannaitic Parables (Robert M. Johnston, "Parabolic Interpretations Attributed to Tannaim," PhD diss., Hartford Seminary Foundation, 1977) is a masterpiece on this subject.
88. John's gospel is famous for not including any parables. But what are the Good Shepherd (John 10:1–18) and the True Vine (John 15:1–8) but parables or allusions to parables?
89. As quoted in Eileen Egan, *Such a Vision of the Street: Mother Teresa, the Spirit and the Work* (Garden City, NY: Image Books, 1986), 413.
90. Luke 10:21 NIV.
91. Matt. 25:40.
92. See Isaiah 55:8; Romans 11:33; Matthew 6:9 KJV.
93. For a few of those twenty times, see Deuteronomy 32:6; Isaiah 63:16; Jeremiah 3:19. For more on God as King, see Marc Zvi Brettler, *God Is King: Understanding an Israelite Metaphor* (Sheffield, UK: JSOT, 1989).
94. The one exception is Matthew 5:35, but this echoes Psalm 47:7.
95. Rev. 19:7, 9, 21.
96. No wonder three of the Gospel writers skipped this story (only John told it).
97. We owe Craig Keener for this insight.
98. Augustine, "Homilies on the Gospel of John," in *A Select Library of the Nicene and Post-Nicene Fathers of the Christian Church*, ed. Philip Schaff (New York: Christian Literature, 1988) 7:57.
99. John 2:6.
100. John 2:5.
101. Mark 9:7.

Chapter 12: The Human Jesus

1. Douglas John Hall, *The Cross in Our Context: Jesus and the Suffering World* (Minneapolis, MN: Fortress, 2003).
2. Einstein's actual quote: "Imagination is more important than knowledge. Knowledge is limited. Imagination encircles the world" (Albert Einstein,

The Ultimate Quotable Einstein, ed. Alice Calaprice [Princeton, NJ: Princeton University Press, 2011], 12. Originally published in an interview with G. S. Viereck, "What Life Means to Einstein," *Saturday Evening Post*, October 26, 1929).

3. Gerald O'Collins is the theologian who gives this subject the most serious attention. See his *Jesus: A Portrait* (Maryknoll, NY: Orbis, 2008), 44ff.
4. See Matthew 7:3–5; see also Luke 6:41–42.
5. "Rabbi Tarfon said, 'I wonder if there is anyone in this generation who knows how to accept reproof. For if one says to another: "Remove the chip of wood from between your eyes," he would answer: "Remove the beam from between *your* eyes!"'" (Talmud, *Arakin* 16b). As quoted in Barry W. Holtz, *Finding Our Way: Jewish Texts and the Lives We Lead Today* (Philadelphia: Jewish Publication Society, 2005), 155.
6. Matt. 6:28.
7. Louis Jacobs, *Jewish Preaching* (Portland, OR: Vallentine Mitchell, 2004), 181.
8. Rudolf Bultmann, *Jesus and the Word*, prepared for Religion Online by Ted and Winnie Brock, introduction, http://media.sabda.org/alkitab-2/Religion-Online.org%20Books/Bultmann,%20Rudolf%20-%20Jesus%20and%20the%20Word.pdf.
9. Confirmed in a personal e-mail from John H. Armstrong, December 30, 2011.
10. Mark 4:37–38.
11. Mark 14:33–34.
12. Matt. 4:2.
13. Mark 1:41; 8:2.
14. John 11:35–37.
15. "When taking on the human condition, he claims no special exemption and treatment; he shares it all with us. He now knows at firsthand what it is to be human—with all our limits, including the final limit of death. As one of us, he can experience and love us" (O'Collins, *Jesus: A Portrait*, 48).
16. Mark 15:23.
17. Matt. 19:24.
18. Matt. 6:2.
19. Thanks to Craig Keener for this thought.
20. Ludwig Wittgenstein, *Culture and Value*, ed. G. H. Von Wright, trans. Peter Winch (Chicago: University of Chicago Press, 1980), 78, 78e.
21. Matt. 25:21.
22. Friedrich Nietzsche, *Thus Spake Zarathustra: A Book for All and None*, trans. Thomas Common, *The Complete Works of Friedrich Nietzsche*, 11 (New York: Macmillan, 1911), 45.
23. While some scholars believe that the eighteen measures were later rabbinic material, they very well may have represented the mind-set during Jesus' day.
24. G. K. Chesterton, "On the Comic Spirit," in *Generally Speaking: A Book of Essays*, 2nd ed. (London: Methuen, 1930), 176.
25. See the Charles Wesley hymn "Gentle Jesus, Meek and Mild." For the words, see John Richard Watson, ed., *An Annotated Anthology of Hymns* (New York: Oxford University Press, 2002), 180. The term used for Jesus'

meekness was also applied to rulers who showed compassion; thus it doesn't mean wimpy. It can mean power expressed mercifully, when applied to persons of power.

26. Matt. 3:7; 9:4, 12–13; 23:1ff.; John 8:44.
27. John 2:15.
28. Matt. 17:17; Mark 3:5; 7:18; 8:16–18; 9:19; Luke 13:6–9; 22:38; 24:25; Mark 11:13–14.
29. Mark 1:43; 3:12; 5:43; 8:30.
30. Luke 4:22; Matt. 11:29.
31. Luke 7:31–35.
32. Mark 2:15–17; Luke 5:33.
33. Mark 3:29.
34. Mark 9:42.
35. Mark 13:26–36.
36. Matt. 23:24–25.
37. Matt. 7:6; Luke 10:10–11; Matt. 21:31. For a commentary on these texts and other examples, see *The Humor of Christ* by Elton Trueblood (New York: Harper & Row, 1964).
38. Matt. 12:27; 23:2–4; Mark 7:9; 15:2; Luke 13:32.
39. Luke 13:32.
40. Matt. 15:27.
41. Matt. 22:22; Luke 20:26, 40.
42. Luke 22:15 NLT.
43. Mark 14:26.
44. See Psalm 149:3; 150:4. There is an apocryphal gospel called the Acts of John that tells of the disciples making a ring around Jesus and dancing. See "The Acts of John," in *The Apocryphal New Testament: A Collection of Apocryphal Christian Literature in an English Translation*, ed. J. K. Elliott (New York: Oxford University Press, 1993), 318–20. See also sections 94–96 in the original 1924 edition as reprinted in "Gnostic Scriptures and Fragments: The Acts of John," The Gnostic Society Library, http://www.gnosis.org/library/actjohn.htm.
45. Luke 19:41; John 11:35. A third time was at Gethsemane (Heb. 5:7).
46. John 11:18.
47. Sweet and Viola, *Jesus Manifesto*, chap. 9.
48. See Leonard Sweet, "The Nerve of Failure," *Theology Today* 34 (July 1977), 143–49.
49. Matt. 11:20–21.
50. Luke 9:51.
51. Matt. 23:37.
52. Heb. 4:15 CEB.
53. Paul said that a person can be angry without sinning (Eph. 4:26).
54. See Paul Ekman's classic research as described on his website, "Dr. Paul Ekman: Cutting-Edge Behavioral Science for Real World Applications," http://www.paulekman.com.
55. 2 Tim. 4:2.
56. Mark 11:14.
57. Mic. 4:4.

58. Gen. 1:22.
59. "Intelligent Design Theory—Squeezing Common Sense out of Science, Creation, Noah's Ark and Jesus Christ," http://www.intelligentdesigntheory.info/god_and_the_size_of_the_universe.htm.
60. See Genesis 2:15.
61. Matt. 7:17.
62. Matt. 7:16.
63. See Matthew 18:6.
64. Gilbert K. Chesterton, "On Certain Modern Writers and the Institution of the Family," in his *Heretics* (New York: John Lane, 1909), 179.
65. Matt. 2:16–18.
66. Luke 10:25–37.
67. John 9:33–37; 10:35–45.
68. See Thomas J. Norris, *The Trinity: Life of God, Hope for Humanity: Towards a Theology of Communion* (Hyde Park, NY: New City Press, 2009), 81. He is quoting Klaus Hemmerle, *Wie Glauben im Leben geht* (München: Verlag Neue Stadt, 1995), 224.
69. An alternative translation of "Let the little children come to me, . . . for it is to such of these that the kingdom of heaven belongs" (Matt. 19:14 NRSV).
70. John 1:12.
71. Mark 11:17; Luke 19:46. See also Isa. 56:7.
72. 1 Cor. 6:19.
73. John 2:19.
74. Acts 5, with thanks to Nazarene pastor James Spruill for helping us make this connection.
75. Matt. 23; John 8:44.
76. Heb. 13:8.
77. John Eldredge, from the front cover of Mark Galli, *Jesus Mean and Wild: The Unexpected Love of an Untamed God* (Grand Rapids: Baker Books, 2008).
78. Dodd, *The Founder of Christianity*, 46 (see intro., n. 6).
79. See Philip Yancey, *What's So Amazing About Grace?* (Grand Rapids: Zondervan, 1997), esp. chap. 3.
80. John 17:1.
81. Ps. 51:15.
82. Luke 1:46–55.
83. Luke 1:46, 52 MOFFATT.
84. Matt. 26:30.
85. See Mark 15:34; Matthew 27:46. Jesus was likely praying/singing Psalm 22 (*Eli, Eli, lama sabachtani*) from the cross.
86. Luke 22:32.
87. Heb. 7:25.
88. Mark 1:35.
89. Mark 6:46.
90. Mark 9:28–29.
91. Matt. 17.
92. Mark 14:32–41.
93. Vance Havner is quoted as saying, "If we don't come 'a-part' and spend time with God, we will 'come apart' emotionally and spiritually." See the preface

to Vance Havner, *When God Breaks Through: Sermons on Revival*, ed. Dennis J. Hester (Grand Rapids: Kregel, 2003), 11.

94. Ps. 121:1 ASV.
95. Matt. 4.
96. H. Richard Niebuhr, *The Meaning of Revelation* (Louisville: Westminster John Knox, 2006), 72. (Originally published New York: MacMillan, 1941, 100.)
97. Matt. 17.
98. Matt. 5–7.
99. Matt. 15.
100. Matt. 28. See Terence L. Donaldson's *Jesus on the Mountain: A Study in Matthean Theology* (Sheffield, UK: JSOT Press, 1985).
101. One thinks here of Moses on Pisgah or Dante climbing Mount Purgatorio to reach paradise.
102. This is what the Greeks called the *kataskapos* or the "looker-downs."
103. See Job 38.
104. Matt. 4:12–13; 9:1.
105. John 2:12.
106. See Nick Page, *What Happened to the Ark of the Covenant? and Other Bible Mysteries* (Colorado Springs: Authentic, 2007), 128. "He was known as, and we still talk about, Jesus of Nazareth. But Jesus from Capernaum was the man who really made an impact."
107. Four disciples had houses at Capernaum: Simon and Andrew (Mark 1:29) and James and John, the sons of Zebedee (Mark 1:20). It may have been that James and John were cousins of Jesus. Peter and Andrew were from Bethsaida, to the north of the lake.
108. See Page, "Where Did Jesus Live?" in *What Happened to the Ark of the Covenant? and Other Bible Mysteries*, 123–28.
109. Mark 2:1–4.
110. Isa. 9:1–2 NLT.
111. For Jesus' description of Capernaum's stubbornness as worse than Sodom's, see Matthew 11:23–24.
112. Augustine, *De Genesi ad Litteram*, VIII, 32, as quoted in Norris, *The Trinity*, 100.
113. Matt. 11:29.
114. 2 Cor. 8:9 NLT.
115. Matt. 12:43.
116. Luke 8:33.
117. Rev. 1:9.
118. See Philippians 2:7–8.
119. Phil. 2:8.
120. 2 Cor. 4:7; authors' paraphrase.
121. Gen. 9:9–10.
122. For a discussion on the spiritual implications of the wilderness experience in the life of a Christian, see Viola, *From Eternity to Here*, pt. 2, "An Eternal Quest: The House of God."
123. Ps. 150:6.
124. See Genesis 1:20–24.
125. Gen. 6:19–22.
126. Hos. 2:20–21.

127. Ex. 23:11–12.
128. Ps. 148:7–12; Rev. 5:13.
129. Isa. 11:6–9; 65:25.
130. See Talmud, Sanhedrin 98a. "I was watching in the night visions, and behold, One like the Son of Man, coming with the clouds of heaven! He came to the Ancient of Days, and they brought Him near before Him" (Dan. 7:13). See also Zechariah 9:9.
131. Ogden Nash, "Barnyard Cogitations," in his *The Bad Parents' Garden of Verse* (New York: Simon and Schuster, 1936), 28.
132. Matt. 3:16; Mark 1:10; John 1:32; Luke 3:22. A dove, of course, is a poetic name for a white pigeon.
133. Mark 1:13. The wild beasts that Jesus Himself created long beforehand served Him in the desert by accompanying Him there. Thus, Jesus was not alone during His wilderness trial.
134. Rev. 5:5; John 1:29.
135. Matt. 10:16.
136. Matt. 10:29.
137. Matt. 21:2, 7 NLT.
138. Mark 11:3 KJV.
139. Matt. 12:11; Luke 14:5.
140. John 2:15.
141. Rom. 8:19–23.

Chapter 13: Jesus' Trial and Crucifixion

1. Erich Sauer, *The Triumph of the Crucified* (Grand Rapids: Eerdmans, 1951), 32.
2. John 19:41.
3. John 18:1 NRSV.
4. In *Jesus Manifesto*, we demonstrated that Bethany was the Lord's favorite place on earth. Jesus spent the last evenings of His life in Bethany.
5. Mark 14:33–34 NIV; see also Psalm 43:5.
6. Luke 22:42.
7. Matt. 26:39.
8. Luke 22:42. Joseph Ratzinger links Jesus' prayer in Gethsemane as well as His prayer on the cross to the text of Hebrews 5:7 (NIV): "During the days of Jesus' life on earth, he offered up prayers and petitions with loud cries and tears to the one who could save him from death, and he was heard because of his reverent submission" (*Jesus of Nazareth, Part Two, Holy Week: From the Entrance into Jerusalem to the Resurrection* [San Francisco: Ignatius, 2011], 162ff).
9. Ps. 16:5; 116:13; 23:5.
10. Ps. 11:6; 75:8; Isa. 51:17; Jer. 49:12–16.
11. Mark 10:38; John 18:11.
12. 1 Cor. 10:16.
13. Matt. 26:13; authors' paraphrase.
14. Gen. 3.
15. Luke 22:47–48.
16. Mark 14:1–11.
17. Mark 14:3–9.

18. Matt. 27:33; Mark 15:22, 29–30.
19. Deut. 21:22–23 NLT.
20. See Karl Barth's *Deliverance to the Captives*, trans. Marguerite Wieser (New York: Harper, 1961).
21. Luke 23:43.
22. While the church is holy and without blame before God, every member is still fallen and in need of transformation.
23. Luke 23:2 NIV (see footnote a).
24. See Matthew 27:11.
25. John 18:38–19:22, esp. 19:19.
26. Matt. 27:37.
27. Matt. 27:24.
28. This is made explicit in John 19.
29. John 19:22.
30. Jesus has redeemed us with His own blood. See 1 Corinthians 6:19–20 and Romans 12:1–2.
31. Phil. 2.
32. THE FIRST WORD: "Father, forgive them, for they do not know what they do" (Luke 23:34). THE SECOND WORD: "Assuredly, I say to you, today you will be with Me in Paradise" (Luke 23:43). THE THIRD WORD: "[Jesus] said to His mother, 'Woman, behold your son!' Then He said to the disciple, 'Behold your mother!'" (John 19:26–27). THE FOURTH WORD: "My God, My God, why have You forsaken Me?" (Matt. 27:46; Mark 15:34). THE FIFTH WORD: "I thirst!" (John 19:28). THE SIXTH WORD: "It is finished!" (John 19:30). THE SEVENTH WORD. "Father, 'into Your hands I commit My spirit'" (Luke 23:46).
33. Luke 23:34.
34. Ibid.
35. Hannah Arendt, *The Human Condition*, 2nd ed. (Chicago: University of Chicago Press, 1958), 238.
36. John 20:22–23.
37. Henri Nouwen, *Return of the Prodigal Son: A Meditation on Fathers, Brothers, and Sons* (New York: Doubleday, 1992).
38. John 19:26–27. Raymond E. Brown, in *The Death of the Messiah: From Gethsemane to the Grave: A Commentary on the Passion Narratives in the Four Gospels* (New York: Doubleday, 1998), 1021, argues that there is a testamentary quality to Jesus' speech from the cross.
39. Matt. 10:37; 8:22; Luke 14:26.
40. Along with this semiotic understanding of Jesus as the new Adam birthing the church, we can also see the conception of the church in the moment of His death. Len suggests that when John says Jesus "gave up his spirit" (Matt. 27:50 NIV), it does not mean He died. Rather, it means that with the creation of this new relationship between John and Mary, Jesus poured out His spirit on them, and at the foot of the cross, sprayed and bathed in the water and blood that spewed from His side, the church universal was conceived. The church, pregnant with the blood and sacrifice of Jesus, became Spirit-breathed and born to resurrection life at the time of Pentecost.

41. Mark 1:29–31.
42. Mark 16:1.
43. The contrasts can be so striking that one scholar who loves to provoke believers, John Dominic Crossan, in his controversial book *Jesus: A Revolutionary Biography* (San Francisco: HarperSanFrancisco, 1994), argues a startling thesis with which we don't agree but which illustrates the power of Markan contrasts. Mark is a mystery, Crossan reminds us, stating that we know no Mark in early church history. Mark's gospel is so partial to women that Crossan suspects the nameless woman of this text to be in fact the real Mark, the author of the gospel. He theorizes that "in remembrance of her" is the author's way of leaving behind a coded signature of authorship.
44. Matt. 26:6.
45. Mark 1:40–44.
46. Prov. 27:9.
47. "Spikenard" was the favorite perfume of antiquity. It got its name from the spikelike shape of the root and spiny stem of the herb plant that was found high up in the Himalayan mountains. The Greeks and Romans loved the smell of this rare unguent (perfume and ointment were virtually indistinguishable) so much that they willingly paid the expense of having nard shipped long distances. The best spikenard was imported from India in sealed alabaster boxes, costly containers that were opened only on very special occasions. The cost of the perfume was three hundred denarii. Since one denarius a day was a worker's usual salary, this one jar of perfume represented one laborer's salary for almost a year—or in today's money, almost forty thousand dollars. If denarii were translated into pieces of silver, Jesus was crucified for one-tenth the cost of this perfume. In Jesus' circles this kind of extravagance—a year's salary for one moment of luxury—was unheard-of.
48. John 12:3 NIV.
49. Mark 10:37.
50. John 12:8. It is generally held that *chronos* time is more or less "clock time"—hours, minutes, etc. *Kairos* is time as experienced by someone. It often means the opportune time, the right time, the important time. *Chronos* looks at time quantitatvely while *kairos* looks at time qualitatively. However, some scholars argue that this isn't technically accurate. Regardless, it doesn't take away from our point.
51. Matt. 26:15.
52. John Charles Ryle, *Expository Thoughts on the Gospel of John* (London: Hodder and Stoughton, 1896), 348.
53. The anointing of Jesus is a much-disputed account in scholarly circles. The woman was unnamed in three out of the four gospel accounts. Only John named her as Mary of Bethany. Luke named her a sinner. While Matthew's and Mark's accounts depicted the woman as pouring oil upon Jesus' head, both Luke and John depicted her pouring it upon Jesus' feet. Witherington noted (*John's Wisdom: A Commentary on the Fourth Gospel* [Louisville: Westminster John Knox, 1995], 207) that the differing focus serves a symbolic purpose in line with each writer's theology: the anointing of the head symbolizes kingship while the anointing of the feet symbolizes Jesus being glorified in death. In Matthew, Mark, and John, the disciples

were outraged at the use of the perfume. In Luke, Simon wondered and was told a parable, not found in the other three. Both Matthew and Mark named Simon "the leper." Luke named the Pharisee only as *Simon*. John's account was without name. The patristic church believed that the woman in Luke 7 was Mary Magadalene. Scholars disagree vigorously on whether the gospel accounts describe three anointings (as believed in the Eastern churches), two anointings (as believed by some scholars), or one anointing (as believed by others). Those who subscribe to the one-anointing, as does Len, call attention to the possibility of a variously described oral account, written differently for variant audiences, and as seen in different perspective by the writers. Those, like Frank, subscribing to the two anointings believe that the Luke account occurred earlier in Jesus' ministry and the other anointing later in Bethany. (See Frank Viola's *From Eternity to Here*, chap. 8, for a reconstruction of one of the accounts.) Whatever you choose, there is the issue of why she anointed His feet in John but in Matthew and Mark, His head. The John passage agrees with Luke. For the purposes of this theography, we have rendered a semiotic reading of the text, calling attention to the truth of Jesus the Messiah and the truth of His identity. Because a semiotic reading is more interested in drawing upon the truth found in the story and not an empirical nailing-down or historical fact-finding, we have striven to view the anointing of Jesus as a revelation of important truths that Jesus would have us understand about His identity and His mission.

54. As quoted in Albert Edward Thompson, *The Life of A. B. Simpson* (New York: Christian Alliance Publishing Co., 1920), 196.
55. Ps. 138.6.
56. Isa. 65:5 NLT.
57. Ex. 30:6; 37:25–28. Exodus 30:6 even may mean that the altar of incense was within the veil, or within the Holy of Holies itself (ref. Heb. 9:4).
58. Henry David Thoreau, *Walden: A Fully Annotated Edition*, ed. Jeffrey S. Cramer (New Haven, CT: Yale University Press, 2004), 71.
59. "Ivory Palaces," words and music by Henry Barraclough, 1915.
60. Mark 15:20.
61. "Father, forgive them; for they know not what they do" (Luke 23:34 KJV).
62. Matt. 26:30; Mark 14:26.
63. Ps. 116:16. The "Last Supper" in view here is regarded by Catholics to be the "first Mass."
64. Versitis is a metaphorical disease to describe the act of approaching the Bible with a scissors mentality, cutting apart verses to build doctrines and justify church practices. A coining of this phrase can be found in Leonard Sweet, *Viral: How Social Media Is Poised to Ignite Revival* (Colorado Springs: WaterBrook, 2012). For a further detailed explanation of the problem and how it emerged, see Frank Viola and George Barna, *Pagan Christianity: Exploring the Roots of Our Church Practices* (Carol Stream, IL: BarnaBooks, 2008), chap. 11; and for a suggested solution, see Viola, *The Untold Story of the New Testament Church* (see intro., n. 80).
65. Mark 15:24 NLT.
66. Psalm 69:20–21: "If only one person would show some pity. . . . But instead . . . they offer me sour wine for my thirst" (NLT); Psalm 34:20: "The

LORD protects the bones of the righteous; not one of them is broken!" (NLT); Psalm 31:5: "I entrust my spirit into your hand" (NLT).

67. Luke 23:36.
68. Matt. 27:54.
69. Ps. 22:15 NIV.
70. Ps. 22:31 NIV.
71. Heb. 9:11–12 NLT; 10:19–20 NIV. According to Hebrews, the curtain that divided the holy place from the Holy of Holies depicted the Lord's own body. Once His body was torn, the curtain was torn as well, and "the way into the Holiest of All" (Heb. 9:8) was made available.

Chapter 14: The Atonement and the Harrowing of Hell

1. Bruce, *Jesus, Lord & Savior*, 114 (see chap. 2, n. 146).
2. N. T. Wright, *Jesus and the Victory of God*, vol. 2 of *Christian Origins and the Question of God*, 370ff., 405ff.; James Edward Talmage and Walter Kasper, *Jesus the Christ* (n.p.: Valde Books, 2009), 117; Raymond E. Brown, *The Death of the Messiah: From Gethsemane to the Grave: A Commentary on the Passion Narratives in the Four Gospels*, vol. 1 (n.p.: Yale Univerity Press, 1998), 460; Witherington, *The Christology of Jesus*, 117–18; Klyne R. Snodgrass, "The Temple Incident," in Bock and Webb, eds., *Key Events in the Life of the Historical Jesus*, chap. 10, pp. 429–80 (see intro., n. 3).
3. 1 Thess. 2:15–16; Luke 11:40–51; Acts 7:51–53.
4. Col. 2:13; Heb. 9:28; 1 Peter 2:24; 1 John 3:5.
5. Col. 2:20; Gal. 6:14.
6. Col. 1:20; 2 Cor. 5:17.
7. Eph. 2:15–16; Gal. 3:10–13; Rom. 7:1ff.
8. Rom. 6:6; 8:3.
9. John 12:31–32; Col. 2:15; Heb. 2:14; 1 John 3:8.
10. Matt. 27:39–40.
11. Matt. 4:3.
12. 2 Cor. 5:21.
13. 1 Cor. 15:26; Rom. 5:12; 2 Tim. 1:10.
14. Nee, *A Table in the Wilderness: Daily Meditations*, May 12 (see chap. 2, n. 184).
15. McKnight, *The King Jesus Gospel*, 51 (see intro., n. 39).
16. Col. 1:20.
17. Eph. 2:13–15.
18. Phil. 4:7.
19. Isa. 11:6.
20. Grenz, *Theology for the Community of God*, 339–40 (see chap. 1, n. 25).
21. Luke 24:25–27.
22. 1 Peter 1:10–11.
23. 1 Cor. 15:3–4. See also Acts 3:18, 24; 17:2–3; 26:22–23.
24. Heb. 9:22.
25. Rev. 3:18.
26. Heb. 9:22. See also Ephesians 1:7.
27. Lev. 17:11, 14.
28. Gen. 6–8; 1 Peter 3:20ff.; 2 Peter 2:5ff.
29. 1 Cor. 5:7.

30. Joseph Ratzinger, *Jesus of Nazareth, Part Two, Holy Week: From the Entrance into Jerusalem to the Resurrection* (San Francisco: Ignatius, 2011), 108. On pages 106–15, Ratzinger discusses the debate among scholars concerning when Jesus took the Lord's Supper and the time of His trial.
31. Romans 10:6–8 compares Israel's salvation with today as an analogy. Israel didn't descend into the sea to save themselves or go up to receive the Torah—it was God's gift. The same is true with believers today. Christ descended into death and rose again to save us. In 1 Corinthians 10:1ff., Paul compared Israel's redemption with ours, including an analogy with Israel being brought through the sea. In Exodus 20, before God gave the commandments, He prefaced His words with grace: I am the LORD who redeemed you . . . God acted and then invited our obedience. We are saved by grace through faith. (We credit Craig Keener for these thoughts.)
32. Col. 1:13.
33. 1 Cor. 10:4.
34. Num. 20:7–12.
35. Heb. 6:6 KJV.
36. Ex. 15:23–25. Scripture says that Jesus was put to death on a "tree" (Acts 13:29; 1 Peter 2:24; Gal. 3:13).
37. The best study of the serpent is a recent one by a Princeton professor. James H. Charlesworth, *The Good and Evil Serpent: How a Universal Symbol Became Christianized* (New Haven, CT: Yale University Press, 2010).
38. Eph. 6:12 KJV.
39. Heb. 2:14.
40. Col. 2:15 KJV.
41. Wright, *Simply Jesus*, 188 (see intro., n. 6).
42. Lucado, *God Came Near*, xiii (see chap. 4, n. 43).
43. Jerusalem finds its origins in the ancient Canaanite site of Salem, the city of the priest-king Melchizedeck (Gen. 14:18). Salem was called "Jebus" until David conquered it and made it "Jerusalem," the capital of Israel (2 Sam. 5:6–10; 1 Chron. 11:4–9). For details on the five stages of David's journey from the cave of Adullam to the founding of Jerusalem, see "A City Whose Builder and Maker Is God" by Frank Viola, audio message, at http://ptmin.podbean.com.
44. Lev. 1:1–17; 6:8–13; Heb. 10:1–8; 9:14.
45. Lev. 2:1–16; 6:14–23.
46. John 6:35, 48–51; 12:24.
47. Lev. 3:1–17; 7:11–38; Eph. 2:13–17; Col. 1:20–21; 2 Cor. 5:21.
48. Lev. 4:1–35; 6:24–30; Rom. 6:6; Gal. 2:20.
49. Lev. 5:1–6:7; 7:1–10; 1 John 1:7–9; 2:1–2; Heb. 9:14.
50. For details, see Scot McKnight's *A Community Called Atonement* and N. T. Wright's *Simply Jesus*, 184–89.
51. Richard B. Hays, *The Conversion of the Imagination: Paul as Interpreter of Israel's Scripture* (Grand Rapids: Eerdmans, 2005), 106.
52. Matt. 12:40 NIV.
53. Acts 2:27 KJV.
54. Acts 2:31 KJV.

55. 1 Peter 3:18–19 NIV; see also 4:6.
56. Eph. 4:8–9 UPDATED NIV. "Lower, earthly regions" has traditionally been interpreted to mean "hell," or the abode of the dead. And this interpretation is not extinct. See F. F. Bruce, *The Epistles to the Colossians, Philemon, and to the Ephesians* (Grand Rapids: Eerdmans, 1984), 344–45; and Clinton Arnold, *Zondervan Exegetical Commentary on the New Testament*, bk. 10, *Ephesians* (Grand Rapids: Zondervan, 2010), 254.
57. The understanding that Jesus descended into hell is firmly rooted in the early Christian tradition. As far as post-apostolic writers go, Christ's descent into hell is first found in Justin Martyr's *Dialogue with Trypho*, trans. Thomas B. Falls, ed. Michael Slusser (Washington, D.C.: Catholic University of America Press, 2003), 112 (chap. 72). From Irenaeus on, it became a common theme in patristic writings. Many modern scholars believe that hades simply refers to the grave while premodern scholars view it as the abode of the dead. Neither interpretation can be proven. Both are plausible and within the realm of Christian orthodoxy. For more, see F. Buchsel's argument in Gerhard Kittel, ed., *Theological Dictionary of the New Testament*, vol. 3, trans. Geoffrey W. Bromiley (Grand Rapids: Eerdmans, 1966), 641–42.
58. John 13:36.
59. It should be understood that we are not universalists. God's judgment is real, and Scripture attests to it abundantly. But Jesus has made provision through His atoning work to save all who repent and believe in Him.
60. George Mackay Brown, "The Harrowing of Hell," in *Northern Lights* (London: John Murray, 1999), 24.
61. "Let All Mortal Flesh Keep Silence" is the title of a hymn from the Liturgy of St. James, 4th century; translated by Gerard Moultrie in 1864.
62. Alan Lewis, *Between Cross and Resurrection: A Theology of Holy Saturday* (Grand Rapids: Eerdmans, 2003), 3.
63. See the *Book of Common Prayer and Administration of the Sacraments and Other Rites and Ceremonies of the Church* (New York: Church Publishing, 2001), 18.
64. "St. John Chrysostom's Easter Sermon," http://anglicansonline.org/special/Easter/chrysostom_easter/html.
65. *The New Testament Apocrypha*, ed. M. R. James (Berkeley, Apocryphile, 2004), 124. Reprint of *The Apocryphal New Testament: Being the Apocryphal Gospels, Epistles, and Apocalypses: With Other Narratives and Fragments*, trans. M. R. James (Oxford, Eng.: Clarendon Press, 1924), 124.
66. Ps. 24:8.
67. Leonard Sweet, "Hell-Busters and Heaven-Raisers" [sermon, n.p., n.d.].
68. Ps. 139:8.
69. Here is an excerpt from an ancient Greek homily for Holy Saturday:

> Something strange is happening—there is a great silence on earth today, a great silence and stillness. The whole earth keeps silence because the King is asleep. The earth trembled and is still because God has fallen asleep in the flesh and he has raised up all who have slept ever since the world began. God has died in the flesh and hell trembles with fear.

He has gone to search for our first parent, as for a lost sheep. Greatly desiring to visit those who live in darkness and in the shadow of death, he has gone to free from sorrow the captives, Adam and Eve, he who is both God and the son of Eve. The Lord approached them bearing the cross, the weapon that had won him the victory. At the sight of him Adam, the first man he had created, struck his breast in terror and cried out to everyone: 'My Lord be with you all.' Christ answered him, 'And with your spirit.' He took him by the hand and raised him up, saying, 'Awake, O sleeper, and rise from the dead, and Christ will give you light . . .

'I order you, O sleeper, to awake. I did not create you to be held a prisoner in hell. Rise from the dead, for I am the life of the dead. Rise up, work of my hands, you who were created in my image. Rise, let us leave this place, for you are in me and I am in you; together we form only one person and we cannot be separated.'"

Liturgy of the Hours: According to the Roman Rite, trans. International Committee on English in the Liturgy (New York: Catholic Book Pub. Co., 1976), 2: 496–97.

70. Daniel O'Leary, "Human Touch of Easter," *The Tablet*, March 24, 2007, 9. See also Daniel O'Leary, "Caught Between Earth and Heaven," *The Tablet*, April 15, 2006, 11.
71. Luke 3:6.
72. Rev. 21:1.
73. Also see Alan E. Lewis, *Between Cross and Resurrection* for further discussion.
74. O'Leary, "Caught Between Earth and Heaven," 11.

Chapter 15: The Resurrection, Ascension, and Pentecost

1. U. A. Fanthorpe, "BC/AD," in her *Standing To* (Liskeard, Cornwall, UK: Harry Chambers/Peterloo Poets, 1982), 56. See also *Journey with Jesus* (webzine), http://danclendenin.com/PoemsAndPrayers/UA_Fanthorpe_BC_AD.shtml.
2. Quoted in Daniel Hillel, *Rivers of Eden: the Struggle for Water and the Quest for Peace in the Middle East* (New York: Oxford University Press, 1994), 296.
3. These are the phrases of first-century historians Josephus and Philo.
4. John 20:8.
5. Charles Wesley, "Hark! the Herald Angels Sing," 1739 (music by Felix Mendelsohn), http://popularhymns.com/hark_the_herald_angels_sing.php.
6. John 20:13.
7. Matt. 28:6.
8. This is the argument of William Placher, *Mark: Belief: A Theological Commentary on the Bible* (Louisville: Westminster John Knox, 2010), 246.
9. *The Church Hymnary*, 3rd edition (New York: Oxford University Press, 1973), 256.
10. Luke 2:17.
11. Matt. 28:10.

12. Ex. 25:20, 22. See also Roger Wagner, "Art and Faith," in *Public Life and the Place of the Church: Reflections to Honour the Bishop of Oxford*, comp. Michael W. Brierley (Burlington, VT: Ashgate, 2006), 130.
13. Col. 1:15.
14. The word *raised* and the phrase *raised up* are used repeatedly in connection with Jesus' resurrection (Acts 2:32–33; 5:30–31; Rom. 4:25; 6:4; 10:9; 1 Cor. 6:14; 15:4; Mark 16:6; Luke 24:34, for example).
15. Col. 1:18.
16. John 20:22.
17. Rom. 8:29ff.; Heb. 2:10.
18. Col. 3:11.
19. See Frank Viola, *Epic Jesus: The Christ You Never Knew*, eBook (Gainesville, FL: Present Testimony Ministry, 2011). Also available at http://www.ptmin.org/epicjesus.
20. Compare John 20 with Acts 2.
21. For an exhaustive treatment of the resurrection of Jesus in all of its multidimensional grandeur, see N. T. Wright's classic work *The Resurrection of the Son of God*, vol. 3 of *Christian Origins and the Question of God* (Minneapolis, MN: Fortress, 2003), as well as Dunn's *Jesus Remembered*, chap. 18 (see intro., n. 3).
22. 1 Tim. 3:16 NIV.
23. Gen. 1:26–28.
24. Rom. 1:4. See also Acts 13:33.
25. Acts 2:24–28 NIV.
26. Acts 2:31 NIV.
27. Gen. 1:9–13.
28. Gen. 6–9; 1 Peter 3:20; 2 Peter 2:5.
29. Heb. 11:19 NIV.
30. Num. 17:8.
31. Ex. 23:16ff.; 1 Cor. 15:23.
32. Rom. 8:29ff; 1 Cor. 15:1ff.
33. 1 Cor. 15:4.
34. Hos. 6:1–2 KJV.
35. Acts 1:3.
36. John 20:30.
37. Acts 1:3 NIV.
38. Luke 24:15–32; Acts 1:3.
39. For a discussion on the significance of Jesus' pattern of appearing and disappearing after His resurrection, see Frank Viola's blog post "A Vanishing God," at http://frankviola.org.
40. 1 Cor. 15:6.
41. John 20:19; Col. 1:27; Rom. 8:9–11.
42. 2 Cor. 5:16.
43. Matt. 28:17.
44. 1 Peter 1:8; John 20:29.
45. Acts 1:3. For Paul's limiting the time Jesus appeared in bodily form, see 1 Corinthians 15:8.
46. John 17:5; also see John 7:39.

47. 2 Kings 2:9–13.
48. Ps. 110:1.
49. Acts 2:33 NKJV.
50. John 7:39 NKJV.
51. It cannot be emphasized too much that the "seated" Son is a significant detail. In Hebrews 10:11–13 the author noted that the Levitical priests continued to stand and serve the Lord with their ineffectual sacrifices, day after day. But since their sacrifices could never "take away sins," they were trapped in a circle of failure, serving without end or results. Christ's once-and-for-all sacrifice accomplished the destruction of the hold of sin and death, and so Christ "sat down at the right hand of God" (Heb. 10:12). There is also the historic privilege of the House of David to "sit" before the Lord, as found in 2 Samuel 7:18.
52. For a fuller treatment on the spiritual and practical implications of the ascension of Jesus, see N. T. Wright's *Surprised by Hope: Rethinking Heaven, the Resurrection, and the Mission of the Church* (New York: HarperCollins, 2008), chap. 7; and Douglas Farrow's volume, *Ascension and Ecclesia* (Edinburgh: T. & T. Clark, 1999).
53. Herbert McCabe, "A Sermon for Easter," in *God Still Matters*, ed. Brian Davies (New York: Continuum, 2002), 227.
54. Isa. 49:16 NIV.
55. Acts 20:28.
56. Personal communication with Leonard Sweet. Used with permission.
57. 1 Cor. 15:3–4; emphasis added.
58. Matt. 22:43–44 NIV.
59. The Emmaus road story is told only by Luke (24:13–35).
60. Origen took this identification of Cleopas (husband of "Mary the wife of Clopas" in John 19:25) for granted, and thus claimed the unnamed disciple walking with Cleopas was his son, Symeon. See Bauckham, *Jesus and the Eyewitnesses*, 43 (see intro., n. 73).
61. Luke 24:16 NIV.
62. Luke 24:18.
63. Luke 24:19.
64. Ibid.
65. Luke 24:25.
66. Luke 24:27 NIV.
67. SERT is a phrase used by Leonard Sweet, but the four components (Scripture, Experience, Reason, Tradition) are known as the "Wesleyan Quadrilateral."
68. Luke 22:14–20.
69. Luke 9:16.
70. Luke 9:7–9.
71. Luke 9:20.
72. Luke 9:31.
73. John 20:17.
74. Matt. 18:20.
75. Luke 24:35.
76. Emphasis added.

77. Luke 24:32.
78. Luke 24:32 NIV. (This is the phrase used in the founding of Methodism.)
79. Ibid.
80. Luke 24:25.
81. Luke 24:34.
82. 1 Cor. 15:6.
83. Matt. 28:19.
84. Matt. 6:10.
85. Matt. 28:18 NLT.
86. Dan. 7:13–14 NLT.
87. Acts 1:4, 8.
88. 1 John 5:6–8.
89. We are aware that *pneuma* in this text primarily refers to the Spirit. However, we are using biblical metaphor. The Spirit is the wind of God (Acts 2:2–4).
90. Compare John 14–16 with Acts 2. Note that we reject modalism. Jesus and the Spirit are distinct, but they are not separate. Christ is now *in* the Spirit. For a thorough discussion on this point, see Andrew Murray's classic book *The Spirit of Christ* (see chap. 10, n. 84).
91. Deut. 34.
92. See Joel 2:28–29.
93. Acts 2:21.
94. Rev. 22.
95. Rom. 1:4.
96. Ex. 19:16–19; 1 Kings 19:11–12; Isa. 6:6.
97. There is also an allusion in Ezekiel 37 to the wind of the Spirit in Acts 2.
98. Paul Evdokimov, as quoted by Nicholas Lash, "Churches, Proper and Otherwise," *The Tablet*, 21 July 2007.
99. Acts 12:1–2.
100. For a further discussion on this subject, see Frank Viola, *Reimagining Church*.
101. Matt. 23:9.
102. 1 Cor. 12:12 ESV.
103. Jer. 31:31.
104. Ezek. 36:26. See also "I will give them an undivided heart and put a new spirit in them; I will remove from them their heart of stone and give them a heart of flesh" (Ezek. 11:19 NIV).
105. Heb. 9:16–17.
106. Eph. 5:25.
107. Acts 20:28.
108. Luke 9:58. See also chapter 9 of our *Jesus Manifesto* for a full discussion on the spiritual meaning of Bethany.

Chapter 16: The Return of the King

1. Gen. 1:31.
2. Pss. 78:69; 104:5; Eccl. 1:4; see also Pss. 93:1; 96:10; 119:90.
3. Rev. 21:1.
4. 2 Peter 3:10–11. The "elements" could refer to the sun and the moon, since neither will be needed when the fullness of the new creation comes, according to Revelation 21. Or they could refer to the surface of the earth,

which has been affected by the curse. Yet the earth itself will remain forever, as Scripture repeatedly declares.

5. 2 Peter 1:4; 1 Cor. 1:21; John 7:7; James 1:27; 4:4; 1 John 5:19.
6. Gal. 1:4.
7. 2 Cor. 4:4.
8. John 12:31.
9. 1 Peter 2:11; Heb. 11:13.
10. Phil. 3:20.
11. Col. 3:2.
12. 1 John 2:17; 2 Cor. 4:18.
13. John 15:19.
14. John 18:36. The popular translation in these texts, "not of this world," is more accurately translated "not from this world."
15. Matt. 6:10.
16. Rev. 21:2–3.
17. Ps. 24:1; Deut. 10:14; Ps. 115:16.
18. Heb. 2:10; Col. 1:16; Rom. 11:36; Ps. 2:7–8.
19. Gen. 1:26.
20. Rom. 8:19–23 NIV.
21. Num. 14:21 KJV.
22. Hab. 2:14 KJV.
23. Isa. 11:6–9 KJV.
24. Isa. 2:4 NIV.
25. Col. 1:18–20; Eph. 1:9–10.
26. Ps. 2:1–2 KJV.
27. Col. 2:14–15; 2 Cor. 2:14; Rom. 8:37.
28. 2 Cor. 6:15.
29. Luke 17:20–21.
30. Luke 17:20; Mark 4:11.
31. Acts 2:33–34; Eph. 1:3; Rom. 14:17; Eph. 1:20–21; 2:5; Rom. 5:17.
32. "Toward a Theology of Hope" in Martin E. Marty and Dean G. Peerman, eds., *New Theology, No. 5* (New York: Macmillan, 1969), 99.
33. Acts 17:31.
34. Dan. 7:13–14; Ps. 2:7–9; Isa. 9:6–7; Phil. 2:10–11.
35. Heb. 13:12–13.
36. Heb. 6:5.
37. Luke 12:32; 16:16; 1 Cor. 4:20; Rom. 14:17.
38. Harry A. Williams, *True Resurrection* (New York: Continuum, 2000).
39. For details on the present-yet-future aspect of the kingdom, see George Ladd's *The Presence of the Future: The Eschatology of Biblical Realism* (Grand Rapids: Eerdmans, 1974): earlier editions (1964–69) published as *Jesus and the Kingdom*; *Last Things: An Eschatology for Laymen* (Grand Rapids: Eerdmans, 1978); *The Blessed Hope* (Grand Rapids: Eerdmans, 1956); and *Theology of the New Testament* (Grand Rapids: Eerdmans, 1974). See also France, *Jesus and the Old Testament*, 161ff. (see intro., n. 22).
40. Luke 13:30; 2 Tim. 2:12; Rom. 8:17.
41. 2 Cor. 1:5; 1 Peter 4:13; Phil. 3:10.
42. 1 Cor. 15:58.

43. Hebrews 11:24–27, which speaks of the "treasures in Egypt" with its "pleasures of sin." For details on how Egypt represents the world system, see Frank Viola, *From Eternity to Here*, chap. 16 (see chap. 1, n. 59).
44. Num. 13:27.
45. Heb. 4:3–11 NIV.
46. Col. 2:16–17.
47. Rom. 14:17.
48. Eph. 3:8.
49. Eph. 1:3 NLT.
50. Eph. 1:3; 3:8, 17–19.
51. Phil. 3:8.
52. John 4:10–14; 7:38.
53. 2 Cor. 4:11–12; 6:9–10.
54. John 12:24–25; Phil. 3:10.
55. John 6:9–13; 1 Cor. 15:22–23.
56. John 15:1–5.
57. Judg. 9:11; Gal. 5:22–23.
58. Ex. 29:7; 30:31; Ps. 133:1–3; Heb. 1:9.
59. 1 Cor. 3:2; Heb. 5:12; 1 Peter 2:2.
60. John 6:48–51.
61. Eph. 1:20–21; 4:10.
62. See Deuteronomy 6 and 8. For details, see Viola, *From Eternity to Here*, chap. 19.
63. Eph. 3:18 KJV.
64. Eph. 3:17; Col. 2:6–7.
65. Eph. 1:3 NIV.
66. Eph. 6:12.
67. Eph. 6:12 KJV.
68. George E. Ladd, *A Theology of the New Testament* (Grand Rapids: Eerdmans, 1993), 601.
69. Heb. 4:8. Interestingly, in Hebrews 4:8, "Jesus" and "Joshua" are the same in the Greek.
70. Acts 14:22.
71. See Wright, *Surprised by Hope*, chaps. 7–10 (see chap. 15, n. 52).
72. See the discussion in Walter Kaiser's *The Messiah in the Old Testament* (Grand Rapids: Zondervan, 1995), 18–23.
73. See George Ladd, *Crucial Questions of the Kingdom of God* (Grand Rapids: Eerdmans, 1952) and *The Blessed Hope* (Grand Rapids: Eerdmans, 1956), as well as Keith Mathison, *When Shall These Things Be? A Reformed Response to Hyper-Preterism* (Phillipsburg, NJ: P&R Pub., 2004). Still others believe that part of the description in the Olivet Discourse applies to the near future (AD 70) and part of it applies to the ultimate future—e.g., Jesus said "within a generation" for some of it (like the temple's destruction), but He also gave some signs and non-signs of the end when He said, "No one knows the day nor the hour" (of His return). Craig Keener is one scholar who holds this view.
74. Rom. 8:18–25; Rev. 21:1; Isa. 65:17; 66:22.
75. Matt. 12:32; Mark 10:30; Luke 18:30; Col. 3:4; 1 John 3:2.
76. 1 Thess. 4:16–17; 1 Cor. 15:22–23, 50–54; Phil. 3:20–21; Col. 3:4; 1 John 3:2.

77. Ibid.
78. Job 19:25–26 KJV; John 6:39–44, 54; 11:24; 12:48.
79. 1 Cor. 1:7–8 (here, the day of "our Lord"); 5:5; 2 Cor. 1:13–14; 1 Thess. 5:2; 2 Thess. 2:2 NIV; Phil. 1:6–10 (here, the day "of Christ"); 2 Peter 3:8–12; see also Zech. 14:1–4; Amos 5:18–20; Joel 2:1–3.
80. For a thorough treatment of the day of the Lord, see Robert Gundry's *The Church and the Tribulation* (Grand Rapids: Zondervan, 1973), chap. 6, and Ben Witherington's *Jesus, Paul, and the End of the World* (Downers Grove, IL: InterVarsity Press, 1992), pt. 5.
81. 1 John 3:2–3; Titus 2:13; Col. 1:27; Rom. 5:2; 8:18–25; Acts 23:6; 1 Peter 5:1, 4; 1 Cor. 15:22–43; 1 Peter 1:13.
82. Eph. 4:30; Luke 21:28; Rom. 8:18–24.
83. Dan. 12:1–3; John 5:28–29; Acts 24:15; 1 Cor. 4:5; 2 Tim. 4:1, 8; Rom. 14:10; 2 Cor. 5:10.
84. 1 Thess. 1:7–10; 3:13; 4:15; 2 Thess. 2:8; verses 14–15 of Jude; 1 Tim. 6:14–15; Rev. 19–22.
85. Eph. 1:10; Col. 1:20; 1 Cor. 15:24–28.
86. C. S. Lewis, "A Summary of the Bible," http://ficotw.org/biblesum.txt; or http://www.believersweb.org/view.cfm?ID=815.
87. Rom. 8.
88. Rev. 21–22.
89. Dan. 7; Rev. 11.
90. 1 Thess. 4:17.
91. 1 Cor. 15:52.
92. Many Christians have been taught a two-stage coming of Christ—a secret rapture followed by Jesus returning to judge the earth. This view has been popularized by the Scofield Bible, *The Late Great Planet Earth* by Hal Lindsey, and the Left Behind series. The origins of this two-stage coming trace back to John Nelson Darby in 1830. To read the history of when and why this doctrine emerged, see *The Incredible Cover-Up* by Dave MacPherson (Medford, OR: Omega Publications, 1975). To read a thorough critique of this view, see Gary DeMar's *Last Days Madness* (Atlanta: American Vision, 1997) and Robert Gundry's *The Church and the Tribulation*, chap. 6.
93. Acts 3:20–21. Other texts on the *parousia* include Paul (1 Thess. 2:19; 3:13; 4:15; 5:23; 2 Thess. 2:1, 8–9), Peter (2 Peter 1:16; 3:4, 12), James (James 5:7–8), John (1 John 3:2–3), and Jude (verse 14). These texts demonstrate that the writers of the Second Testament speak with great consistency in describing the Lord's second coming.
94. Grenz, *Theology for the Community of God*, 659 (see chap. 1, n. 25).
95. Col. 2:16–17 NIV.
96. Lev. 23:4–5.
97. 1 Cor. 5:7 NIV.
98. Lev. 23:6–8.
99. Rom. 6:4; Col. 2:12; 1 Cor. 5:8.
100. Lev. 23:9–14.
101. 1 Cor. 15:23.
102. Lev. 23:15–22.
103. Acts 2.

104. John 14–16.
105. Lev. 23:23–25.
106. 1 Cor. 15:52; 1 Thess. 4:16. Some believe that the Feast of Trumpets looked forward to the battle of Jericho, when trumpets were blown and a shout was uttered. Both a trumpet and a shout are mentioned in 1 Thessalonians 4 in reference to Christ's second coming.
107. Lev. 23:26–32.
108. Hab. 2:14; Heb. 8–11; Eph. 5:27; Rev. 21:11; Rom. 8:19–24.
109. Lev. 23:33–44.
110. Hos. 6:11; Joel 3:13; Matt. 13:39; Rev. 14:14–20; 1 John 3:2–3; Col. 1:27; Rom. 5:2; 8:18–25; Acts 23:6; 1 Peter 5:1, 4; 1 Cor. 15:22–43; 1 Peter 1:13. Of course, Jesus is Sukkoth (John 1:14, "He tabernacled with us," Greek literal).
111. Lev. 23:15–16.
112. Luke 4:16–21.
113. Rom. 8:18–15; Rev. 21–22. The Year of Jubilee was the Sabbath of Sabbaths. It corresponds to Daniel's seventy weeks in Daniel 9: 70 x 7 = the greatest Sabbath coming, the ultimate Jubilee.
114. Heb. 9:28 NIV.
115. Heb. 10:37.
116. 1 Cor. 1:30; Col. 1:27.
117. Heb. 9:28.
118. Karl Barth as paraphrased by Cornelius Plantinga, "Between Two Advents: In the Interim (Luke 21:28)," *Christian Century*, December 6, 2000, 1270–72.
119. 1 Cor. 16:22 NASB; Rev. 22:20 NASB.

Conclusion: The Jesus Spirit

1. Phil. 2:5 NASB.
2. Ambrose, *Exposition of the Holy Gospel According to Saint Luke: With Fragments on the Prophecy of Isaias*, trans. Theodosia Tomkinson (Etna, CA: Center for Traditionalist Orthodox Studies, 2003), 52.II, 41.
3. Matt. 12:3–8.
4. Matt. 11:29 YLT.
5. Blaise Pascal, *Pascal: Pensées*, trans. W. F. Trotter (Charleston, SC: Forgotten Books, 2008), 113.
6. John Calvin, *Commentary on the Book of Psalms*, trans. James Anderson (Grand Rapids: Eerdmans, 1949), 5:109: "their minds repose in the stillness of faith."
7. Luke 2:49.
8. See the discussion on "Abba" in Joseph Ratzinger's *Jesus of Nazareth, Part Two, Holy Week: From the Entrance into Jerusalem to the Resurrection* (San Francisco: Ignatius, 2011), 161ff.
9. Luke 2:52.
10. Robert Jenson is insightful here: "You cannot accurately pick out Jesus of Nazareth without simultaneously picking out the second person of the Trinity, and you cannot accurately pick out the second person of the Trinity without in fact simultaneously picking out Jesus of Nazareth . . . When we ask about the identity of Jesus, historical and systematic questions cannot be separated" (Robert Jenson, "Identity, Jesus and Exegesis," in *Seeking the*

Identity of Jesus: A Pilgrimage, eds. Beverly Roberts Gaventa and Richard B. Hays [Grand Rapids: Eerdmans, 2008], 46–47).

11. John 8:58.
12. For an excellent exploration of the self-understanding of Jesus, see Gaventa and Hays, *Seeking the Identity of Jesus*. See also Keener, *The Historical Jesus of the Gospels*, 256ff.; and Sigurd Grindheim, *God's Equal: What Can We Know About Jesus' Self-Understanding?* (London: T. & T. Clark, 2011).
13. See Daniel 7:13–14; David L. Edwards, *Yes: A Positive Faith* (London: Darton, Longman and Todd, 2006), 47.
14. John 5:39; authors' paraphrase.
15. R. T. France, *Jesus and the Old Testament*, 75, 79–80; also see F. F. Bruce's *Jesus, Lord & Savior* (Vancouver, BC: Regent College Pub., 1998), chap. 18.
16. See Bono's introduction to *Selections from the Book of Psalms: Authorized King James Version* (New York: Grove, 1999), x.
17. Mark 2:23–28; Matt. 12:3–4; Luke 6:3–4.
18. Matt. 1:1, 6, 17, 20; Luke 3:31; 2:4, 11; 1:27–32, 69.
19. Mark 10:47–48; Mark 12:35–37; Luke 18:38–39; John 7:42; Rom. 1:3.
20. Recall the parable of the tenants in Matthew 21:33ff. The husbandman said, "I will now send my son, for they will respect him" (v. 37, paraphrased) meaning that he expected the tenants to regard the son the same way they regarded the father, since it was him in another form.
21. Mark 2:23–26. Also see Jesus' dialogue with the Pharisees about Psalm 110:1 in Matthew 22:41ff.
22. 2 Sam. 7:12–14.
23. Craig Keener, *The Historical Jesus of the Gospels*, 200ff. See also F. F. Bruce, "The Humanity of Jesus Christ," in his *A Mind for What Matters: Collected Essays* (Grand Rapids: Eerdmans, 1990), 255. Bruce argues that while "Son of Man" points to Daniel 7, it also points to the humanity of Jesus as the representative man.
24. T. W. Manson, *Ethics and the Gospel* (New York: Scribner, 1961), 68.
25. Mark 8:31. See also McKnight, *The King Jesus Gospel*, 108 (see intro., n. 39).
26. N. T. Wright confirms this point in *Simply Jesus*, 148ff. (see intro., n. 6).
27. John 6:31–58.
28. John 6:53–56; compare with John 1:29, 36.
29. One of us developed this point in detail in a message titled "Vantage Point: The Story We Haven't Heard." See http://ptmin.podbean.com. See also Beale, *The Temple and the Church's Mission* (see intro., n. 78).
30. Matt. 12:42.
31. Matt. 5–7.
32. Luke 4:25–27; Mark 6:35ff; Matt. 14:15ff.; Luke 9:12ff; 2 Kings 4:42–44.
33. Matt. 12:40.
34. Matt. 12:8.
35. Matt. 12:41 NLT.
36. Matt. 12:42 NLT.
37. Matt. 12:6 NLT.
38. Heb. 7:3.
39. Heb. 5–9.
40. Heb. 4:6–10.

41. Heb. 3–12.
42. Ex. 1:22–2:10; Matt. 2:13–18.
43. Ex. 2:15; 7:6–7; Matt. 2:13–21.
44. Acts 7:25–27; John 1:10–11; Luke 12:14.
45. Ex. 19:13; Matt. 5–7.
46. Ex. 24:1ff.; Matt. 26:28; 1 Tim. 2:5.
47. Ex. 34:28; Matt. 4:2.
48. Compare the full storyline of Exodus with Matthew; see also John 1:17. For an in-depth treatment of the biblical parallels between Jesus and Moses, see Ada R. Habershon's *The Study of the Types* (Grand Rapids: Kregel, 1974), 165–74.
49. Moses is called a priest in Psalm 99:6. He's called a prophet, a shepherd, and a ruler often.
50. Deut. 18:18–19; John 1:45; 6:14. Interestingly, some scholars believe that the name "Moses" is an Egyptian name that means "child of God." See Ogden Goelet, "Moses' Egyptian Name," *Bible Review* 19, no. 3 (June 2003): 12–17, 50–51.
51. Mark 9:7.
52. 2 Peter 1:16–18.
53. Heb. 3:2–6 NIV.
54. Gen. 30:22–24; Matt.1:25.
55. Gen. 37:3; Matt. 3:17; 12:18.
56. Gen. 37:5–11; Dan. 7:13–14; Mic. 4:7; 5:2; Ps. 2.
57. Gen. 37:4–5, 11; John 7:3–5; 15:18–19.
58. Gen. 37:28; Matt. 26:15.
59. Gen. 37:18–28; Acts 2:22–23.
60. Gen. 37:21–22; Matt. 27:24.
61. Gen. 37:28; Matt. 2:13–15.
62. Gen. 39:1; Phil. 2:7.
63. Gen. 41:40–44; Acts 2:32–33; 1 Cor. 15:27–28.
64. Gen. 41:43; Phil. 2:10.
65. Gen. 42:8; John 1:10.
66. Gen. 45:3; Zech. 12:10; Matt. 24:30–31; Rev. 1:7.
67. Gen. 45:5–8; 50:20; Acts 3:12–18.
68. Gen. 47:25; Acts 13:23. For an in-depth treatment of the biblical parallels between Joseph and Jesus, see Ada R. Habershon's *The Study of the Types*, 169–74.
69. John 1:18; Heb. 11:17.
70. Gen. 17:16; Gal. 3:16.
71. Gen. 17:17–19.
72. Matt. 1:18–25.
73. Gen. 22:1–2.
74. John 3:16; Rom. 8:32.
75. Gen. 22:1–2.
76. Heb. 13:12.
77. Gen. 22:5–12.
78. Phil. 2:5–8.
79. Gen. 22:1–4ff.
80. 1 Cor. 15:3–4.

81. Gen. 22:6.
82. John 19:17–18.
83. Gen. 23:1.
84. Rom. 9–11.
85. Gen. 25:5.
86. Eph. 1:22; Heb. 1:2.
87. See A. B. Simpson, *The Christ in the Bible Commentary:* Book 1, for examples of each (see chap. 2, n. 120).
88. Witherington, *The Christology of Jesus*, 266, 270. Witherington's book is a powerful treatment demonstrating that Jesus did in fact know that He was the Messiah. See also Dunn, *Jesus Remembered*, chaps. 15–16 (see intro., n. 3); and Christopher J. H. Wright, *Knowing Jesus Through the Old Testament*, 108ff. (see intro., n. 55).
89. John 5:39.
90. John 13:16; Matt. 10:25.
91. Mark 11.
92. See Sweet and Viola, *Jesus Manifesto*, chap. 3.
93. In addition, the Roman emperor was expected to bring justice, peace, prosperity, and blessings to the world. He was also called "Pontifex Maximus," which means "chief priest." The Romans also believed that when an emperor ascended into heaven, he was enthroned as being divine. Thus the emperor (at his death) was also called "son of God."
94. See Acts 17:7, as an example.
95. Isa. 52:7.
96. C. S. Lewis, *Mere Christianity*, rev. ed., 221 (see chap. 1, n. 2).
97. The gospel is also bound up with the eternal purpose of God in Christ—which is not separate from Jesus—or as Paul called it, "the mystery." Romans 16:25; Ephesians 6:19; and Ephesians 3:7–11 also associate the preaching of "the mystery" and "the unsearchable riches of Christ" with the gospel. This point is often missed among those who teach about the gospel today, for the eternal purpose ("the mystery") gets very little airplay in evangelical circles today—even though it's at the heart of Second Testament revelation.
98. T. S. Eliot, "The Dry Salvages," pt. 5, lines 215–17, in *Four Quartets* (n. p.: Mariner Books, 1968), 44.
99. While many modern Christians reduce the gospel to two verses in 1 Corinthians 15 (vv. 3–4), Paul's "definition" of the gospel in that passage actually extends to verse 28, when God becomes "all in all." See McKnight, *The King Jesus Gospel*, 53ff.; 81ff (see intro., n. 39).
100. Matt. 23:1–35.
101. Heb. 13:8.
102. Heb. 1:1–3.
103. Wright, *Surprised by Hope*, 281 (see chap. 15, n. 52).
104. 2 Cor. 4:6.

Appendix: Post-Apostolic Witnesses

1. *Dialogue of Justin, Philosopher and Martyr with Trypho, a Jew,* in *The Ante-Nicene Fathers: Translations of the Writings of the Fathers Down to A.D. 325*, eds.

Alexander Roberts, James Donaldson, and Arthur Cleveland Coxe (New York: Cosimo Classics, 2007), 1: 262.

2. Tertullian, *Adversus Marcionem*, ed. and trans. Ernest Evans (Oxford, UK: Clarendon Press, 1972), 159 (2.26), http://www.tertullian.org/articles/evans_marc/evans_marc_06book2_eng.htm.
3. The first quote is from Augustine, *Concerning the City of God Against the Pagans* (Harmondsworth, UK: Penguin Books, 1972), 652. The second quote is from "Ten Homilies on the First Epistle General of St. John: Second Homily," in *Augustine: Later Works*, ed. John Burnaby, Library of Christian Classics (Philadelphia: Westminster, 1955), 270.
4. Irenaeus, *Five Books of S. Irenaeus, Bishop of Lyons, Against Heresies* (James Parker, 1872). Translated from Latin—"The Treasure Hid in the Scriptures Is Christ," http://www.bible-researcher.com/irenaeus.html.
5. John Chrysostom, "Homily on 1 Corinthians 10.1ff.," trans. Ben Witherington from the original Greek text, http://benwitherington.blogspot.com/2007/08/relationship-of-ot-to-nt-according-to.html.
6. Robinson Thornton, *St. Ambrose: His Life, Times and Teaching* (London: Society for Promoting Christian Knowledge, 1898), 145.
7. John Cassian, *Conferences*, trans. Colm Luibheld, Classics of Western Spirituality (New York: Paulist Press, 1985), 161.
8. Thomas Aquinas, *Summa Theologica*, in *Basic Writings of Saint Thomas Aquinas*, ed. Anton C. Pegis (Indianapolis: Hackett, 1997), 2: 858 (Q. 101, art. 4) and 2: 961 (Q.107, art. 2).
9. The first two quotes are from John Calvin, *Commentary on the Gospel According to John* (Grand Rapids: Eerdmans, 1956), 1:218. The third quote is from John Calvin, *Calvin: Commentaries*, trans. and ed. Joseph Haroutunian (Philadelphia: Westminster Press, 1958), 70.
10. The first quote is from Ewald M. Plass, comp., *What Luther Says: An Anthology* (St. Louis: Concordia), 70. The remaining quotes are quoted in Sidney Greidanus, *Preaching Christ from the Old Testament*, 120 (see intro., n. 44).
11. The first quote is from George Whitefield, "Neglect of Christ, the Killing Sin," in his *Sermons on Important Subjects* (London: Thomas Tegg, 1841), 1: 739. The second quote is from Whitefield, "The Gospel Supper," ibid., 1: 384. Also available at http://www.ccel.org/ccel/whitefield/sermons.xxxv.html?highlight=christ,old%20testament#highlight.
12. John Wesley, "Notes on the Second Book of Moses, called Exodus," in his *Explanatory Notes upon the Old Testament* (Salem, OR: Schmul Publishers, 1975; facsim. ed. Bristol, UK: printed by William Fine, 1765), 195.
13. Jonathan Edwards, *A History of the Work of Redemption* in *The Works of President Edwards* (New York: S. Converse, 1829), 3:278–79.
14. The first quote is from J. C. Ryle, *Holiness (Abridged): Its Nature, Hindrances, Difficulties and Roots* (Chicago: Moody Bible Institute, 2010), 253. The second quote is from Ryle, *How Readest Thou?* in Jay P. Green, *Why Read the Bible Through & How Readest Thou?* (Lexington, KY: Sovereign Grace Publishers, 2002), 56.
15. The first quote is from C. H. Spurgeon, "The Dew of Christ's Youth," in *Sermons of the Rev. C. H. Spurgeon of London*, 6th series (New York: Robert

Carter and Brothers, 1863), 255. The second quote, from the same book, is from Spurgeon's sermon "Christ Precious to Believers," 357.

16. John Newton, "On Searching the Scriptures," in *The Works of the Rev. John Newton . . . to Which Are Prefixed Memoirs of His Life, &c.*, by Richard Cecil (New York: Robert Carter, 1847), 1: 405.
17. A. B. Simpson, *Christ in the Tabernacle* (Harrisburg, PA: Christian Publications, n.d.), 5–6.
18. Sinclair B. Ferguson, "Preaching Christ from the Old Testament" (see intro., n. 35).
19. The first quote is from Arthur Washington Pink, "The Typical Significance of the Scriptures Declare Their Divine Authorship," in his *Divine Inspiration of the Bible* (Swengel, PA: Bible Truth Depot, 1917), 65–66. Available also as "The Typical Significance of the Scriptures Declare Their Divine Authorship," http://www.ccel.org/ccel/pink/inspiration.ch6.html?highlight=christ,old%20testament#highlight. The second quote is from "The Ordained Lamp," in *A. W. Pink's Studies in the Scriptures, 1932–1933: Volume 6 of 17* (repr. Lafayette, IN: Sovereign Grace Publishers, 2001), 21.
20. The first quote is from Dietrich Bonhoeffer, *Creation and Fall: A Theological Interpretation of Genesis 1–3*, eds. John W. de Gruchy, Martin Rüter, and Ilse Tödt; trans. Douglas Stephen Bax (Minneapolis: Fortress, 1997), 22. The second and third quotes are quoted in Martin Kuske, *The Old Testament as the Book of Christ: An Appraisal of Bonhoeffer's Interpretation*, trans. S. T. Kimbrough (Philadelphia: Westminster, 1976), 45, 49. "For Bonhoeffer, the Old Testament was certainly the Hebrew Bible, but it was also part of the Christian canon. Therefore it had to be read in the light of God's self-disclosure in Jesus Christ. . . . Bonhoeffer understood the Old Testament as the book of Christ at all times." John DeGruchy, "Editor's Introduction to the English Edition," and Martin Rüter and Ilse Tödt, "Editor's Afterword to the German Edition," in Bonhoeffer, *Creation and Fall*, 9 and 173.
21. The first quote is from Karl Barth, *Homiletics* (Louisville: Westminster John Knox, 1991), 80–81. The second quote is from Barth, *Church Dogmatics*, vol. 1, pt. 2, trans. G. W. Bromiley and G. T. Thomson (Edinburgh: T. & T. Clark International, 2004), 489.
22. The first quote is from F. F. Bruce, "The Dead Sea Scrolls and Early Christianity" in *A Mind for What Matters*, 54. The second quote is from Bruce, *The Books and the Parchments: Some Chapters on the Transmission of the Bible*, rev. ed. (Westwood, NJ: Fleming H. Revell, 1963), 77. The third quote is from Bruce, *The Christian Approach to the Old Testament* (London: Inter-Varsity Fellowship, 1955), 5.
23. Erich Sauer, *From Eternity to Eternity: An Outline of Divine Purpose*, trans. G. H. Lang (Grand Rapids: Eerdmans, 1954), 41.
24. E. E. Ellis, "How Jesus Interpreted His Bible," 345–46 (see intro., n. 33).
25. Stanley Grenz, *A Theology for the Community of God* (Nashville: Broadman & Holman, 1994), 392–93.
26. Wilhelm Vischer, *The Witness of the Old Testament to Christ*, trans. A. B. Crabtree (London: Lutterworth, 1949), 28, n. 1, 7, 27.

27. Brevard Childs, "Jesus Christ the Lord and the Scriptures of the Church" in *The Rule of Faith: Scripture, Canon, and Creed in a Critical Age*, eds. Ephraim Radner and George Sumner (Harrisburg, PA: Morehouse Publishing, 1998), 6, 11.
28. Richard Longnecker, *Biblical Exegesis in the Apostolic Period*, rev. ed. (Grand Rapids: Eerdmans, 1999), 206.
29. R. T. France, *Jesus and the Old Testament*, 40, 75 (see intro., n. 19).
30. John Goldingay, "The Old Testament and Christian Faith," Part I, *Themelios*, 8:1 (Sept. 1984): 4–10, http://www.biblicalstudies.org.uk/article_ot1_goldingay.html.
31. N. T. Wright, *Surprised by Hope*, 237 (see chap. 15, n. 52); second quote is from Tom [i.e., N. T.] Wright, *Luke for Everyone* (London: SPCK, 2001), 294–95; third quote is Tom Wright, *Paul for Everyone: Romans* (Louisville: Westminster John Knox, 2004), 2: 51.
32. James D. G. Dunn, *Unity and Diversity in the New Testament: An Inquiry into the Character of Earliest Christianity* (Philadelphia: Westminster Press, 1977), 94, 101–2.
33. Donald Bloesch, "A Christological Hermeneutic," 84–85 (see intro., n. 41). Also available as "A Christological Hermeneutic," http://www.religion-online.org/showarticle.asp?title=0.
34. Joseph Ratzinger, foreword to his *Jesus of Nazareth*, xix (see chap. 7, n. 18).
35. Norman Geisler, *To Understand the Bible, Look for Jesus* (Grand Rapids: Baker, 1968), 83.
36. John Stott, *The Incomparable Christ* (Downers Grove, IL: InterVarsity, 2001), 15.
37. J. Todd Billings in "Theological Interpretation in Action," *Christianity Today*, October 29, 2011.
38. J. I. Packer, foreword to Edmund Clowney's *The Unfolding Mystery: Discovering Christ in the Old Testament* (Colorado Springs: Navpress, 1988), 8.
39. Christopher J. H. Wright, *Knowing Jesus Through the Old Testament*, 29, 44, 56, 108 (see intro., n. 55).
40. Edmund Clowney, *The Unfolding Mystery*, 9, 116 (see n. 38 above).
41. Michelle A. Vu, "Mohler: Without Old Testament, Jesus Story Incomplete," http://www.christianpost.com/news/mohler-without-old-testament-jesus-story-incomplete-49812.
42. Jon Zens, "How Does the New Testament Use the Old Testament?" *Searching Together* 14:2 (Summer 1985): 18–19.
43. D. A. Carson, *The Cross and Christian Ministry: Leadership Lessons from 1 Corinthians* (Grand Rapids: Baker Books, 1993), 49.
44. Timothy Dalrymple, "Eugene Peterson: Would Jesus Condemn Rob Bell?" ChurchLeaders.com, http://www.churchleaders.com/pastors/pastor-articles/149653-eugene-peterson-would-jesus-condemn-rob-bell.html.
45. John Piper, "How Christ Fulfilled and Ended the Old Testament Regime," February 23, 2005, http://www.desiringgod.org/resource-library/taste-see-articles/how-christ-fulfilled-and-ended-the-old-testament-regime.
46. Tim Keller, "There Are Two Ways to Read the Bible," [posted] July 13, 2010, Reformed University Fellowship at Louisiana State University, http://www.lsu.ruf.org/posts/6001.
47. Graeme Goldsworthy, *Gospel-Centered Hermenutics: Foundations and Principles*

of *Evangelical Biblical Interpretation* (Downers Grove, IL: InterVarsity Press, 2007), 62, 63.

48. Scot McKnight, *The King Jesus Gospel*, 50–51 (see intro., n. 39).
49. Richard Hays, *The Conversion of the Imagination*, 11, 24, 84 (see chap. 14, n. 51).
50. G. K. Beale, *The Temple and the Church's Mission*, 26, 379–80 (see intro., n. 78).
51. Christian Smith, *The Bible Made Impossible*, 97–98 (see intro., n. 68).
52. C. S. Lewis, To "Mrs. Ashton": from Magdalen College, November 8, 1952, in *Letters of C. S. Lewis*, rev. and enl. ed., ed. Walter Hooper (San Diego: Harcourt Brace, 1993), 248.
53. Robert D. Brinsmead, "A Freedom from Biblicism" in *The Christian Verdict: Justification by Faith Reexamined* (Fallbrook, CA: Verdict, 1984), 12.
54. Article I of "The Dallas Seminary Doctrinal Statement," http://www.dts.edu/about/doctrinalstatement.

About the Authors

Leonard Sweet is the E. Stanley Jones Professor of Evangelism at Drew University (NJ), a Distinguished Visiting Professor at George Fox University (OR), and a weekly contributor to sermons.com and the podcast *Napkin Scribbles*. With some of the highest "influence" rankings of any religious figure in the worlds of social media (Twitter, Facebook), and a pioneer in online learning, he has authored numerous articles, sermons, and more than fifty books.

leonardsweet.com

Frank Viola is a popular conference speaker and the best-selling author of numerous books on the deeper Christian life, including *Epic Jesus*, *Revise Us Again*, *From Eternity to Here*, and *Jesus Manifesto* (coauthored with Leonard Sweet). His blog *Beyond Evangelical* is rated as one of the most popular in Christian circles today.

frankviola.org

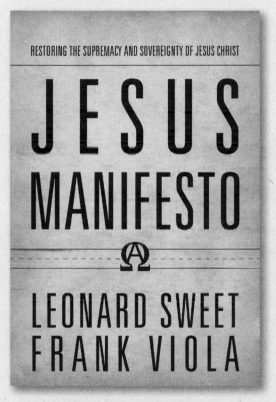